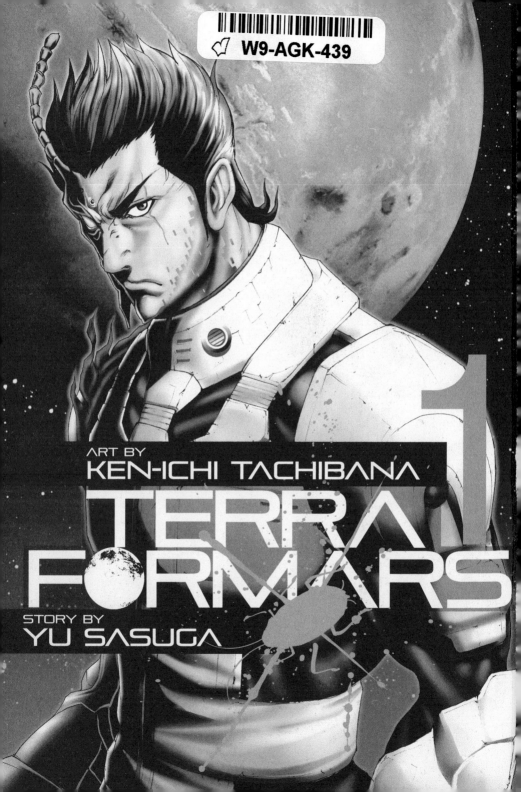

ART BY
KEN-ICHI TACHIBANA

TERRA
FORMARS

STORY BY
YU SASUGA

1

TERRA FORMARS 1

CONTENTS

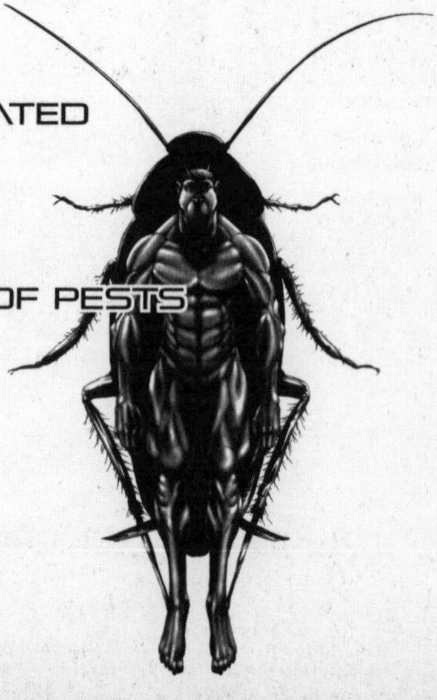

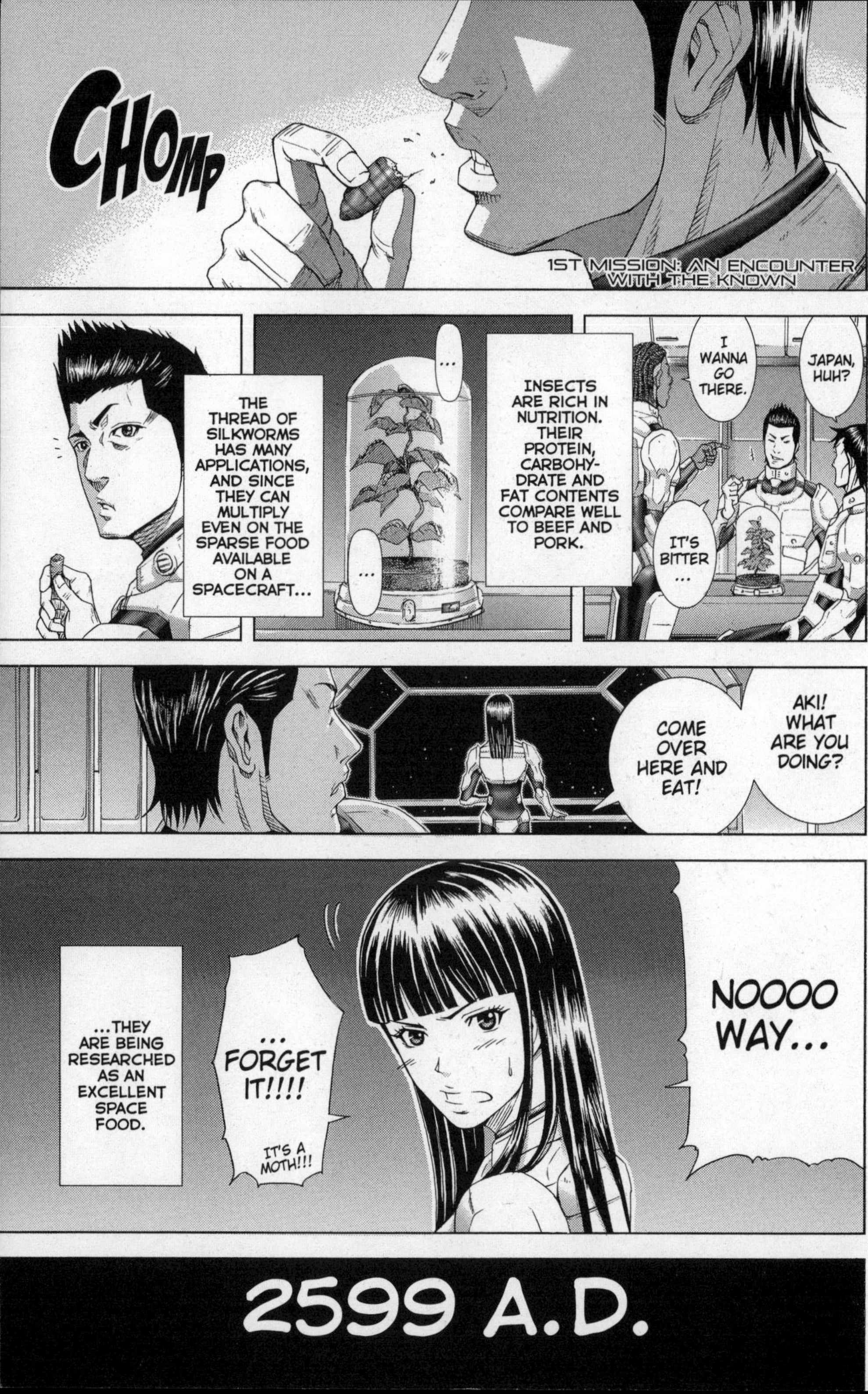
CHOMP
1ST MISSION: AN ENCOUNTER WITH THE KNOWN
JAPAN, HUH?
I WANNA GO THERE.
IT'S BITTER...
INSECTS ARE RICH IN NUTRITION. THEIR PROTEIN, CARBOHYDRATE AND FAT CONTENTS COMPARE WELL TO BEEF AND PORK.
...
...
THE THREAD OF SILKWORMS HAS MANY APPLICATIONS, AND SINCE THEY CAN MULTIPLY EVEN ON THE SPARSE FOOD AVAILABLE ON A SPACECRAFT...
AKI! WHAT ARE YOU DOING?
COME OVER HERE AND EAT!
NOOOO WAY...
...FORGET IT!!!!
IT'S A MOTH!!!
...THEY ARE BEING RESEARCHED AS AN EXCELLENT SPACE FOOD.
2599 A.D.

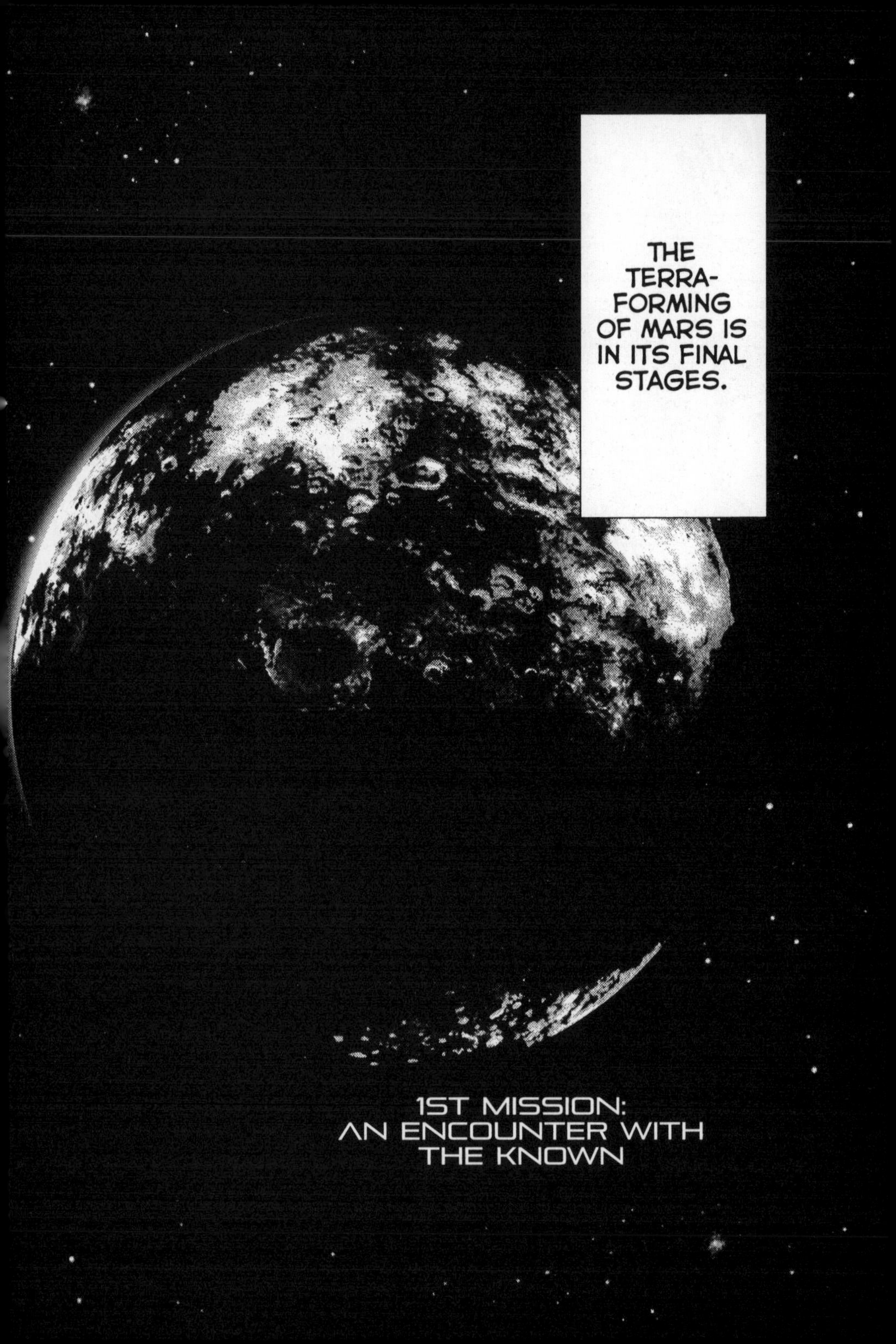
THE TERRA-FORMING OF MARS IS IN ITS FINAL STAGES.
1ST MISSION: AN ENCOUNTER WITH THE KNOWN

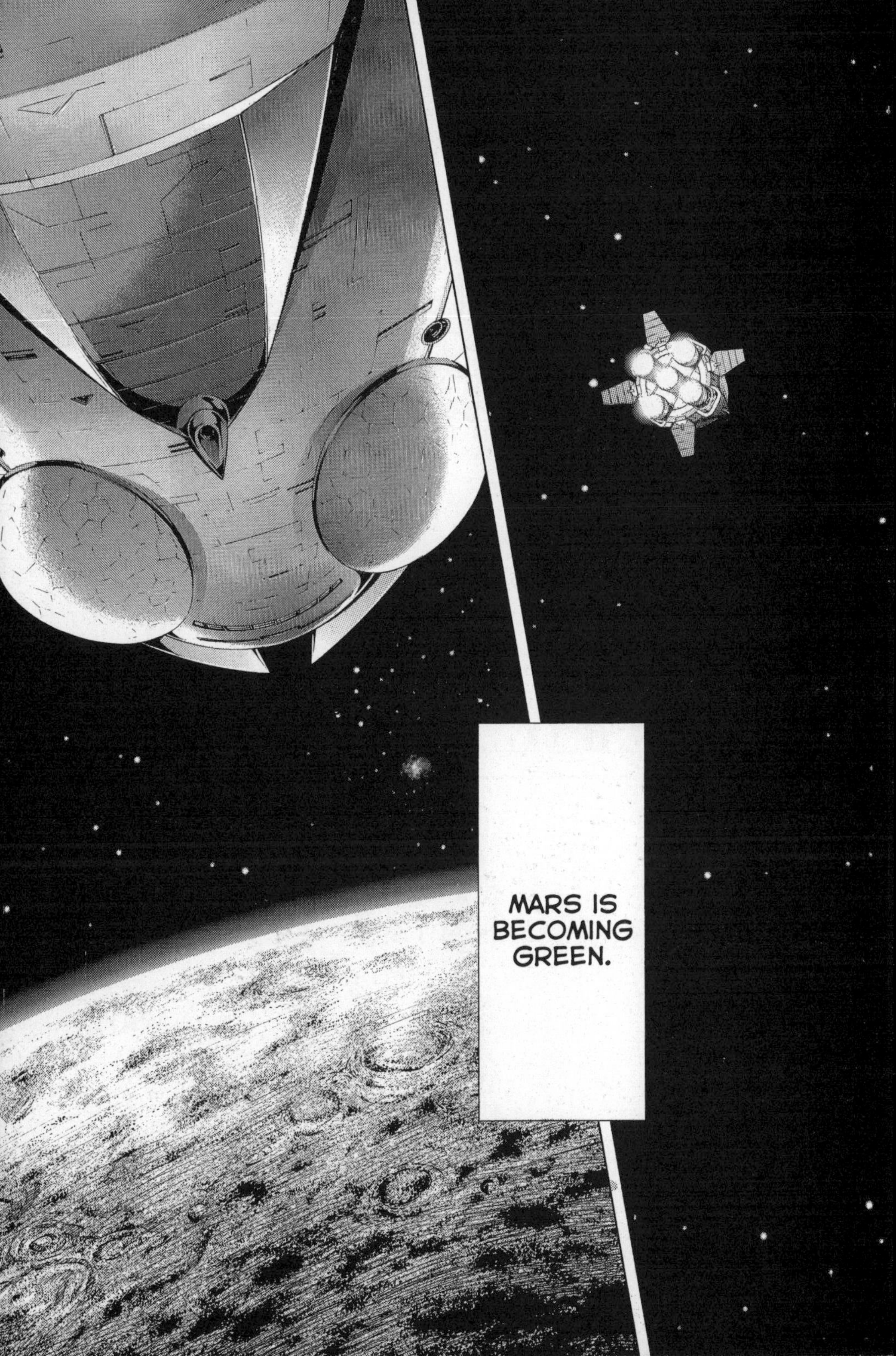
MARS IS BECOMING GREEN.

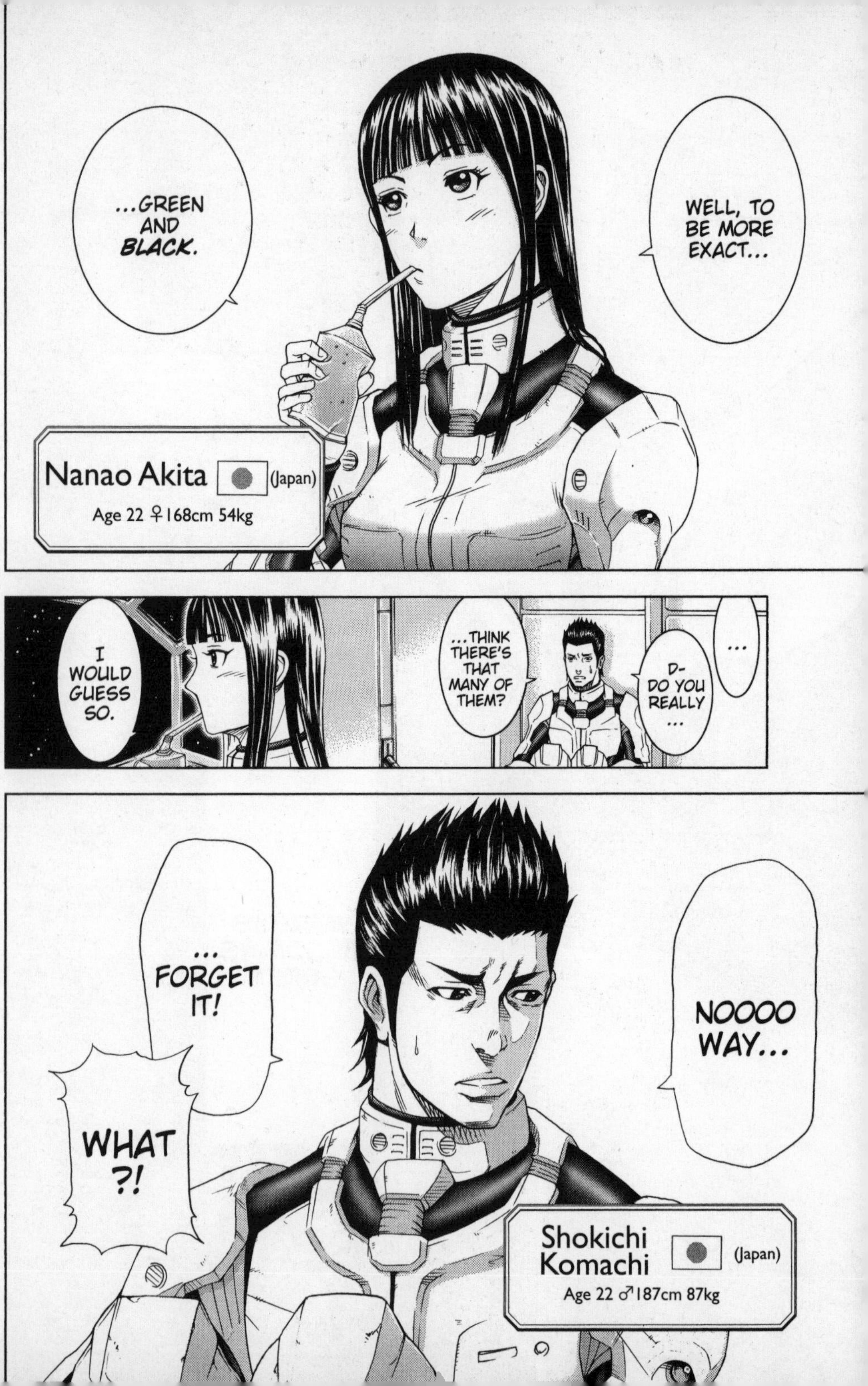
WELL, TO BE MORE EXACT...
...GREEN AND BLACK.
Nanao Akita (Japan)
Age 22 ♀168cm 54kg
...
D-DO YOU REALLY...
...THINK THERE'S THAT MANY OF THEM?
I WOULD GUESS SO.
NOOOO WAY...
...FORGET IT!
WHAT?!
Shokichi Komachi (Japan)
Age 22 ♂187cm 87kg

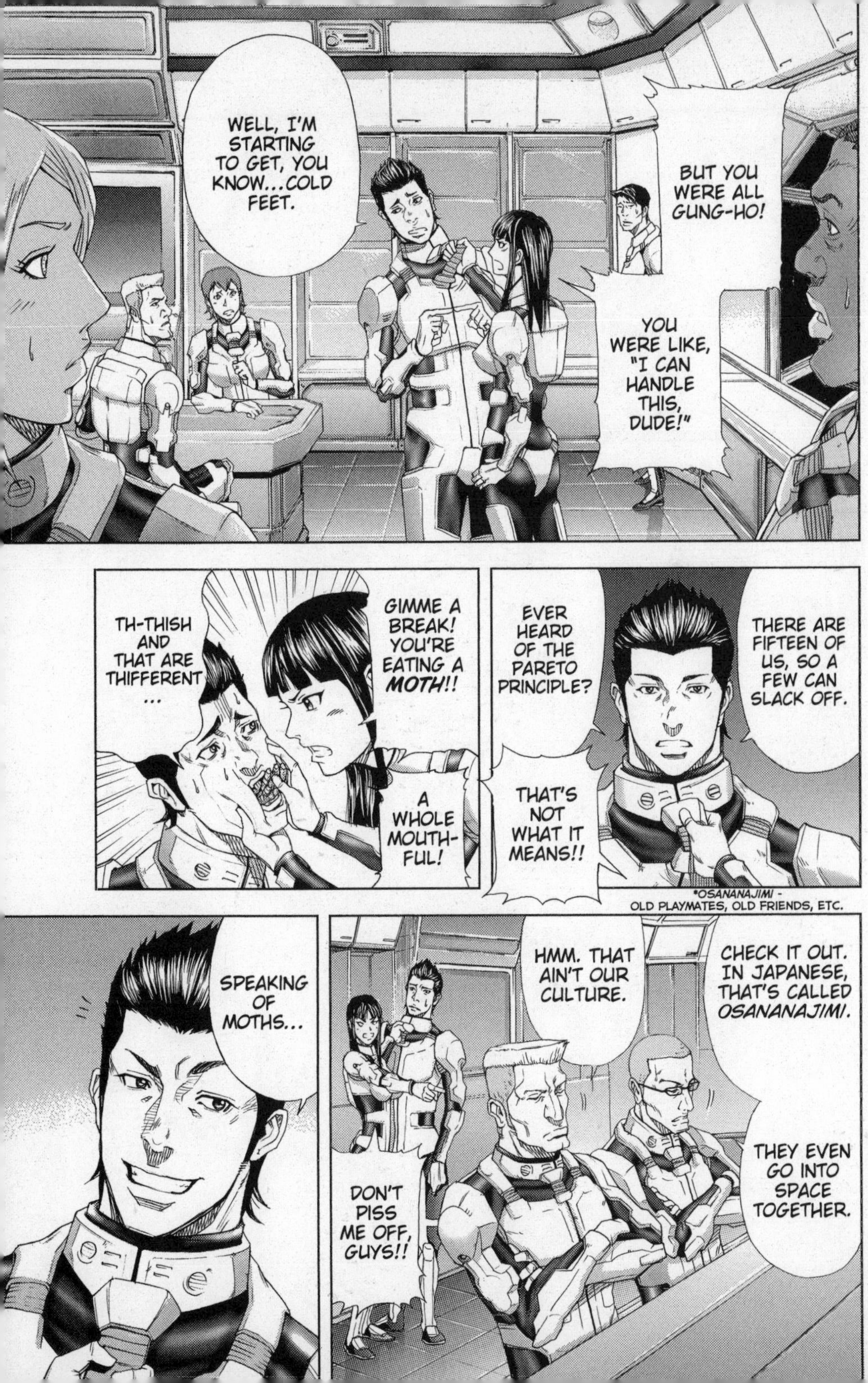
BUT YOU WERE ALL GUNG-HO!
YOU WERE LIKE, "I CAN HANDLE THIS, DUDE!"
WELL, I'M STARTING TO GET, YOU KNOW...COLD FEET.
THERE ARE FIFTEEN OF US, SO A FEW CAN SLACK OFF.
EVER HEARD OF THE PARETO PRINCIPLE?
THAT'S NOT WHAT IT MEANS!!
GIMME A BREAK! YOU'RE EATING A *MOTH*!!
A WHOLE MOUTHFUL!
TH-THISH AND THAT ARE THIFFERENT...
CHECK IT OUT. IN JAPANESE, THAT'S CALLED *OSANANAJIMI*.
HMM. THAT AIN'T OUR CULTURE.
THEY EVEN GO INTO SPACE TOGETHER.
DON'T PISS ME OFF, GUYS!!
SPEAKING OF MOTHS...

*OSANANAJIMI - OLD PLAYMATES, OLD FRIENDS, ETC.

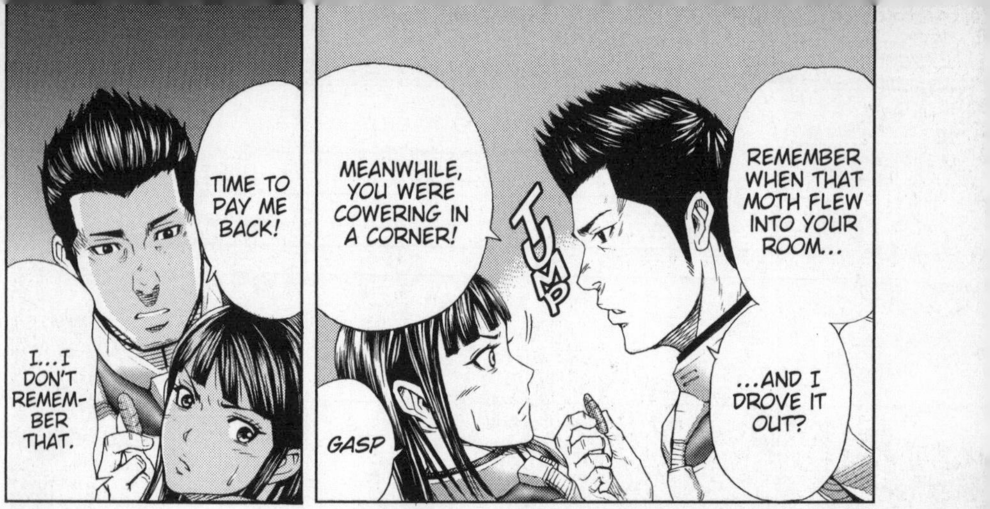
REMEMBER WHEN THAT MOTH FLEW INTO YOUR ROOM...
JUMP
...AND I DROVE IT OUT?
MEANWHILE, YOU WERE COWERING IN A CORNER!
GASP
TIME TO PAY ME BACK!
I...I DON'T REMEMBER THAT.

*JINGI - DUTY

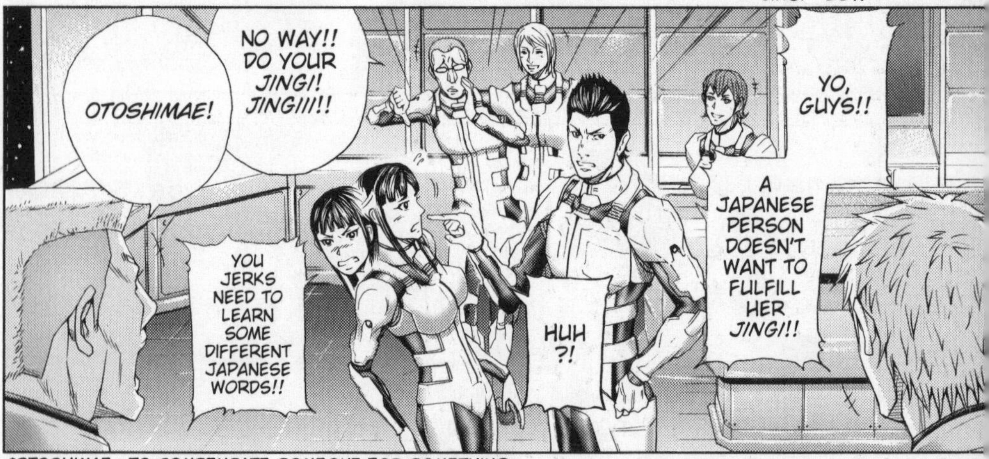
YO, GUYS!!
A JAPANESE PERSON DOESN'T WANT TO FULFILL HER JINGI!!
NO WAY!! DO YOUR JINGI! JINGI!!!!
HUH?!
OTOSHIMAE!
YOU JERKS NEED TO LEARN SOME DIFFERENT JAPANESE WORDS!!

*OTOSHIMAE - TO COMPENSATE SOMEONE FOR SOMETHING

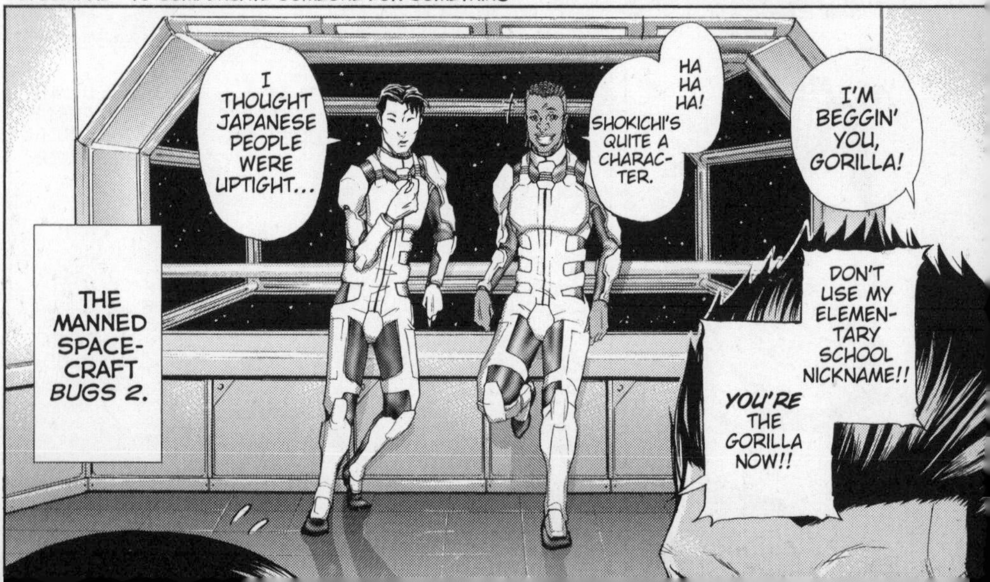
I'M BEGGIN' YOU, GORILLA!
DON'T USE MY ELEMENTARY SCHOOL NICKNAME!!
YOU'RE THE GORILLA NOW!!
HA HA HA! SHOKICHI'S QUITE A CHARACTER.
I THOUGHT JAPANESE PEOPLE WERE UPTIGHT...
THE MANNED SPACECRAFT BUGS 2.

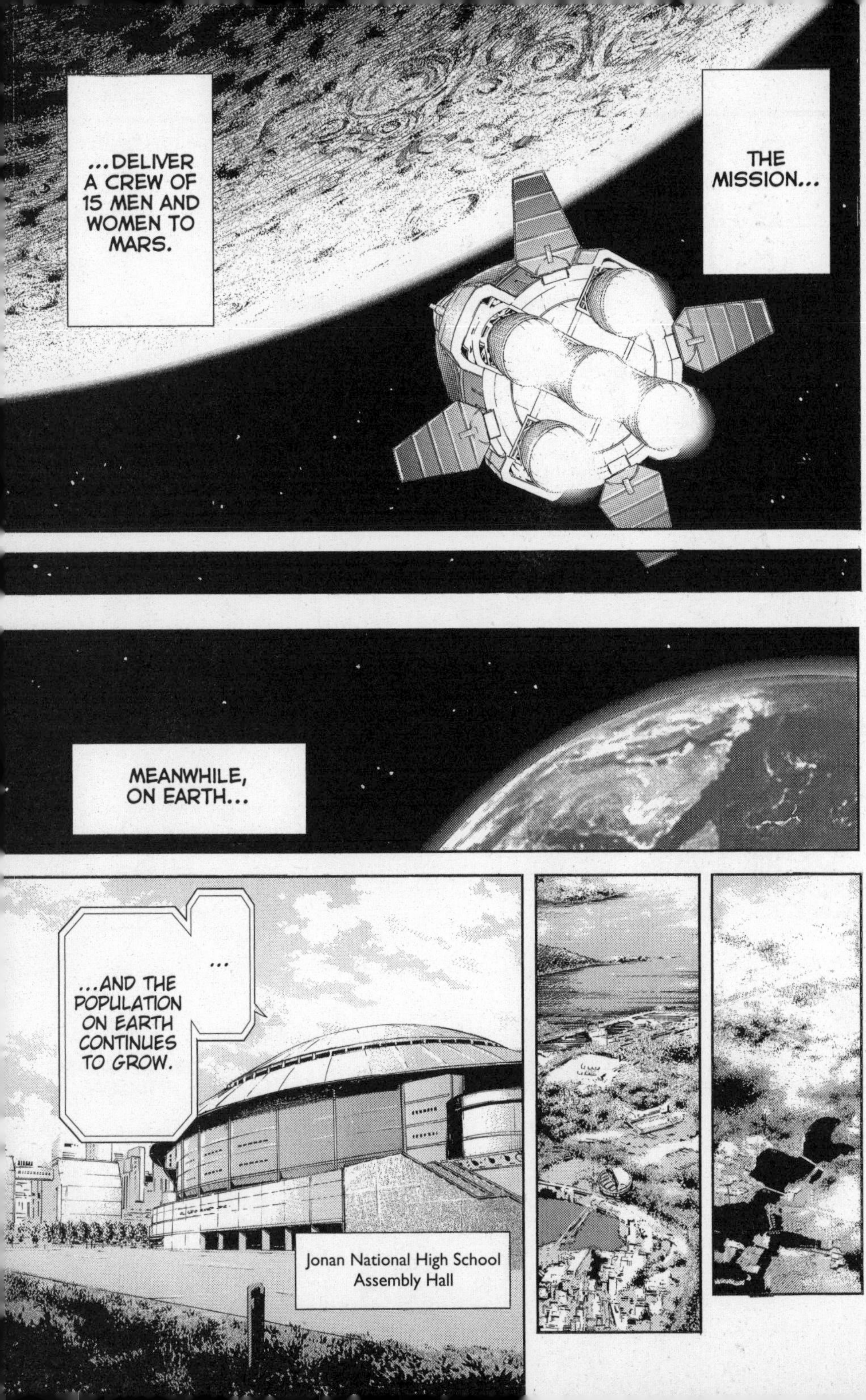
THE MISSION...
...DELIVER A CREW OF 15 MEN AND WOMEN TO MARS.
MEANWHILE, ON EARTH...
...
...AND THE POPULATION ON EARTH CONTINUES TO GROW.
Jonan National High School Assembly Hall

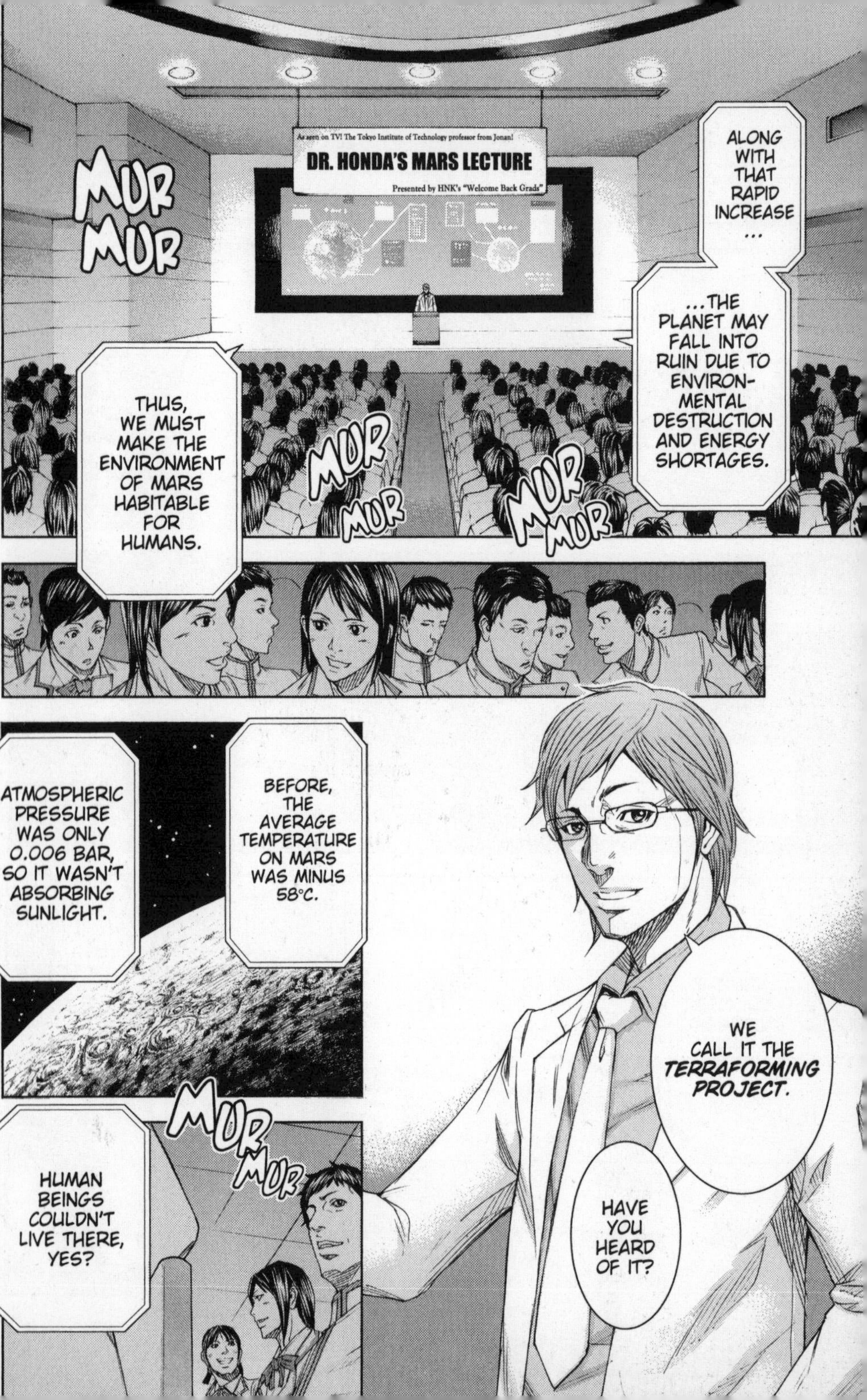

As seen on TV! The Tokyo Institute of Technology professor from Jonan!
DR. HONDA'S MARS LECTURE
Presented by HNK's "Welcome Back Grads"
ALONG WITH THAT RAPID INCREASE ...
...THE PLANET MAY FALL INTO RUIN DUE TO ENVIRON-MENTAL DESTRUCTION AND ENERGY SHORTAGES.
MUR MUR
MUR MUR
THUS, WE MUST MAKE THE ENVIRONMENT OF MARS HABITABLE FOR HUMANS.
MUR MUR
WE CALL IT THE *TERRAFORMING PROJECT*.
HAVE YOU HEARD OF IT?
BEFORE, THE AVERAGE TEMPERATURE ON MARS WAS MINUS 58°C.
ATMOSPHERIC PRESSURE WAS ONLY 0.006 BAR, SO IT WASN'T ABSORBING SUNLIGHT.
MUR MUR
HUMAN BEINGS COULDN'T LIVE THERE, YES?

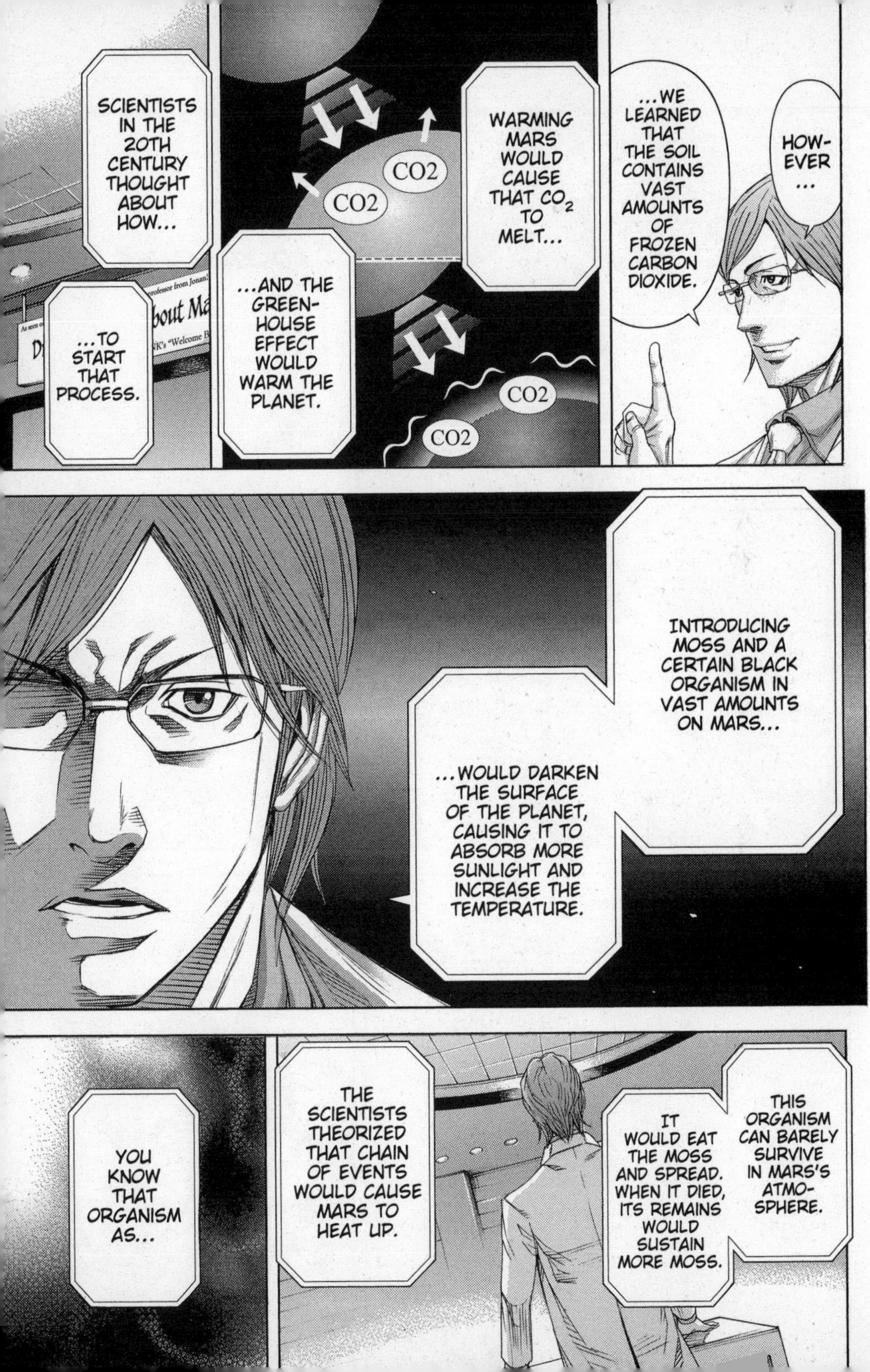
HOW-EVER...
...WE LEARNED THAT THE SOIL CONTAINS VAST AMOUNTS OF FROZEN CARBON DIOXIDE.
WARMING MARS WOULD CAUSE THAT CO_2 TO MELT...
CO2
CO2
...AND THE GREENHOUSE EFFECT WOULD WARM THE PLANET.
CO2
CO2
SCIENTISTS IN THE 20TH CENTURY THOUGHT ABOUT HOW...
...TO START THAT PROCESS.
INTRODUCING MOSS AND A CERTAIN BLACK ORGANISM IN VAST AMOUNTS ON MARS...
...WOULD DARKEN THE SURFACE OF THE PLANET, CAUSING IT TO ABSORB MORE SUNLIGHT AND INCREASE THE TEMPERATURE.
THIS ORGANISM CAN BARELY SURVIVE IN MARS'S ATMOSPHERE.
IT WOULD EAT THE MOSS AND SPREAD. WHEN IT DIED, ITS REMAINS WOULD SUSTAIN MORE MOSS.
THE SCIENTISTS THEORIZED THAT CHAIN OF EVENTS WOULD CAUSE MARS TO HEAT UP.
YOU KNOW THAT ORGANISM AS...

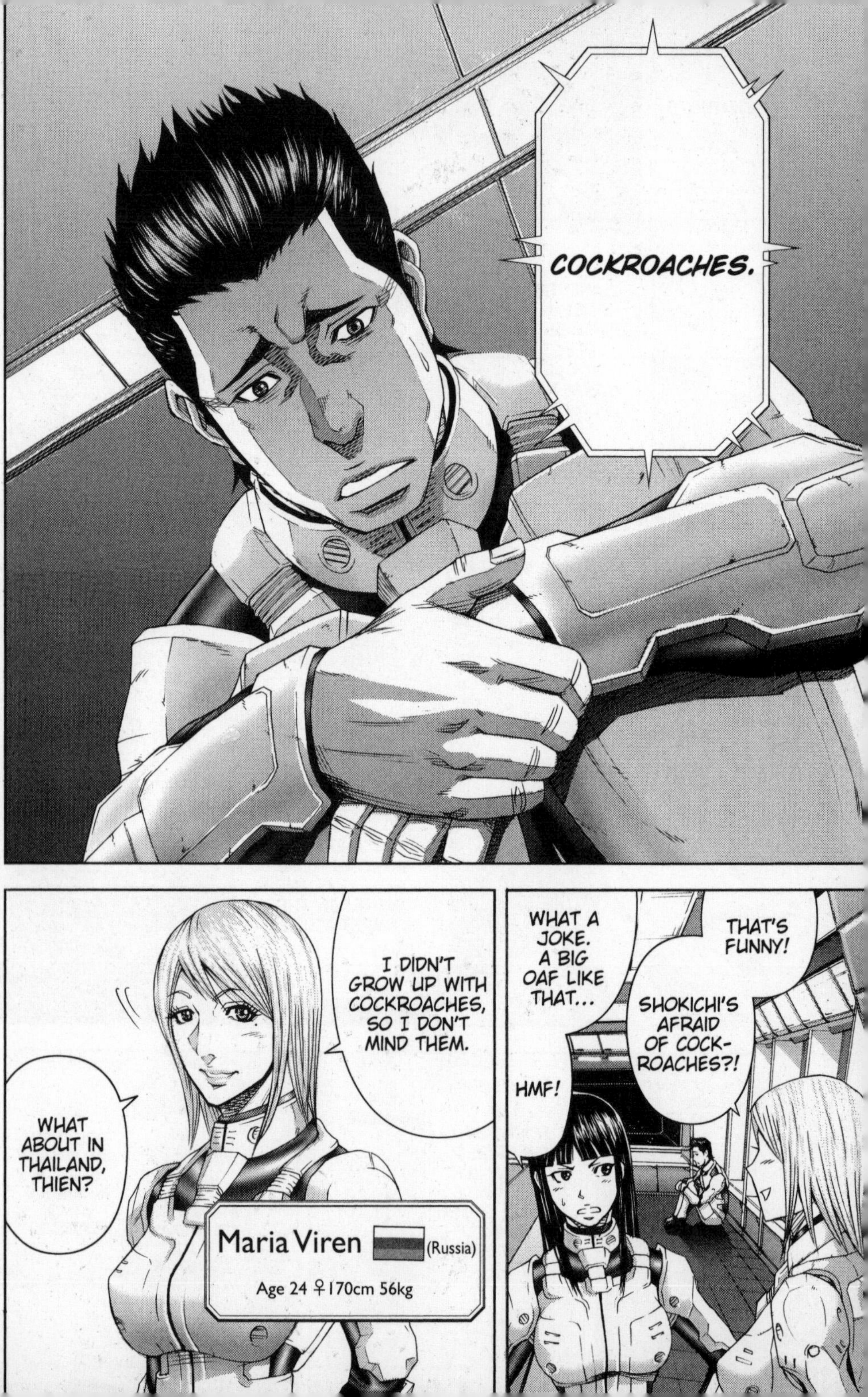

COCKROACHES.
THAT'S FUNNY!
SHOKICHI'S AFRAID OF COCK-ROACHES?!
WHAT A JOKE. A BIG OAF LIKE THAT...
HMF!
I DIDN'T GROW UP WITH COCKROACHES, SO I DON'T MIND THEM.
WHAT ABOUT IN THAILAND, THIEN?
Maria Viren (Russia)
Age 24 ♀170cm 56kg

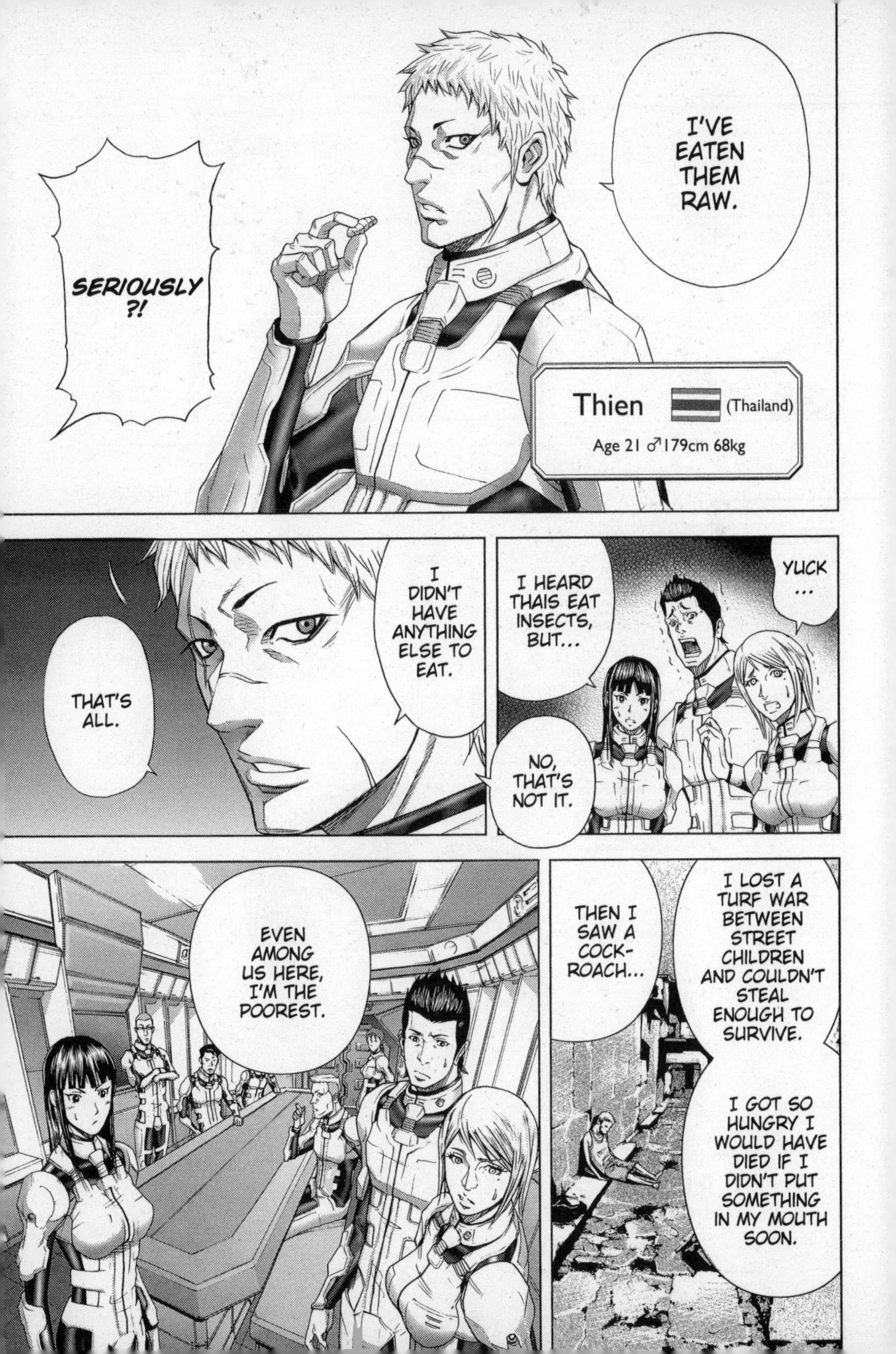
I'VE EATEN THEM RAW.
SERIOUSLY?!
Thien (Thailand)
Age 21 ♂179cm 68kg
YUCK...
I HEARD THAIS EAT INSECTS, BUT...
NO, THAT'S NOT IT.
I DIDN'T HAVE ANYTHING ELSE TO EAT.
THAT'S ALL.
I LOST A TURF WAR BETWEEN STREET CHILDREN AND COULDN'T STEAL ENOUGH TO SURVIVE.
I GOT SO HUNGRY I WOULD HAVE DIED IF I DIDN'T PUT SOMETHING IN MY MOUTH SOON.
THEN I SAW A COCK-ROACH...
EVEN AMONG US HERE, I'M THE POOREST.

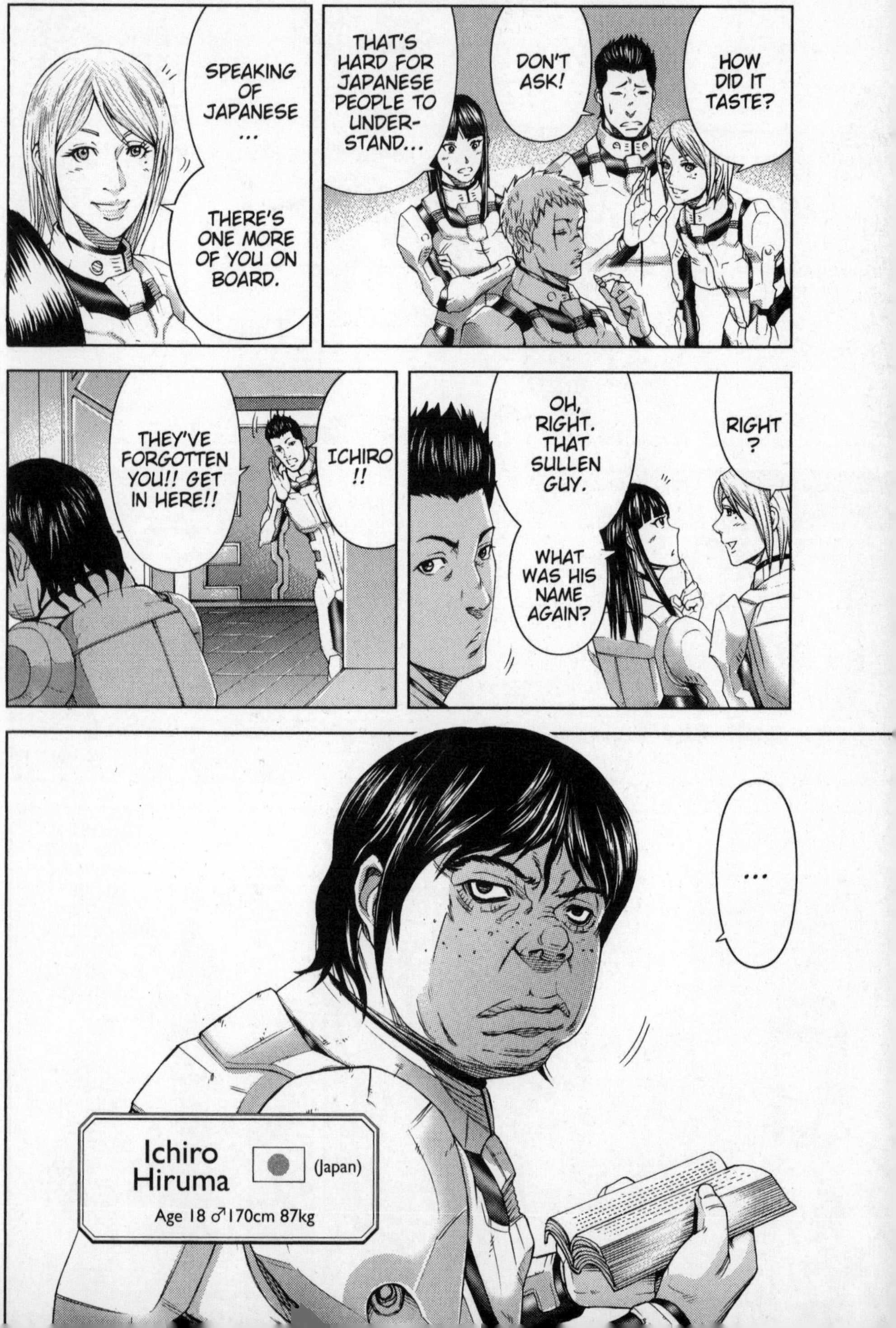
HOW DID IT TASTE?
DON'T ASK!
THAT'S HARD FOR JAPANESE PEOPLE TO UNDERSTAND...
SPEAKING OF JAPANESE...
THERE'S ONE MORE OF YOU ON BOARD.
RIGHT?
OH, RIGHT. THAT SULLEN GUY.
WHAT WAS HIS NAME AGAIN?
ICHIRO!!
THEY'VE FORGOTTEN YOU!! GET IN HERE!!
...
Ichiro Hiruma (Japan)
Age 18 ♂170cm 87kg

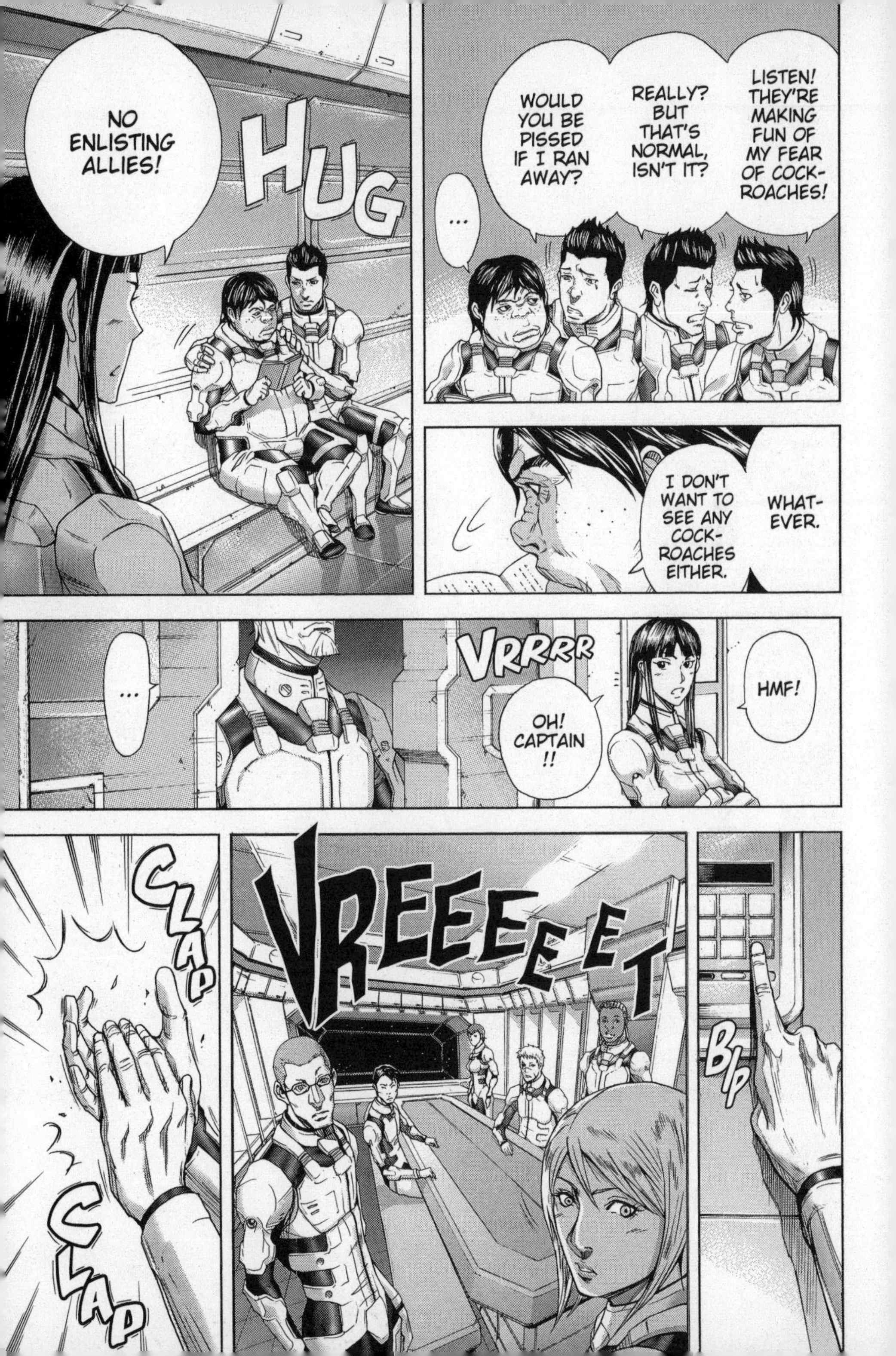
LISTEN! THEY'RE MAKING FUN OF MY FEAR OF COCK-ROACHES!
REALLY? BUT THAT'S NORMAL, ISN'T IT?
WOULD YOU BE PISSED IF I RAN AWAY?
...
WHAT-EVER.
I DON'T WANT TO SEE ANY COCK-ROACHES EITHER.
HUG
NO ENLISTING ALLIES!
HMF!
OH! CAPTAIN !!
VRRRR
...
BIP
VREEEEET
CLAP
CLAP

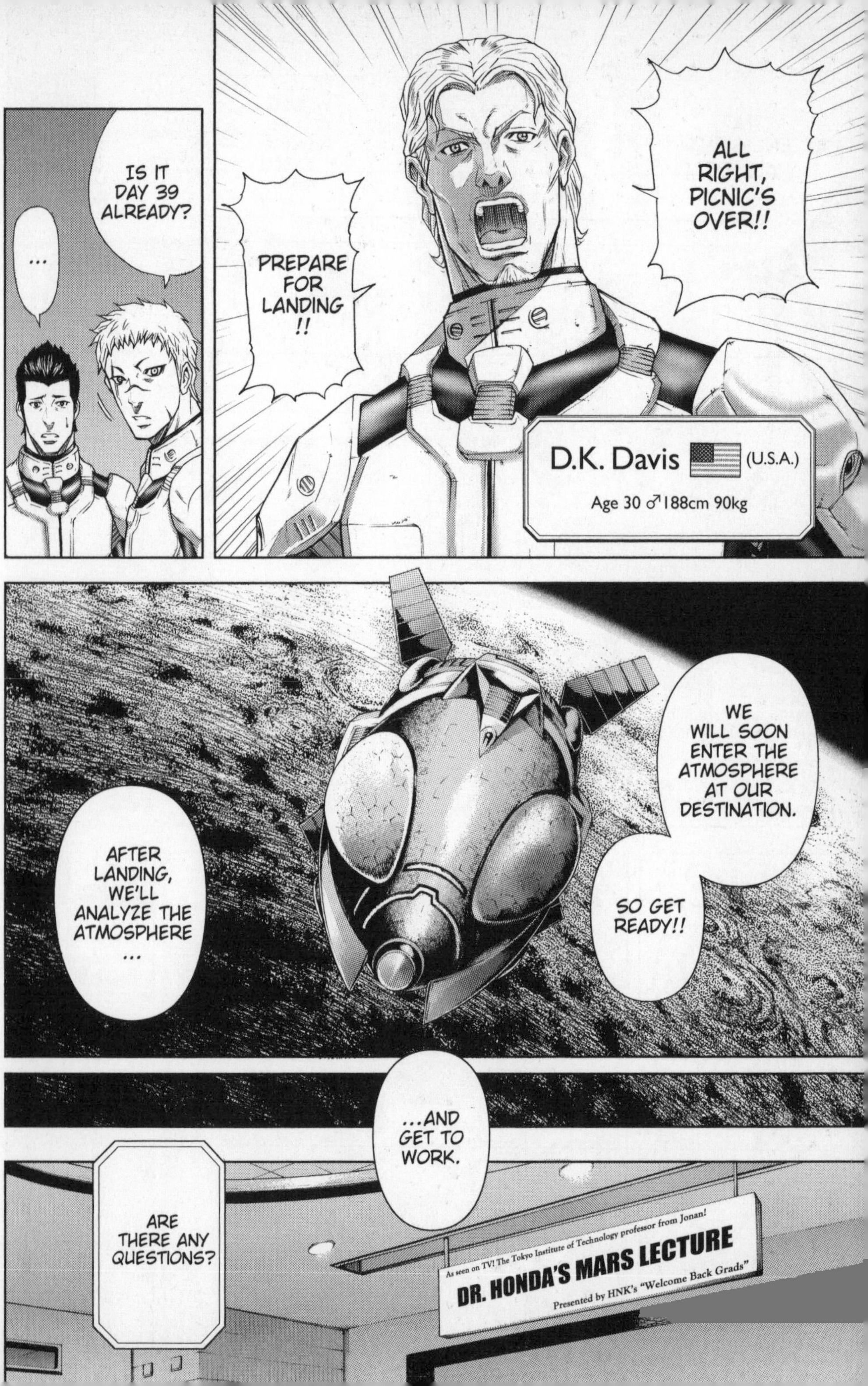

ALL RIGHT, PICNIC'S OVER!!
PREPARE FOR LANDING!!
D.K. Davis (U.S.A.)
Age 30 ♂188cm 90kg
IS IT DAY 39 ALREADY?
...
WE WILL SOON ENTER THE ATMOSPHERE AT OUR DESTINATION.
SO GET READY!!
AFTER LANDING, WE'LL ANALYZE THE ATMOSPHERE...
...AND GET TO WORK.
As seen on TV! The Tokyo Institute of Technology professor from Jonan!
DR. HONDA'S MARS LECTURE
Presented by HNK's "Welcome Back Grads"
ARE THERE ANY QUESTIONS?

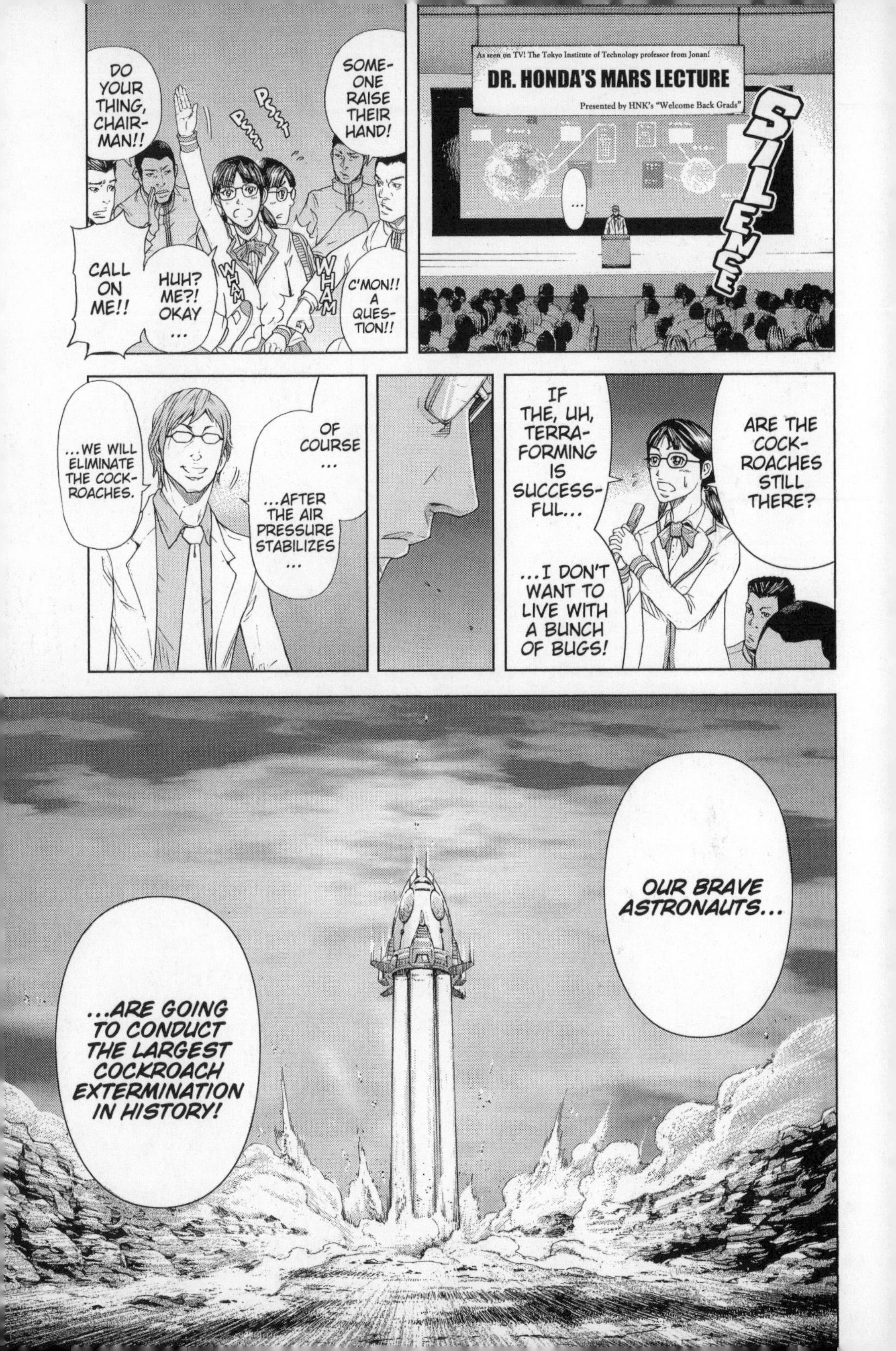
As seen on TV! The Tokyo Institute of Technology professor from Jonan!
DR. HONDA'S MARS LECTURE
Presented by HNK's "Welcome Back Grads"
SILENCE
...
SOME-ONE RAISE THEIR HAND!
DO YOUR THING, CHAIR-MAN!!
C'MON!! A QUES-TION!!
WHAM
WHAM
HUH? ME?! OKAY...
CALL ON ME!!
ARE THE COCK-ROACHES STILL THERE?
IF THE, UH, TERRA-FORMING IS SUCCESS-FUL...
...I DON'T WANT TO LIVE WITH A BUNCH OF BUGS!
OF COURSE...
...AFTER THE AIR PRESSURE STABILIZES...
...WE WILL ELIMINATE THE COCK-ROACHES.
OUR BRAVE ASTRONAUTS...
...ARE GOING TO CONDUCT THE LARGEST COCKROACH EXTERMINATION IN HISTORY!

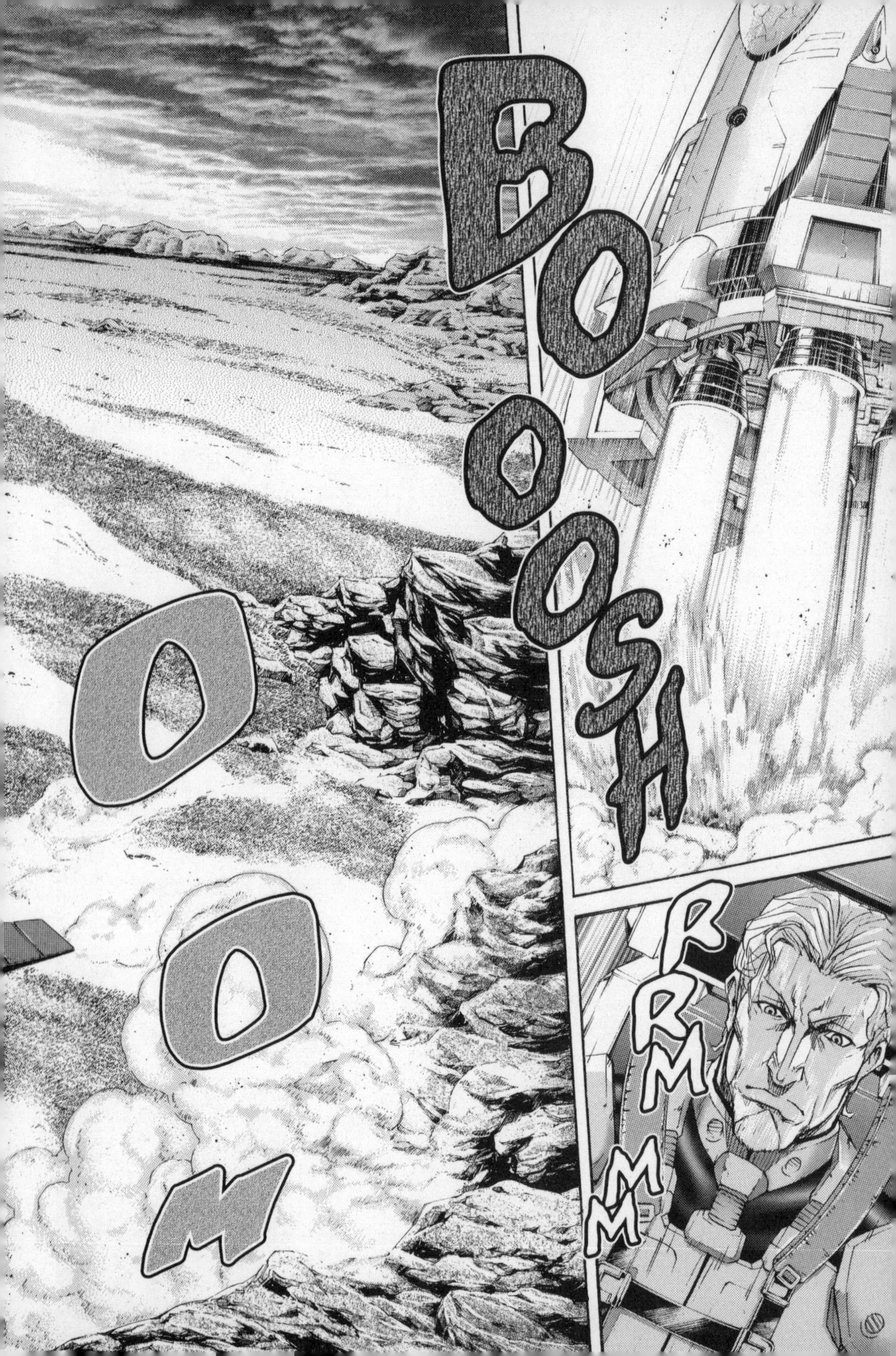

BOOOOSH
RRMMM
OOM

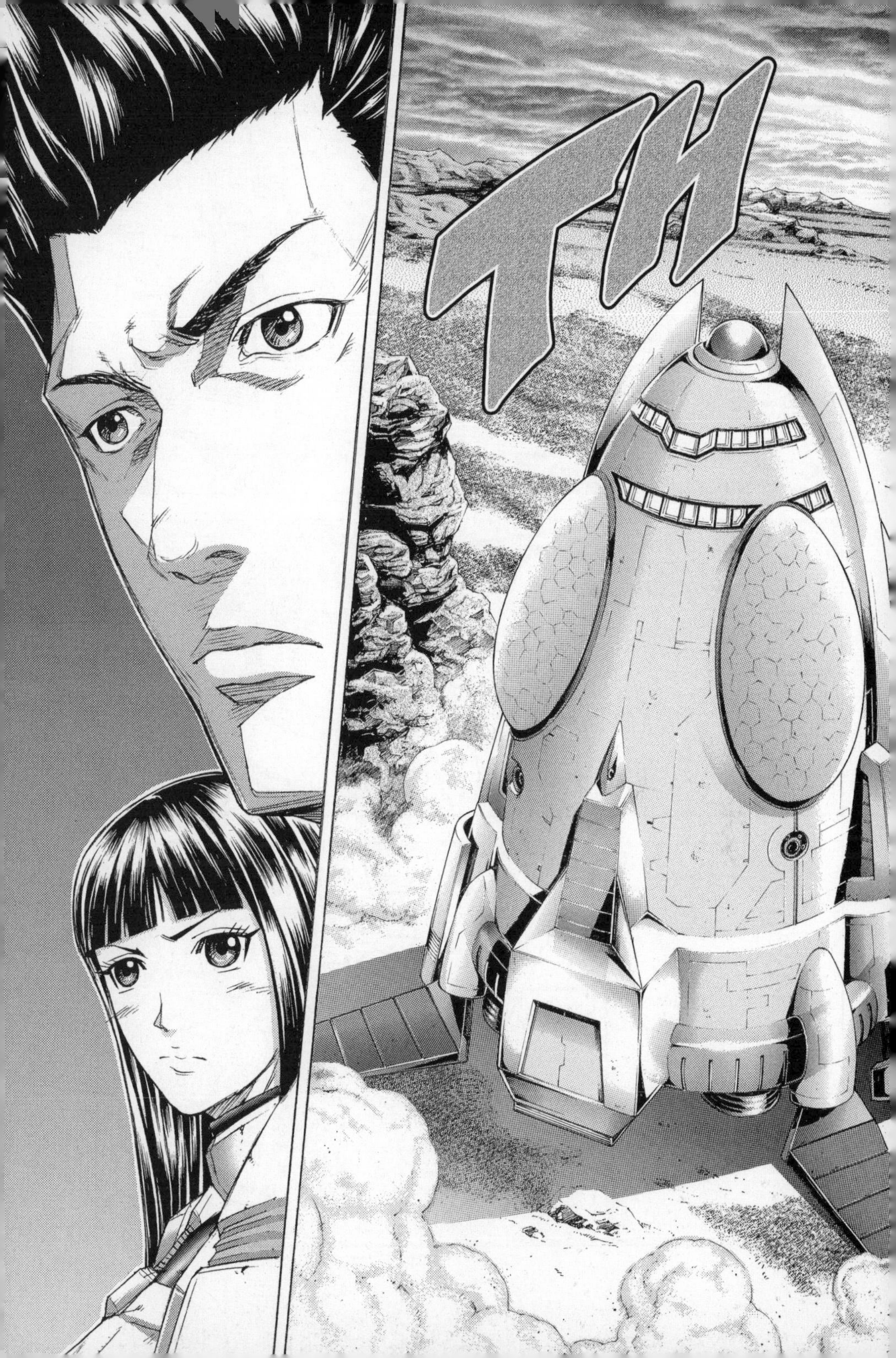

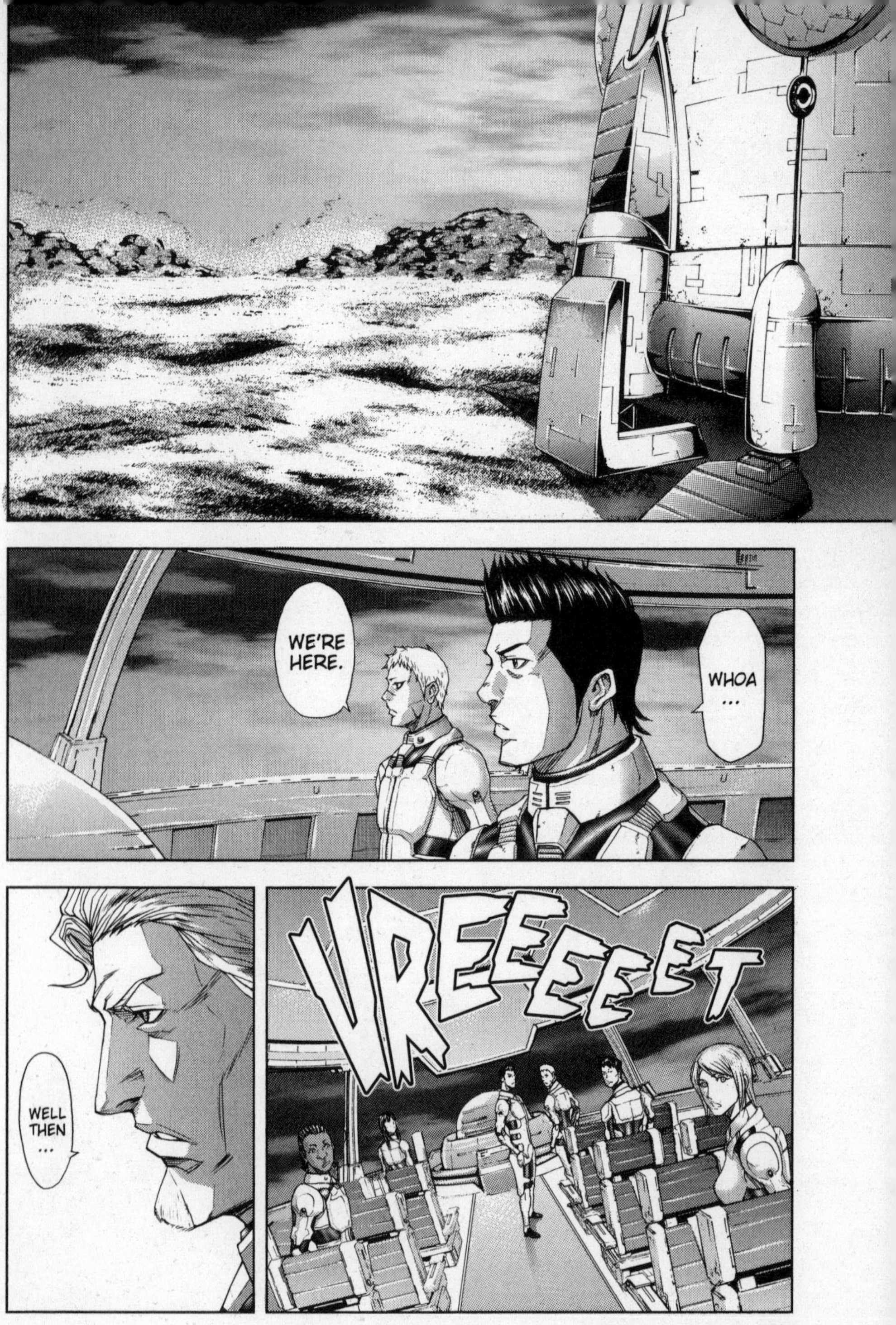
WHOA ...
WE'RE HERE.
VREEEEET
WELL THEN ...

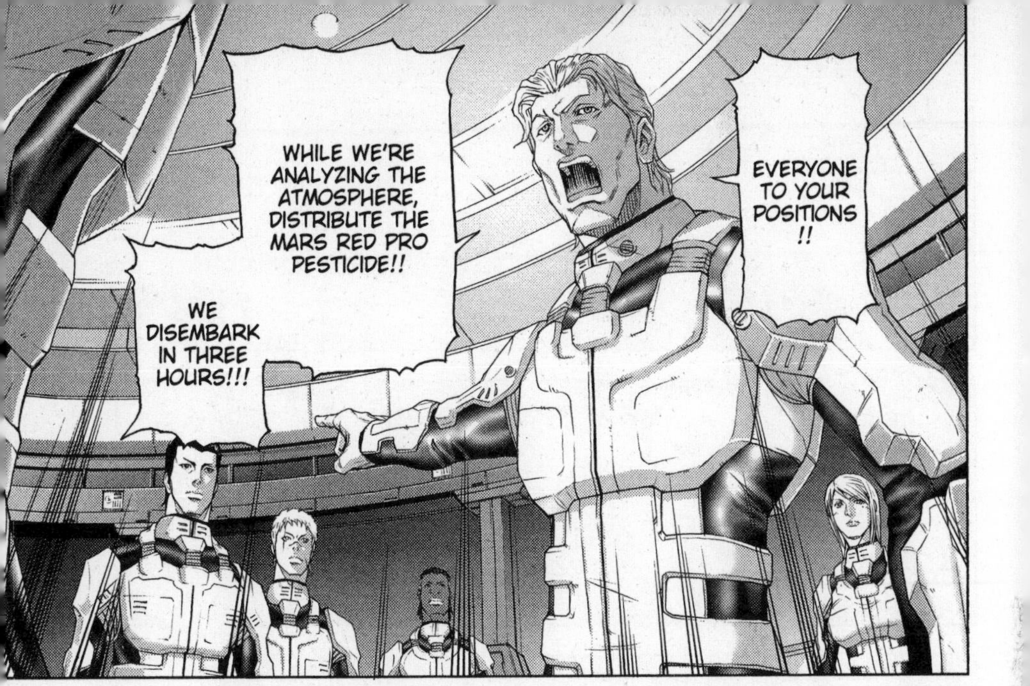
EVERYONE TO YOUR POSITIONS !!
WHILE WE'RE ANALYZING THE ATMOSPHERE, DISTRIBUTE THE MARS RED PRO PESTICIDE!!
WE DISEMBARK IN THREE HOURS!!!

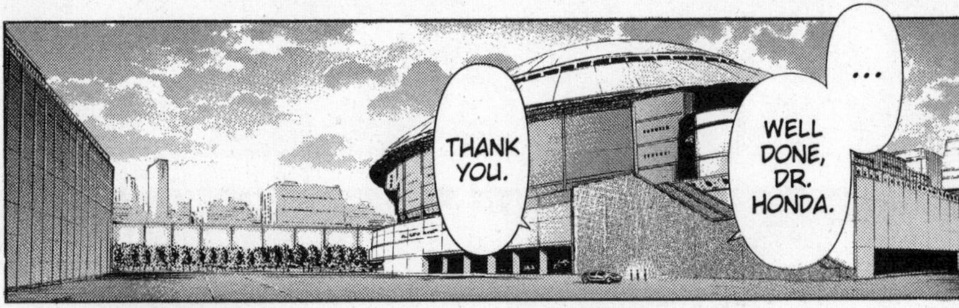
...
WELL DONE, DR. HONDA.
THANK YOU.

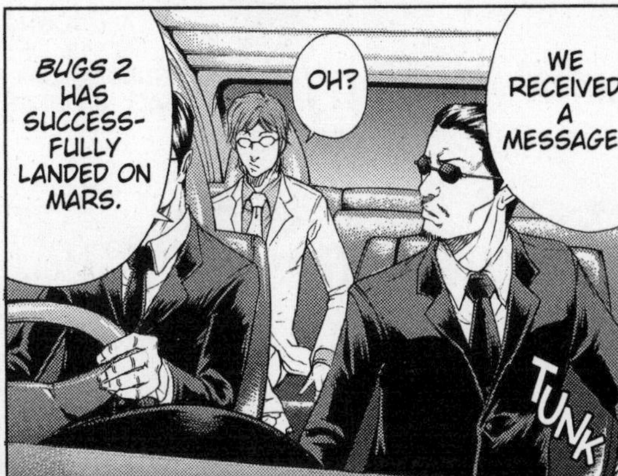
WE RECEIVED A MESSAGE.
OH?
BUGS 2 HAS SUCCESS-FULLY LANDED ON MARS.
TUNK

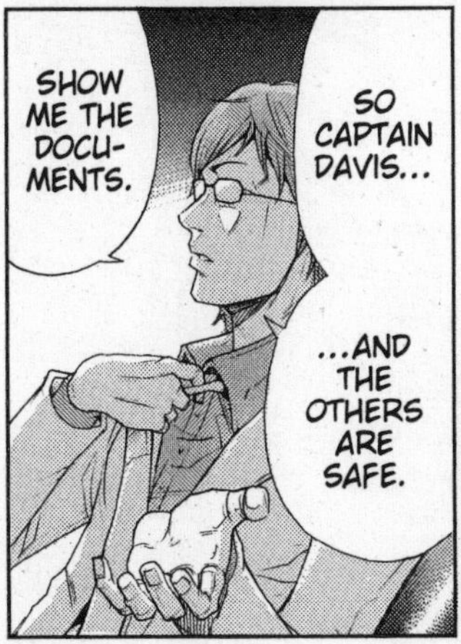
SO CAPTAIN DAVIS...
...AND THE OTHERS ARE SAFE.
SHOW ME THE DOCU-MENTS.

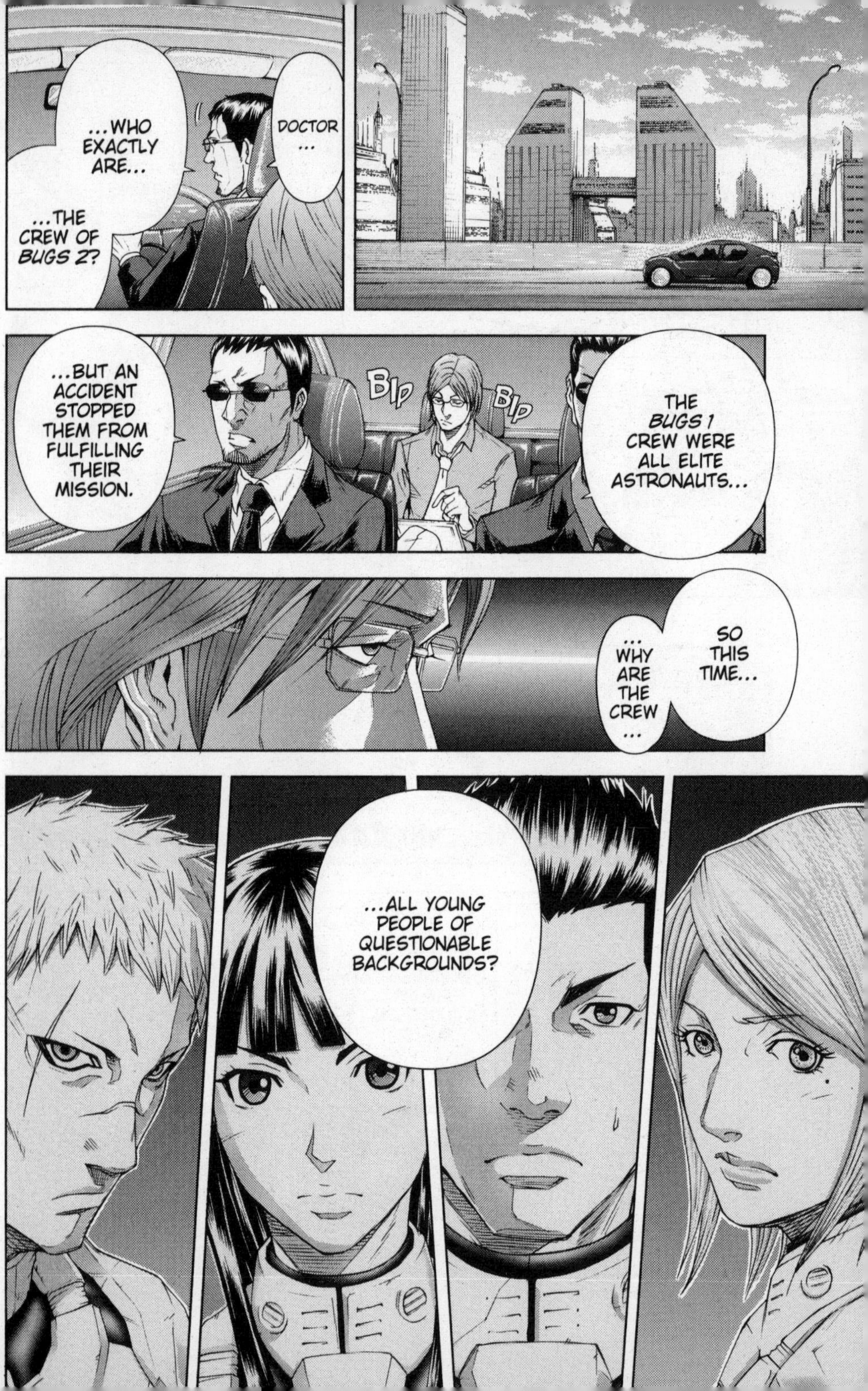
DOCTOR...
...WHO EXACTLY ARE... ...THE CREW OF BUGS 2?
THE BUGS 1 CREW WERE ALL ELITE ASTRONAUTS...
BIP
BIP
...BUT AN ACCIDENT STOPPED THEM FROM FULFILLING THEIR MISSION.
SO THIS TIME...
...WHY ARE THE CREW...
...ALL YOUNG PEOPLE OF QUESTIONABLE BACKGROUNDS?

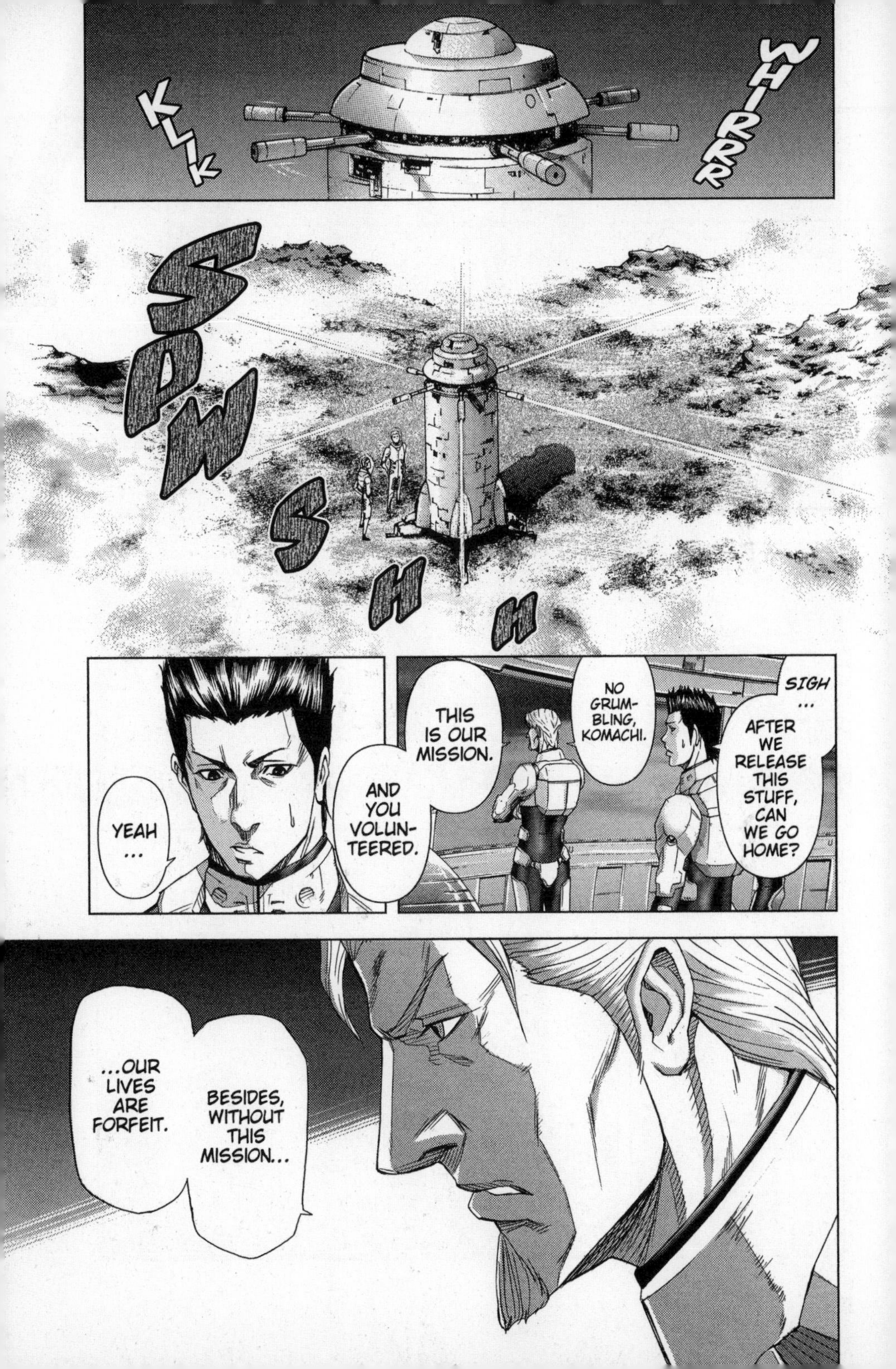
WHIRRR
KLIK
SPWSHH
SIGH...
AFTER WE RELEASE THIS STUFF, CAN WE GO HOME?
NO GRUM-BLING, KOMACHI.
THIS IS OUR MISSION.
AND YOU VOLUN-TEERED.
YEAH...
BESIDES, WITHOUT THIS MISSION...
...OUR LIVES ARE FORFEIT.

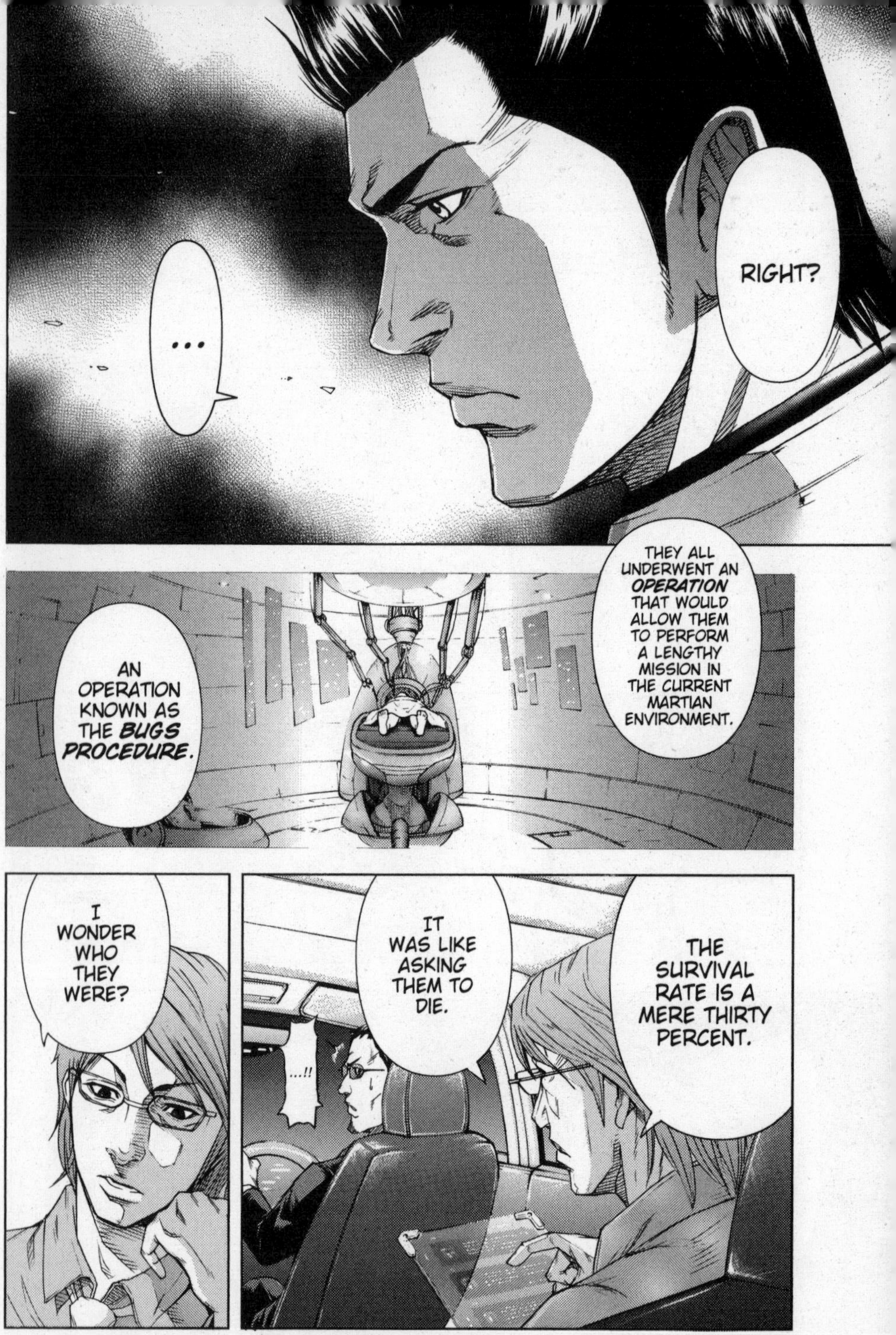
RIGHT?
...
THEY ALL UNDERWENT AN OPERATION THAT WOULD ALLOW THEM TO PERFORM A LENGTHY MISSION IN THE CURRENT MARTIAN ENVIRONMENT.
AN OPERATION KNOWN AS THE BUGS PROCEDURE.
THE SURVIVAL RATE IS A MERE THIRTY PERCENT.
IT WAS LIKE ASKING THEM TO DIE.
...!!
I WONDER WHO THEY WERE?

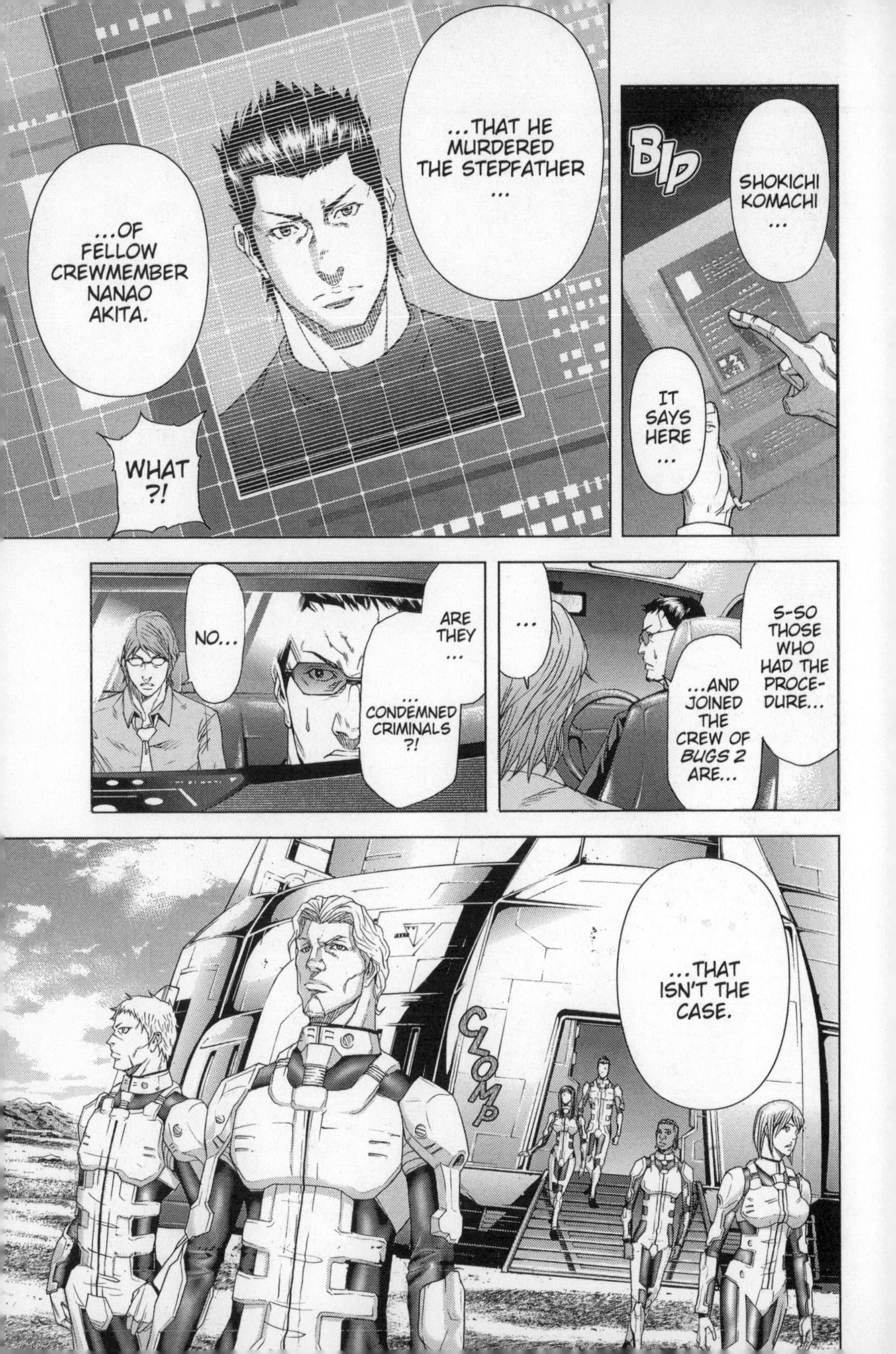
BIP
SHOKICHI KOMACHI...
IT SAYS HERE...
...THAT HE MURDERED THE STEPFATHER...
...OF FELLOW CREWMEMBER NANAO AKITA.
WHAT?!
S-SO THOSE WHO HAD THE PROCEDURE...
...AND JOINED THE CREW OF BUGS 2 ARE...
...
ARE THEY...
...CONDEMNED CRIMINALS?!
NO...
...THAT ISN'T THE CASE.
CLOMP

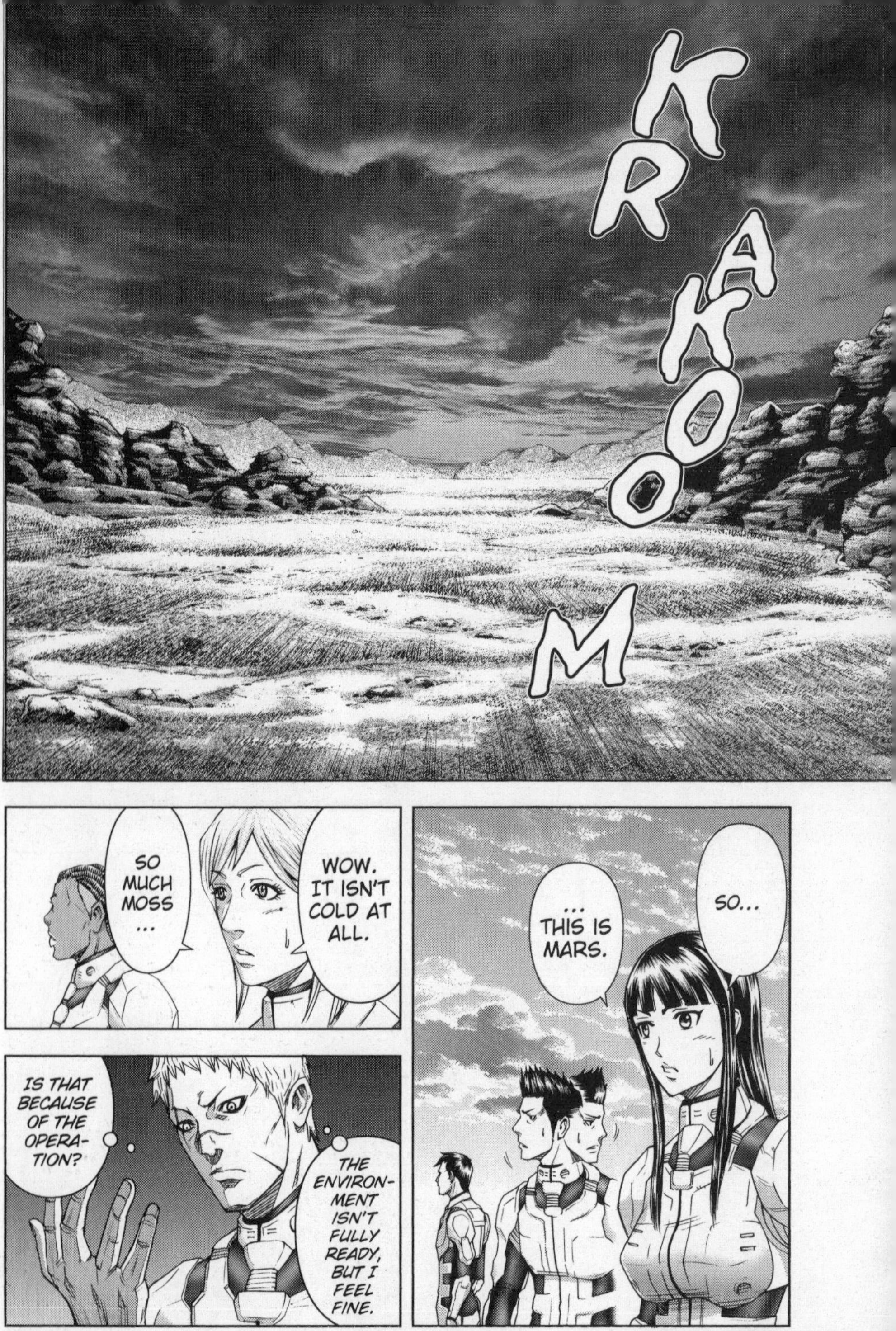
KRAKOOM
SO...
... THIS IS MARS.
WOW. IT ISN'T COLD AT ALL.
SO MUCH MOSS ...
THE ENVIRONMENT ISN'T FULLY READY, BUT I FEEL FINE.
IS THAT BECAUSE OF THE OPERATION?

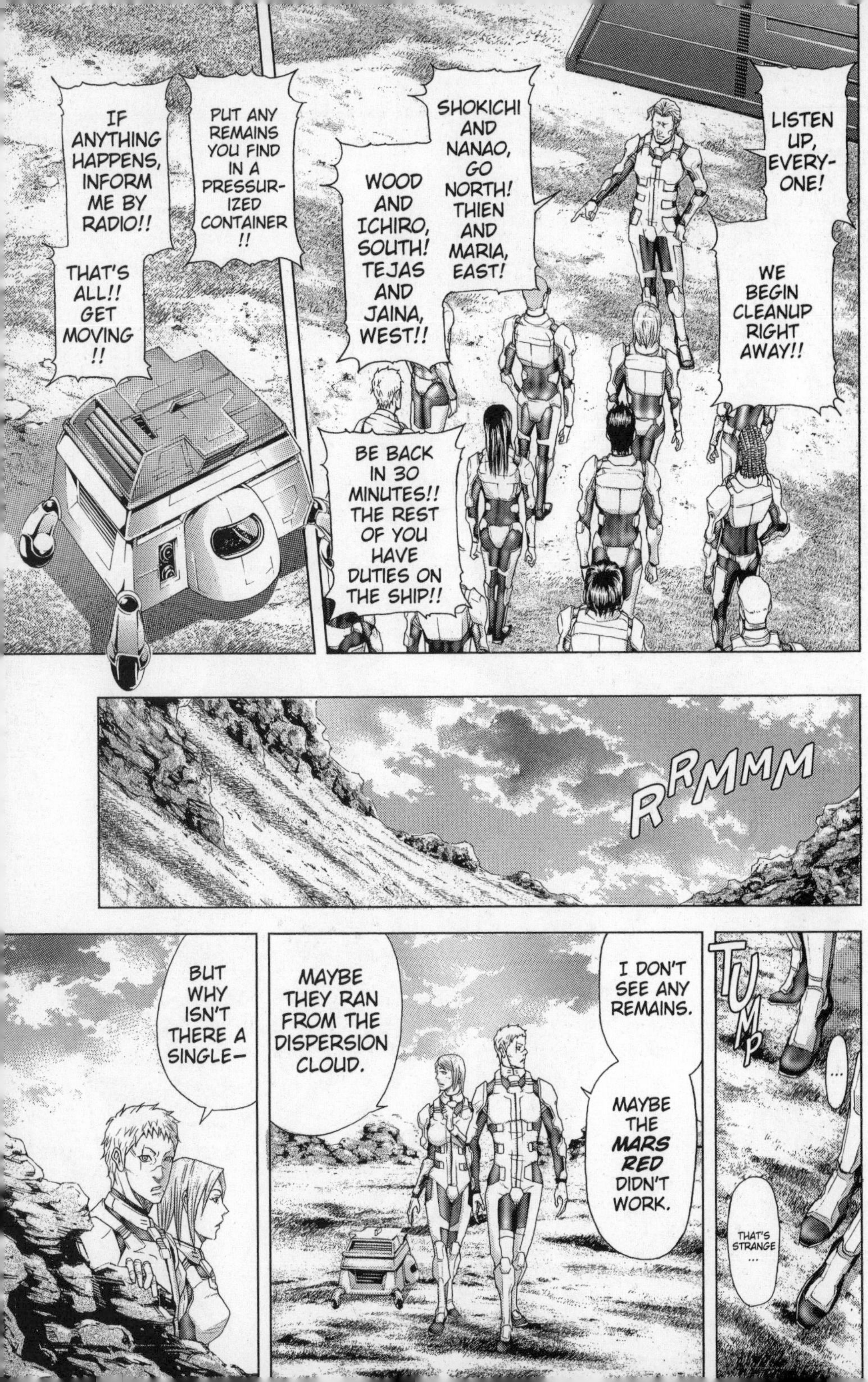
LISTEN UP, EVERYONE!
WE BEGIN CLEANUP RIGHT AWAY!!
SHOKICHI AND NANAO, GO NORTH! THIEN AND MARIA, EAST!
WOOD AND ICHIRO, SOUTH! TEJAS AND JAINA, WEST!!
BE BACK IN 30 MINUTES!! THE REST OF YOU HAVE DUTIES ON THE SHIP!!
PUT ANY REMAINS YOU FIND IN A PRESSURIZED CONTAINER!!
IF ANYTHING HAPPENS, INFORM ME BY RADIO!!
THAT'S ALL!! GET MOVING!!
RRMMMM
TUMP
...
THAT'S STRANGE...
I DON'T SEE ANY REMAINS.
MAYBE THE **MARS RED** DIDN'T WORK.
MAYBE THEY RAN FROM THE DISPERSION CLOUD.
BUT WHY ISN'T THERE A SINGLE—

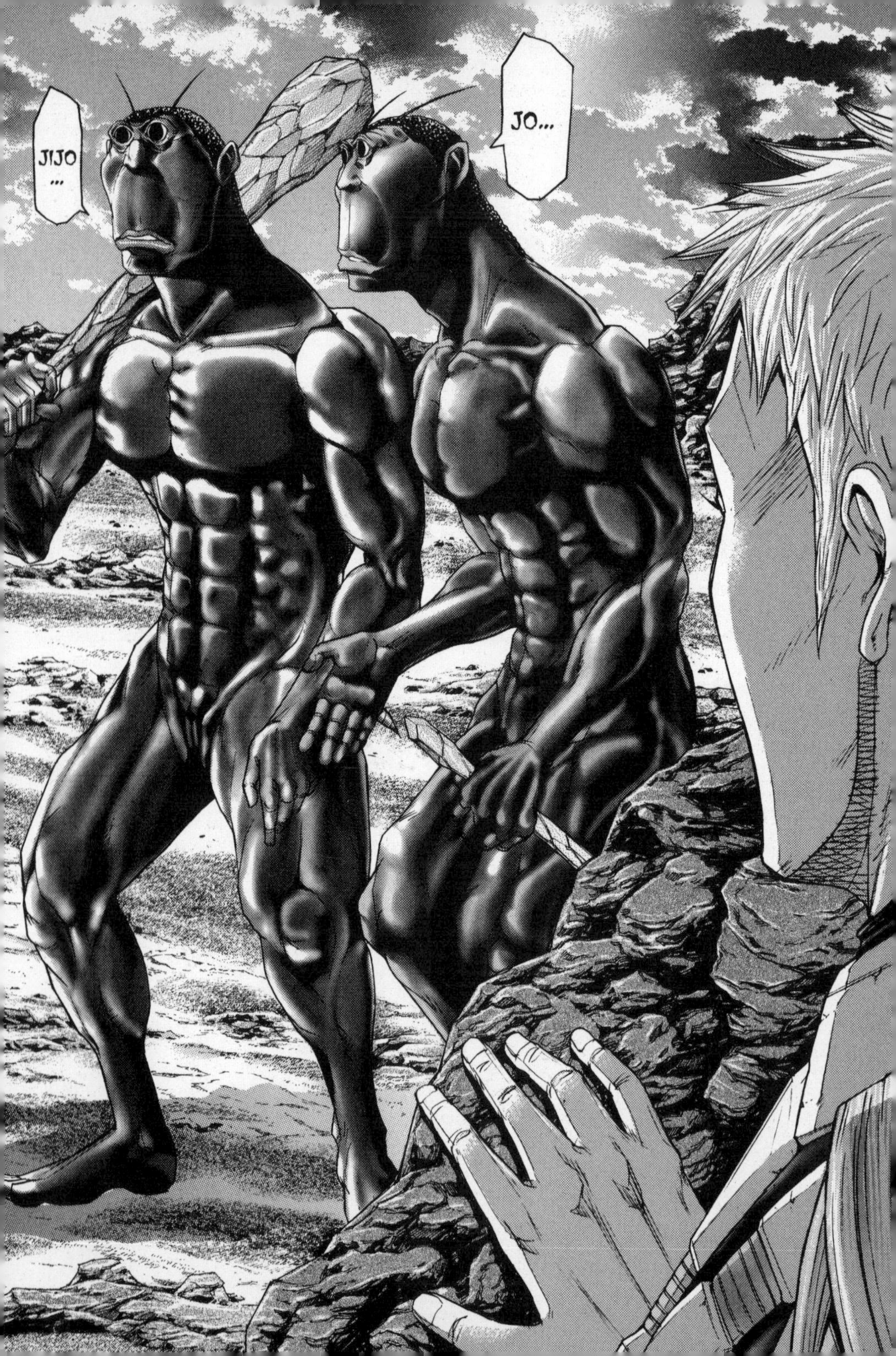
JO...
JIJO ...

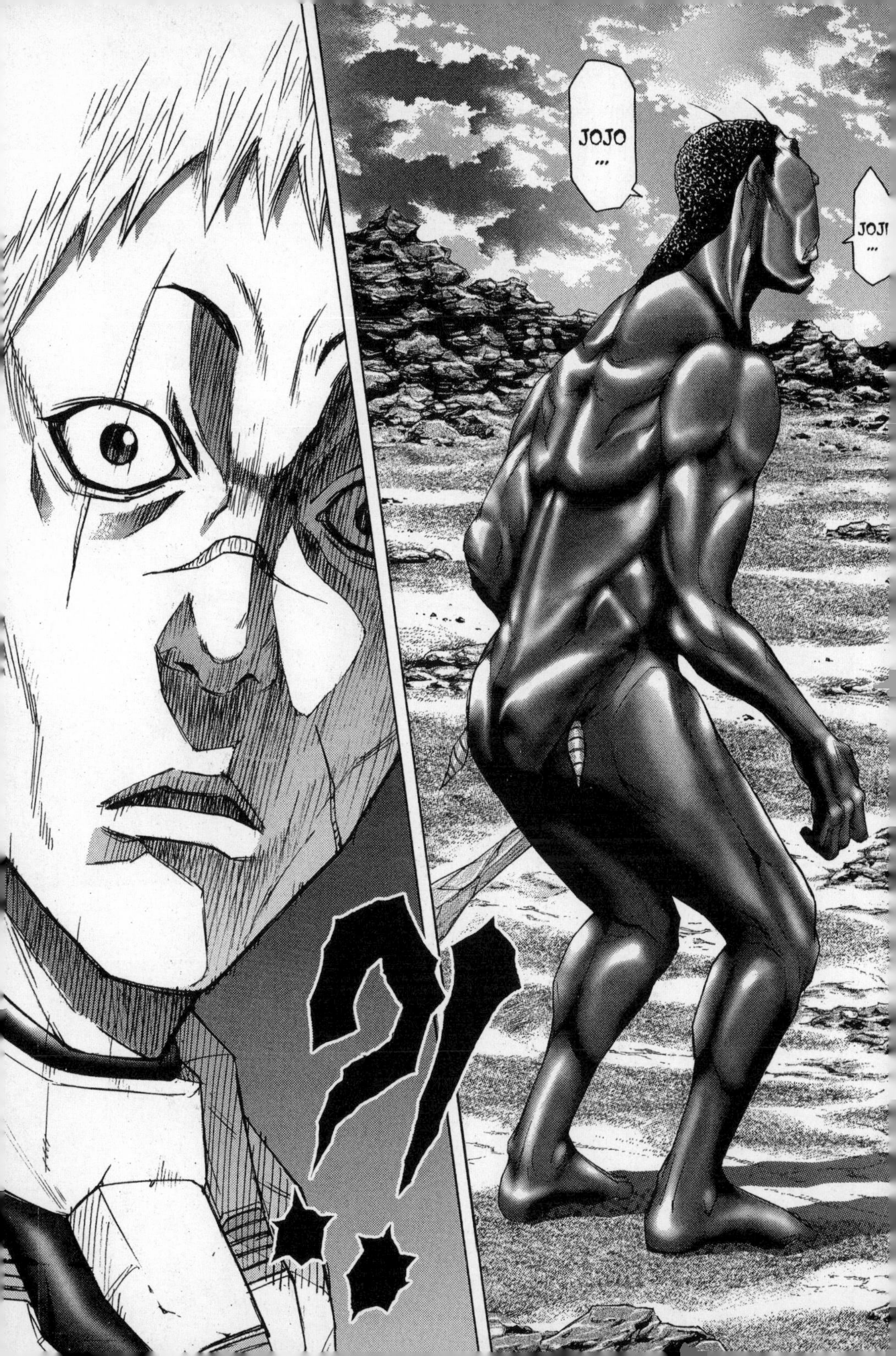
JOJ ...
JOJO ...

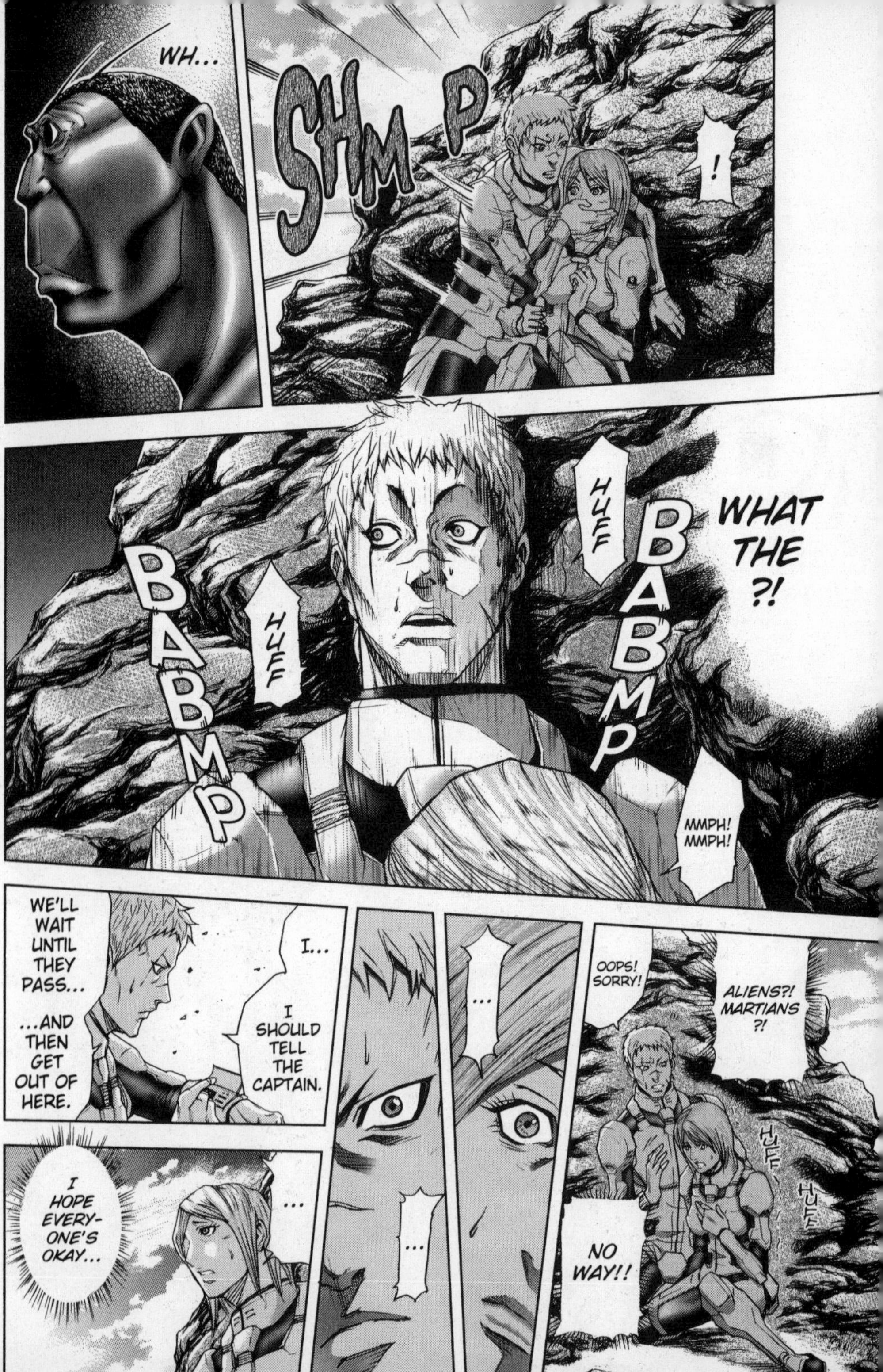
SHMP
!
WH...
WHAT THE ?!
BABMP
HUFF
MMPH! MMPH!
HUFF
BABMP
ALIENS?! MARTIANS ?!
OOPS! SORRY!
HUFF HUFF
NO WAY!!
!
...
...
I...
I SHOULD TELL THE CAPTAIN.
WE'LL WAIT UNTIL THEY PASS...
...AND THEN GET OUT OF HERE.
...
I HOPE EVERYONE'S OKAY...

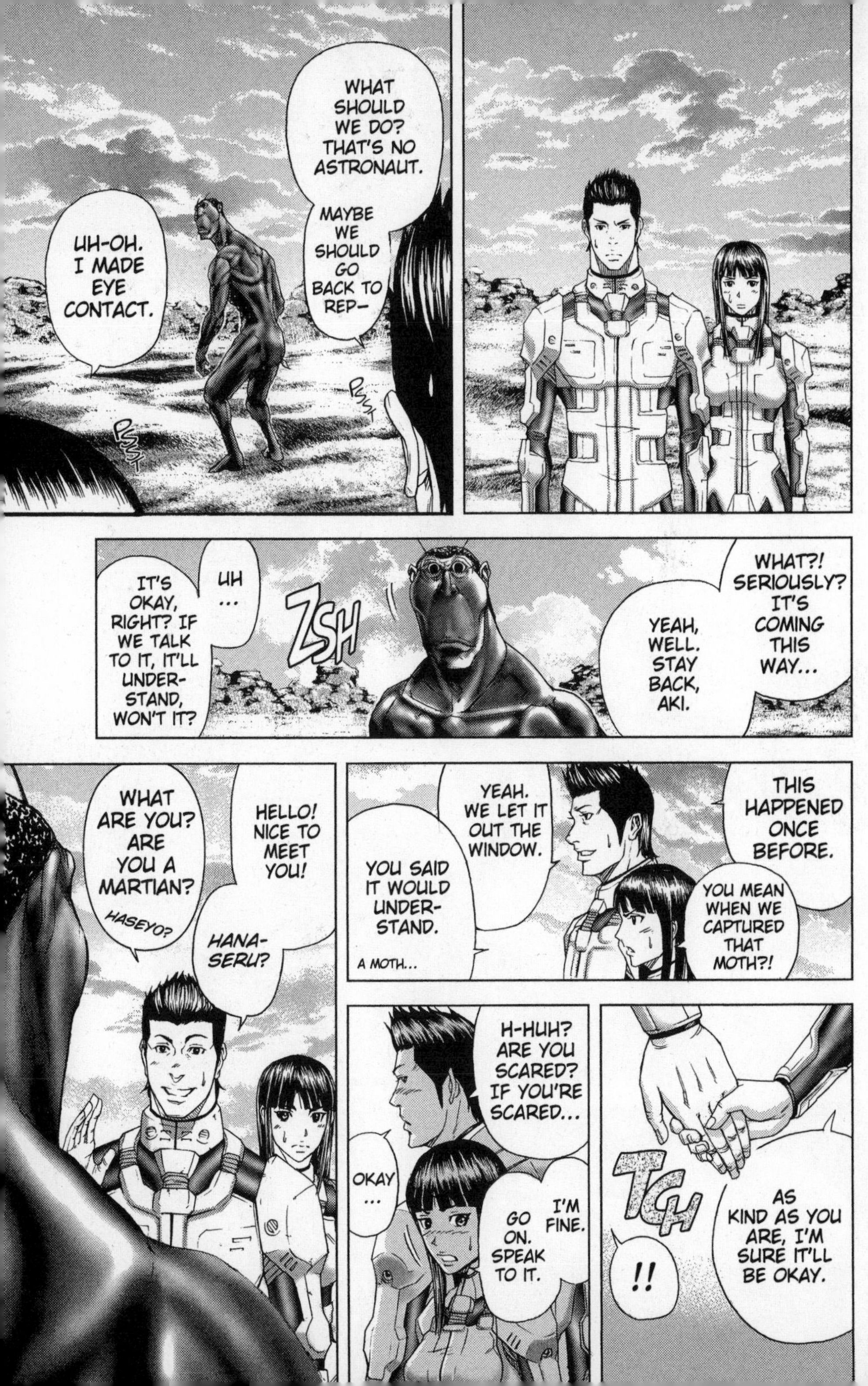
WHAT SHOULD WE DO? THAT'S NO ASTRONAUT.
MAYBE WE SHOULD GO BACK TO REP–
PSSST
UH-OH. I MADE EYE CONTACT.
PSSST
WHAT?! SERIOUSLY? IT'S COMING THIS WAY...
YEAH, WELL. STAY BACK, AKI.
ZSH
UH ...
IT'S OKAY, RIGHT? IF WE TALK TO IT, IT'LL UNDER-STAND, WON'T IT?
THIS HAPPENED ONCE BEFORE.
YOU MEAN WHEN WE CAPTURED THAT MOTH?!
YEAH. WE LET IT OUT THE WINDOW.
YOU SAID IT WOULD UNDER-STAND.
A MOTH...
AS KIND AS YOU ARE, I'M SURE IT'LL BE OKAY.
TCH
!!
H-HUH? ARE YOU SCARED? IF YOU'RE SCARED...
I'M FINE.
GO ON. SPEAK TO IT.
OKAY ...
HELLO! NICE TO MEET YOU!
HANA-SERU?
WHAT ARE YOU? ARE YOU A MARTIAN?
HASEYO?

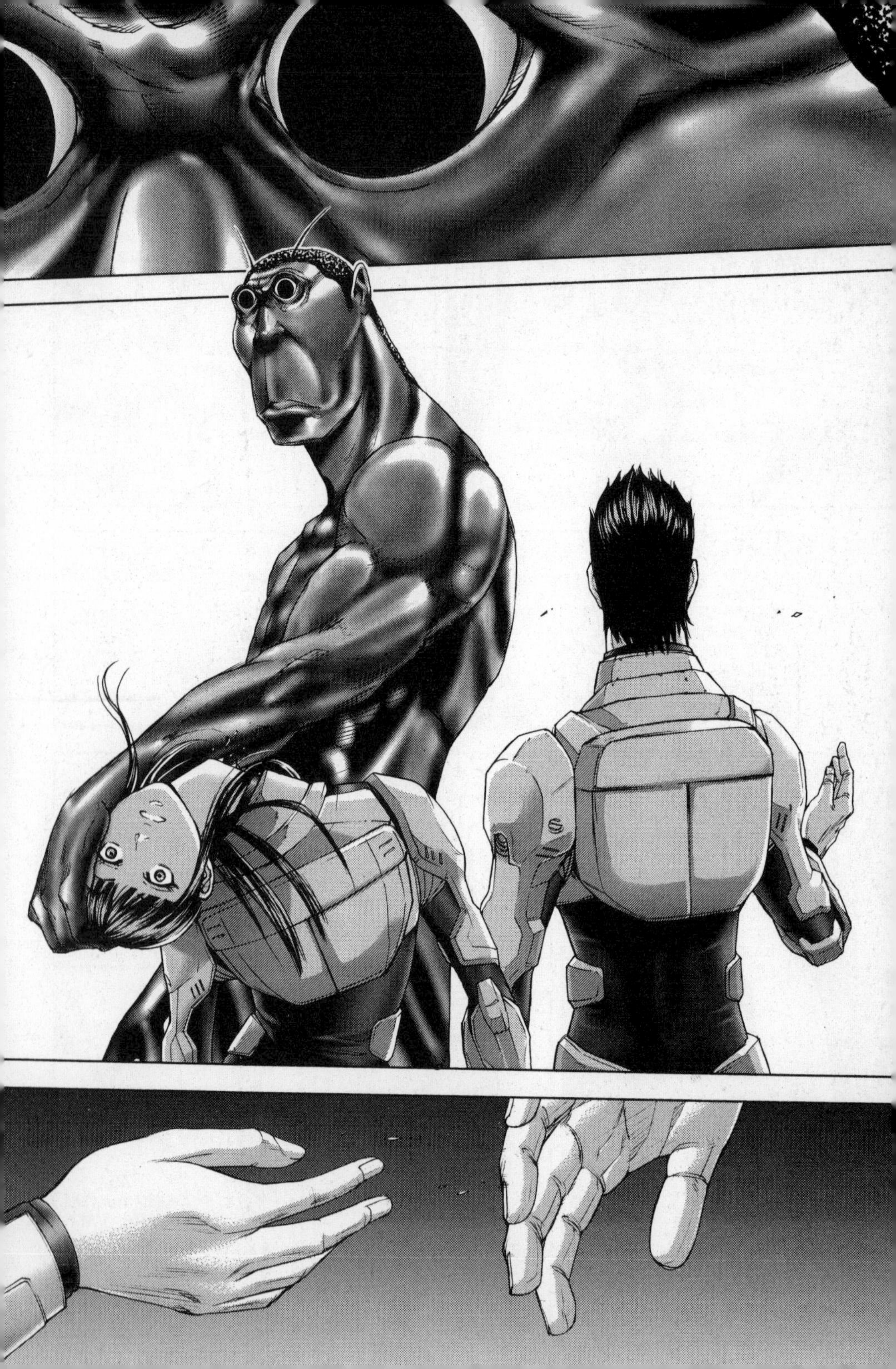

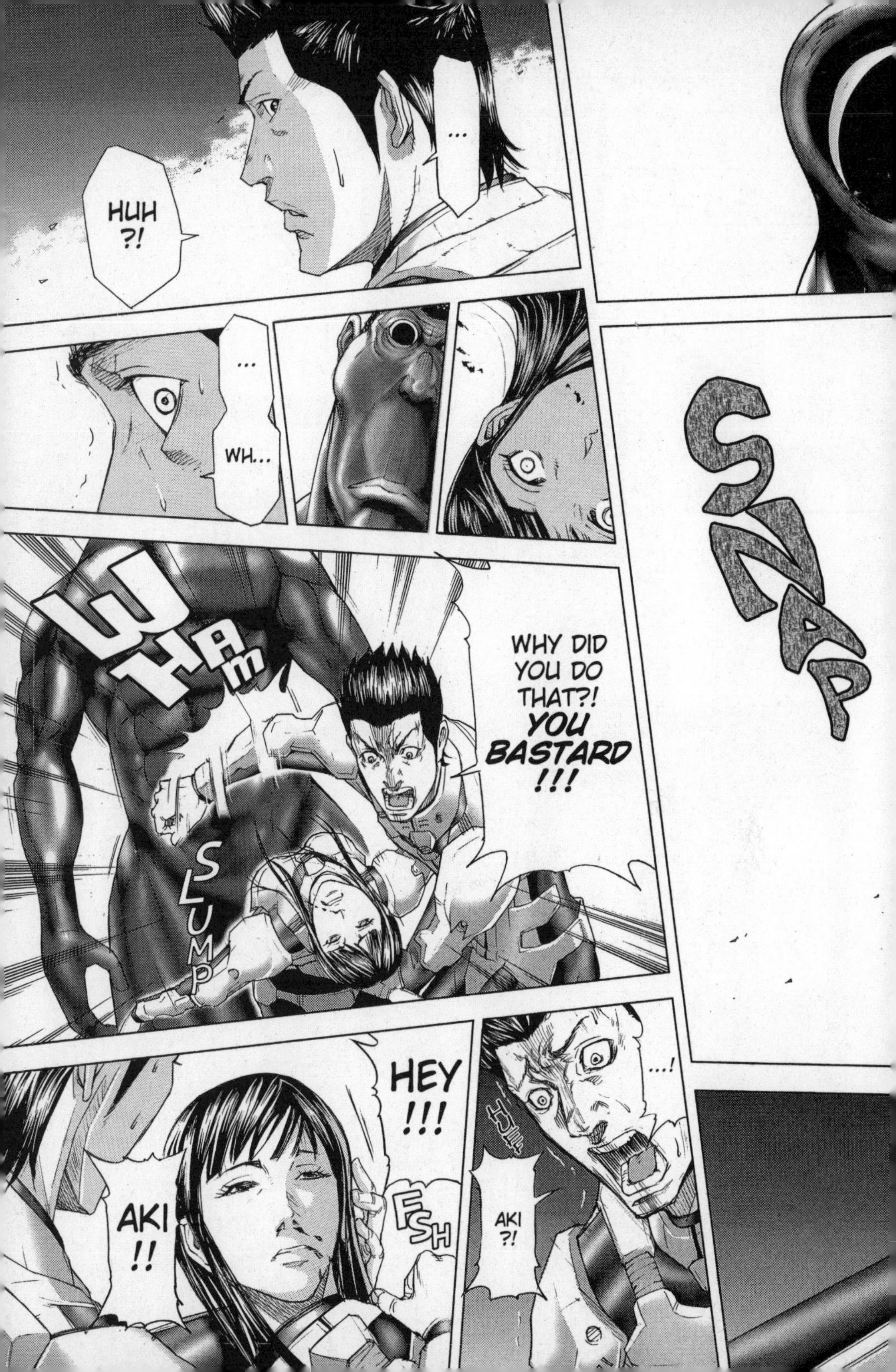
...
HUH ?!
SZAP
...
WH...
WHY DID YOU DO THAT?! YOU BASTARD !!!
WHAM
SLUMP
...!
AKI ?!
HEY !!!
FSH
AKI !!

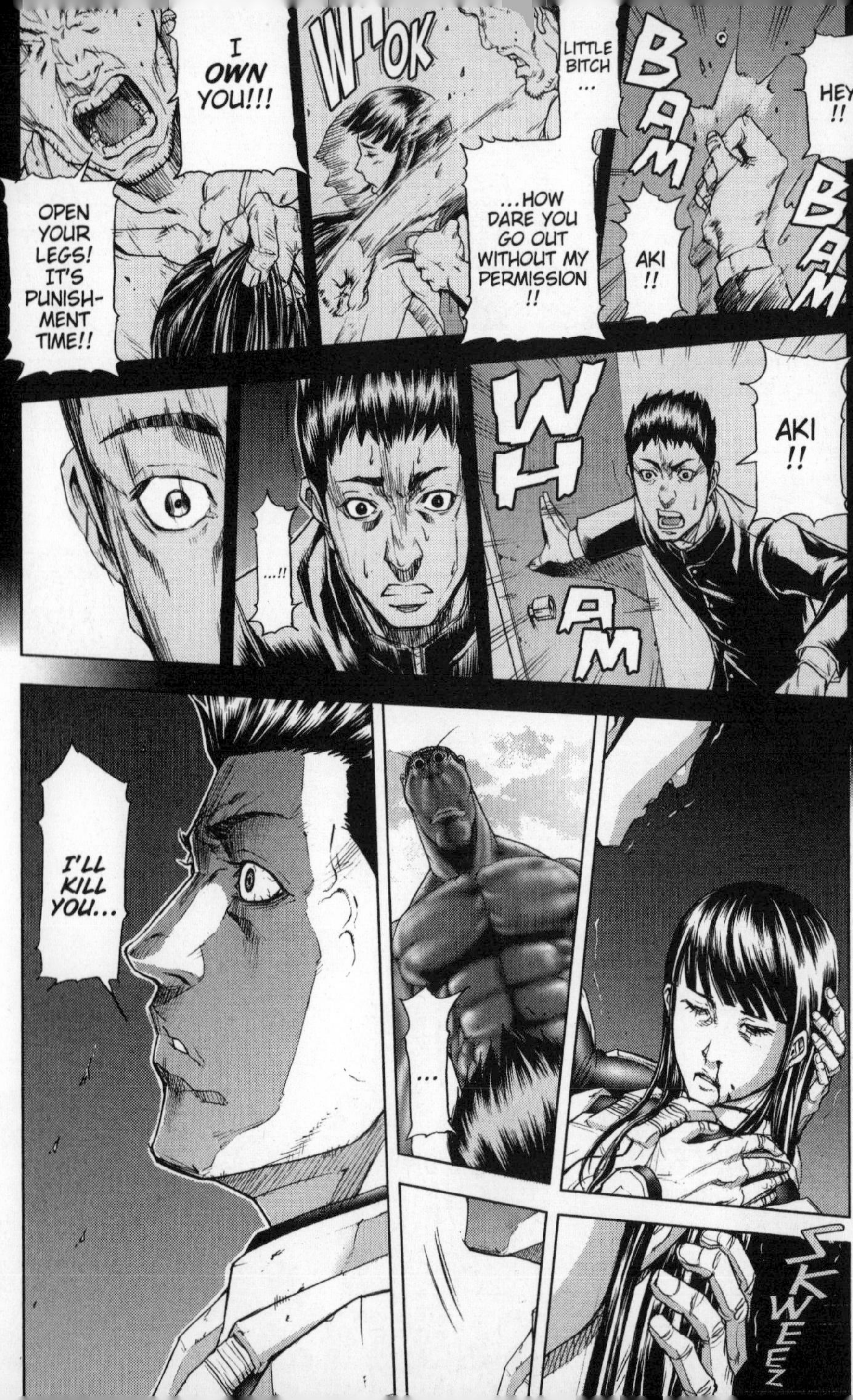

HEY!!
BAM
BAM
AKI!!
LITTLE BITCH...
WHOK
...HOW DARE YOU GO OUT WITHOUT MY PERMISSION!!
I OWN YOU!!!
OPEN YOUR LEGS! IT'S PUNISHMENT TIME!!
AKI!!
WHAM
...!!
...
SKWEEZ
I'LL KILL YOU...

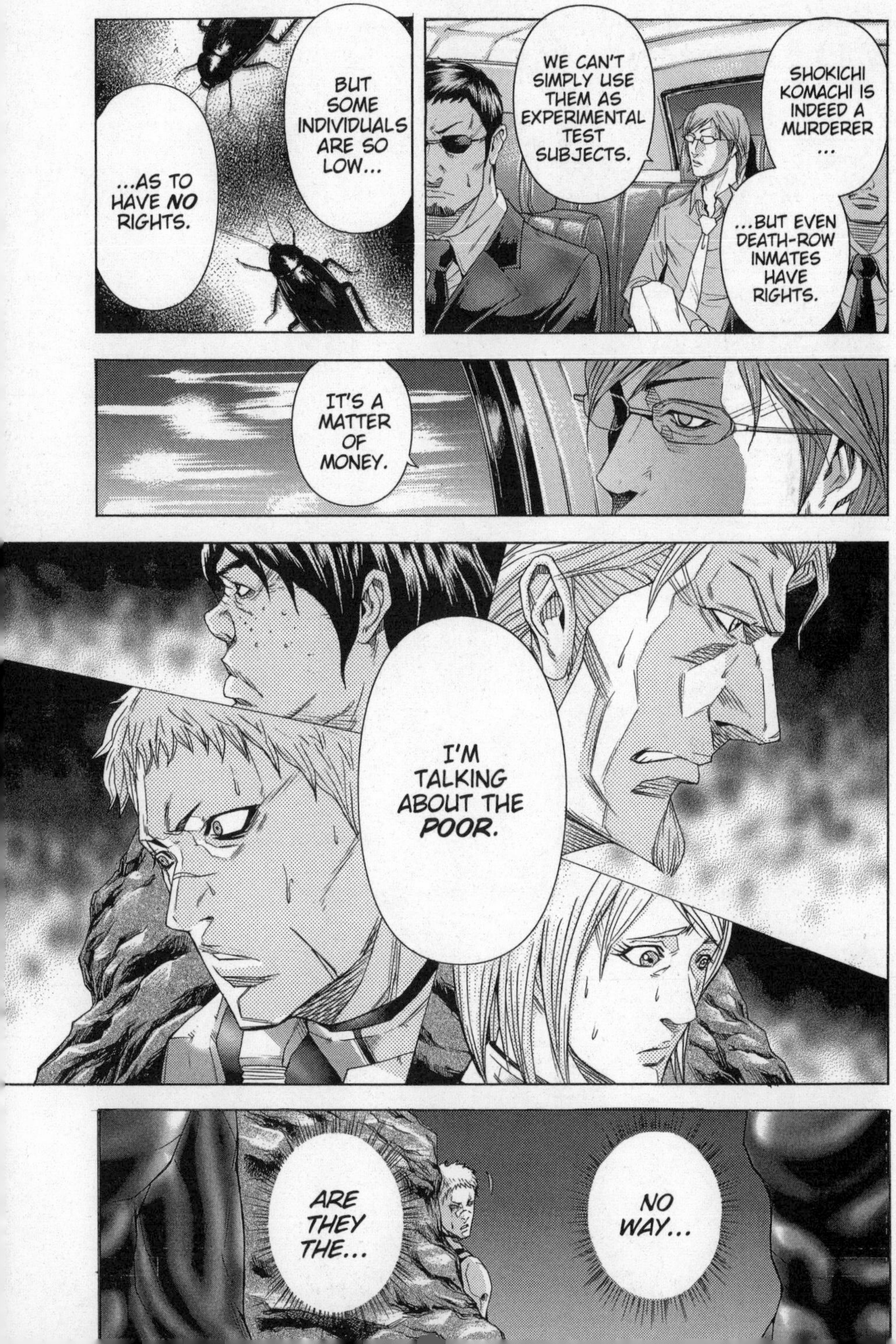
SHOKICHI KOMACHI IS INDEED A MURDERER...
...BUT EVEN DEATH-ROW INMATES HAVE RIGHTS.
WE CAN'T SIMPLY USE THEM AS EXPERIMENTAL TEST SUBJECTS.
BUT SOME INDIVIDUALS ARE SO LOW...
...AS TO HAVE ***NO*** RIGHTS.
IT'S A MATTER OF MONEY.
I'M TALKING ABOUT THE ***POOR.***
NO WAY...
ARE THEY THE...

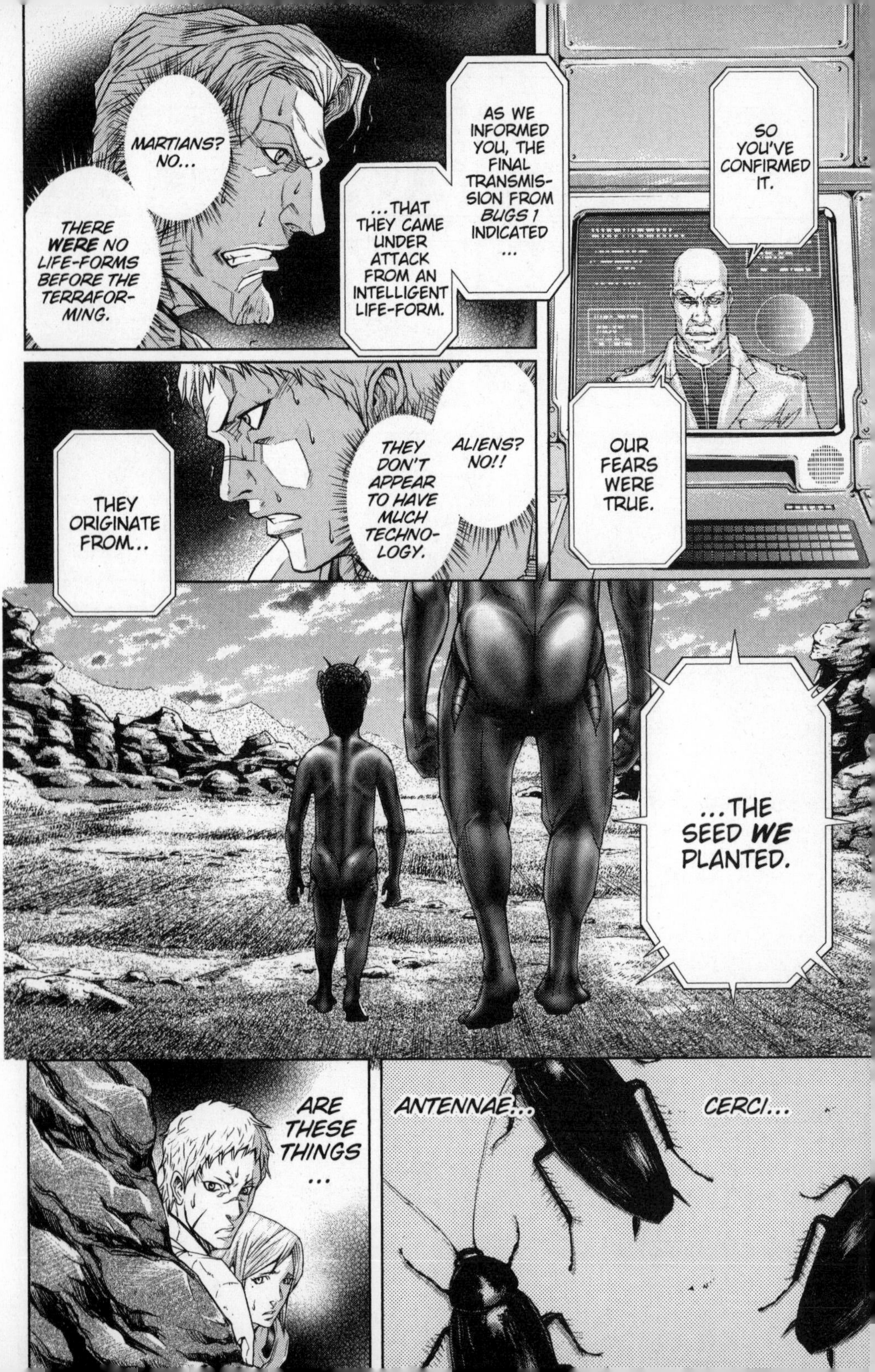
SO YOU'VE CONFIRMED IT.
OUR FEARS WERE TRUE.
AS WE INFORMED YOU, THE FINAL TRANSMISSION FROM *BUGS 1* INDICATED...
...THAT THEY CAME UNDER ATTACK FROM AN INTELLIGENT LIFE-FORM.
MARTIANS? NO...
*THERE **WERE** NO LIFE-FORMS BEFORE THE TERRAFORMING.*
ALIENS? NO!!
THEY DON'T APPEAR TO HAVE MUCH TECHNOLOGY.
THEY ORIGINATE FROM...
...THE SEED ***WE*** PLANTED.
CERCI...
ANTENNAE...
ARE THESE THINGS...

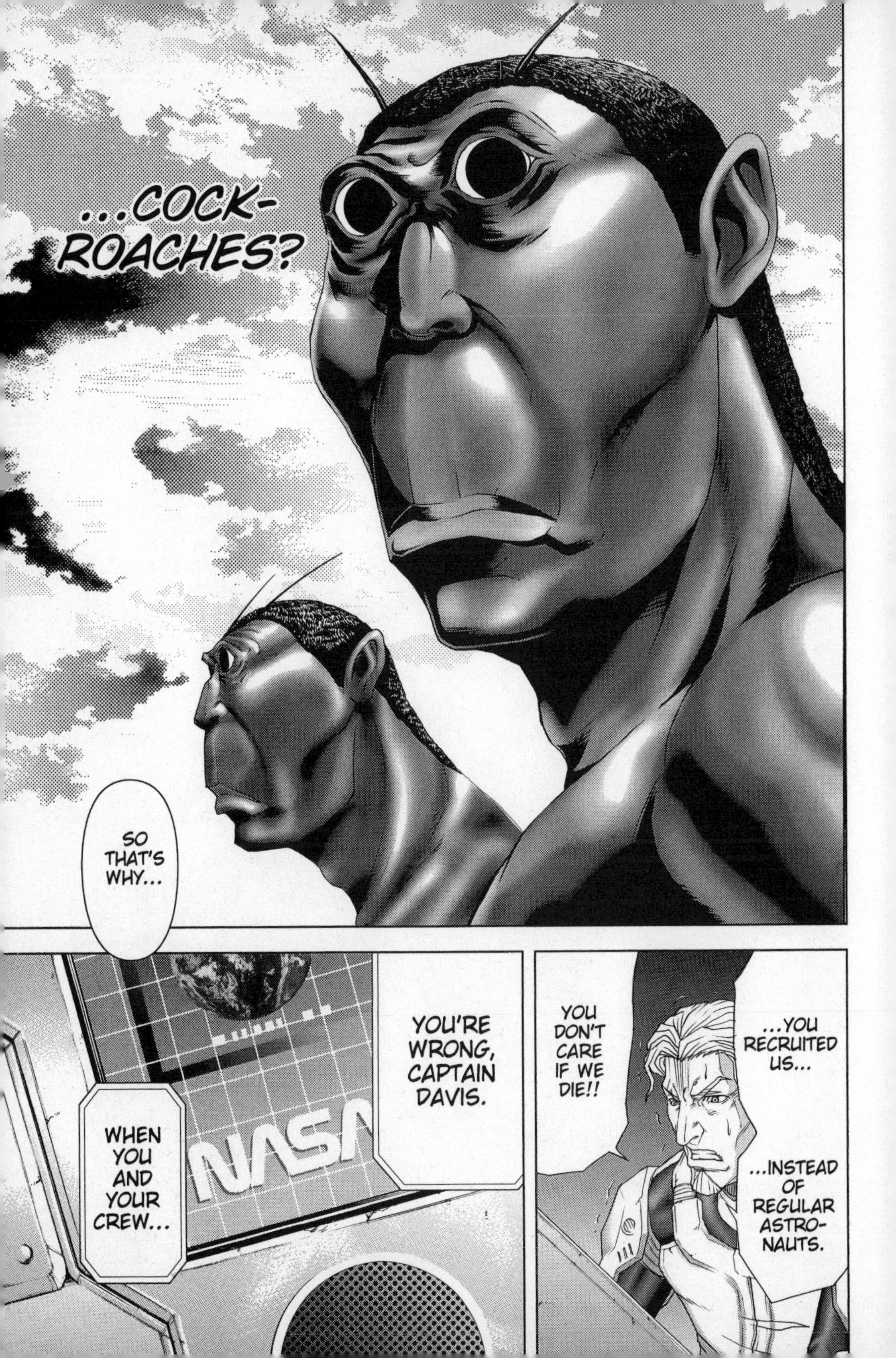
...COCK-ROACHES?
SO THAT'S WHY...
YOU DON'T CARE IF WE DIE!!
...YOU RECRUITED US...
...INSTEAD OF REGULAR ASTRO-NAUTS.
YOU'RE WRONG, CAPTAIN DAVIS.
WHEN YOU AND YOUR CREW...
NASA

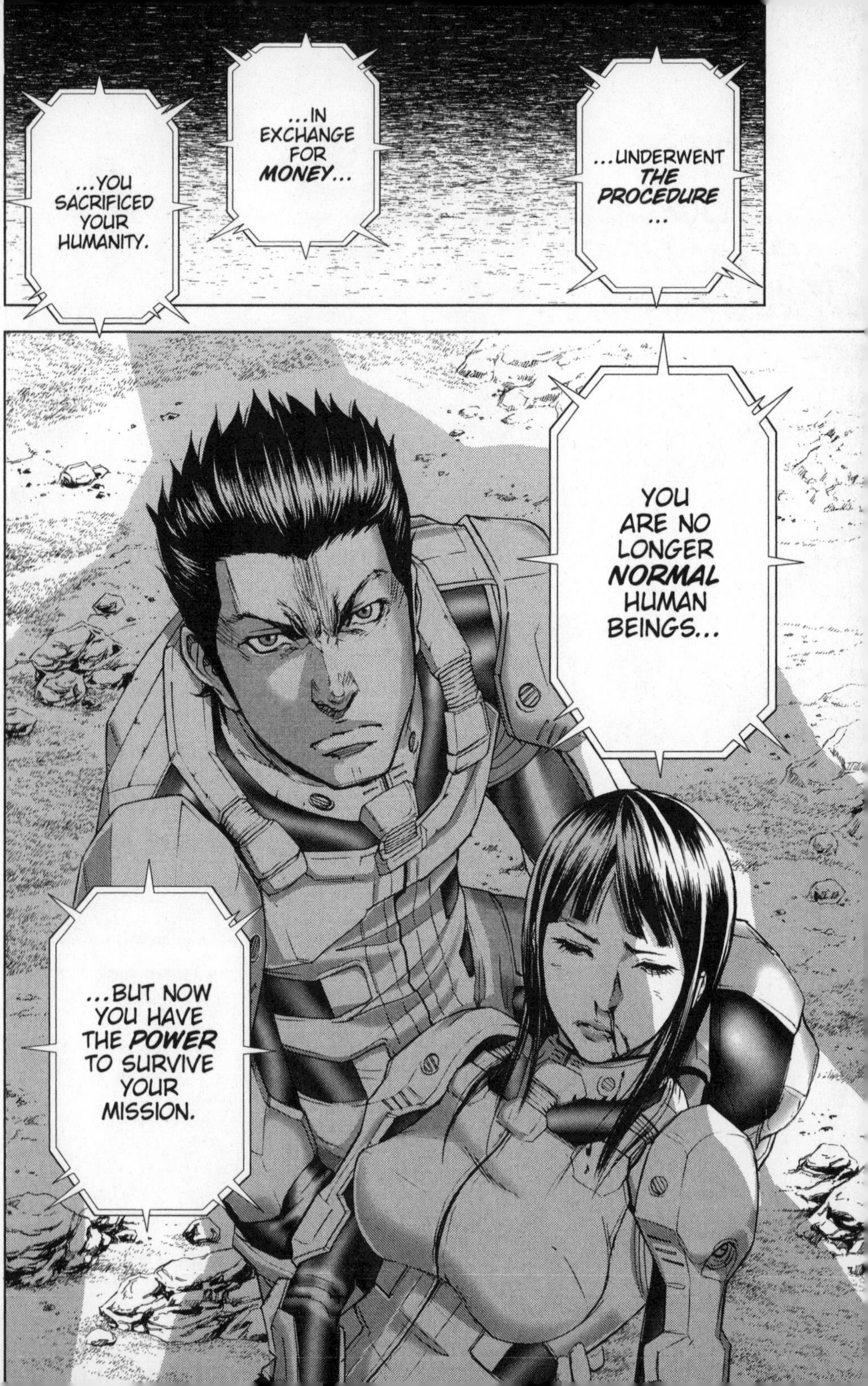
...UNDERWENT THE PROCEDURE...
...IN EXCHANGE FOR MONEY...
...YOU SACRIFICED YOUR HUMANITY.
YOU ARE NO LONGER NORMAL HUMAN BEINGS...
...BUT NOW YOU HAVE THE POWER TO SURVIVE YOUR MISSION.

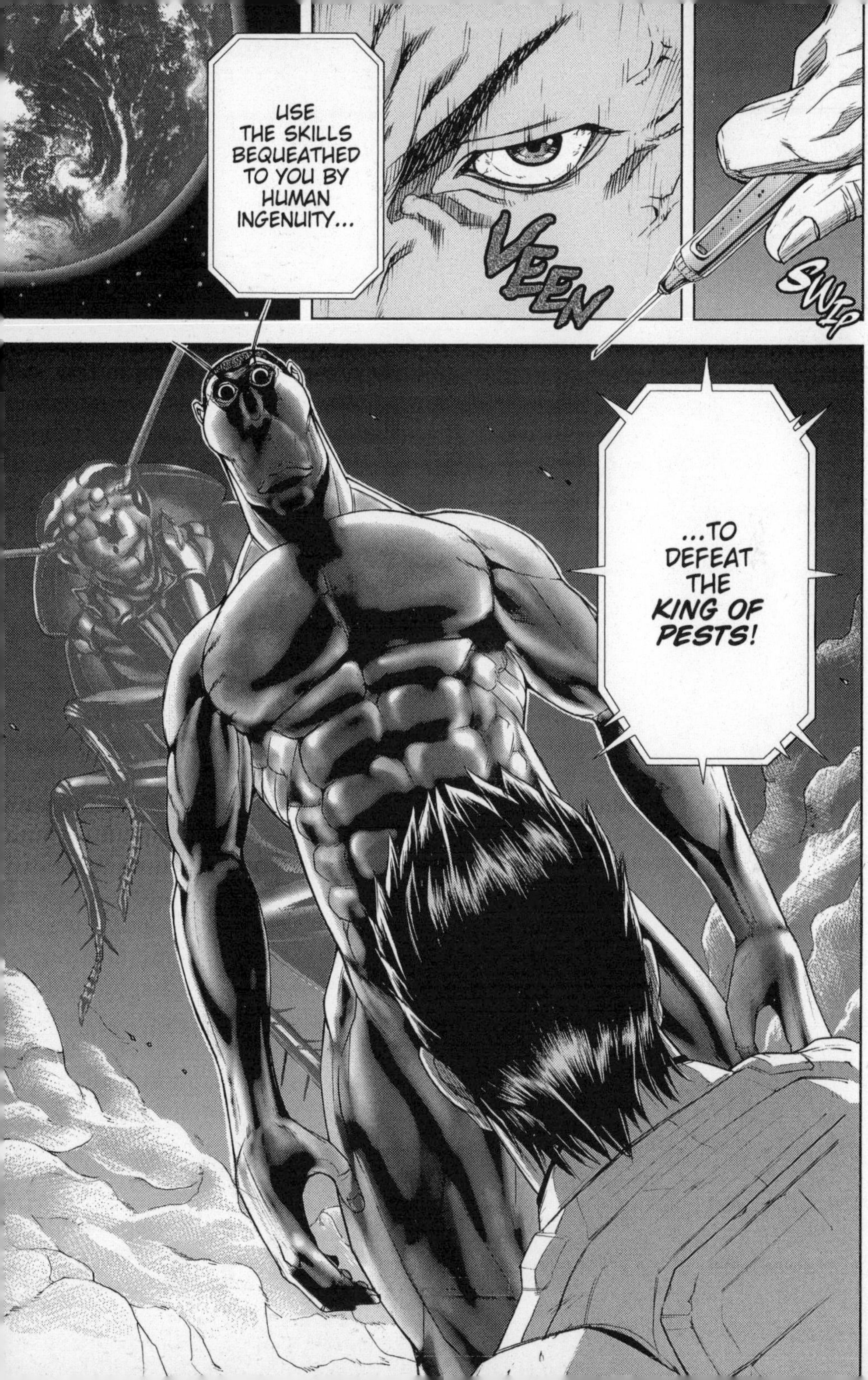
SWIP
VEEN
USE THE SKILLS BEQUEATHED TO YOU BY HUMAN INGENUITY...
...TO DEFEAT THE KING OF PESTS!

TERRA FORMARS

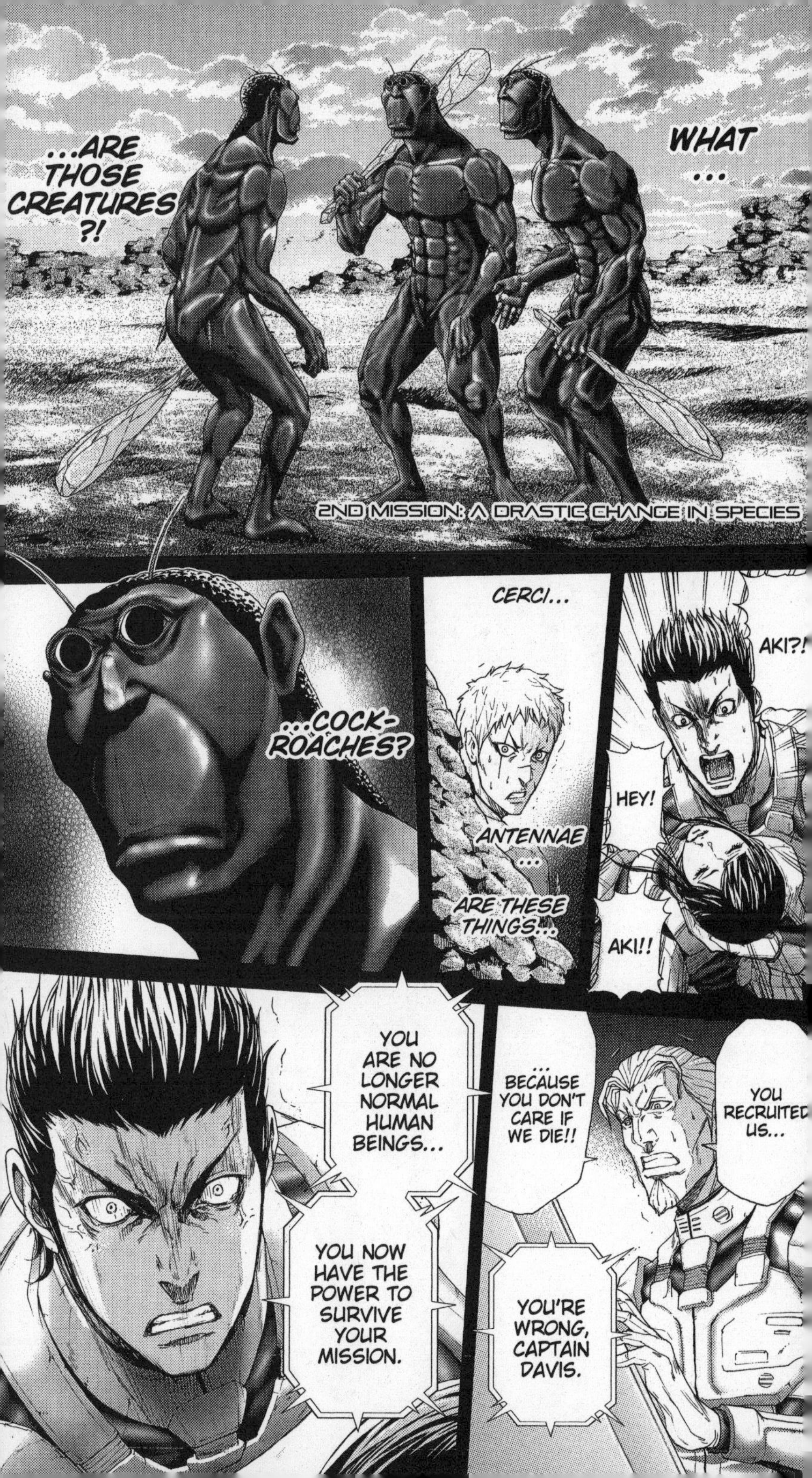
WHAT...
...ARE THOSE CREATURES?!
2ND MISSION: A DRASTIC CHANGE IN SPECIES
AKI?!
HEY!
AKI!!
CERCI...
ANTENNAE...
ARE THESE THINGS...
...COCK-ROACHES?
YOU RECRUITED US...
...BECAUSE YOU DON'T CARE IF WE DIE!!
YOU'RE WRONG, CAPTAIN DAVIS.
YOU ARE NO LONGER NORMAL HUMAN BEINGS...
YOU NOW HAVE THE POWER TO SURVIVE YOUR MISSION.

2ND MISSION: A DRASTIC CHANGE IN SPECIES

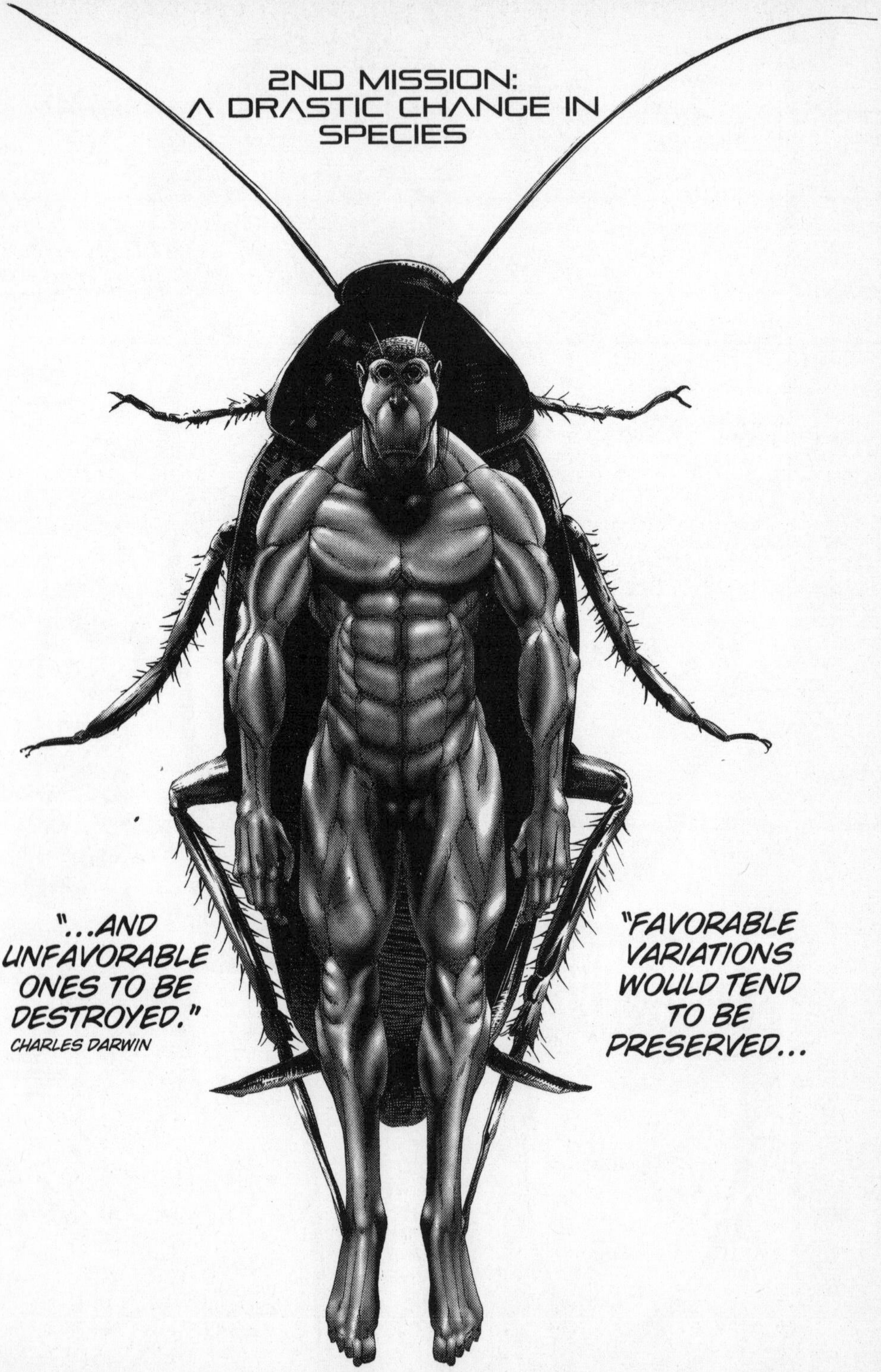
"FAVORABLE VARIATIONS WOULD TEND TO BE PRESERVED...
"...AND UNFAVORABLE ONES TO BE DESTROYED."
CHARLES DARWIN

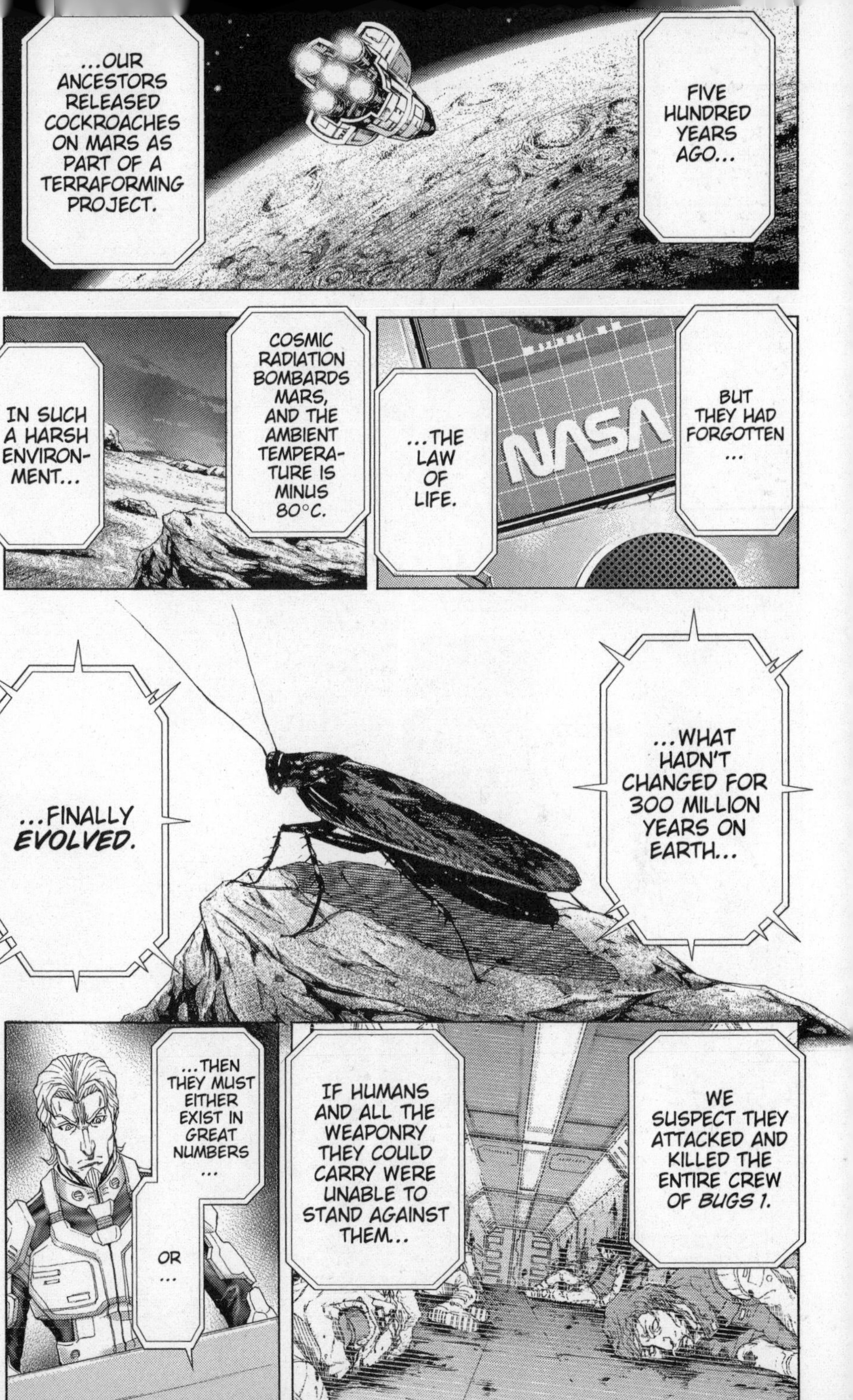
FIVE HUNDRED YEARS AGO...
...OUR ANCESTORS RELEASED COCKROACHES ON MARS AS PART OF A TERRAFORMING PROJECT.
BUT THEY HAD FORGOTTEN ...
...THE LAW OF LIFE.
COSMIC RADIATION BOMBARDS MARS, AND THE AMBIENT TEMPERATURE IS MINUS 80°C.
IN SUCH A HARSH ENVIRONMENT...
...WHAT HADN'T CHANGED FOR 300 MILLION YEARS ON EARTH...
...FINALLY *EVOLVED.*
WE SUSPECT THEY ATTACKED AND KILLED THE ENTIRE CREW OF *BUGS 1*.
IF HUMANS AND ALL THE WEAPONRY THEY COULD CARRY WERE UNABLE TO STAND AGAINST THEM...
...THEN THEY MUST EITHER EXIST IN GREAT NUMBERS ...
OR ...

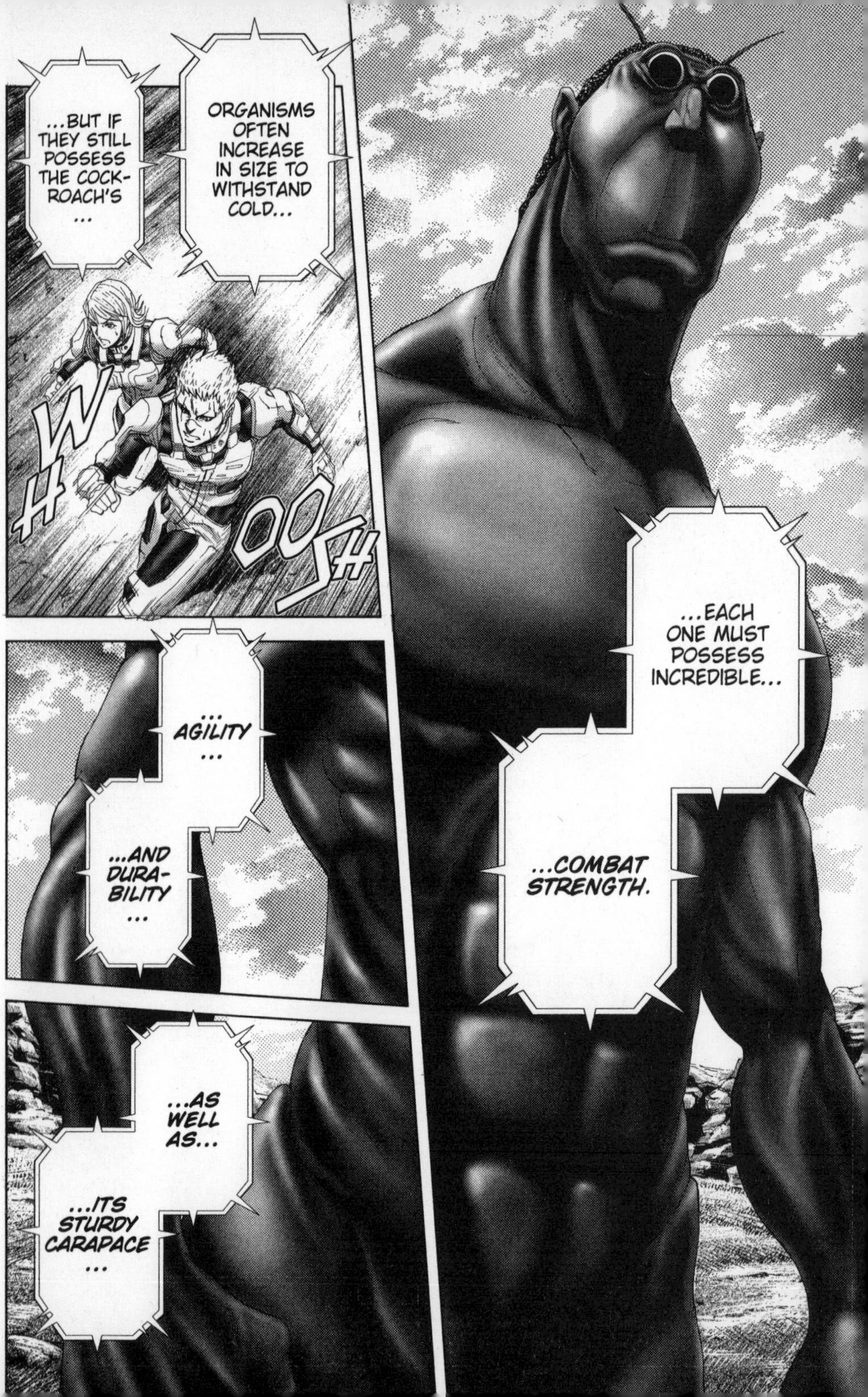
ORGANISMS OFTEN INCREASE IN SIZE TO WITHSTAND COLD...
...BUT IF THEY STILL POSSESS THE COCK-ROACH'S ...
WHOOSH
... AGILITY ...
...AND DURA-BILITY ...
...AS WELL AS...
...ITS STURDY CARAPACE ...
...EACH ONE MUST POSSESS INCREDIBLE...
...COMBAT STRENGTH.

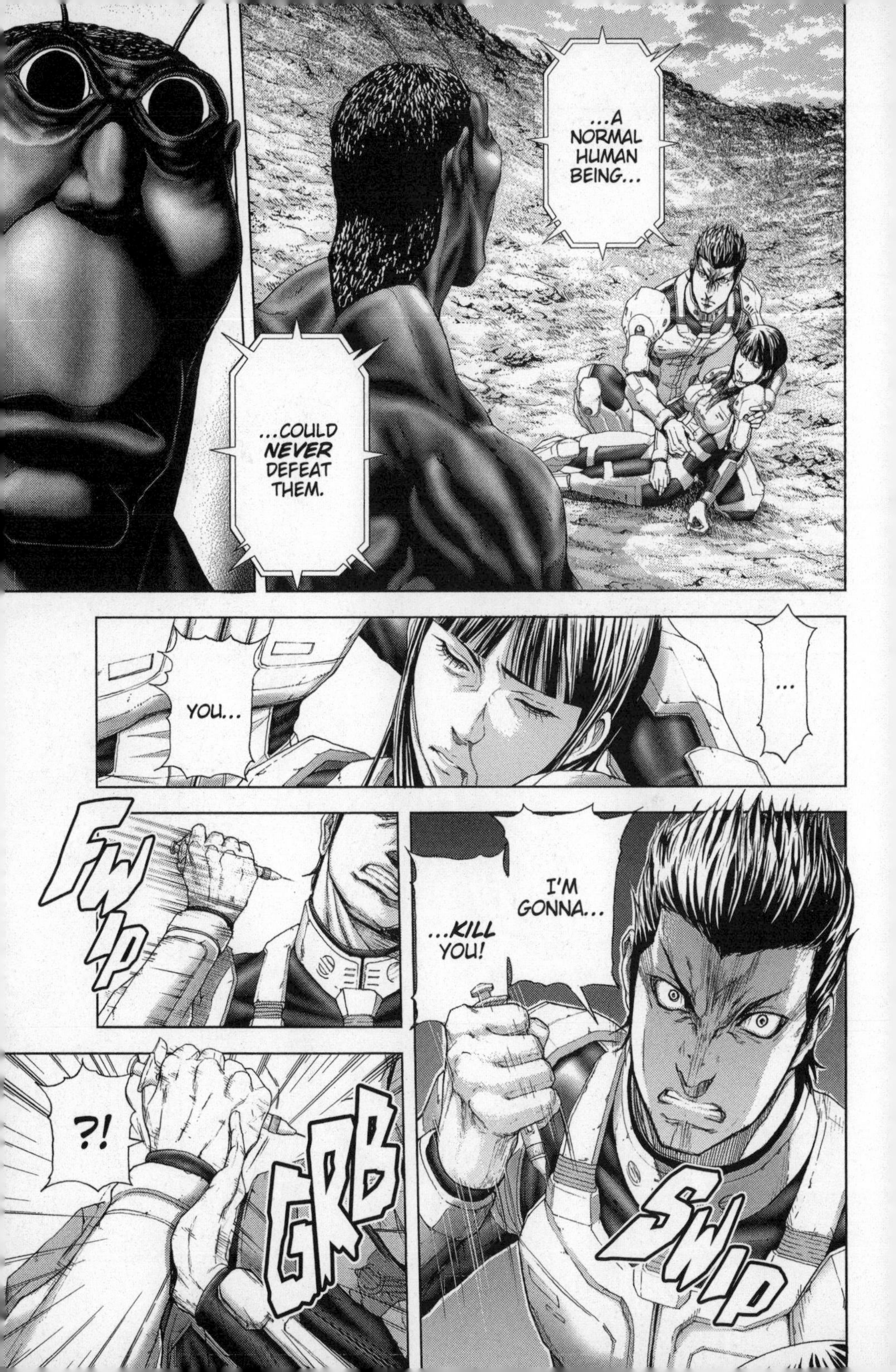
...A NORMAL HUMAN BEING...
...COULD NEVER DEFEAT THEM.
...
YOU...
I'M GONNA...
...KILL YOU!
SWIP
FWIP
?!
GRB

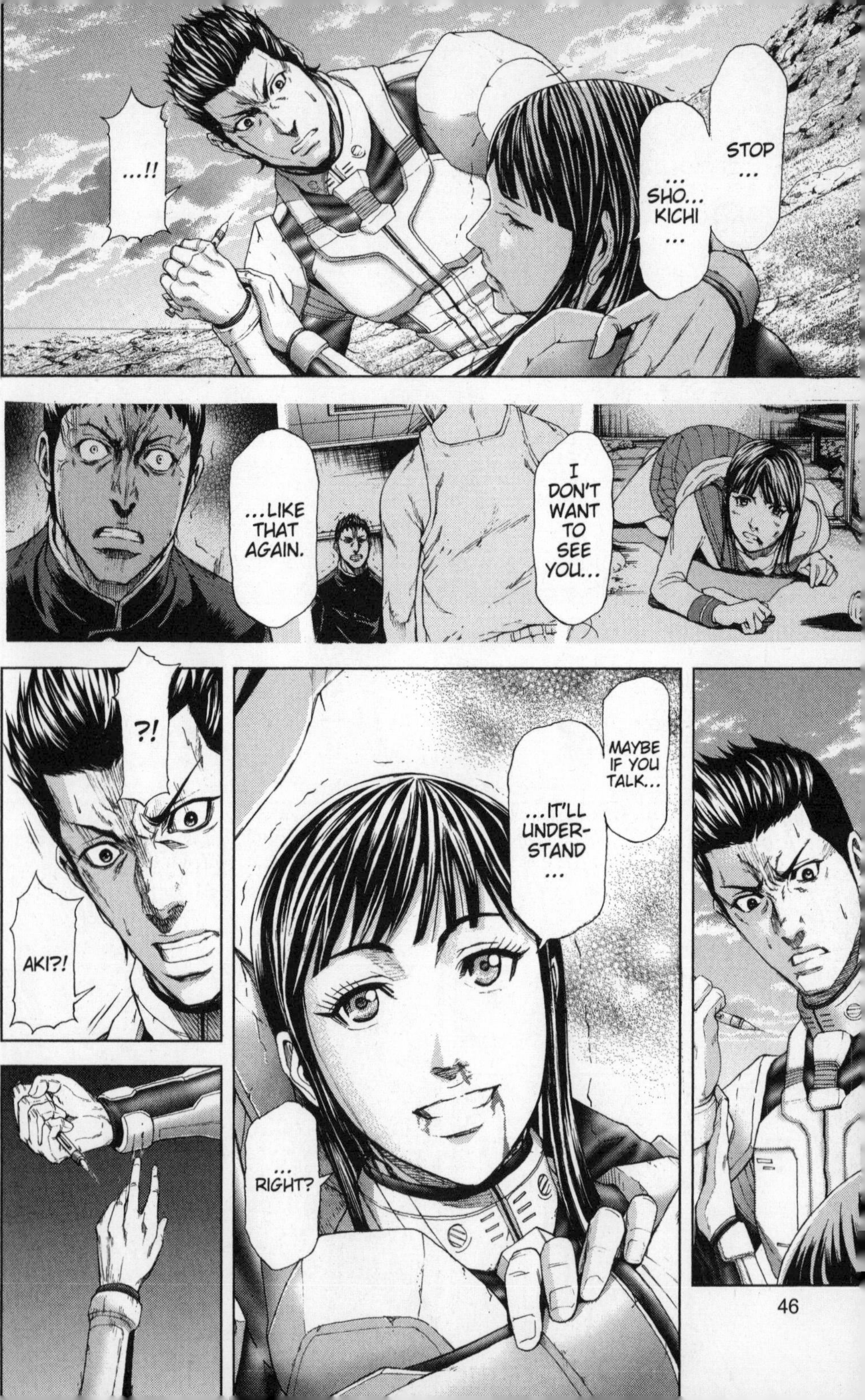

STOP ...
... SHO... KICHI ...
...!!
I DON'T WANT TO SEE YOU...
...LIKE THAT AGAIN.
MAYBE IF YOU TALK...
...IT'LL UNDER-STAND ...
... RIGHT?
?!
AKI?!

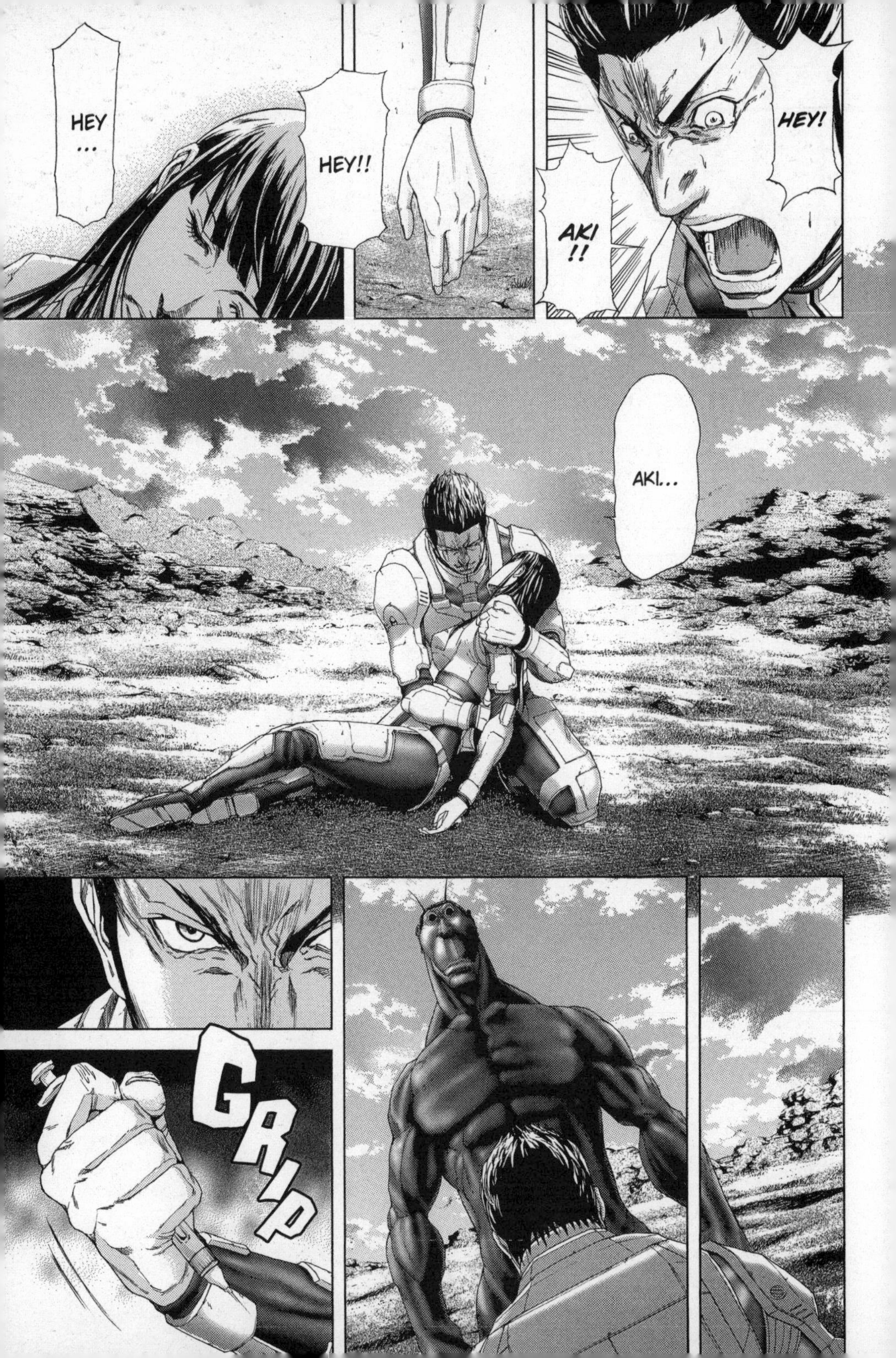
HEY!
AKI !!
HEY!!
HEY ...
AKI...
GRIP

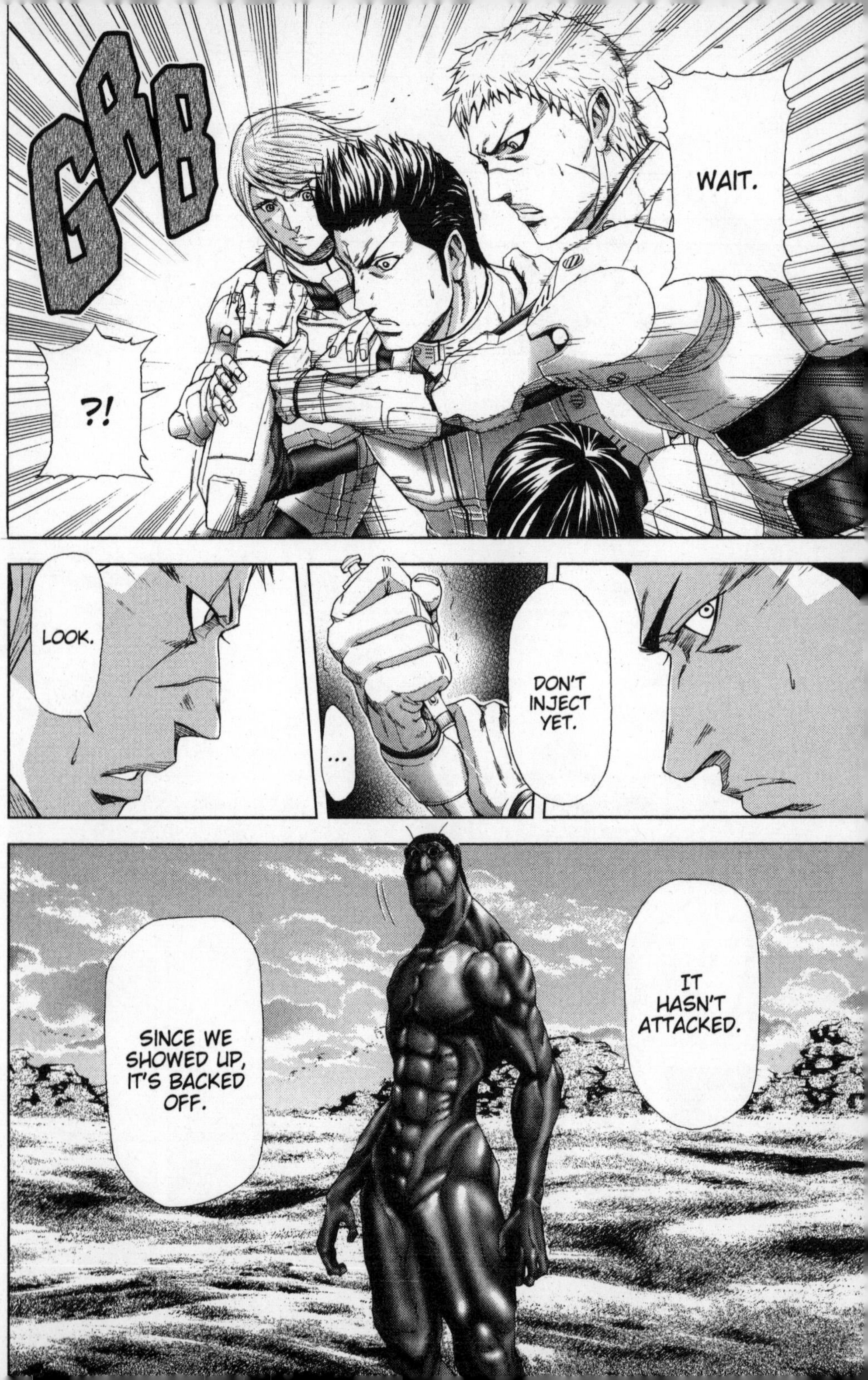
WAIT.
GRB
?!
DON'T INJECT YET.
...
LOOK.
IT HASN'T ATTACKED.
SINCE WE SHOWED UP, IT'S BACKED OFF.

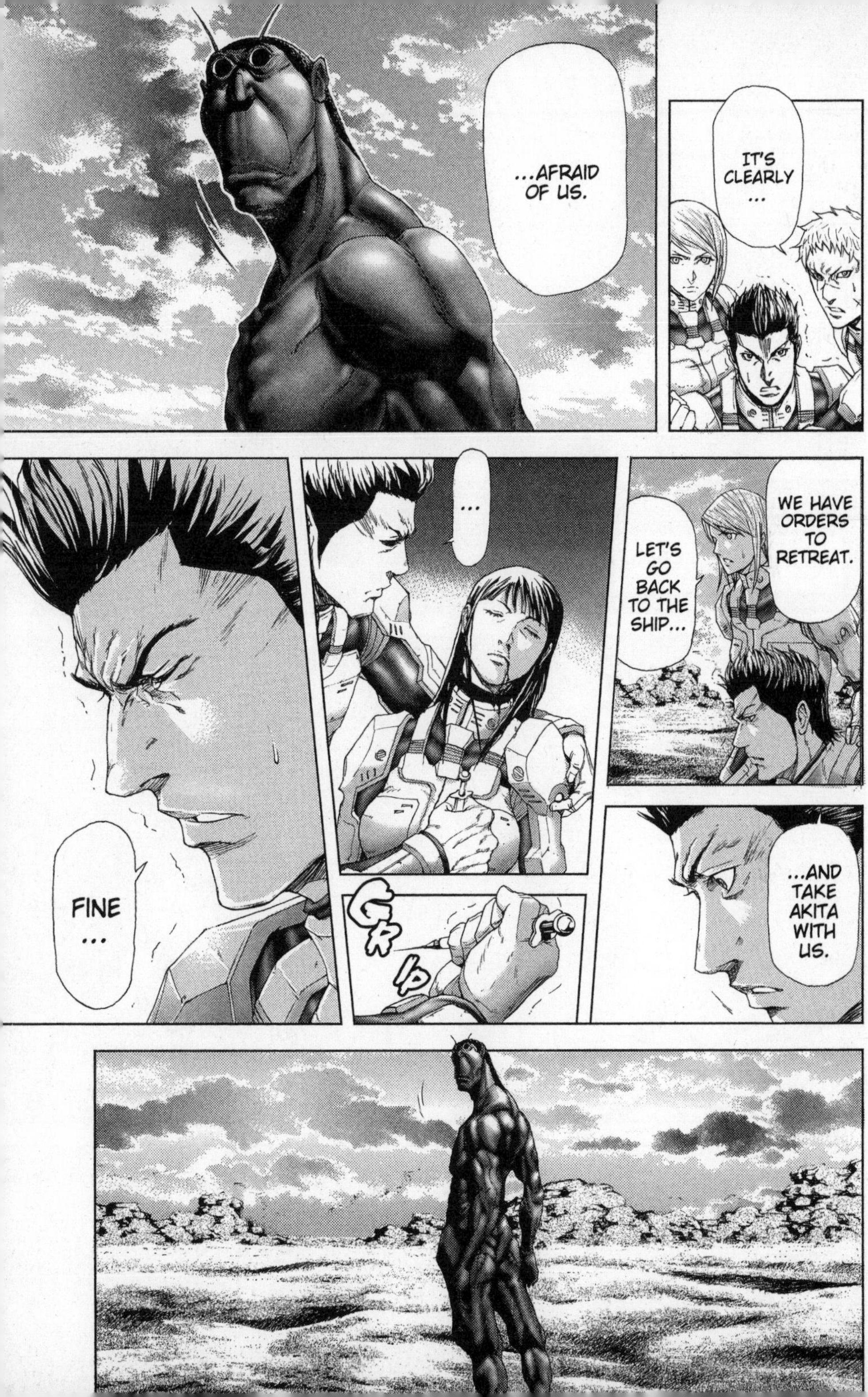
IT'S CLEARLY ...
...AFRAID OF US.
WE HAVE ORDERS TO RETREAT.
LET'S GO BACK TO THE SHIP...
...AND TAKE AKITA WITH US.
...
GRIP
FINE ...

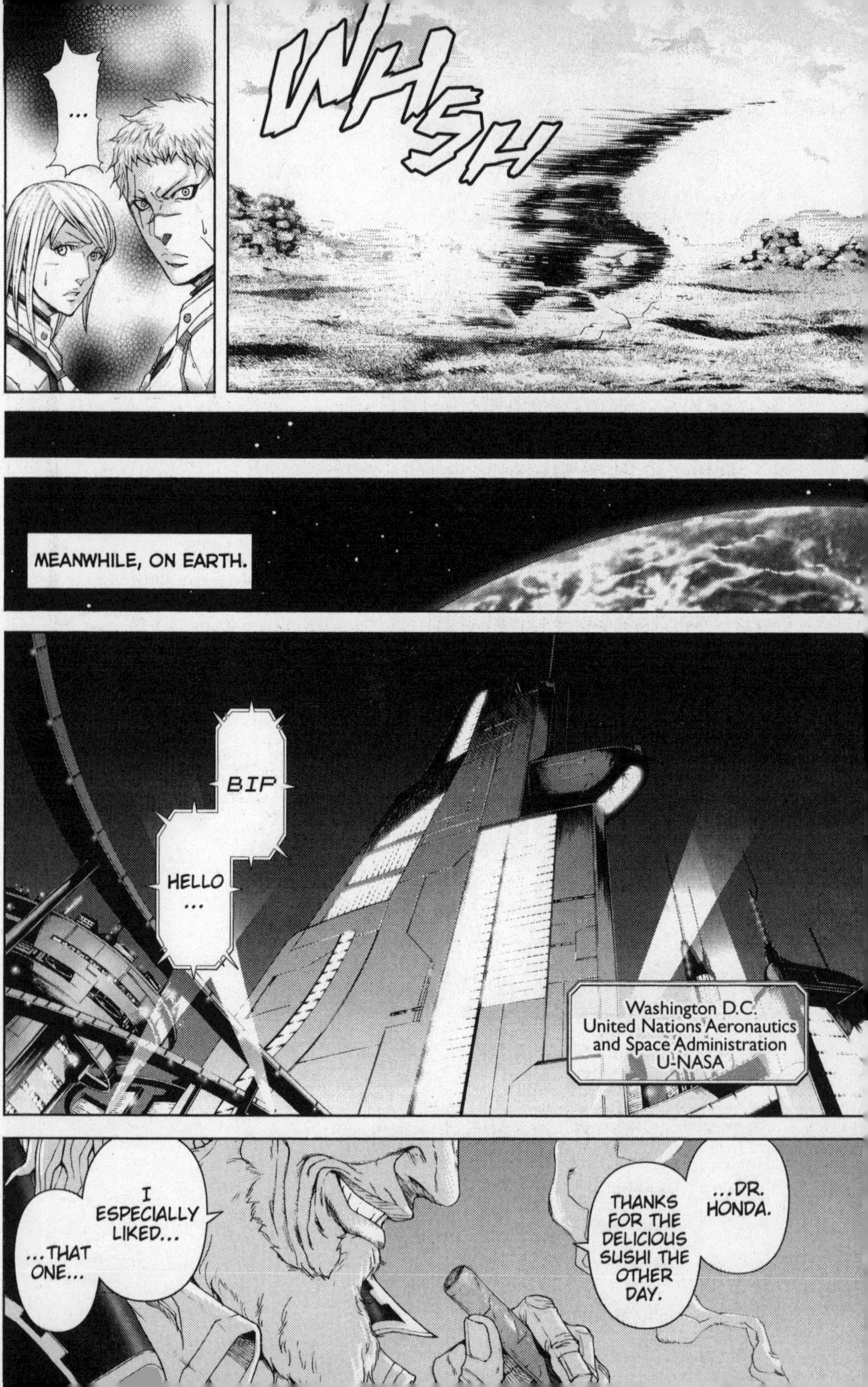
WHSH
...
MEANWHILE, ON EARTH.
BIP
HELLO ...
Washington D.C. United Nations Aeronautics and Space Administration U-NASA
...DR. HONDA.
THANKS FOR THE DELICIOUS SUSHI THE OTHER DAY.
I ESPECIALLY LIKED...
...THAT ONE...

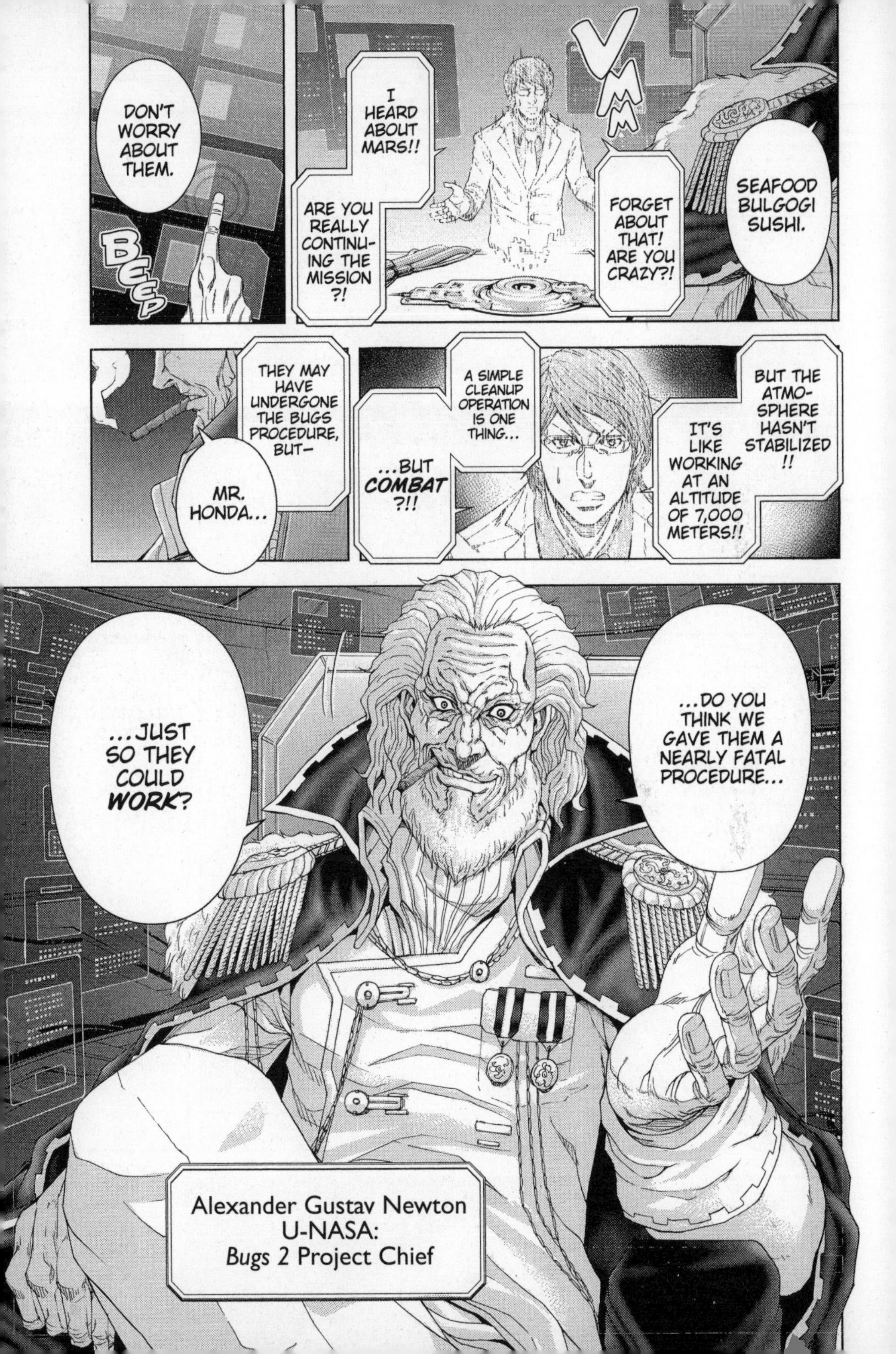
VMM
I HEARD ABOUT MARS!!
ARE YOU REALLY CONTINUING THE MISSION?!
SEAFOOD BULGOGI SUSHI.
FORGET ABOUT THAT! ARE YOU CRAZY?!
DON'T WORRY ABOUT THEM.
BEEP
BUT THE ATMOSPHERE HASN'T STABILIZED!!
IT'S LIKE WORKING AT AN ALTITUDE OF 7,000 METERS!!
A SIMPLE CLEANUP OPERATION IS ONE THING...
...BUT *COMBAT*?!!
THEY MAY HAVE UNDERGONE THE BUGS PROCEDURE, BUT—
MR. HONDA...
...DO YOU THINK WE GAVE THEM A NEARLY FATAL PROCEDURE...
...JUST SO THEY COULD *WORK*?
Alexander Gustav Newton
U-NASA:
Bugs 2 Project Chief

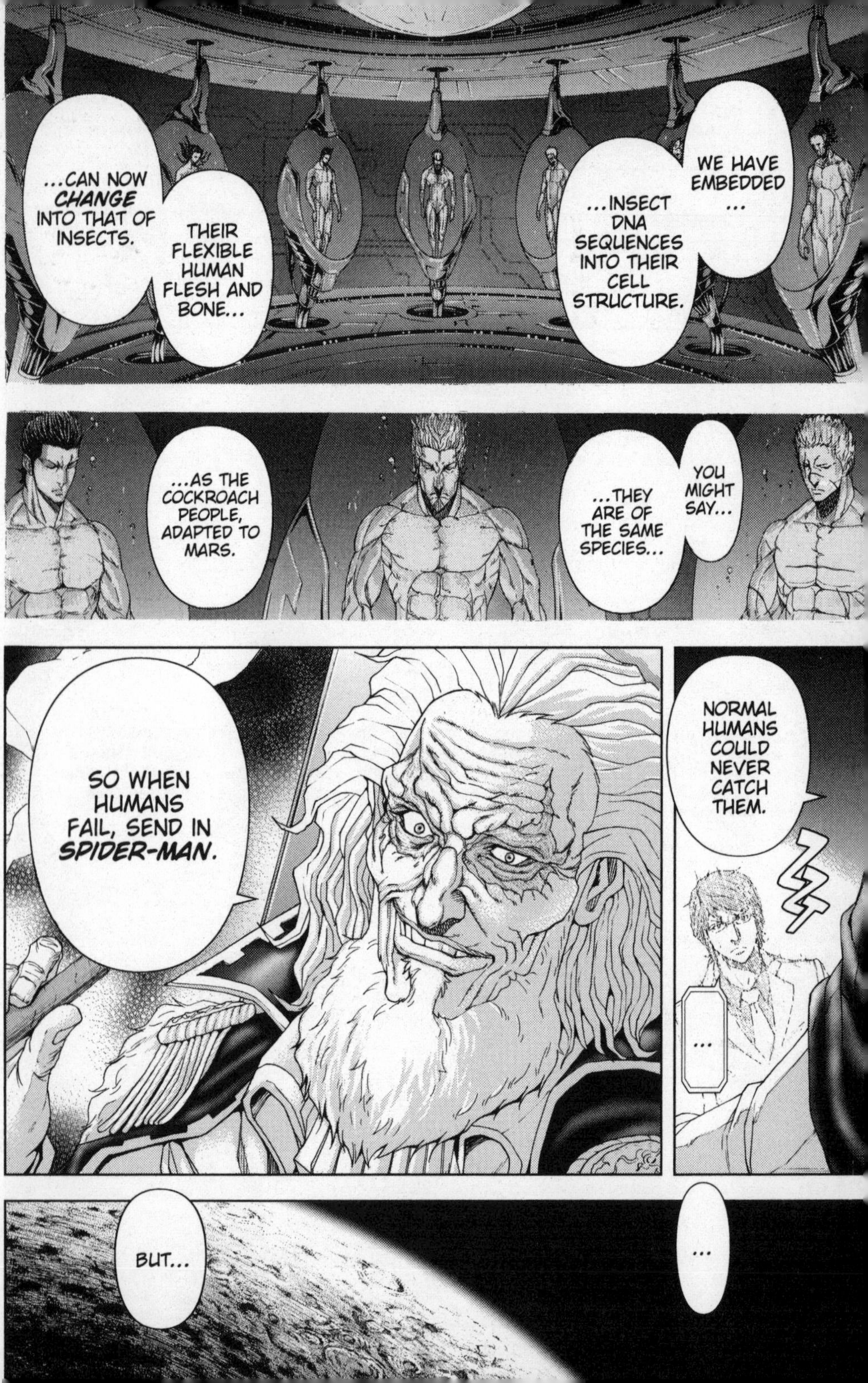
WE HAVE EMBEDDED...
...INSECT DNA SEQUENCES INTO THEIR CELL STRUCTURE.
THEIR FLEXIBLE HUMAN FLESH AND BONE...
...CAN NOW *CHANGE* INTO THAT OF INSECTS.
YOU MIGHT SAY...
...THEY ARE OF THE SAME SPECIES...
...AS THE COCKROACH PEOPLE, ADAPTED TO MARS.
NORMAL HUMANS COULD NEVER CATCH THEM.
...
SO WHEN HUMANS FAIL, SEND IN *SPIDER-MAN*.
...
BUT...

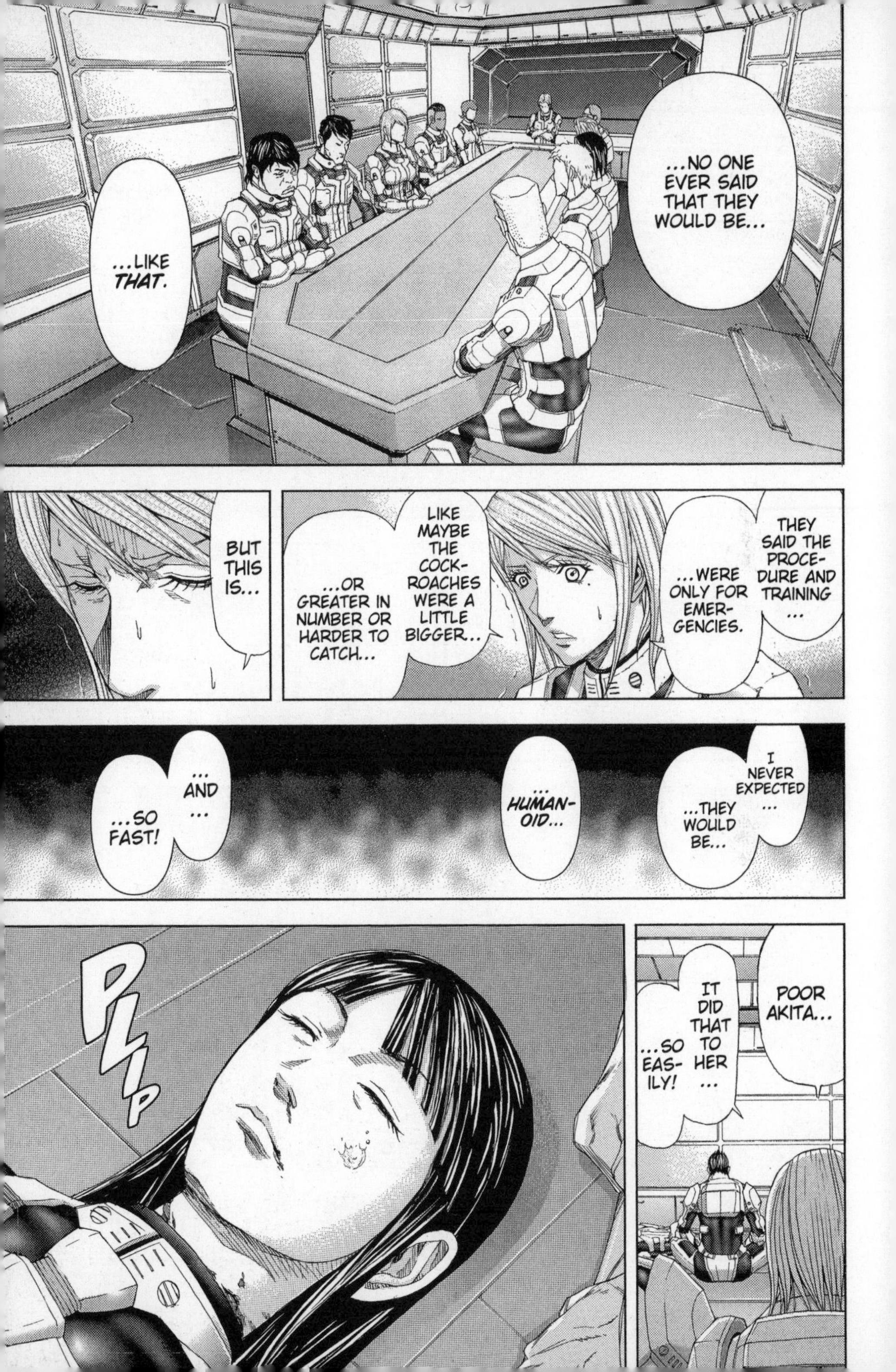
...NO ONE EVER SAID THAT THEY WOULD BE...
...LIKE *THAT*.
THEY SAID THE PROCEDURE AND TRAINING...
...WERE ONLY FOR EMERGENCIES.
LIKE MAYBE THE COCKROACHES WERE A LITTLE BIGGER...
...OR GREATER IN NUMBER OR HARDER TO CATCH...
BUT THIS IS...
I NEVER EXPECTED...
...THEY WOULD BE...
...*HUMANOID*...
...AND...
...SO FAST!
POOR AKITA...
IT DID THAT TO HER...
...SO EASILY!
PLIP

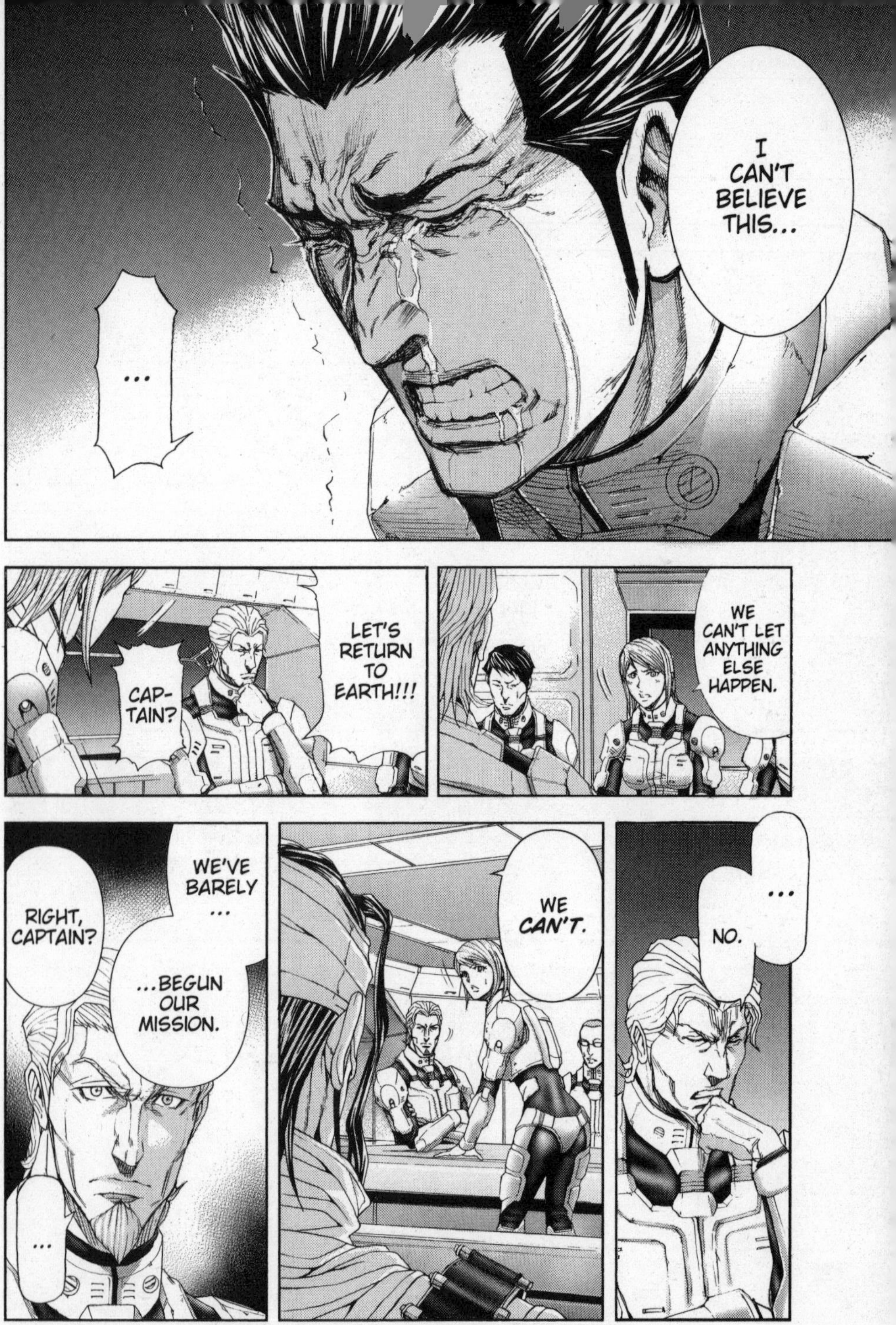
I CAN'T BELIEVE THIS...
...
WE CAN'T LET ANYTHING ELSE HAPPEN.
LET'S RETURN TO EARTH!!!
CAP-TAIN?
...
NO.
WE *CAN'T*.
WE'VE BARELY ...
...BEGUN OUR MISSION.
RIGHT, CAPTAIN?
...

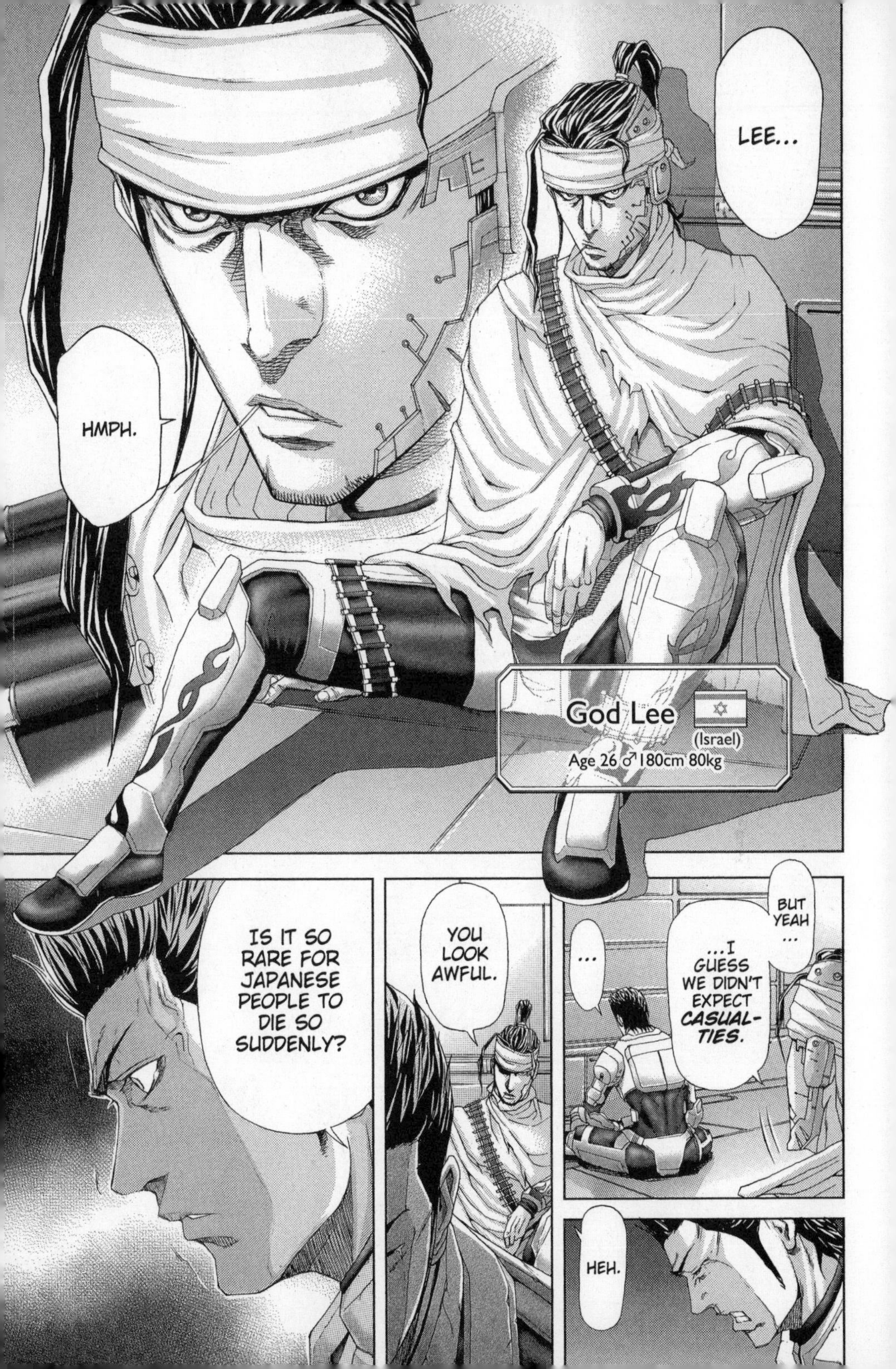
LEE...
HMPH.
God Lee
(Israel)
Age 26 ♂180cm 80kg
BUT YEAH...
...I GUESS WE DIDN'T EXPECT CASUALTIES.
...
HEH.
YOU LOOK AWFUL.
IS IT SO RARE FOR JAPANESE PEOPLE TO DIE SO SUDDENLY?

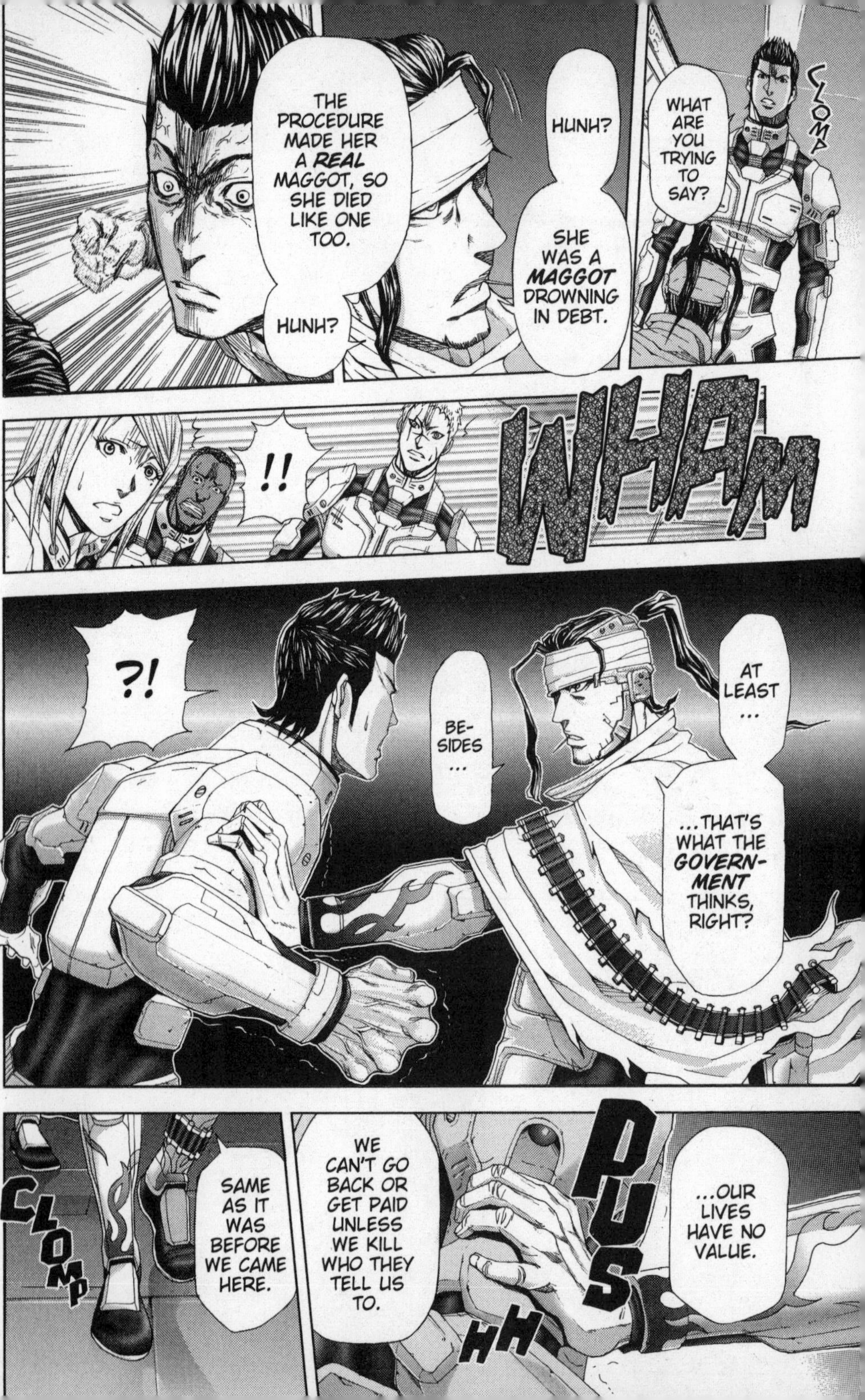
CLOMP
WHAT ARE YOU TRYING TO SAY?
HUNH?
SHE WAS A MAGGOT DROWNING IN DEBT.
THE PROCEDURE MADE HER A REAL MAGGOT, SO SHE DIED LIKE ONE TOO.
HUNH?
WHAM
!!
AT LEAST...
...THAT'S WHAT THE GOVERNMENT THINKS, RIGHT?
BESIDES...
?!
PUSHH
...OUR LIVES HAVE NO VALUE.
WE CAN'T GO BACK OR GET PAID UNLESS WE KILL WHO THEY TELL US TO.
SAME AS IT WAS BEFORE WE CAME HERE.
CLOMP

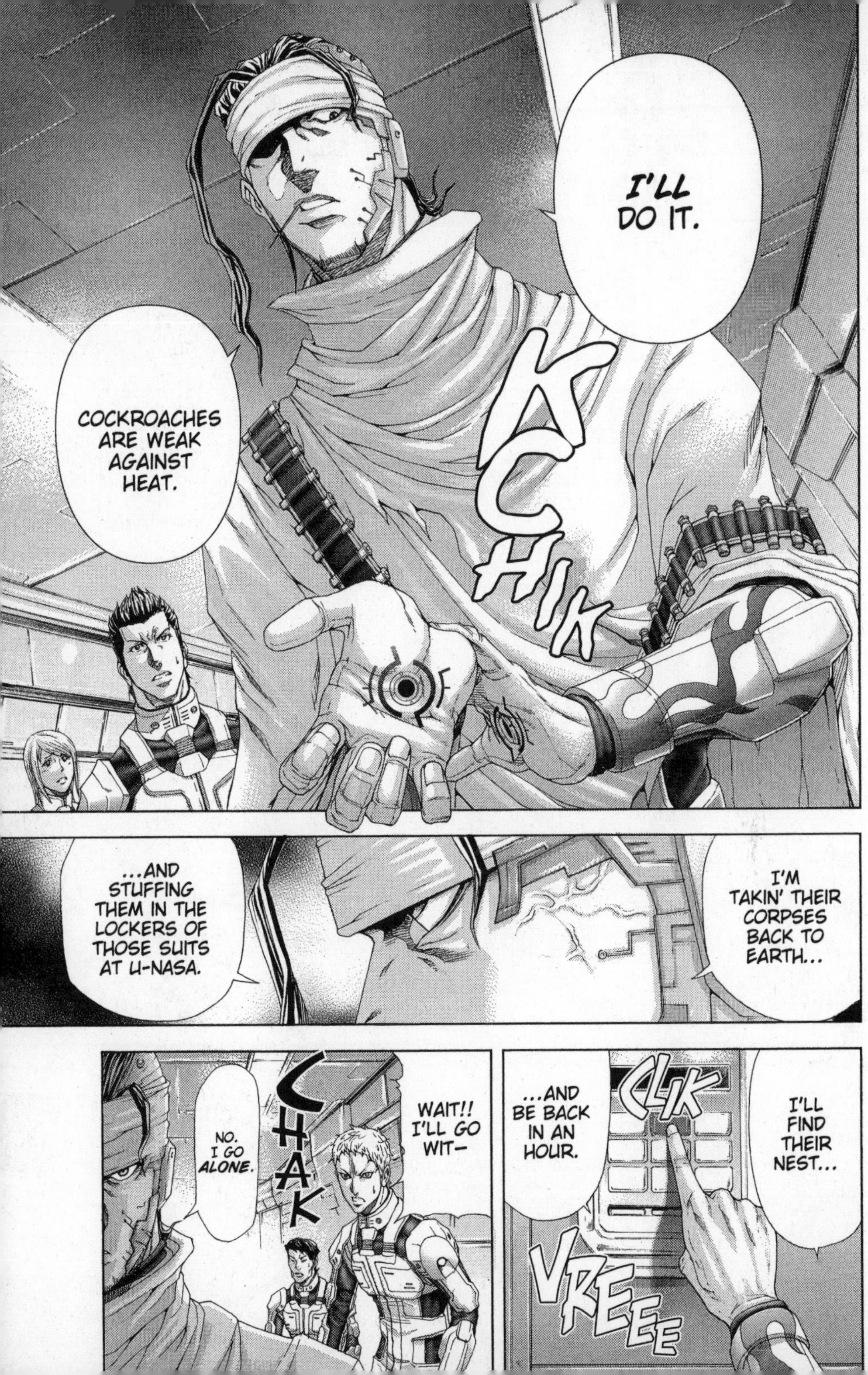
I'LL DO IT.
KCHIK
COCKROACHES ARE WEAK AGAINST HEAT.
I'M TAKIN' THEIR CORPSES BACK TO EARTH...
...AND STUFFING THEM IN THE LOCKERS OF THOSE SUITS AT U-NASA.
I'LL FIND THEIR NEST...
CLIK
...AND BE BACK IN AN HOUR.
VREEEE
WAIT!! I'LL GO WIT—
CHAK
NO. I GO ALONE.

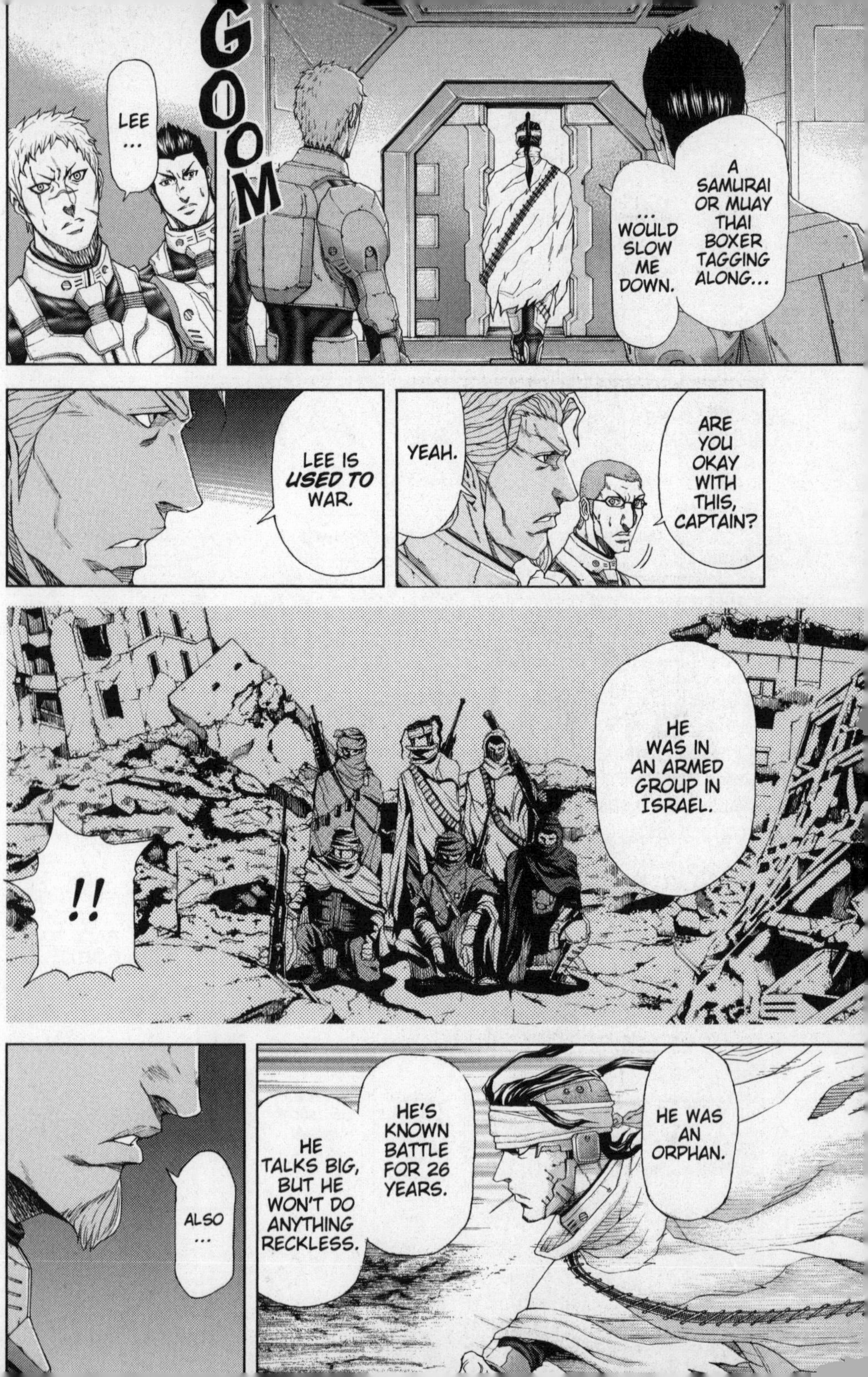
A SAMURAI OR MUAY THAI BOXER TAGGING ALONG...
...WOULD SLOW ME DOWN.
GOOM
LEE...
ARE YOU OKAY WITH THIS, CAPTAIN?
YEAH.
LEE IS *USED TO* WAR.
HE WAS IN AN ARMED GROUP IN ISRAEL.
!!
HE WAS AN ORPHAN.
HE'S KNOWN BATTLE FOR 26 YEARS.
HE TALKS BIG, BUT HE WON'T DO ANYTHING RECKLESS.
ALSO...

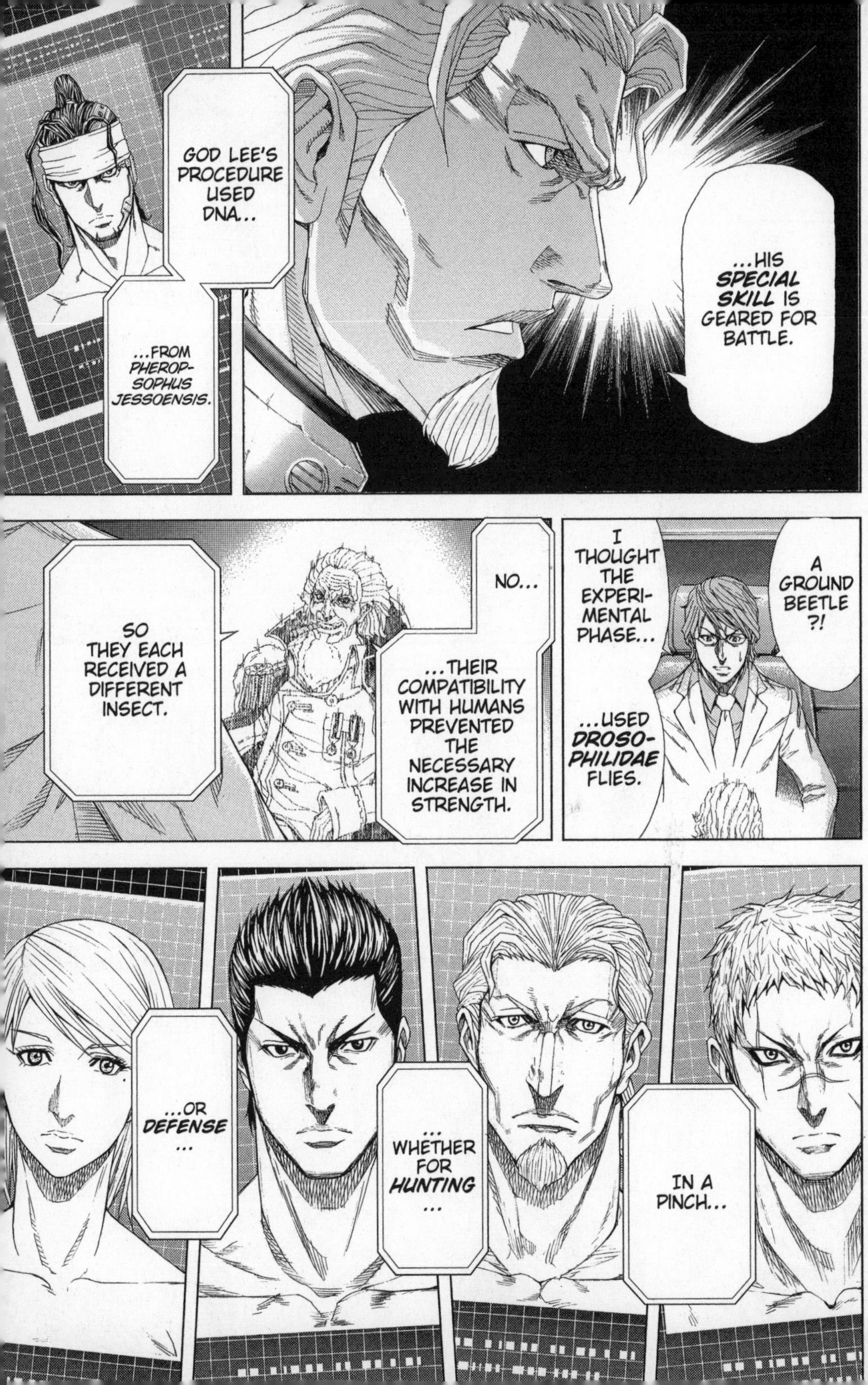
GOD LEE'S PROCEDURE USED DNA...
...FROM PHEROPSOPHUS JESSOENSIS.
...HIS SPECIAL SKILL IS GEARED FOR BATTLE.
A GROUND BEETLE?!
I THOUGHT THE EXPERIMENTAL PHASE...
...USED DROSOPHILIDAE FLIES.
NO...
...THEIR COMPATIBILITY WITH HUMANS PREVENTED THE NECESSARY INCREASE IN STRENGTH.
SO THEY EACH RECEIVED A DIFFERENT INSECT.
IN A PINCH...
...WHETHER FOR HUNTING...
...OR DEFENSE...

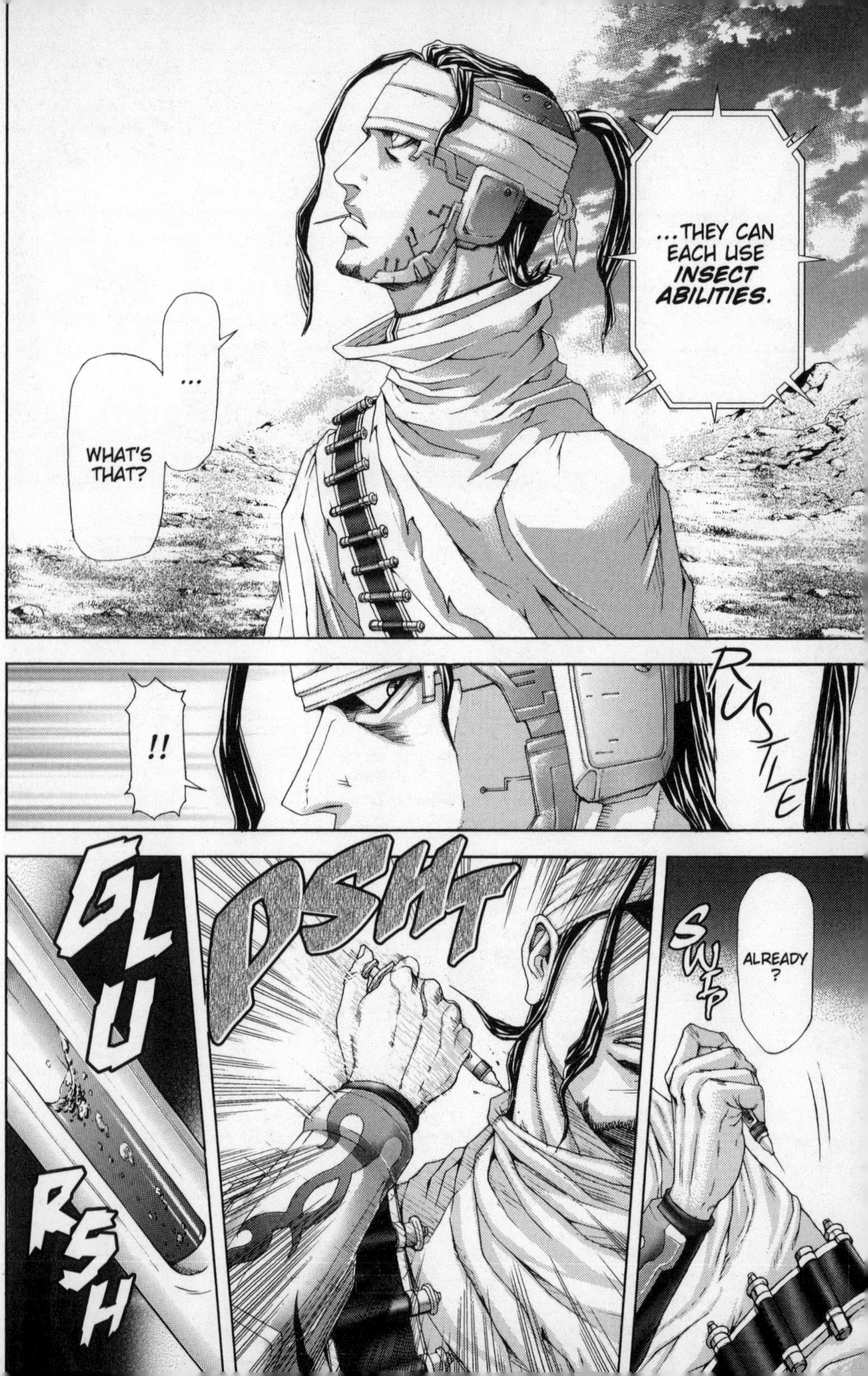
...THEY CAN EACH USE INSECT ABILITIES.
...
WHAT'S THAT?
RUSTLE
!!
SWIP
ALREADY?
DSHT
GLURSH

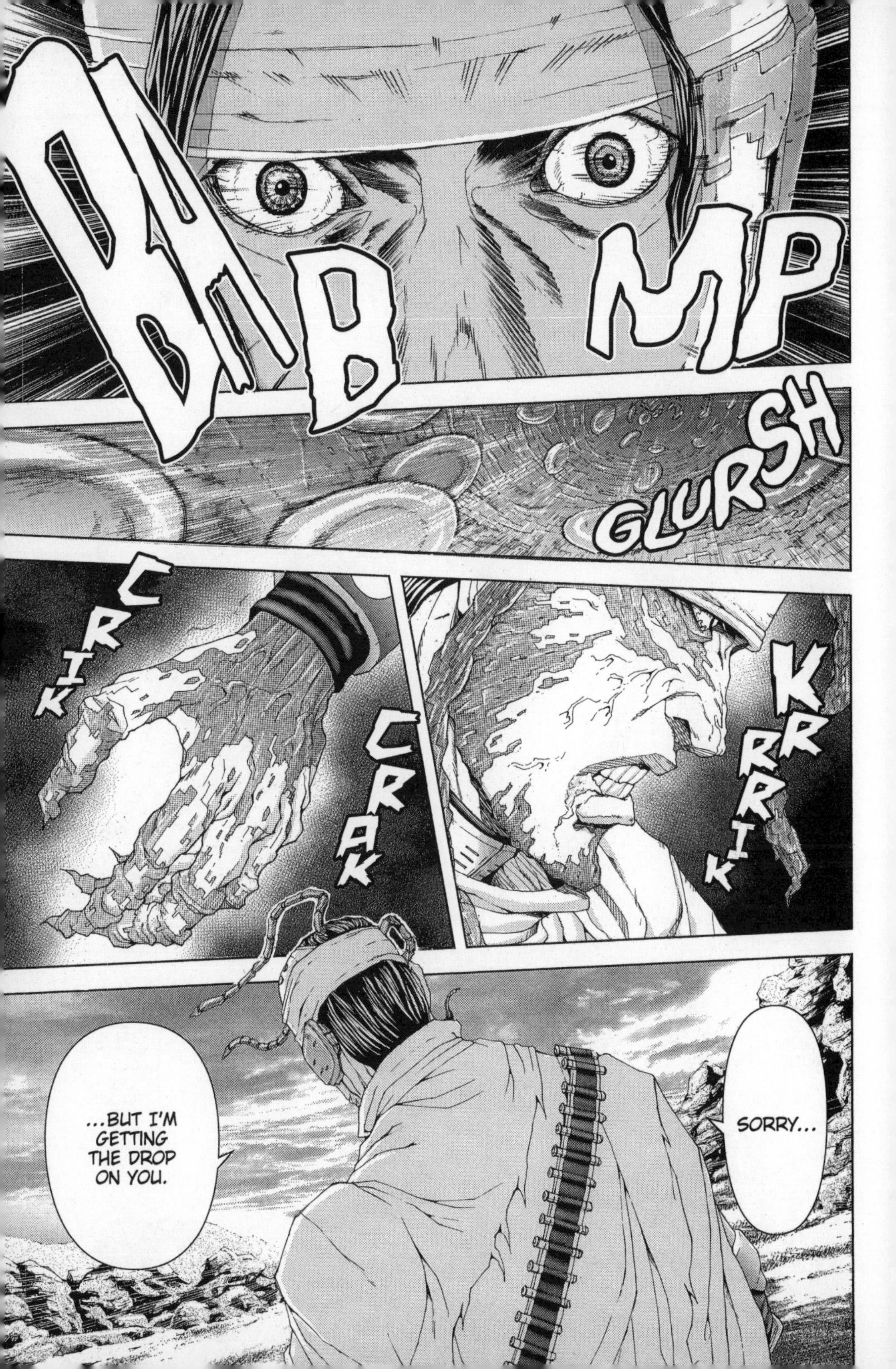

B MP
GLURSH
KRRRRIK
CRAK
CRIK
SORRY...
...BUT I'M GETTING THE DROP ON YOU.

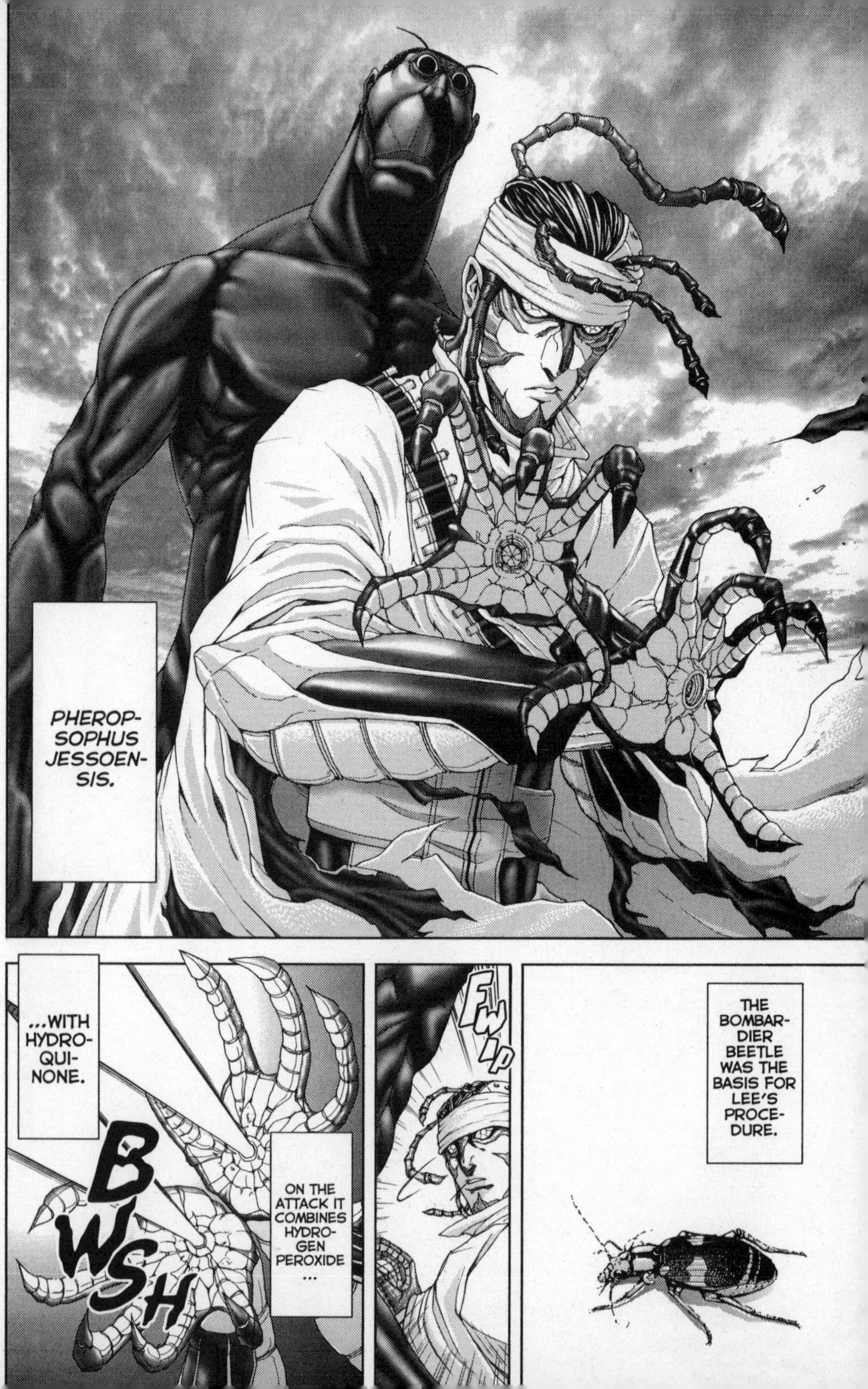
PHEROPSOPHUS JESSOENSIS.
THE BOMBARDIER BEETLE WAS THE BASIS FOR LEE'S PROCEDURE.
FWIP
ON THE ATTACK IT COMBINES HYDROGEN PEROXIDE...
...WITH HYDROQUINONE.
BWSH

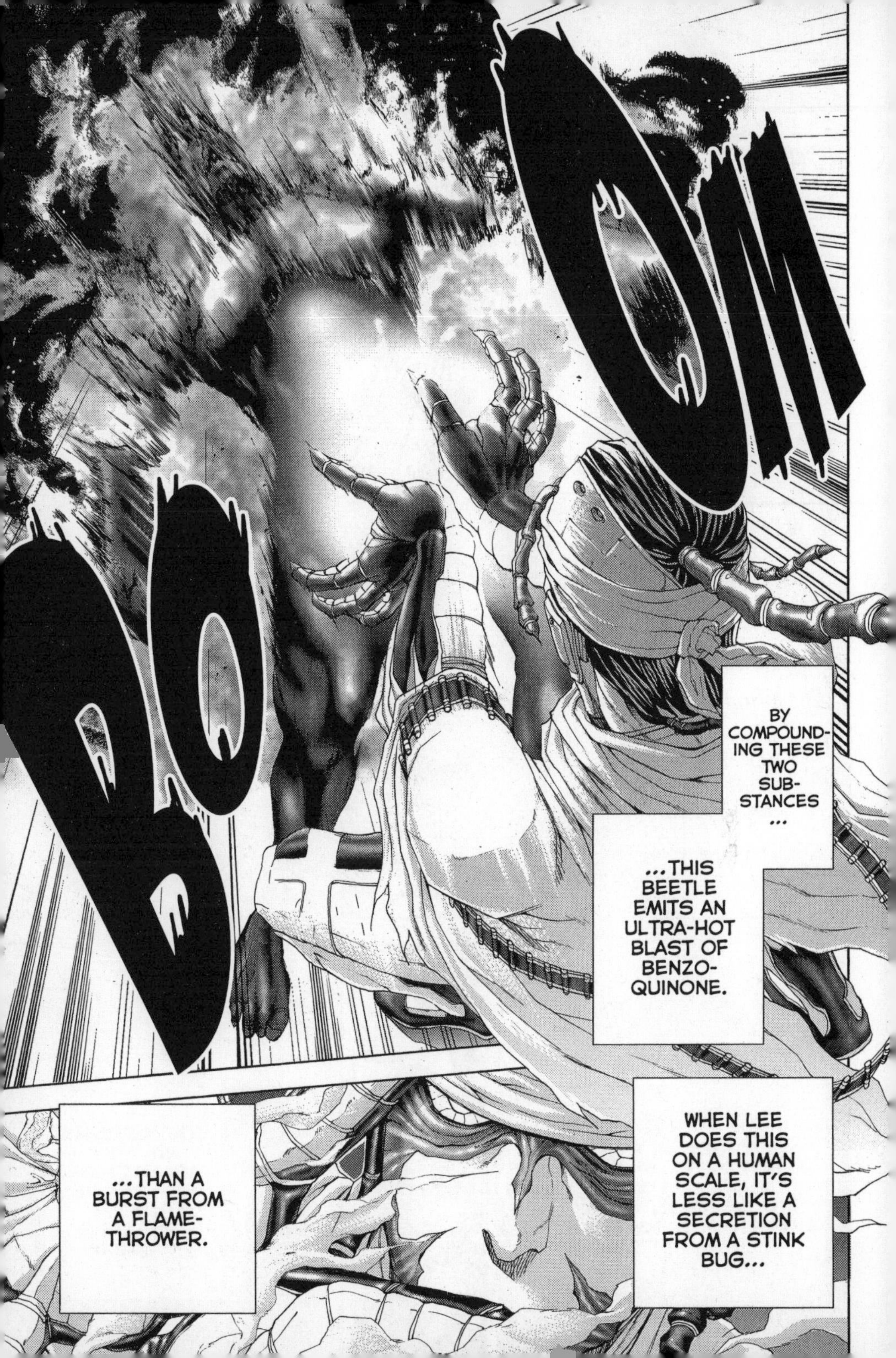
BOOM
BY COMPOUNDING THESE TWO SUBSTANCES...
...THIS BEETLE EMITS AN ULTRA-HOT BLAST OF BENZOQUINONE.
WHEN LEE DOES THIS ON A HUMAN SCALE, IT'S LESS LIKE A SECRETION FROM A STINK BUG...
...THAN A BURST FROM A FLAMETHROWER.

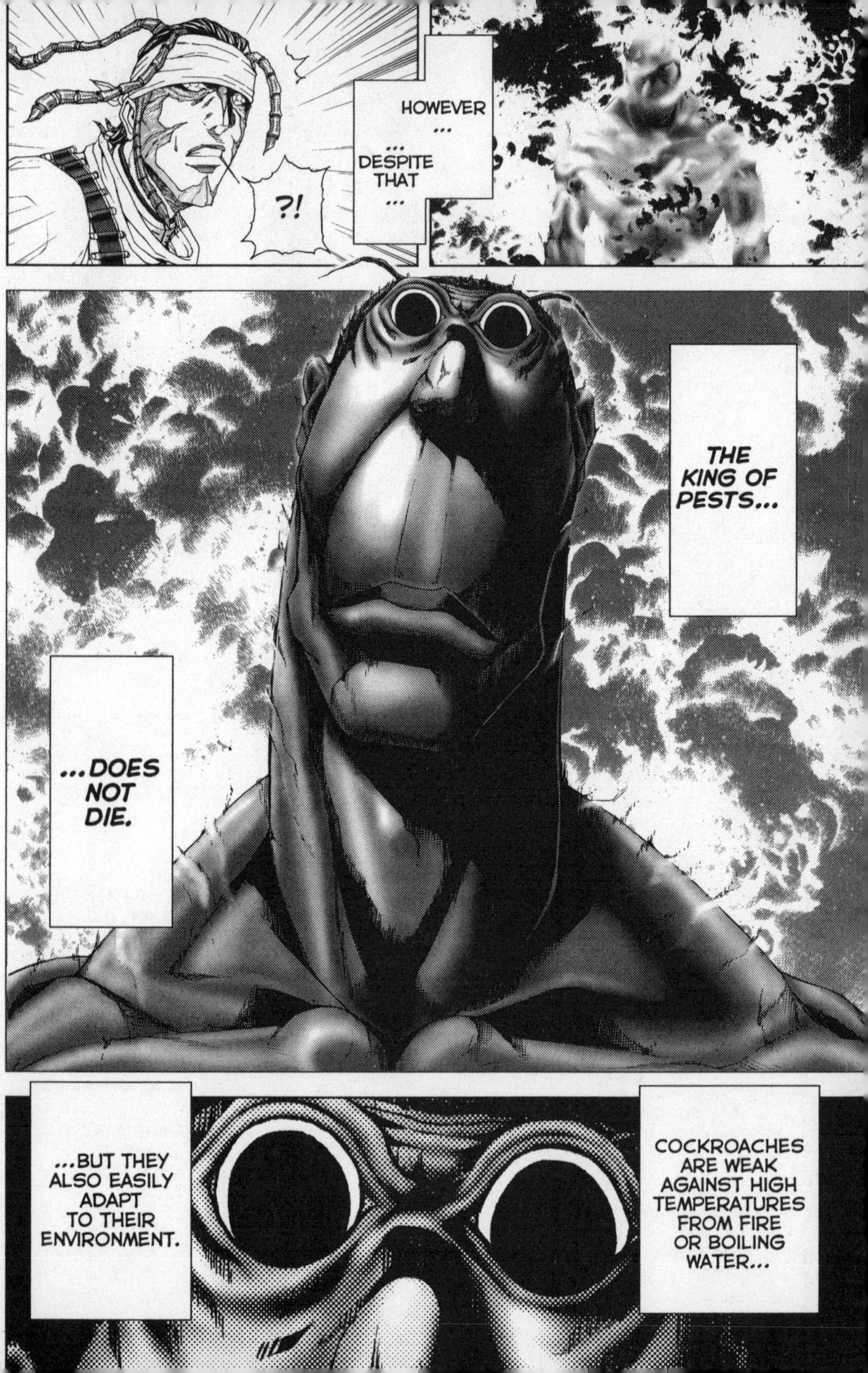
HOWEVER ...
... DESPITE THAT ...
?!
THE KING OF PESTS...
...DOES NOT DIE.
COCKROACHES ARE WEAK AGAINST HIGH TEMPERATURES FROM FIRE OR BOILING WATER...
...BUT THEY ALSO EASILY ADAPT TO THEIR ENVIRONMENT.

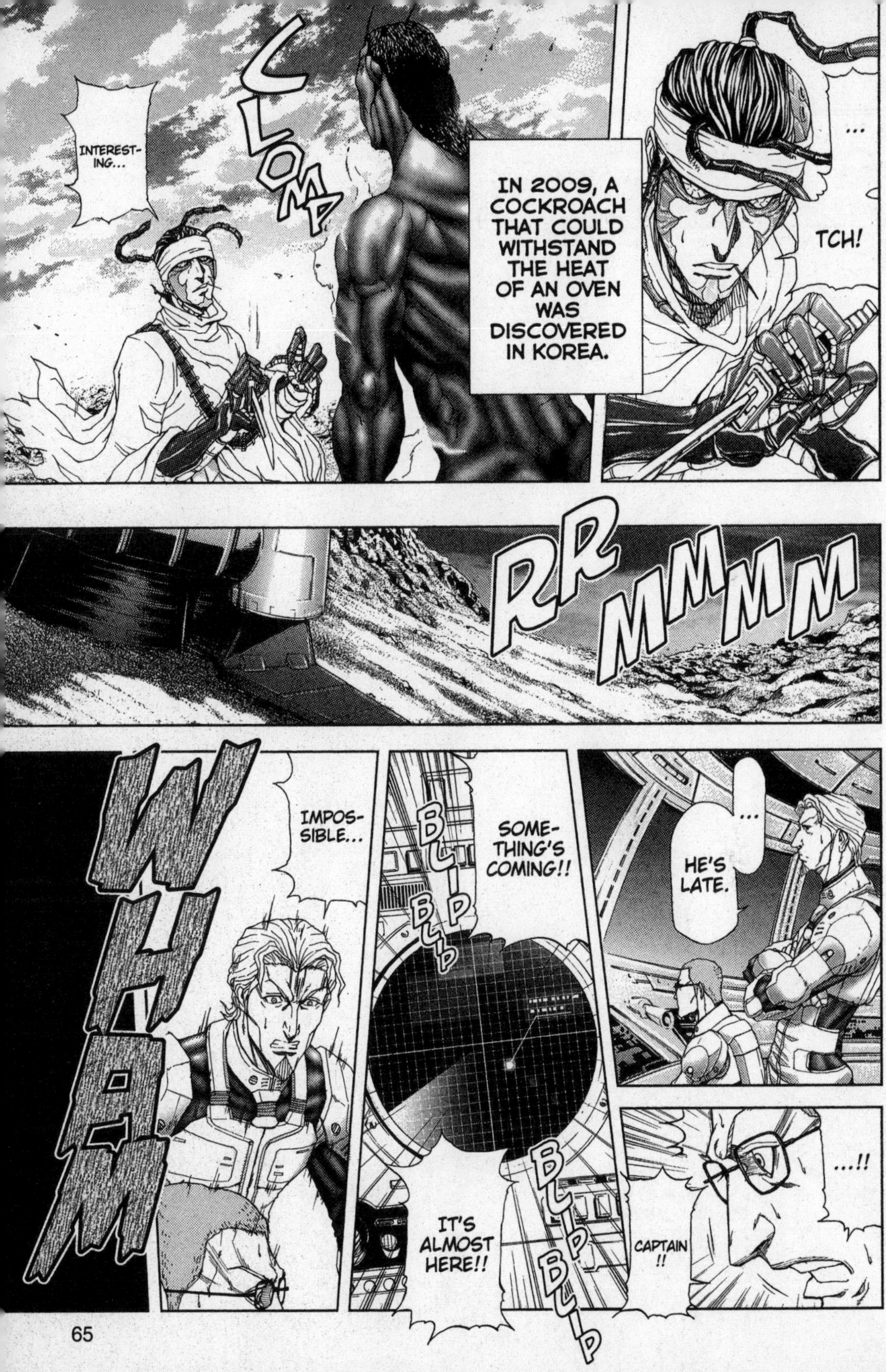
...
IN 2009, A COCKROACH THAT COULD WITHSTAND THE HEAT OF AN OVEN WAS DISCOVERED IN KOREA.
TCH!
CLOMP
INTERESTING...
RRMMMMM
...
HE'S LATE.
...!!
CAPTAIN!!
SOMETHING'S COMING!!
BLIP BLIP
IT'S ALMOST HERE!!
BLIP BLIP
IMPOSSIBLE...
WHAM

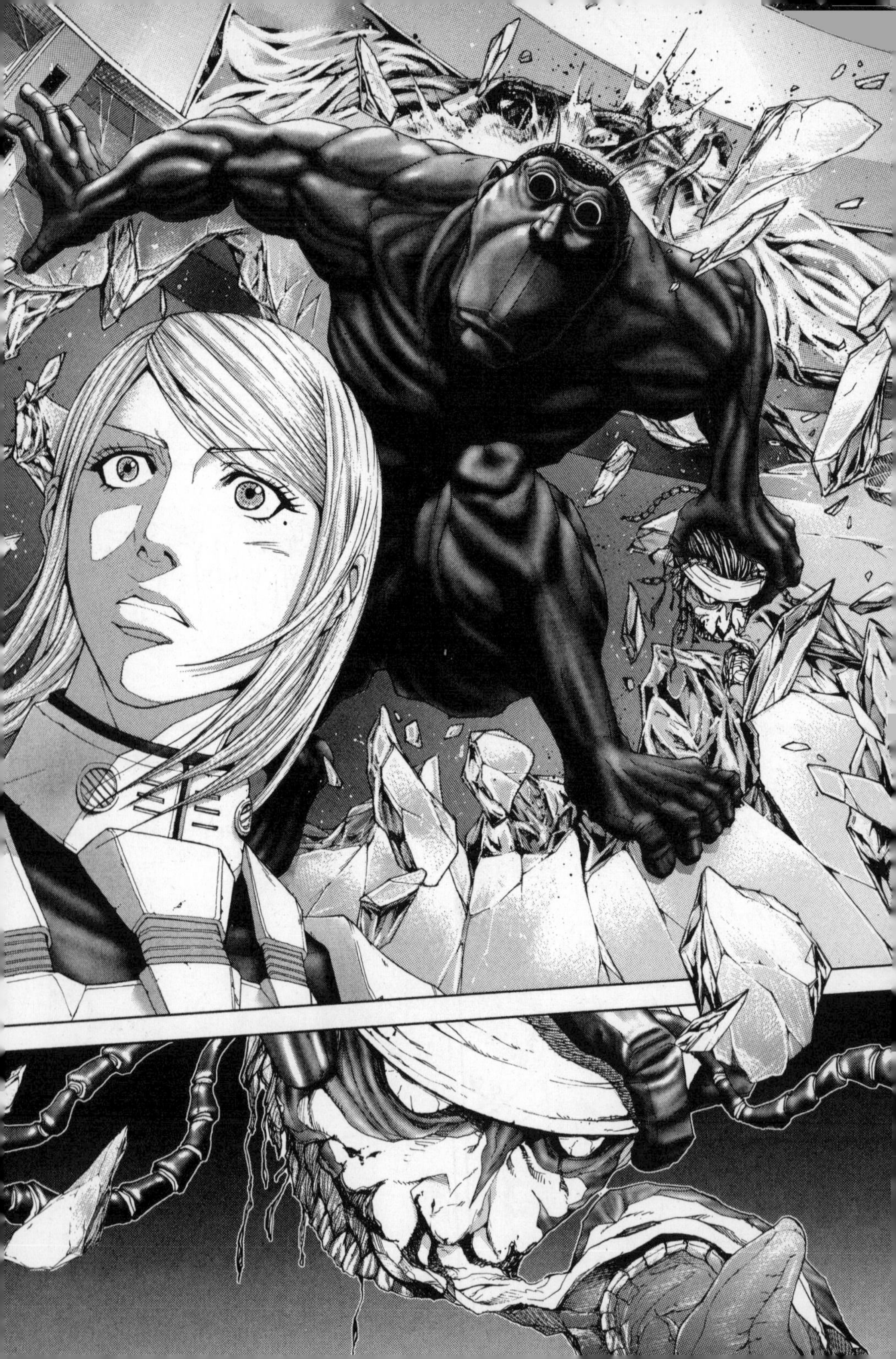

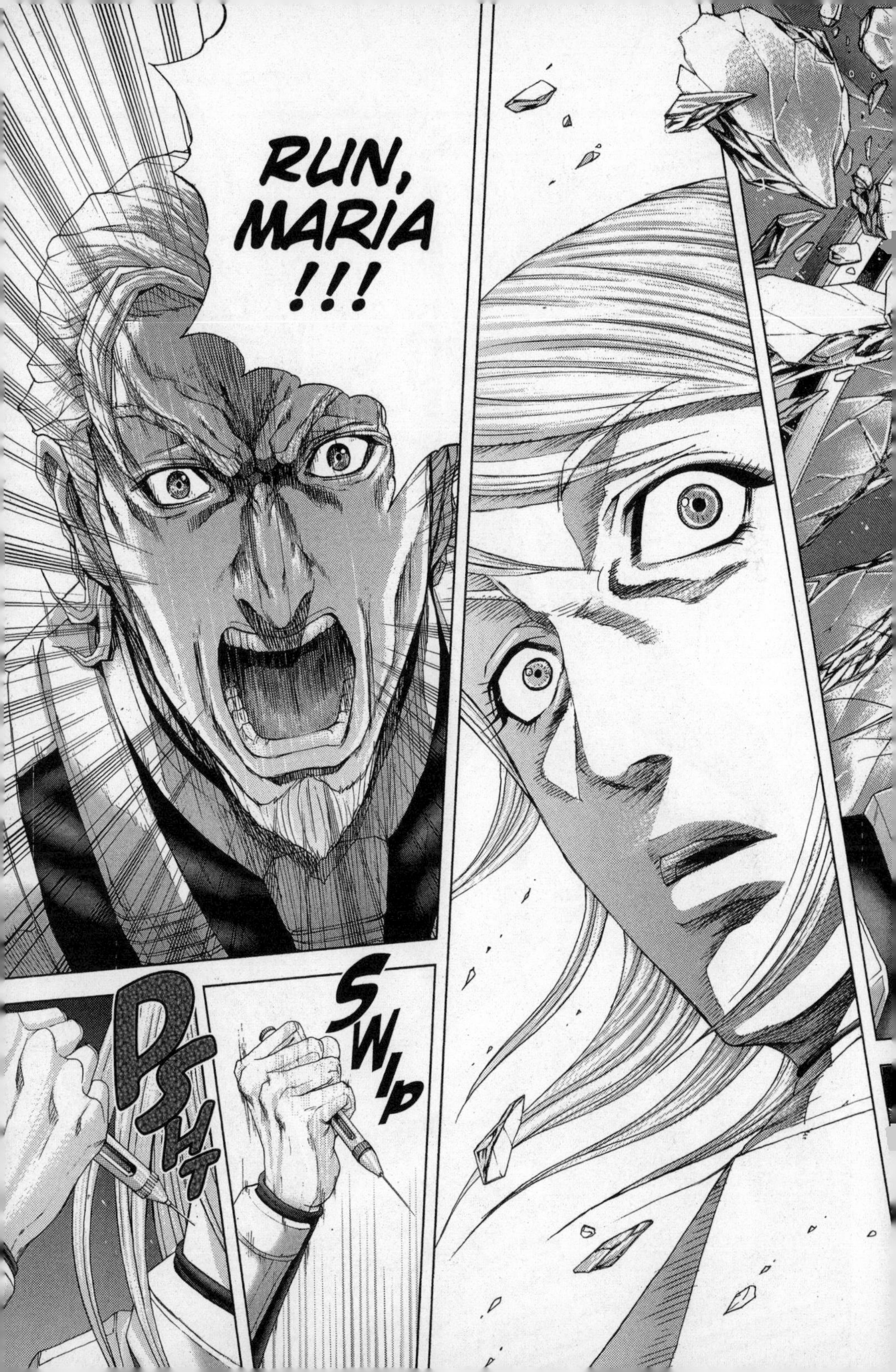
RUN, MARIA!!!
SWIP
PSHT

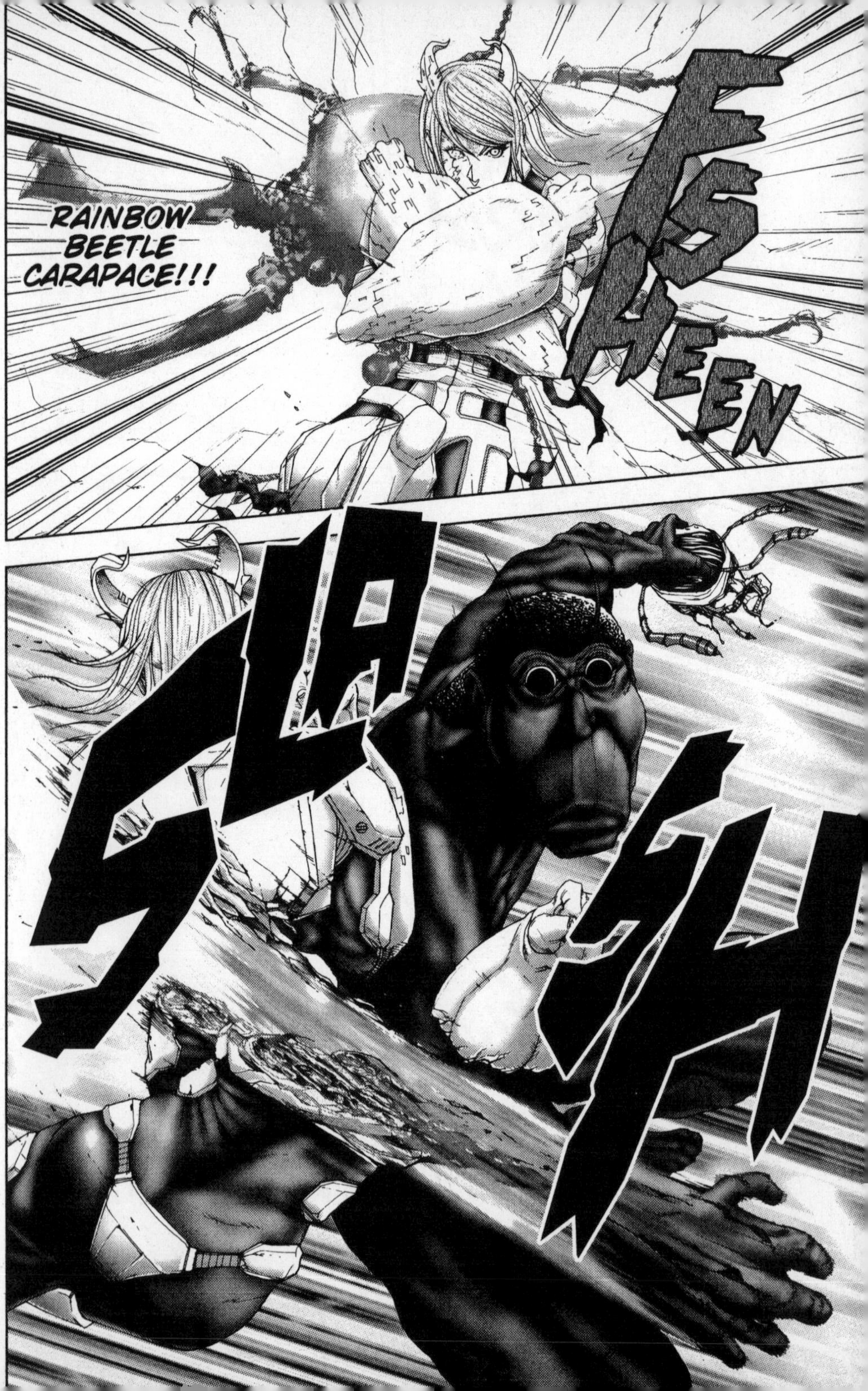
FSHEEN
RAINBOW BEETLE CARAPACE!!!
SLASH

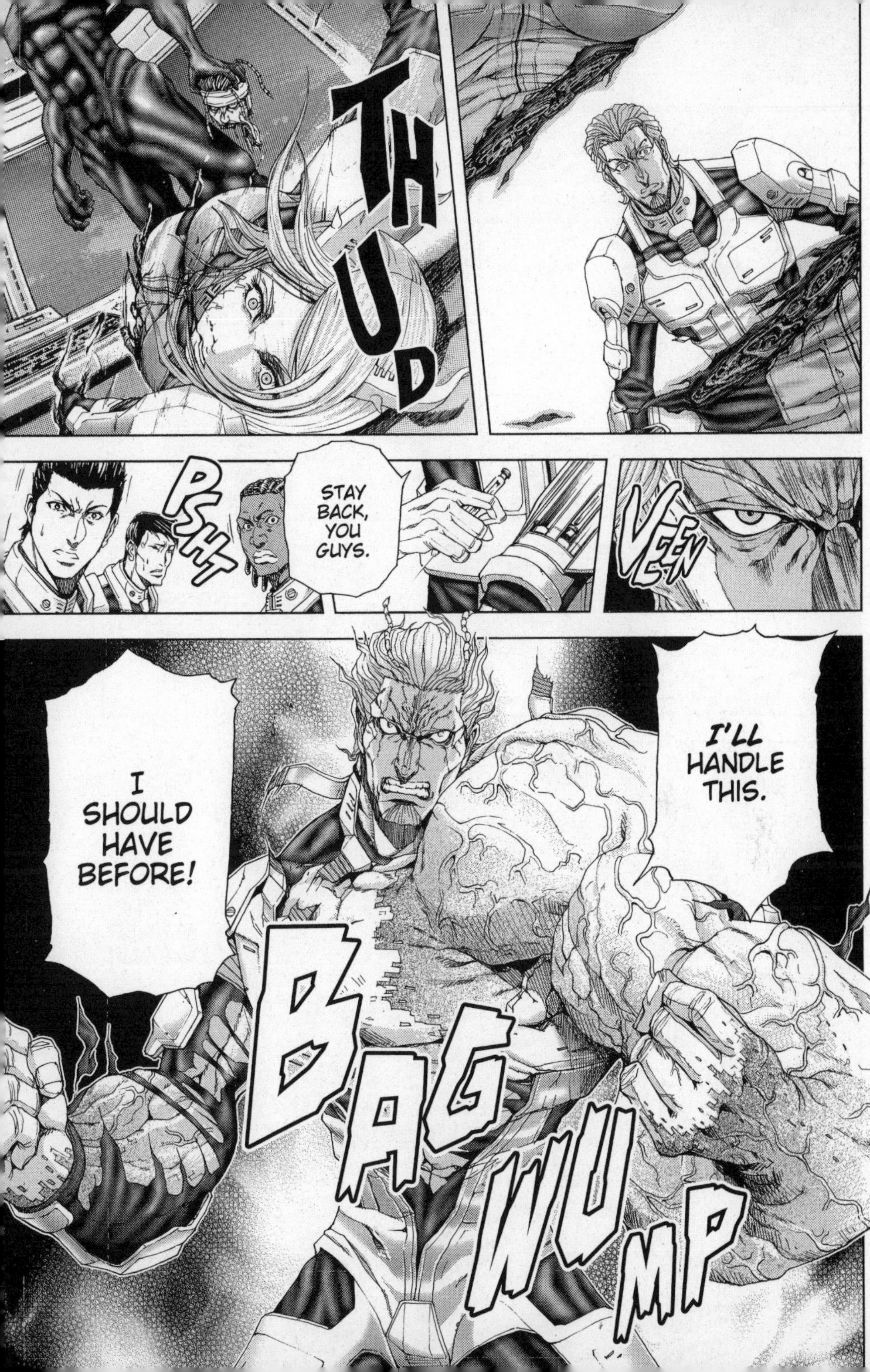
THUD
VEEN
STAY BACK, YOU GUYS.
PSHT
I'LL HANDLE THIS.
I SHOULD HAVE BEFORE!
BAGWUMP

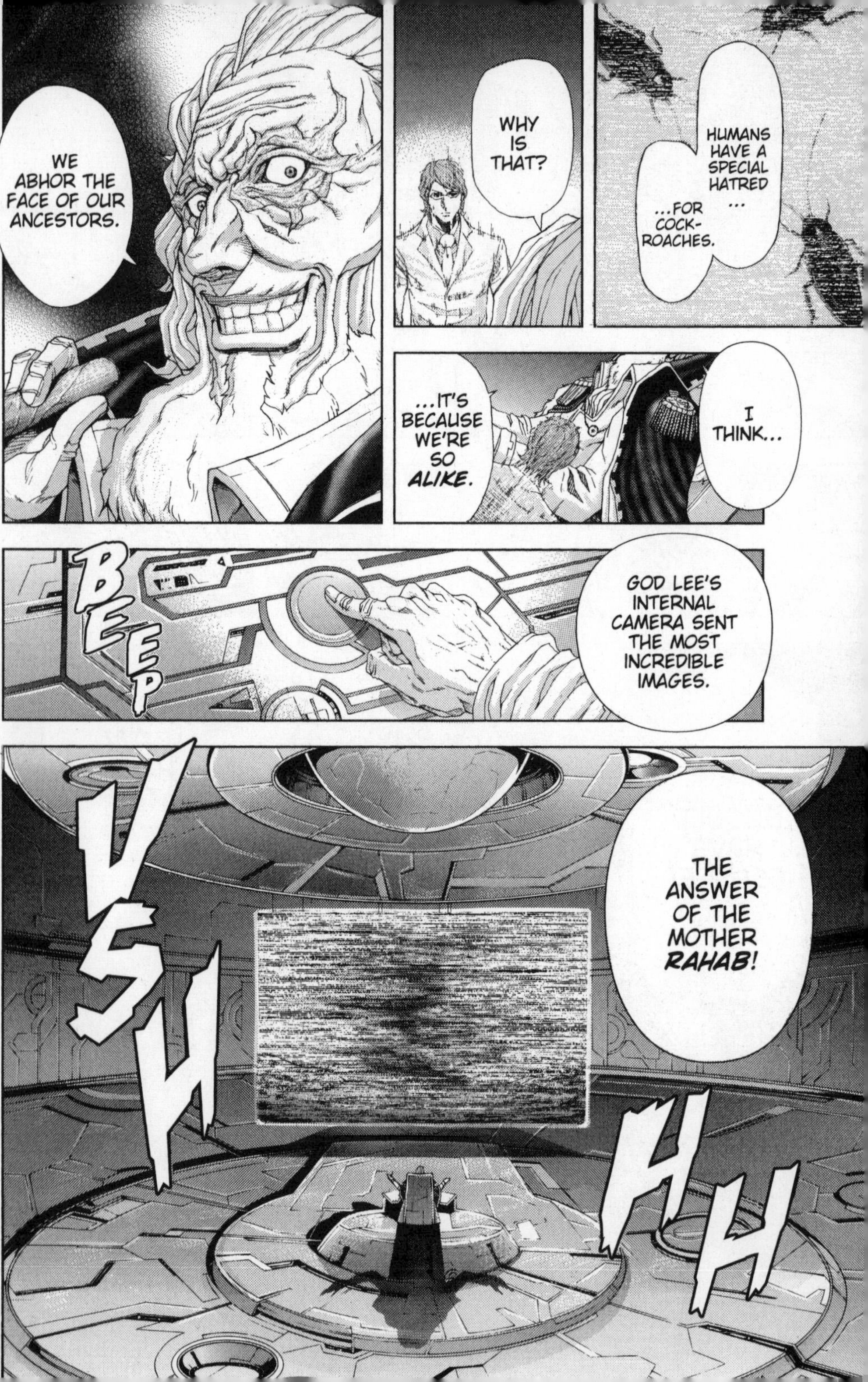
HUMANS HAVE A SPECIAL HATRED...
...FOR COCKROACHES.
WHY IS THAT?
I THINK...
...IT'S BECAUSE WE'RE SO *ALIKE*.
WE ABHOR THE FACE OF OUR ANCESTORS.
GOD LEE'S INTERNAL CAMERA SENT THE MOST INCREDIBLE IMAGES.
BEEP
THE ANSWER OF THE MOTHER *RAHAB*!
VSHHH

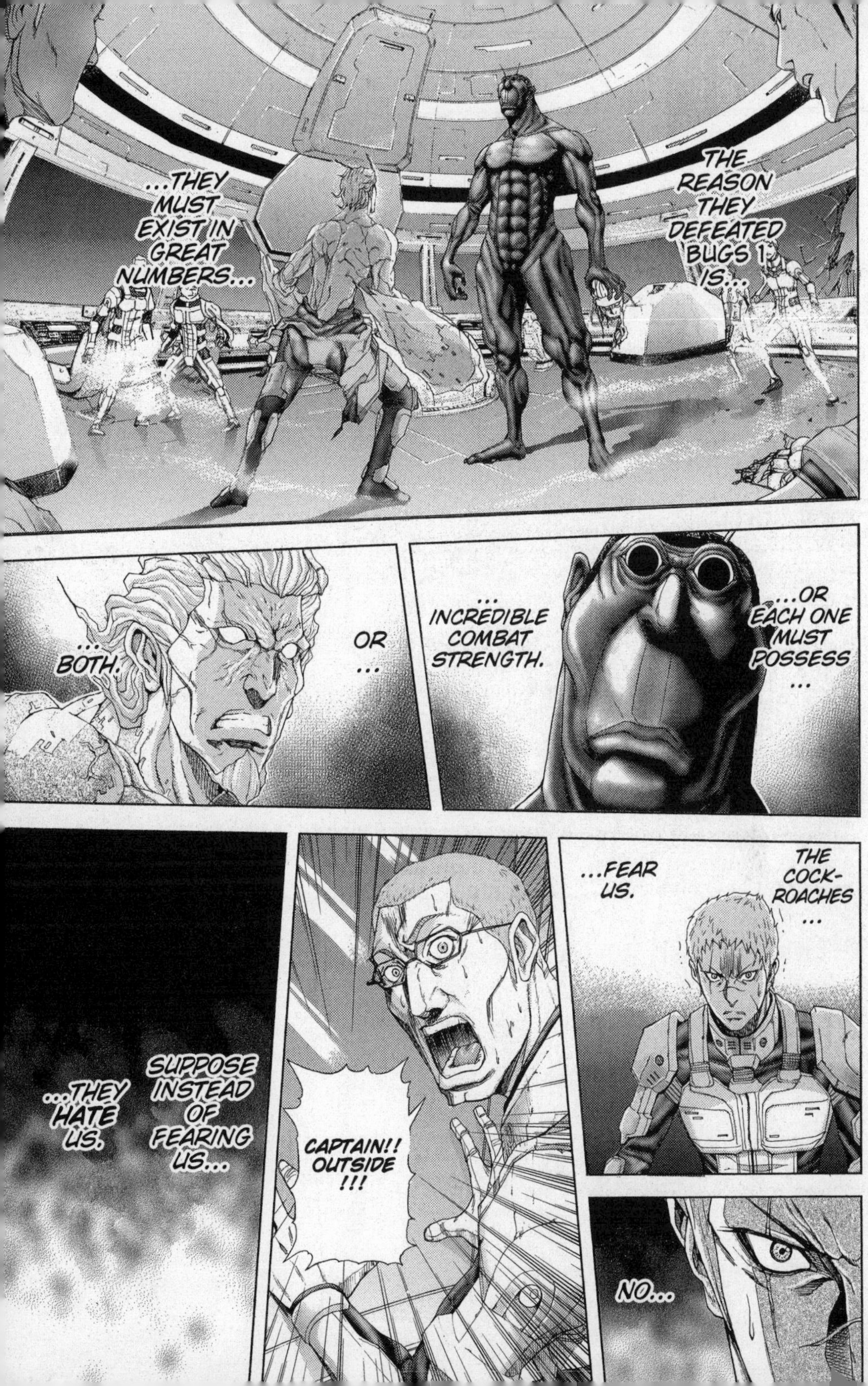
THE REASON THEY DEFEATED BUGS 1 IS...
...THEY MUST EXIST IN GREAT NUMBERS...
...OR EACH ONE MUST POSSESS ...
... INCREDIBLE COMBAT STRENGTH.
OR ...
... BOTH.
THE COCK-ROACHES ...
...FEAR US.
NO...
CAPTAIN!! OUTSIDE !!!
SUPPOSE INSTEAD OF FEARING US...
...THEY HATE US.

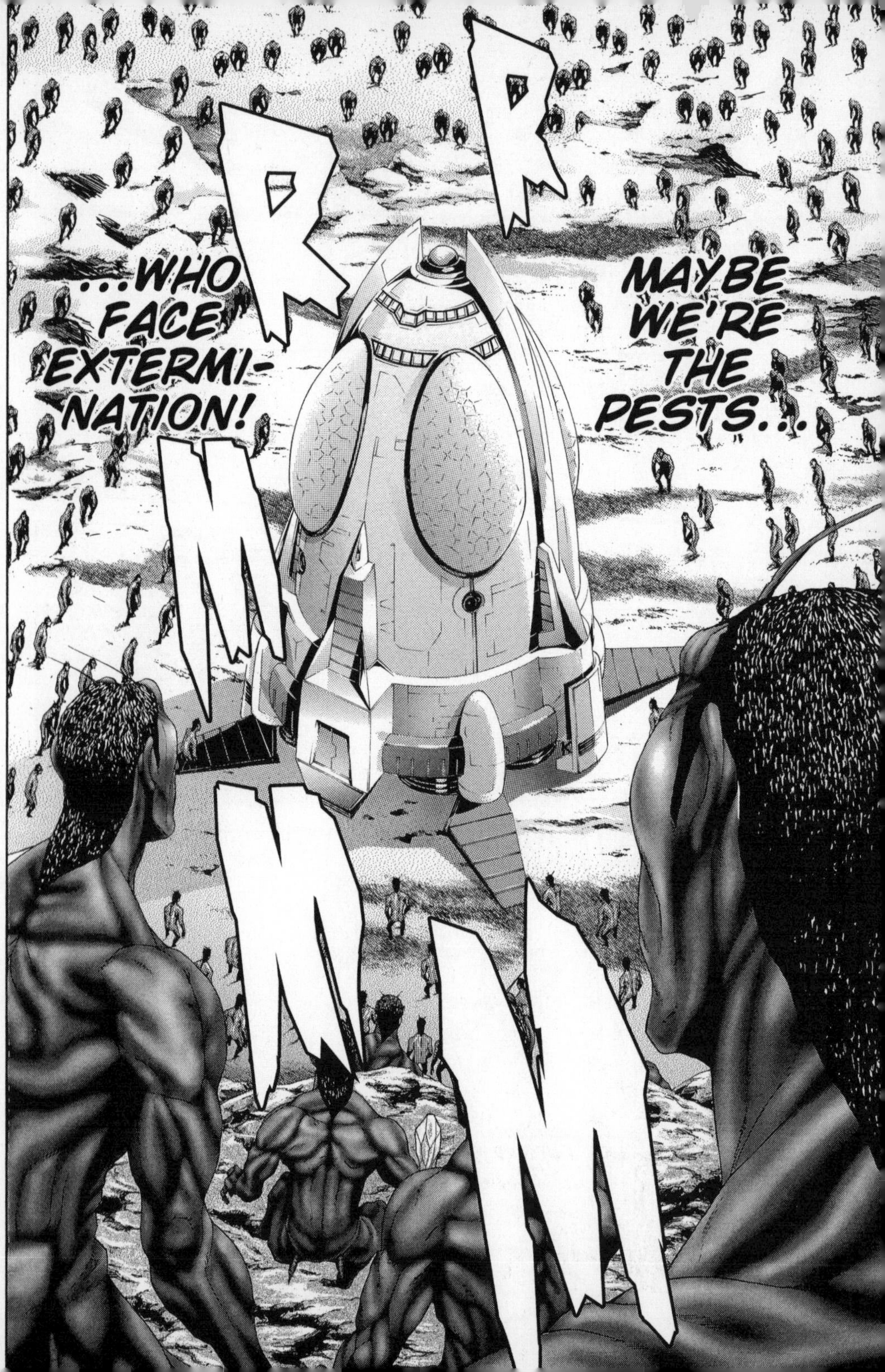
MAYBE WE'RE THE PESTS...
...WHO FACE EXTERMI-NATION!
RRMMM

TERRA
FORMARS

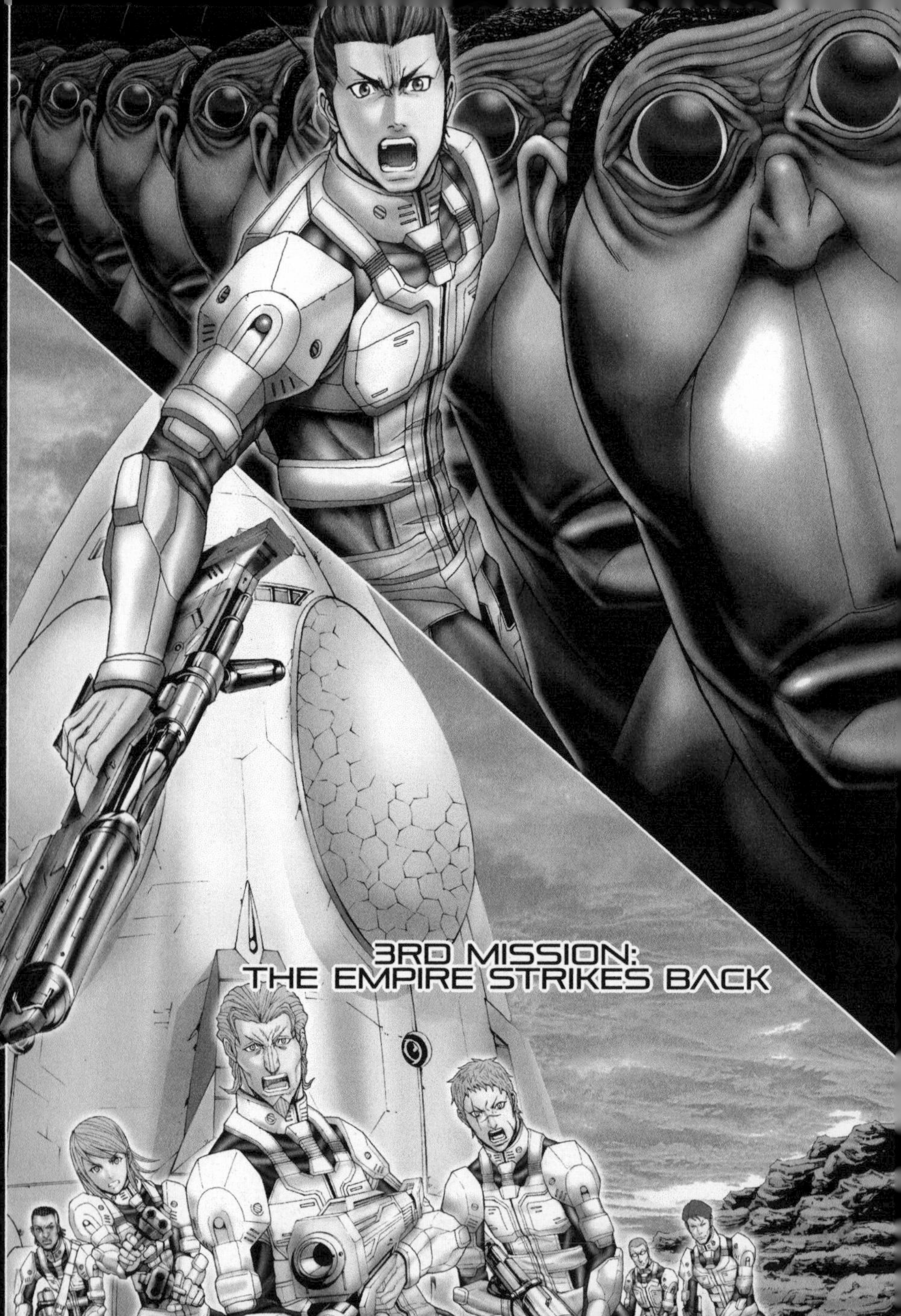
3RD MISSION:
THE EMPIRE STRIKES BACK

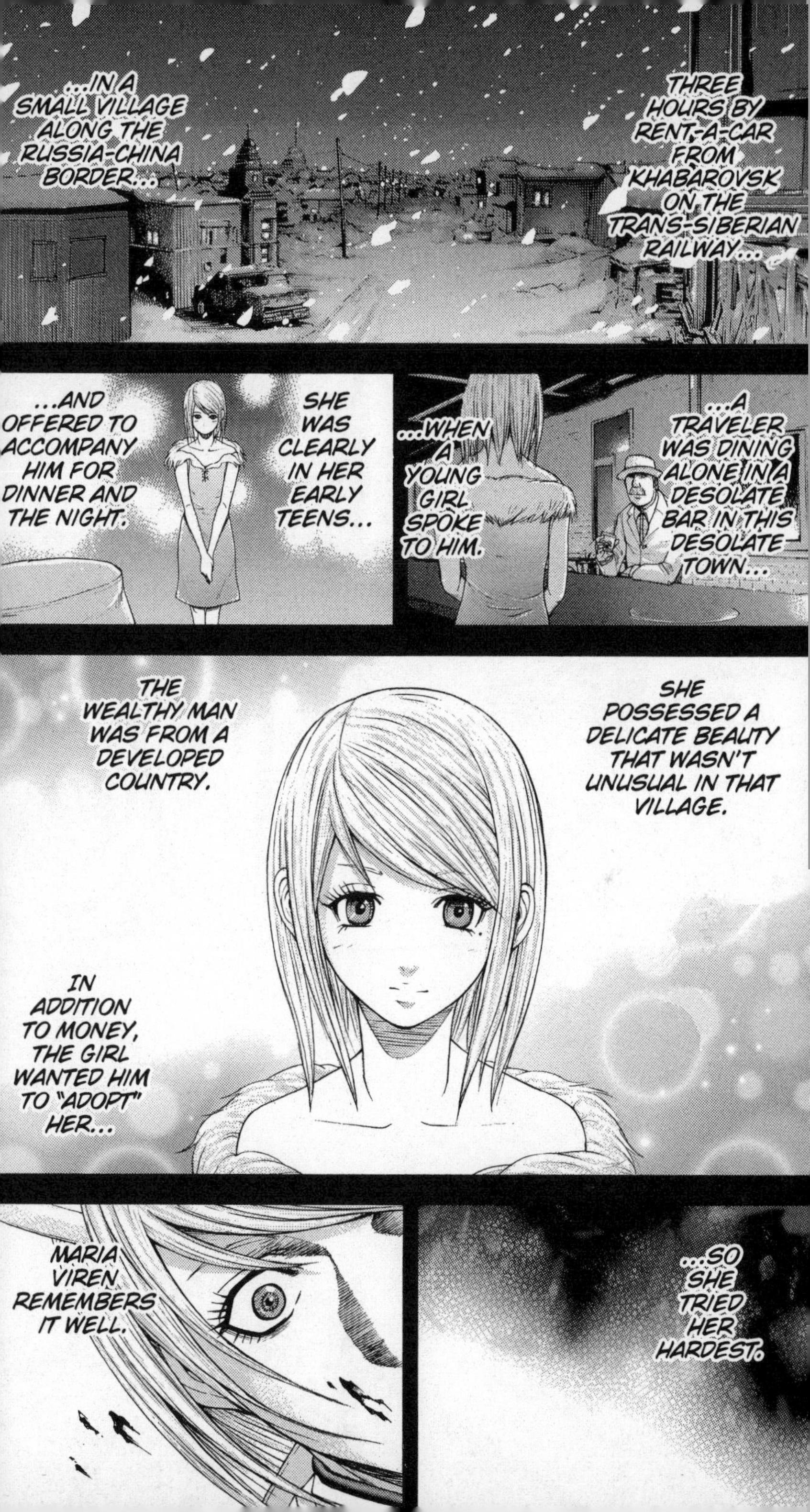
THREE HOURS BY RENT-A-CAR FROM KHABAROVSK ON THE TRANS-SIBERIAN RAILWAY...
...IN A SMALL VILLAGE ALONG THE RUSSIA-CHINA BORDER...
...A TRAVELER WAS DINING ALONE IN A DESOLATE BAR IN THIS DESOLATE TOWN...
...WHEN A YOUNG GIRL SPOKE TO HIM.
SHE WAS CLEARLY IN HER EARLY TEENS...
...AND OFFERED TO ACCOMPANY HIM FOR DINNER AND THE NIGHT.
SHE POSSESSED A DELICATE BEAUTY THAT WASN'T UNUSUAL IN THAT VILLAGE.
THE WEALTHY MAN WAS FROM A DEVELOPED COUNTRY.
IN ADDITION TO MONEY, THE GIRL WANTED HIM TO "ADOPT" HER...
...SO SHE TRIED HER HARDEST.
MARIA VIREN REMEMBERS IT WELL.

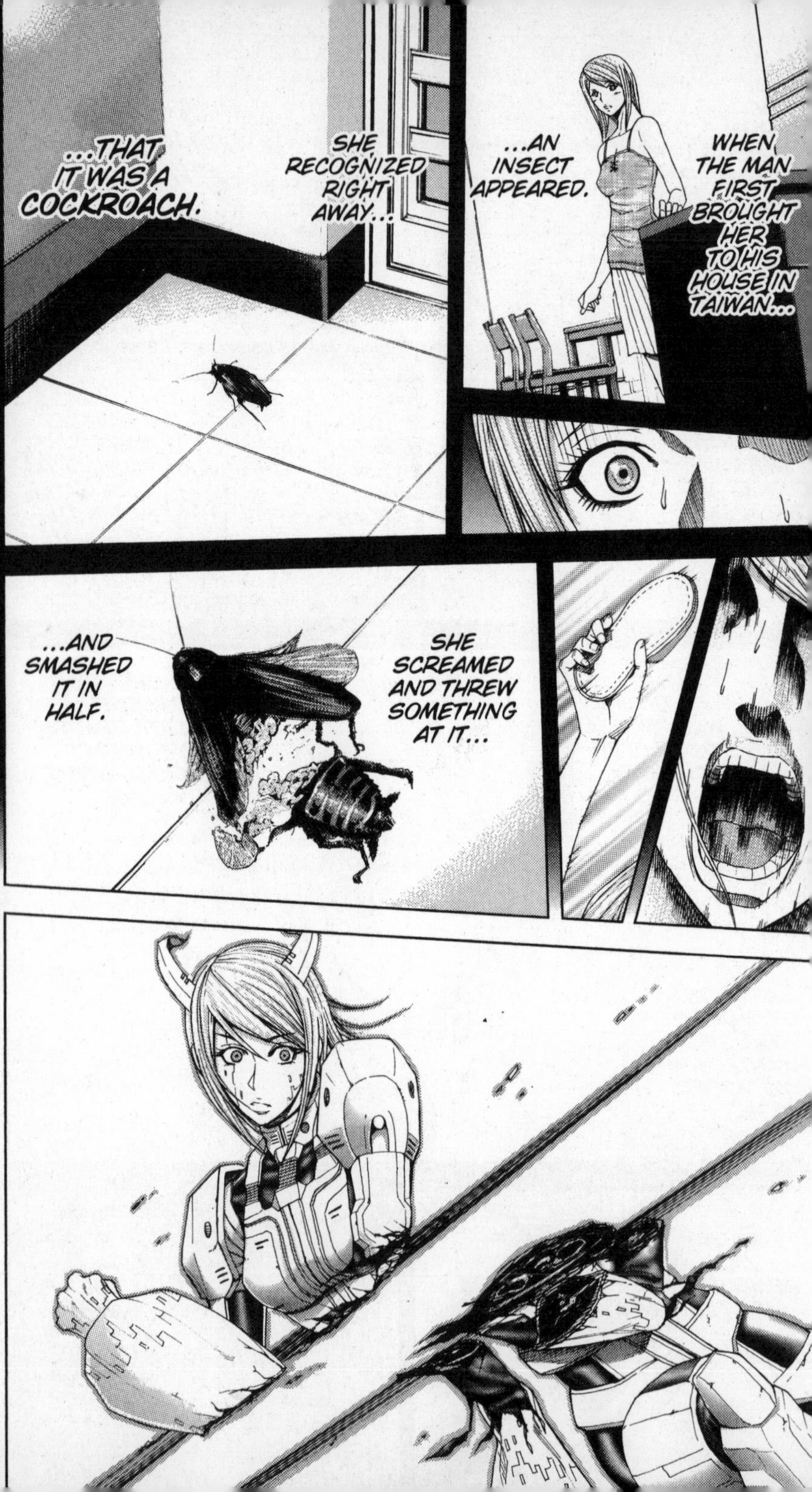
WHEN THE MAN FIRST BROUGHT HER TO HIS HOUSE IN TAIWAN...
...AN INSECT APPEARED.
SHE RECOGNIZED RIGHT AWAY...
...THAT IT WAS A COCKROACH.
SHE SCREAMED AND THREW SOMETHING AT IT...
...AND SMASHED IT IN HALF.

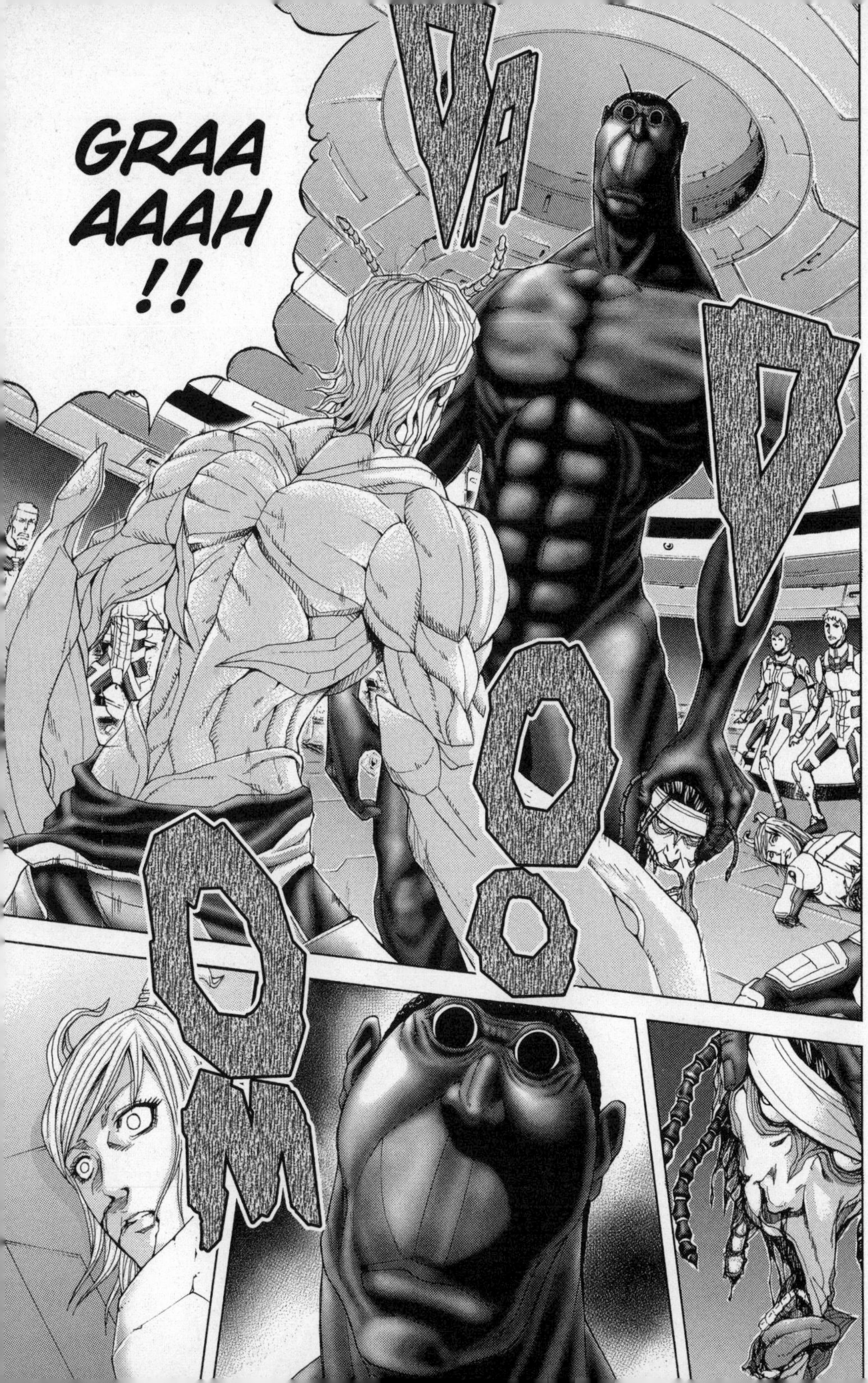
DADOOOM
GRAA
AAAH
!!

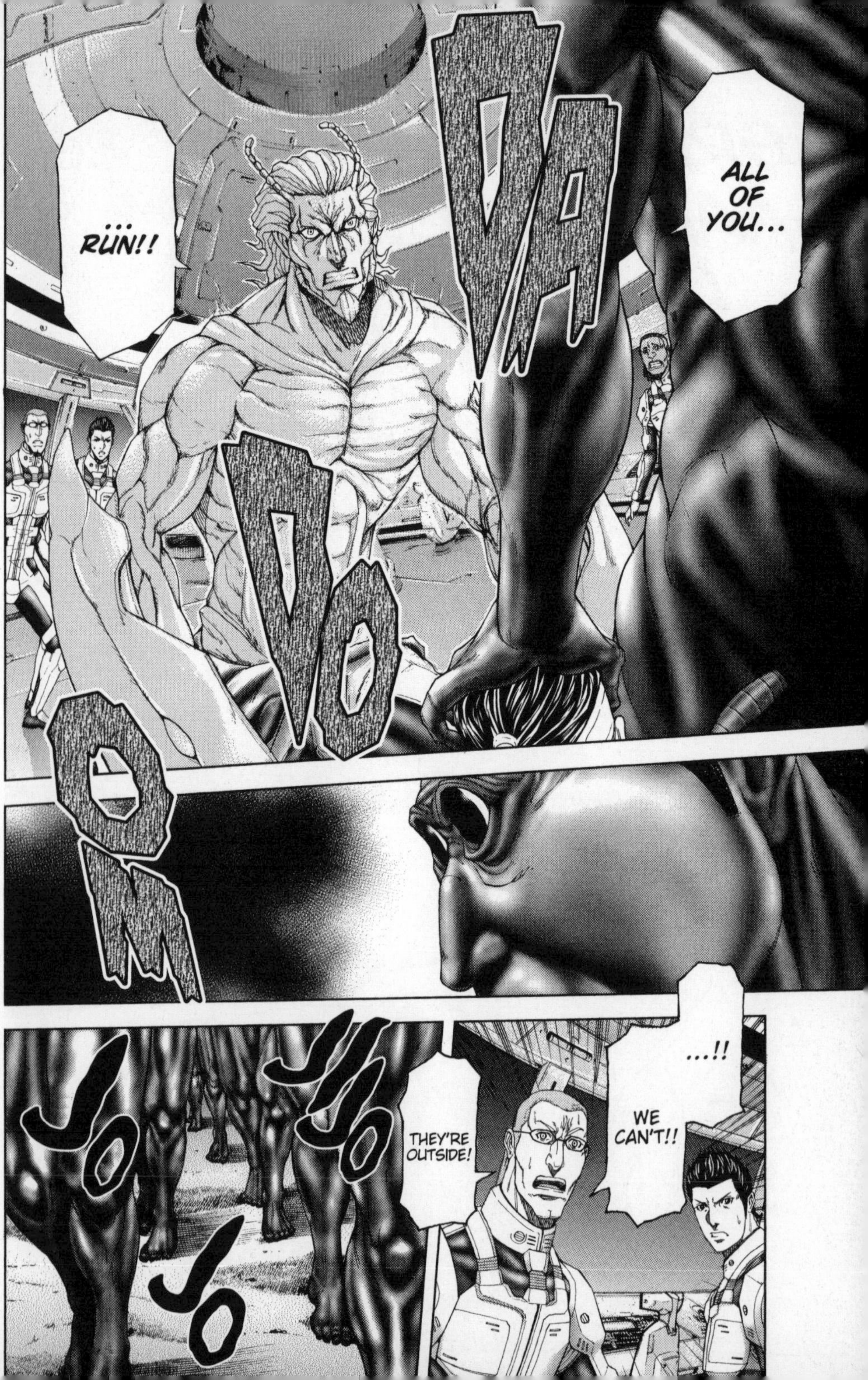
ALL OF YOU...
...RÜN!!
...!!
WE CAN'T!!
THEY'RE OUTSIDE!

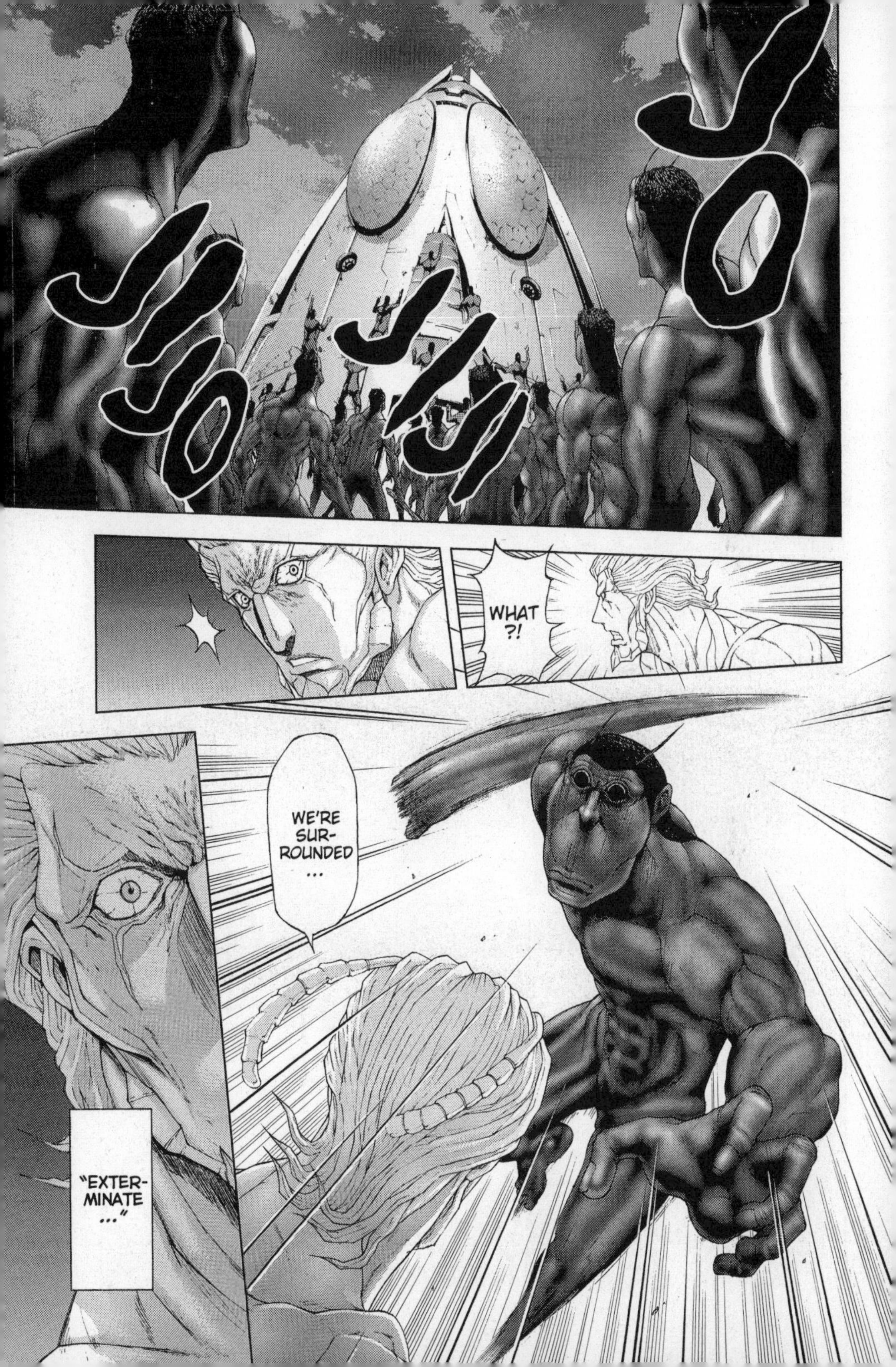
WHAT ?!
WE'RE SUR-ROUNDED ...
"EXTER-MINATE ..."

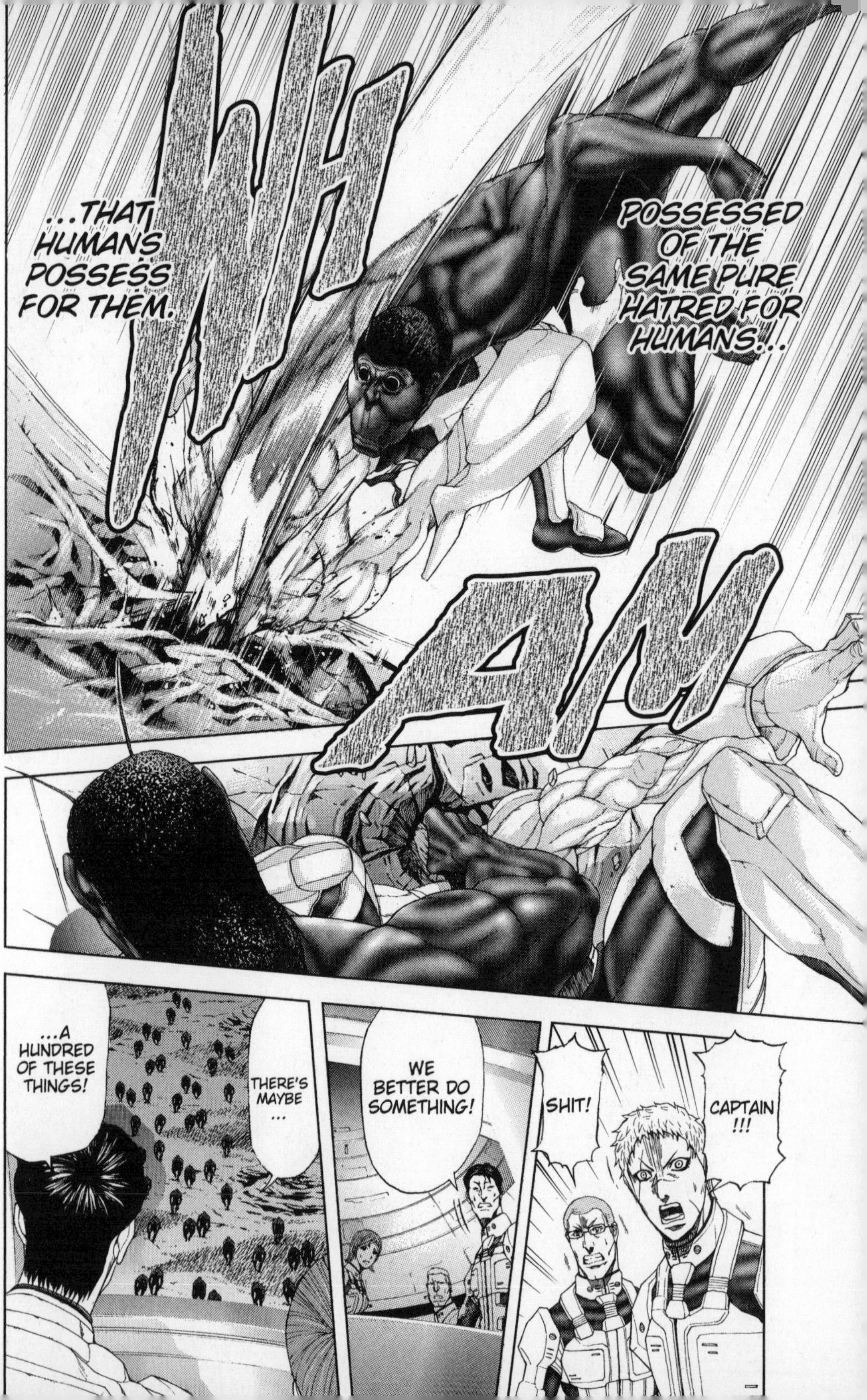
POSSESSED OF THE SAME PURE HATRED FOR HUMANS...
...THAT HUMANS POSSESS FOR THEM.
WHAM
CAPTAIN!!!
SHIT!
WE BETTER DO SOMETHING!
THERE'S MAYBE ...
...A HUNDRED OF THESE THINGS!

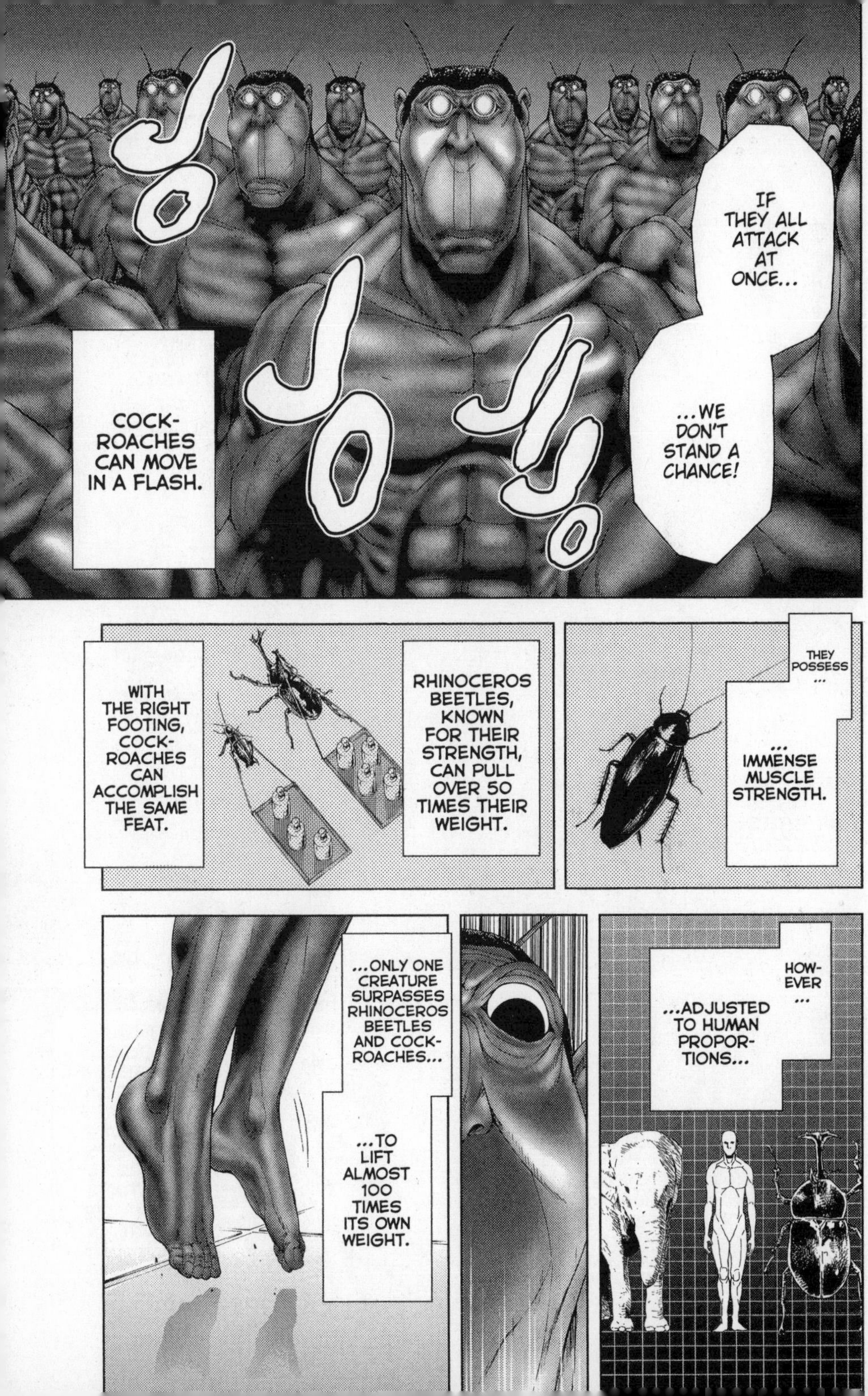
IF THEY ALL ATTACK AT ONCE...
...WE DON'T STAND A CHANCE!
JJO
JO
JO
COCK-ROACHES CAN MOVE IN A FLASH.
THEY POSSESS...
...IMMENSE MUSCLE STRENGTH.
RHINOCEROS BEETLES, KNOWN FOR THEIR STRENGTH, CAN PULL OVER 50 TIMES THEIR WEIGHT.
WITH THE RIGHT FOOTING, COCK-ROACHES CAN ACCOMPLISH THE SAME FEAT.
HOW-EVER...
...ADJUSTED TO HUMAN PROPOR-TIONS...
...ONLY ONE CREATURE SURPASSES RHINOCEROS BEETLES AND COCK-ROACHES...
...TO LIFT ALMOST 100 TIMES ITS OWN WEIGHT.

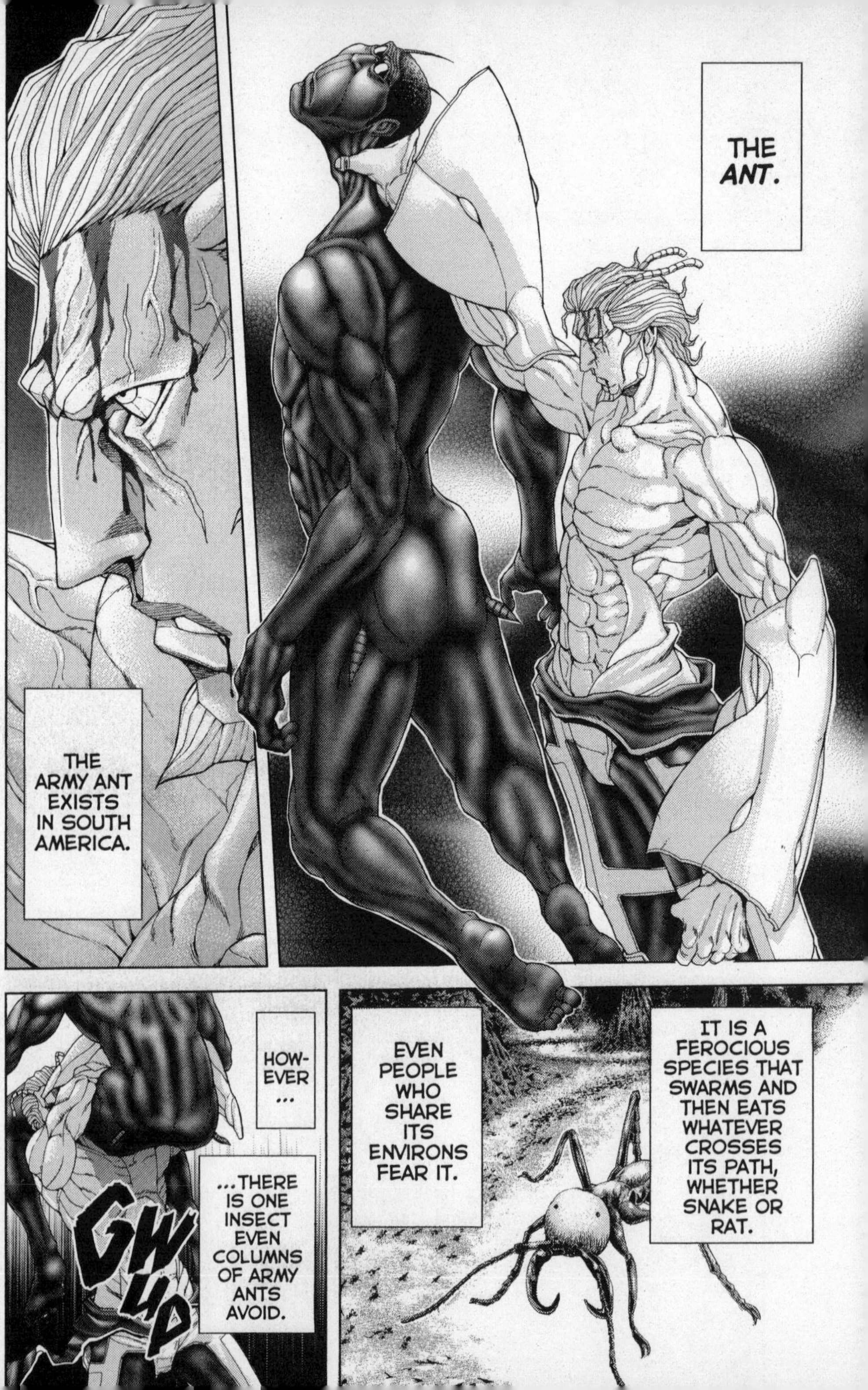
THE ANT.
THE ARMY ANT EXISTS IN SOUTH AMERICA.
IT IS A FEROCIOUS SPECIES THAT SWARMS AND THEN EATS WHATEVER CROSSES ITS PATH, WHETHER SNAKE OR RAT.
EVEN PEOPLE WHO SHARE ITS ENVIRONS FEAR IT.
HOW-EVER ...
...THERE IS ONE INSECT EVEN COLUMNS OF ARMY ANTS AVOID.
GWUD

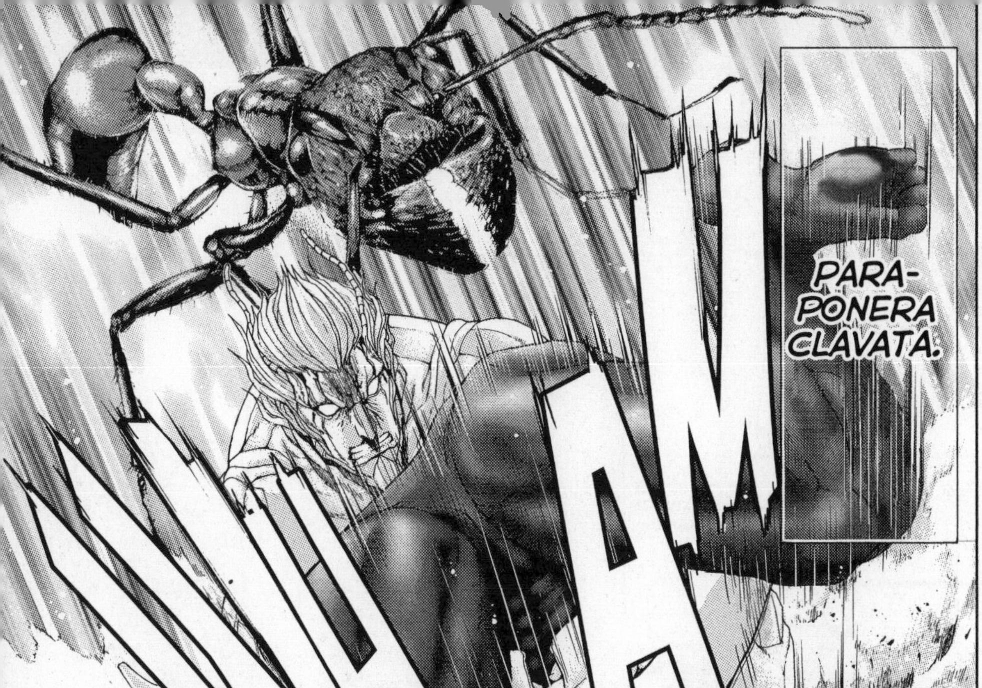
PARA-
PONERA
CLAVATA.
WHAM
IT IS THE
STRONGEST
ANT AND THE
STRONGEST
INSECT.

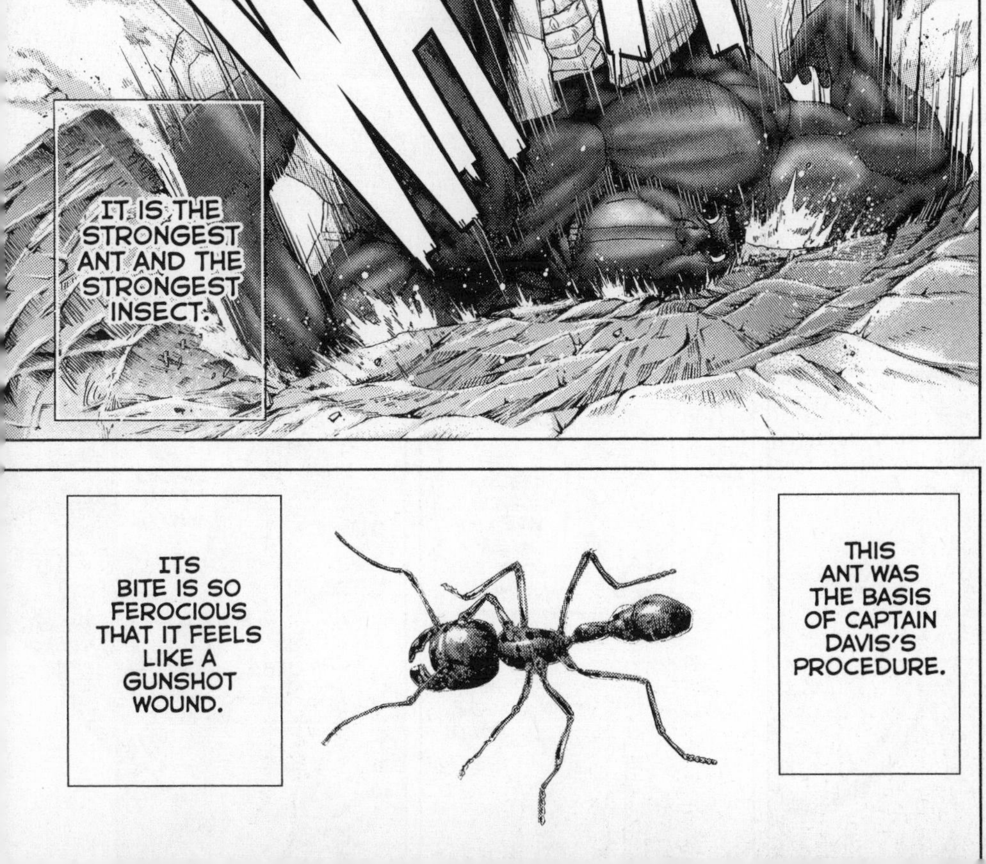
THIS
ANT WAS
THE BASIS
OF CAPTAIN
DAVIS'S
PROCEDURE.
ITS
BITE IS SO
FEROCIOUS
THAT IT FEELS
LIKE A
GUNSHOT
WOUND.

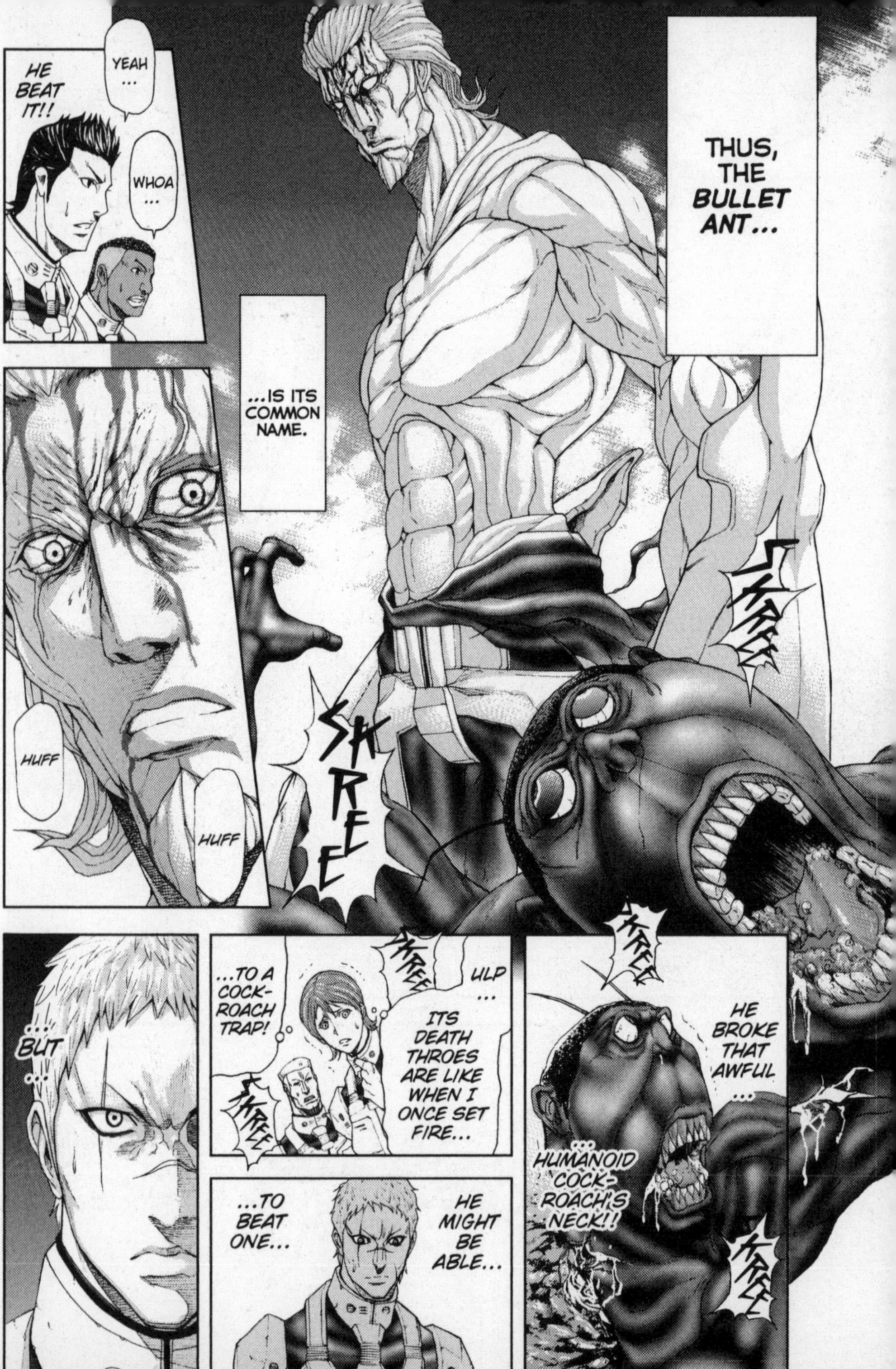
THUS, THE BULLET ANT...
...IS ITS COMMON NAME.
SKREE
SKREE
YEAH...
HE BEAT IT!!
WHOA...
HUFF
HUFF
SKREE
HE BROKE THAT AWFUL...
...HUMANOID COCKROACH'S NECK!!
KREE
SKREE
ULP...
ITS DEATH THROES ARE LIKE WHEN I ONCE SET FIRE...
...TO A COCKROACH TRAP!
SKREE
HE MIGHT BE ABLE...
...TO BEAT ONE...
...BUT...

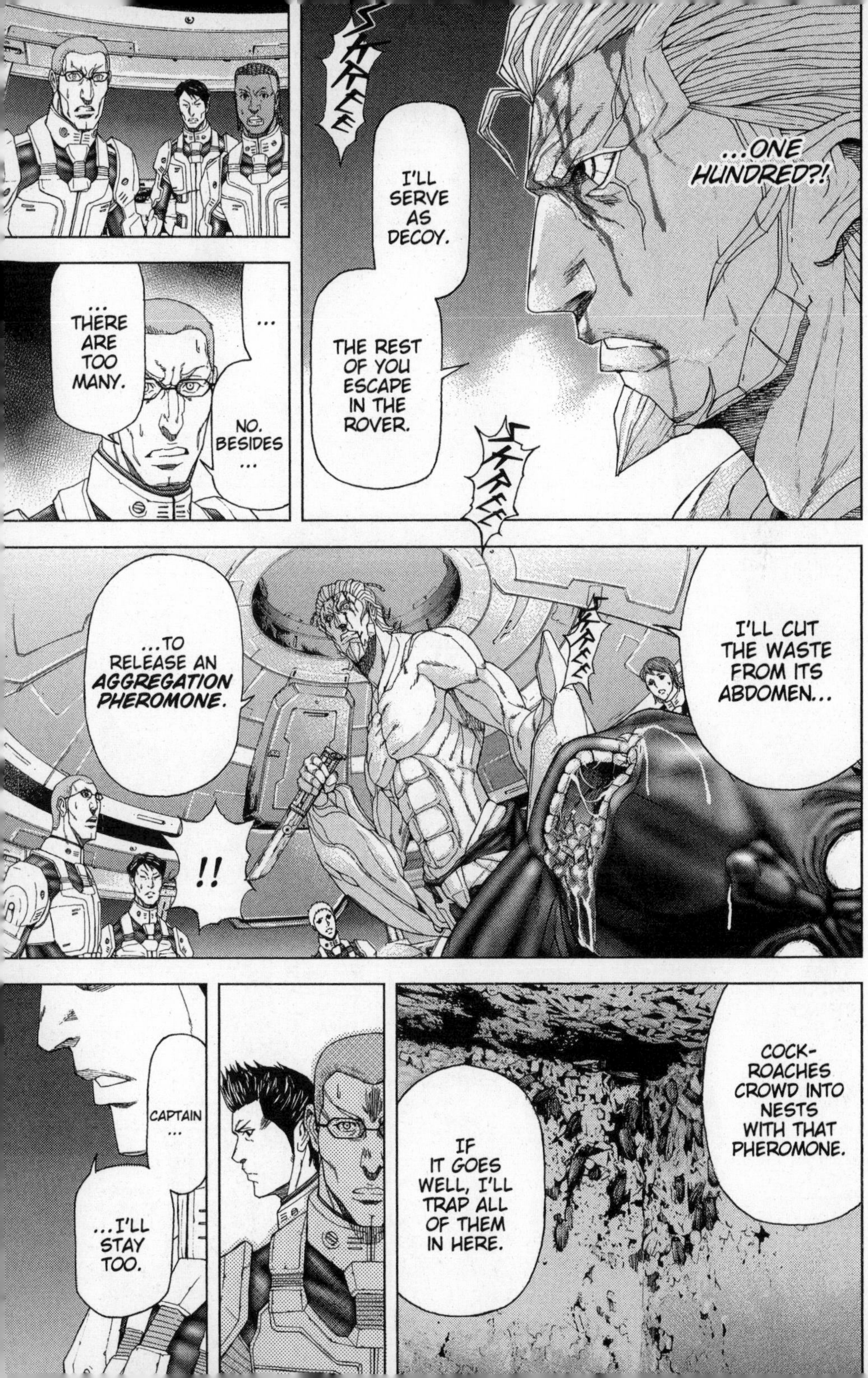
...ONE HUNDRED?!
SKREE
I'LL SERVE AS DECOY.
THE REST OF YOU ESCAPE IN THE ROVER.
SKREE
...
NO. BESIDES ...
... THERE ARE TOO MANY.
I'LL CUT THE WASTE FROM ITS ABDOMEN...
SKREE
...TO RELEASE AN *AGGREGATION PHEROMONE*.
!!
COCK-ROACHES CROWD INTO NESTS WITH THAT PHEROMONE.
IF IT GOES WELL, I'LL TRAP ALL OF THEM IN HERE.
CAPTAIN ...
...I'LL STAY TOO.

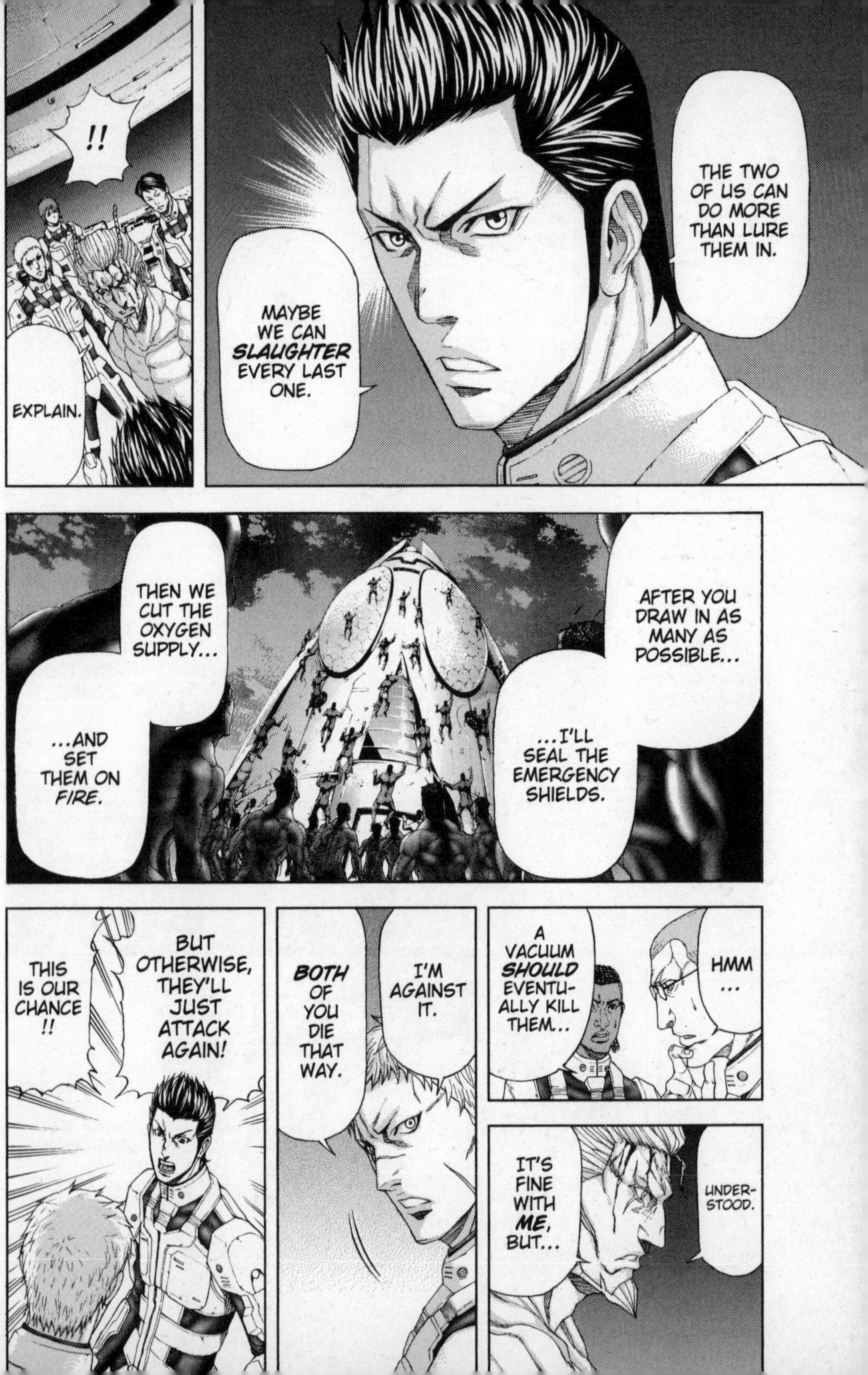
THE TWO OF US CAN DO MORE THAN LURE THEM IN.
MAYBE WE CAN SLAUGHTER EVERY LAST ONE.
!!
EXPLAIN.
AFTER YOU DRAW IN AS MANY AS POSSIBLE...
...I'LL SEAL THE EMERGENCY SHIELDS.
THEN WE CUT THE OXYGEN SUPPLY...
...AND SET THEM ON FIRE.
HMM...
A VACUUM SHOULD EVENTUALLY KILL THEM...
UNDERSTOOD.
IT'S FINE WITH ME, BUT...
I'M AGAINST IT.
BOTH OF YOU DIE THAT WAY.
BUT OTHERWISE, THEY'LL JUST ATTACK AGAIN!
THIS IS OUR CHANCE!!

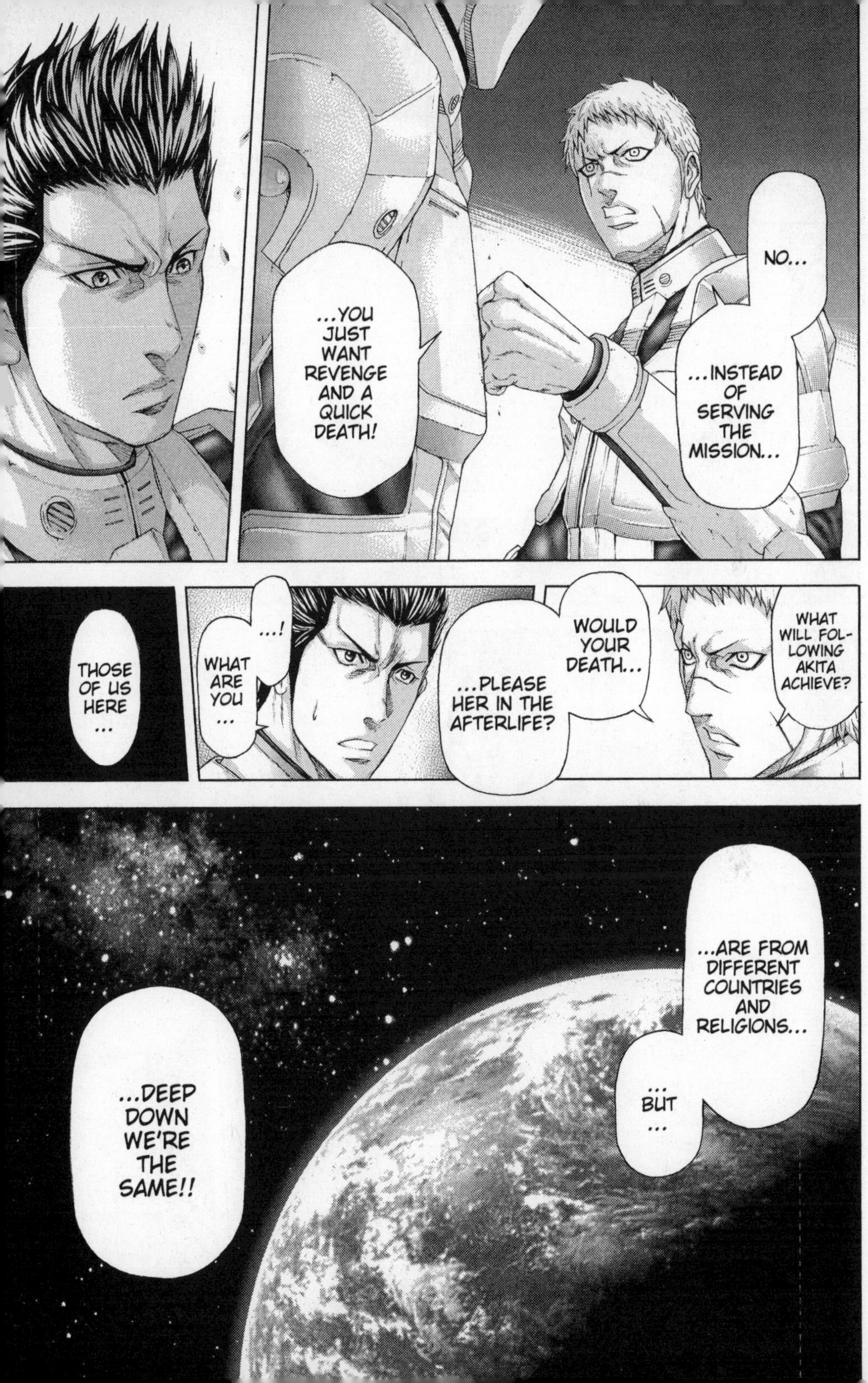
NO...
...INSTEAD OF SERVING THE MISSION...
...YOU JUST WANT REVENGE AND A QUICK DEATH!
WHAT WILL FOL-LOWING AKITA ACHIEVE?
WOULD YOUR DEATH...
...PLEASE HER IN THE AFTERLIFE?
...!
WHAT ARE YOU ...
THOSE OF US HERE ...
...ARE FROM DIFFERENT COUNTRIES AND RELIGIONS...
... BUT ...
...DEEP DOWN WE'RE THE SAME!!

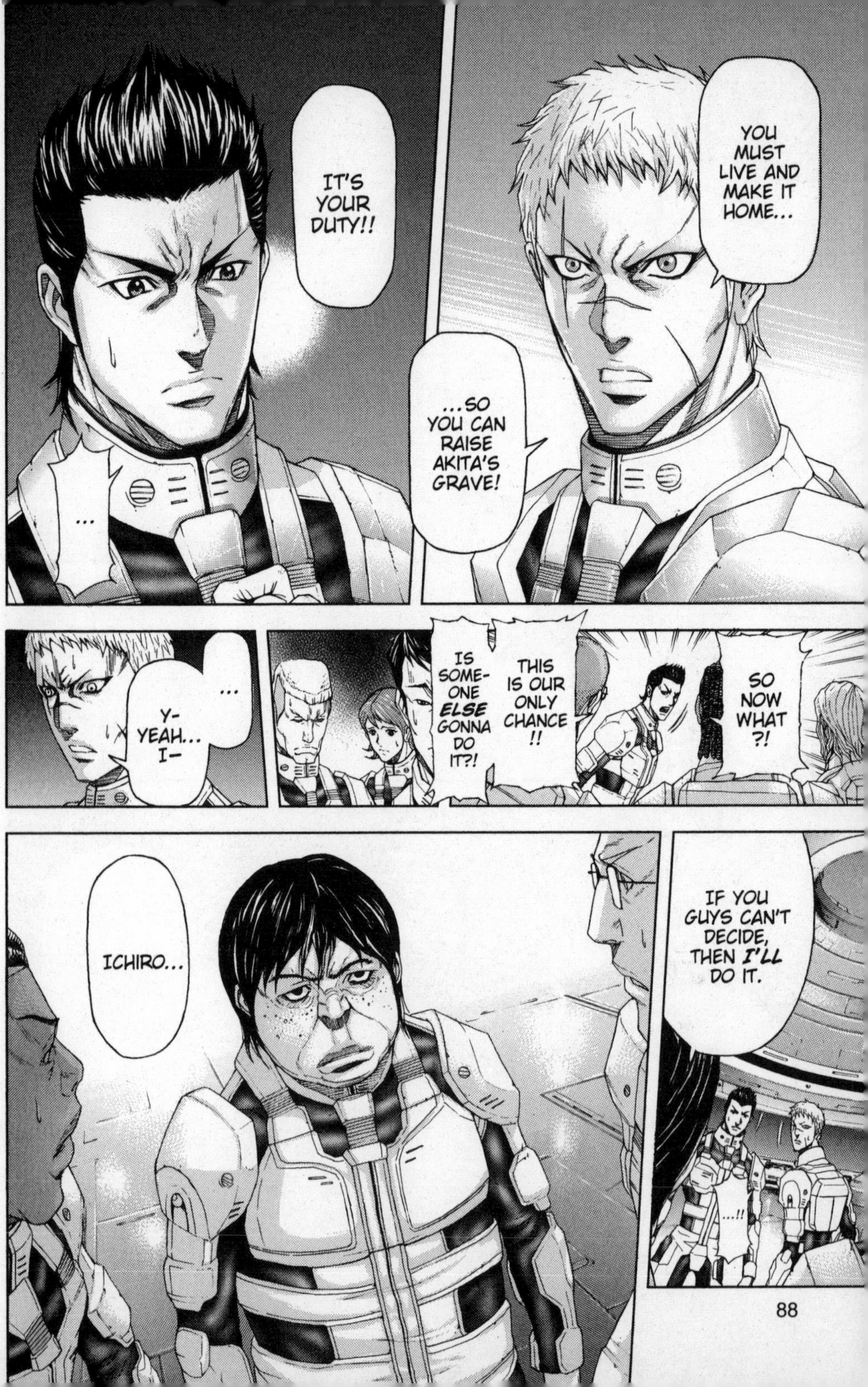
YOU MUST LIVE AND MAKE IT HOME...
...SO YOU CAN RAISE AKITA'S GRAVE!
IT'S YOUR DUTY!!
...
SO NOW WHAT?!
THIS IS OUR ONLY CHANCE!!
IS SOMEONE **ELSE** GONNA DO IT?!
...
Y-YEAH... I—
IF YOU GUYS CAN'T DECIDE, THEN ***I'LL*** DO IT.
...!!
ICHIRO...

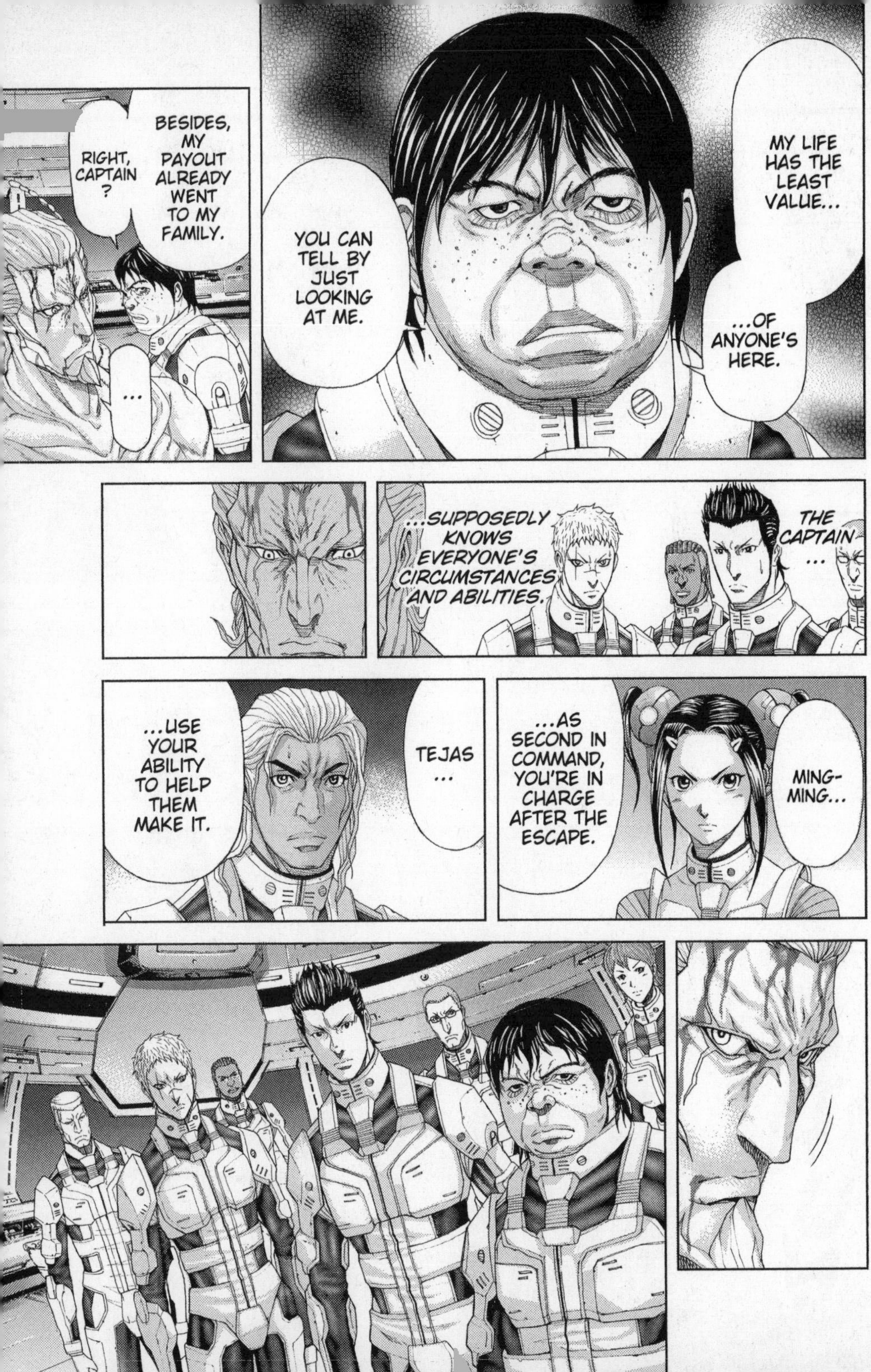
MY LIFE HAS THE LEAST VALUE...
...OF ANYONE'S HERE.
YOU CAN TELL BY JUST LOOKING AT ME.
BESIDES, MY PAYOUT ALREADY WENT TO MY FAMILY.
RIGHT, CAPTAIN ?
...
THE CAPTAIN ...
...SUPPOSEDLY KNOWS EVERYONE'S CIRCUMSTANCES AND ABILITIES.
MING-MING...
...AS SECOND IN COMMAND, YOU'RE IN CHARGE AFTER THE ESCAPE.
TEJAS ...
...USE YOUR ABILITY TO HELP THEM MAKE IT.

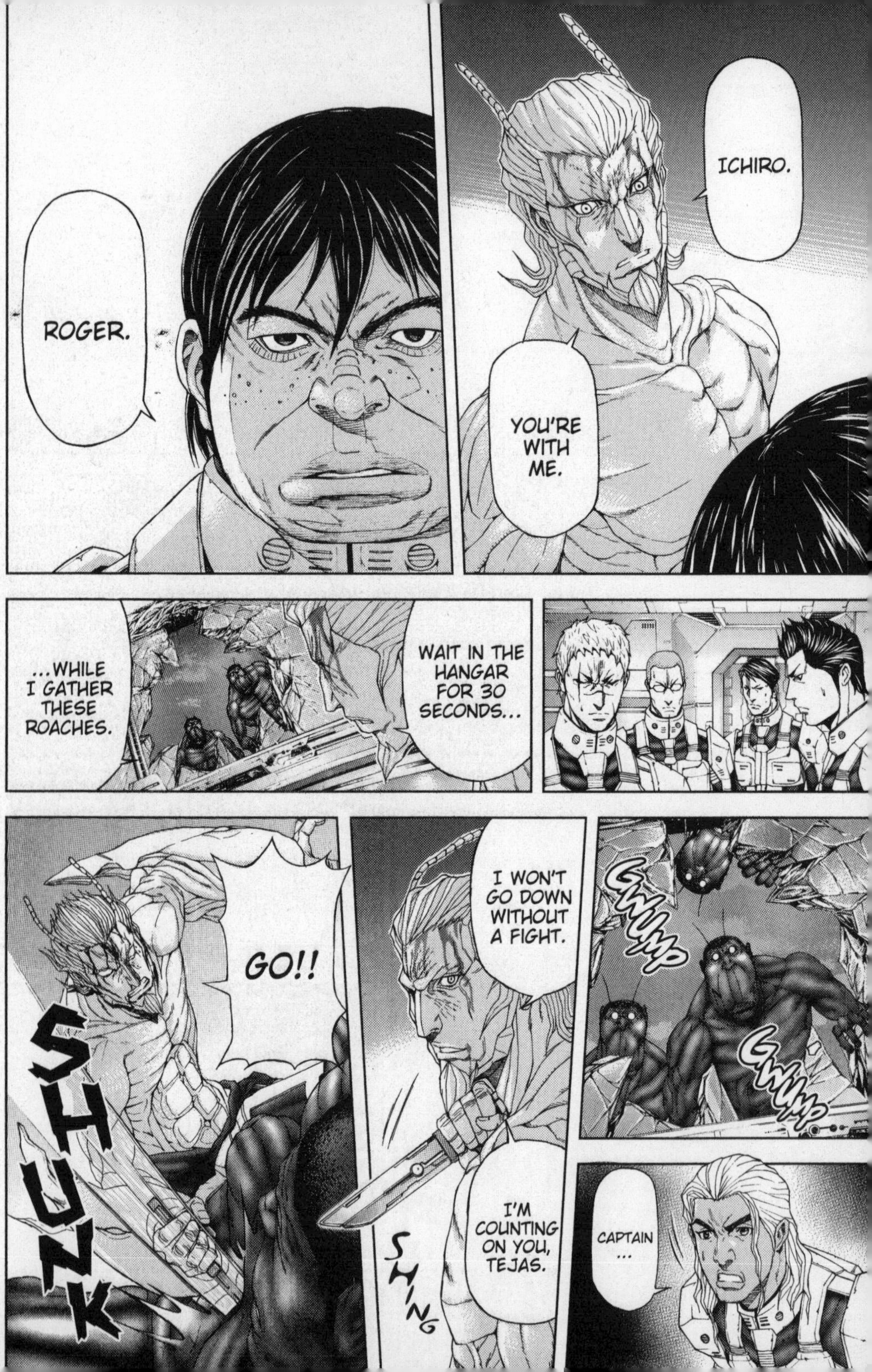
ICHIRO.
YOU'RE WITH ME.
ROGER.
WAIT IN THE HANGAR FOR 30 SECONDS...
...WHILE I GATHER THESE ROACHES.
GWUMP
GWUMP
CAPTAIN ...
I WON'T GO DOWN WITHOUT A FIGHT.
I'M COUNTING ON YOU, TEJAS.
SHING
GO!!
SHUNK

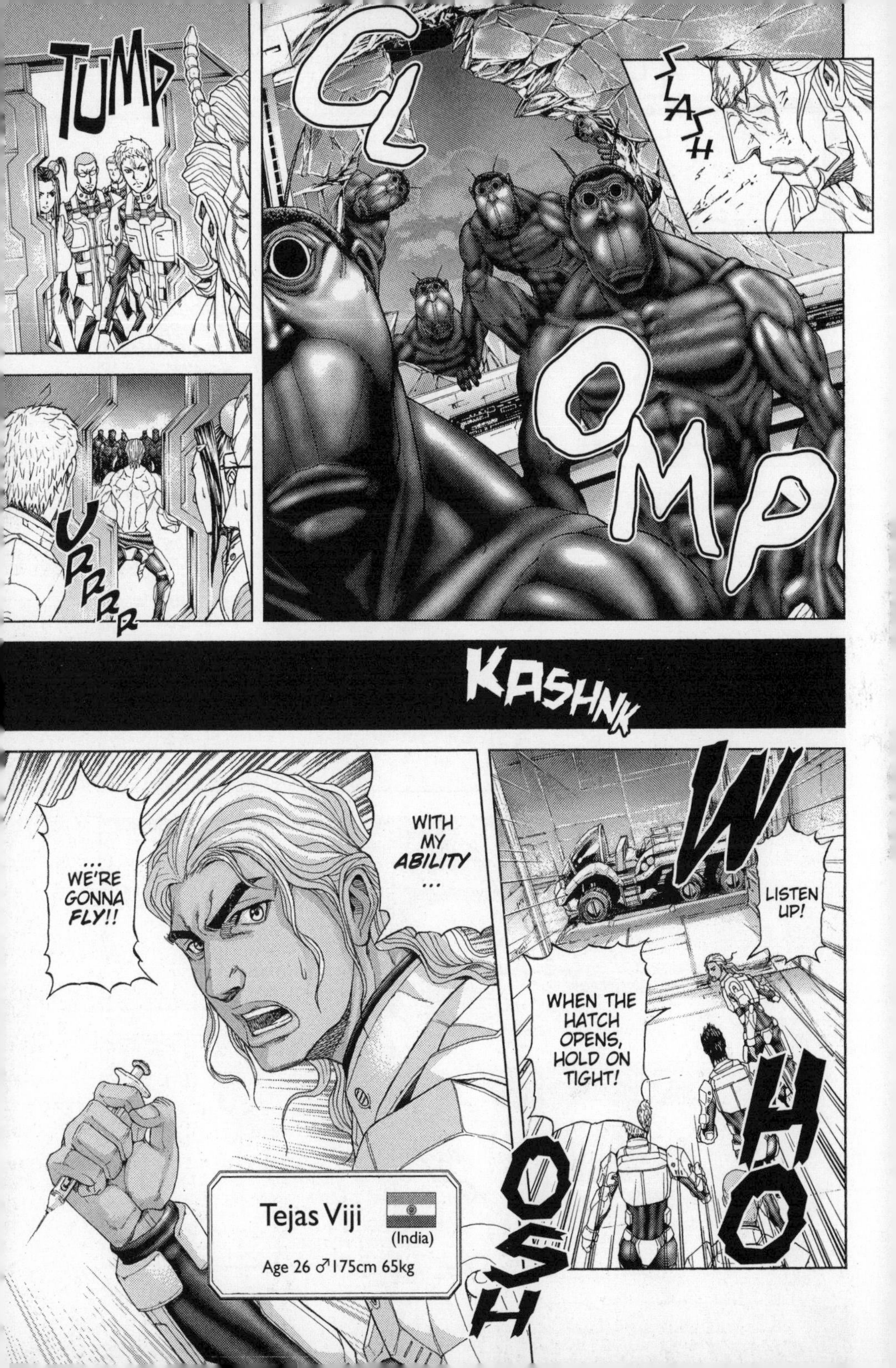
SLASH
CLOMP
TUMP
URRRR
KASHNK
WHOOSH
LISTEN UP!
WHEN THE HATCH OPENS, HOLD ON TIGHT!
WITH MY *ABILITY* ...
... WE'RE GONNA *FLY!!*
Tejas Viji
(India)
Age 26 ♂175cm 65kg

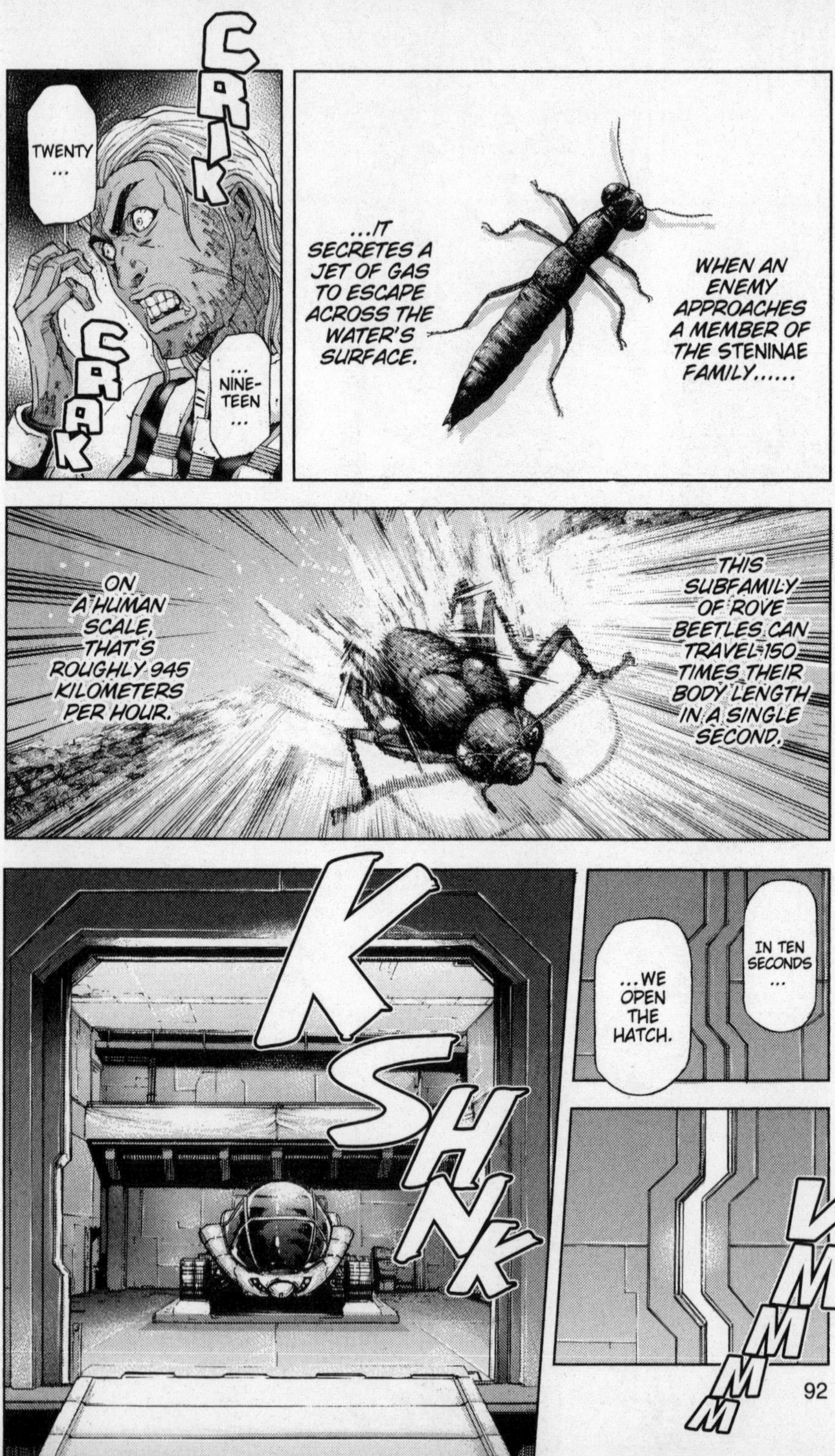
WHEN AN ENEMY APPROACHES A MEMBER OF THE STENINAE FAMILY......
...IT SECRETES A JET OF GAS TO ESCAPE ACROSS THE WATER'S SURFACE.
CRIK
TWENTY ...
CRAK
... NINETEEN ...
THIS SUBFAMILY OF ROVE BEETLES CAN TRAVEL 150 TIMES THEIR BODY LENGTH IN A SINGLE SECOND.
ON A HUMAN SCALE, THAT'S ROUGHLY 945 KILOMETERS PER HOUR.
IN TEN SECONDS ...
...WE OPEN THE HATCH.
VMMMMM
KSHNK

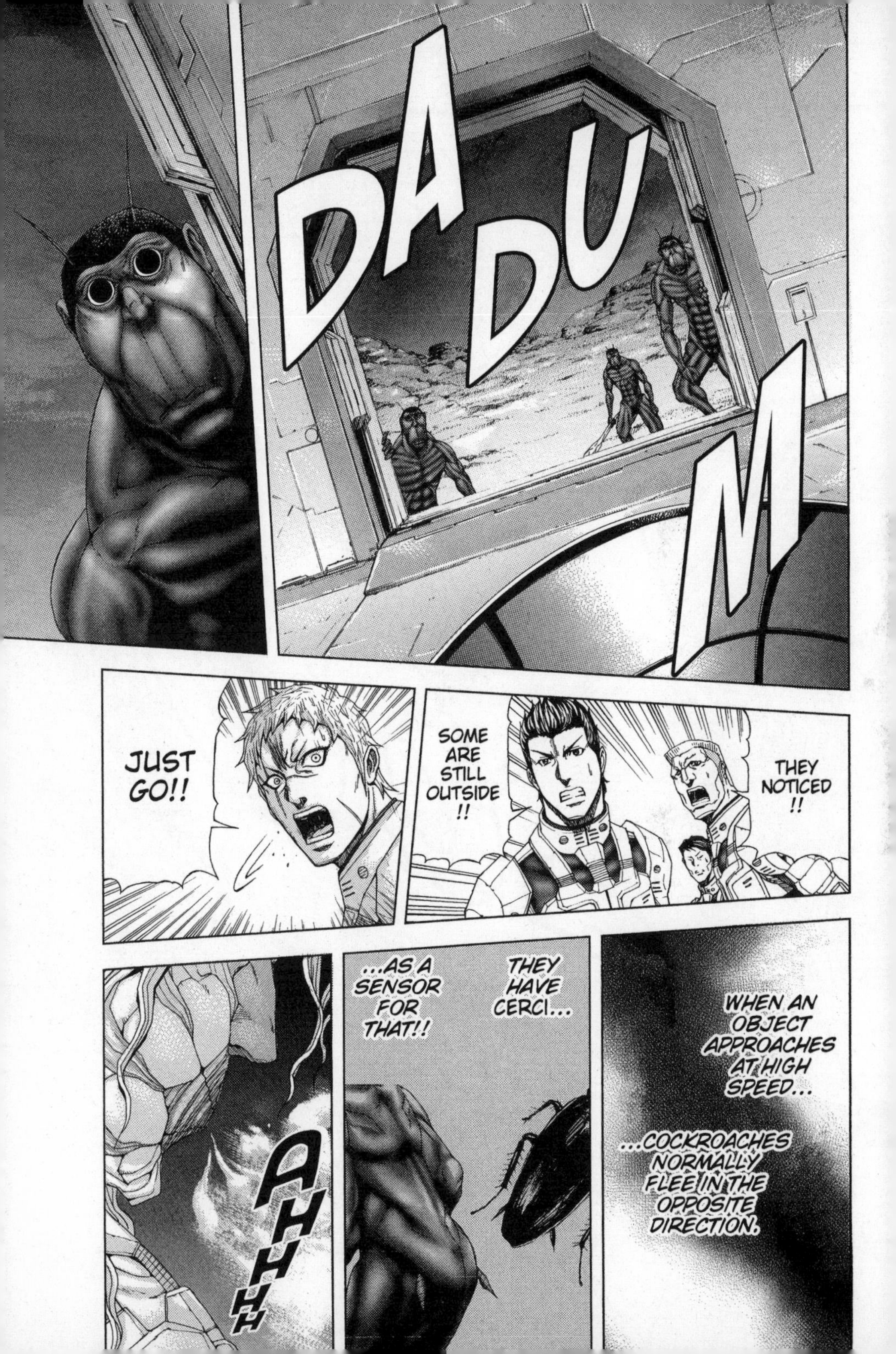
DA
DU
M
THEY NOTICED !!
SOME ARE STILL OUTSIDE !!
JUST GO!!
WHEN AN OBJECT APPROACHES AT HIGH SPEED...
...COCKROACHES NORMALLY FLEE IN THE OPPOSITE DIRECTION.
THEY HAVE CERCI...
...AS A SENSOR FOR THAT!!
AHHHHH

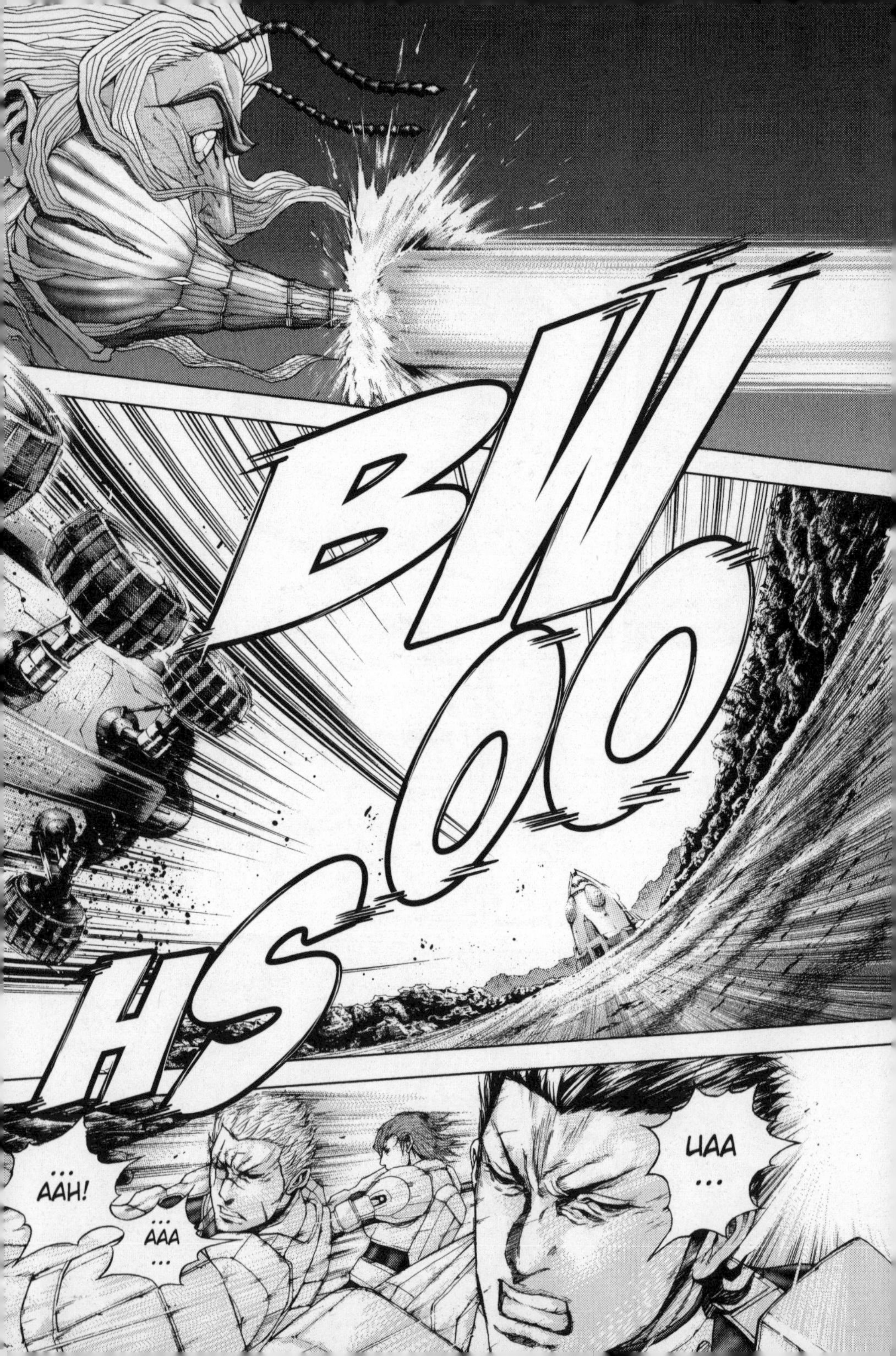
BWOOSH
UAA ...
ÄÄH!
ÄÄA ...

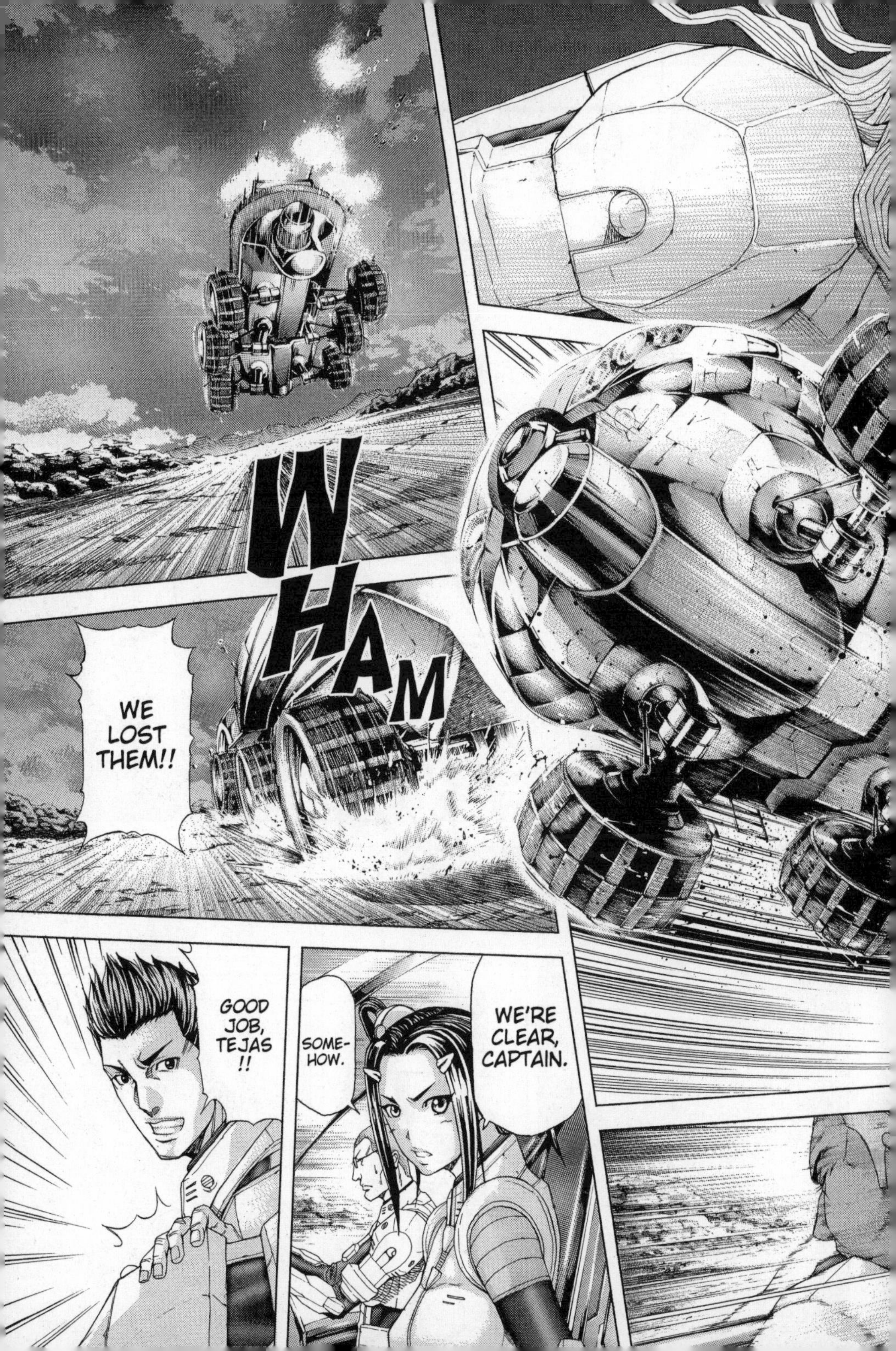
WHAM
WE LOST THEM!!
WE'RE CLEAR, CAPTAIN.
SOME-HOW.
GOOD JOB, TEJAS!!

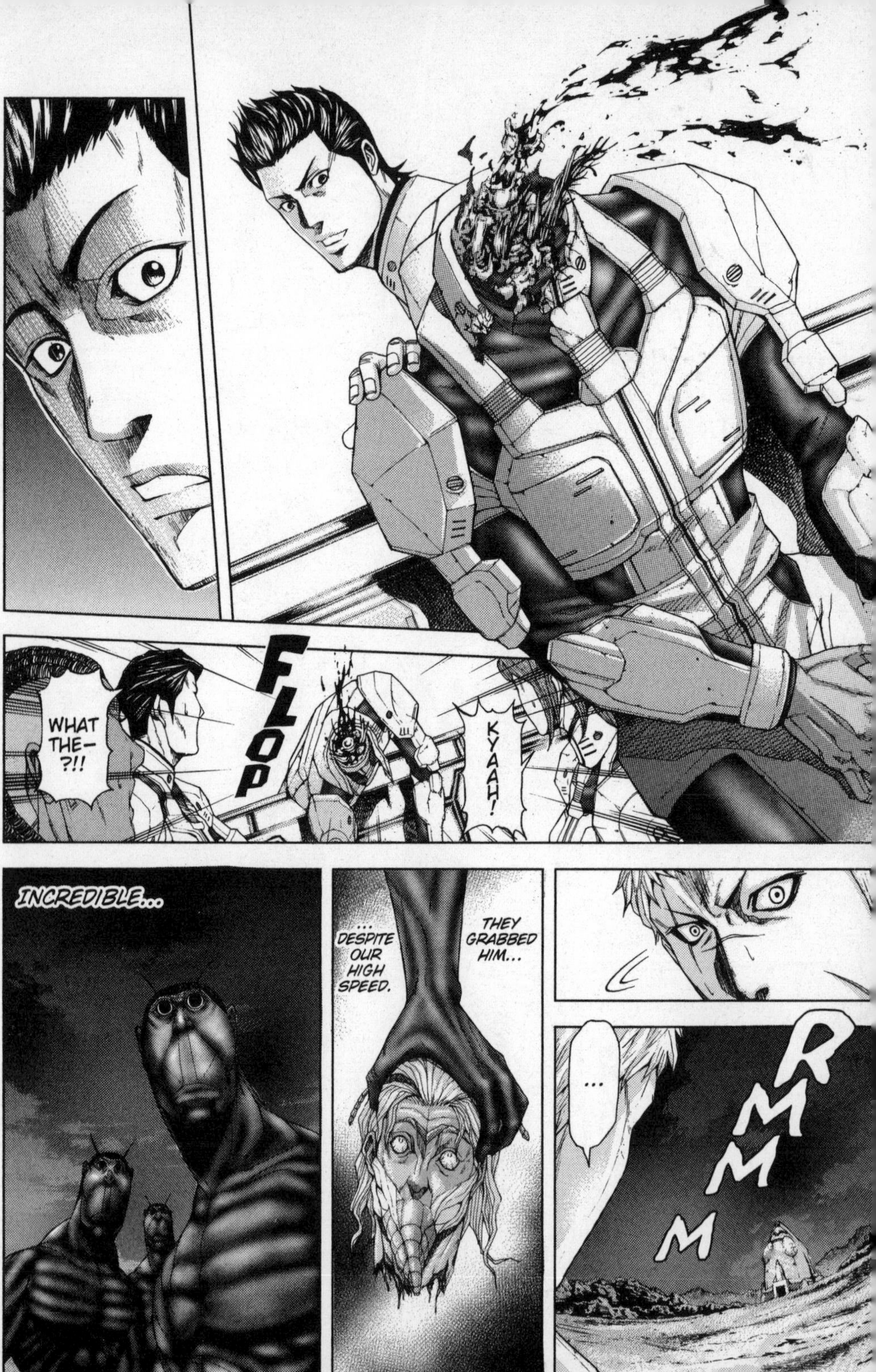
KYAAH!
FLOP
WHAT THE—?!!
...
RMMMM
THEY GRABBED HIM...
...DESPITE OUR HIGH SPEED.
INCREDIBLE...

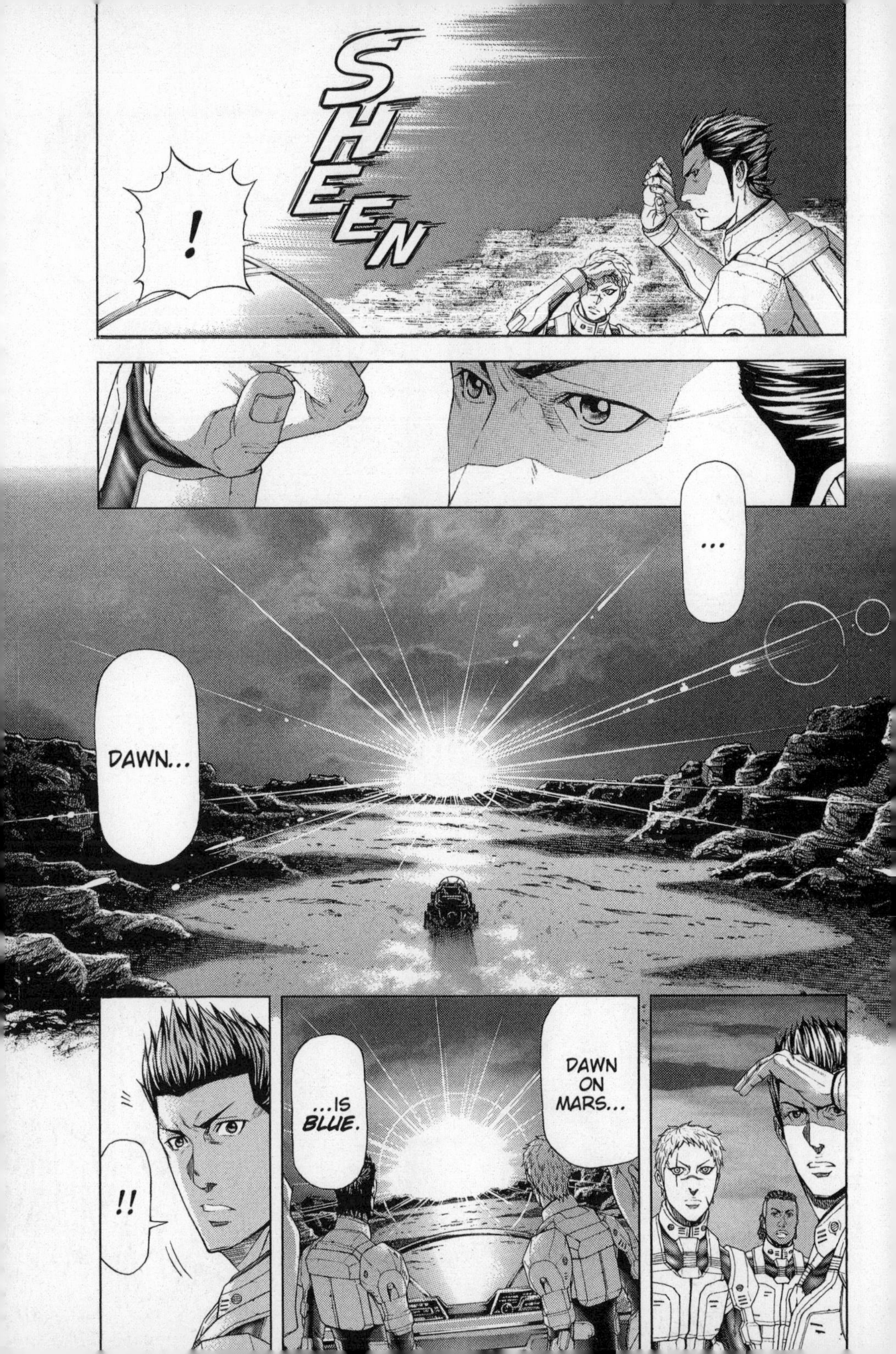
SHEEEN
!
...
DAWN...
DAWN ON MARS...
...IS BLUE.
!!

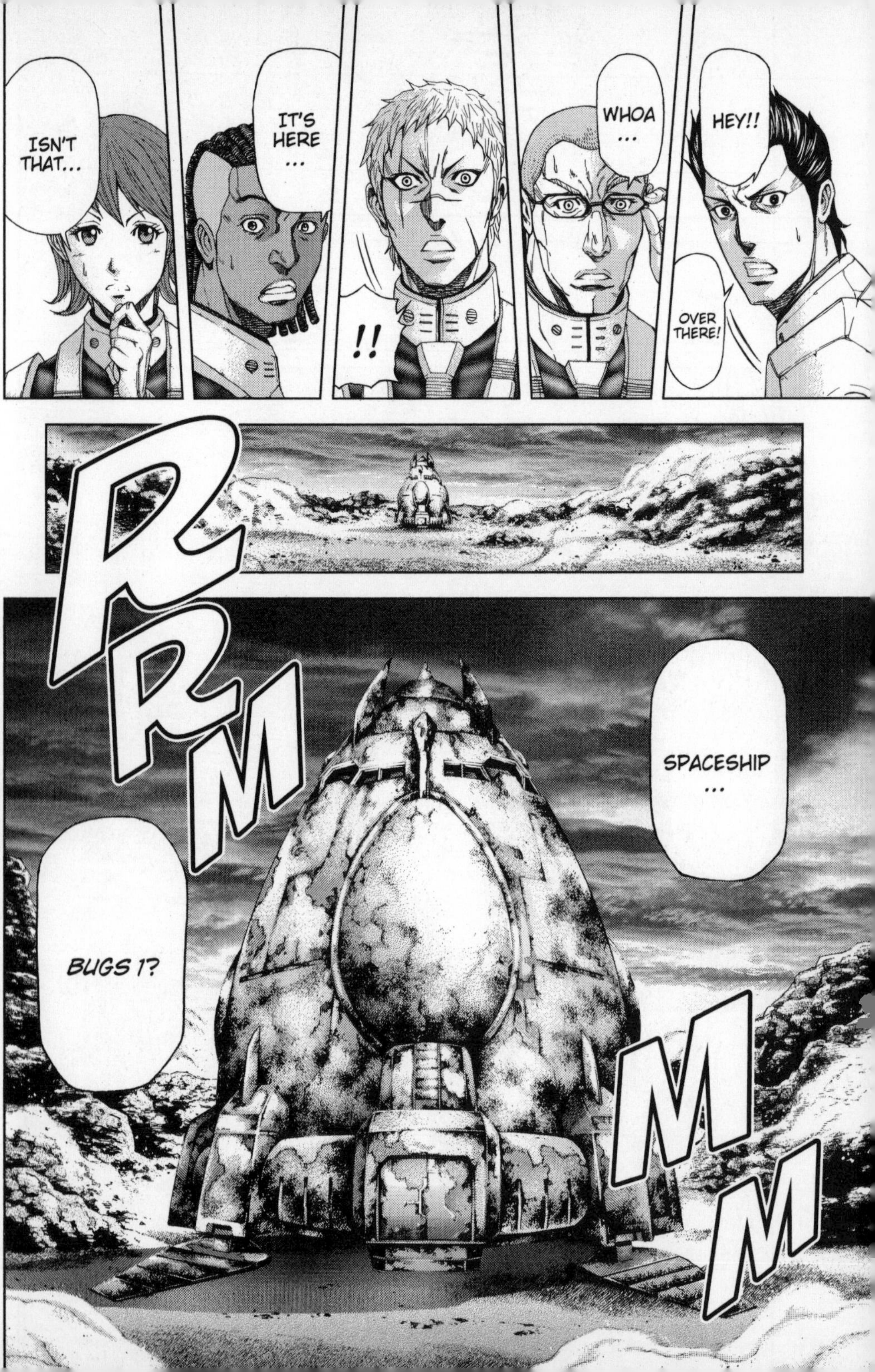
HEY!!
OVER THERE!
WHOA ...
!!
IT'S HERE ...
ISN'T THAT...
RRMMM
SPACESHIP ...
BUGS 1?

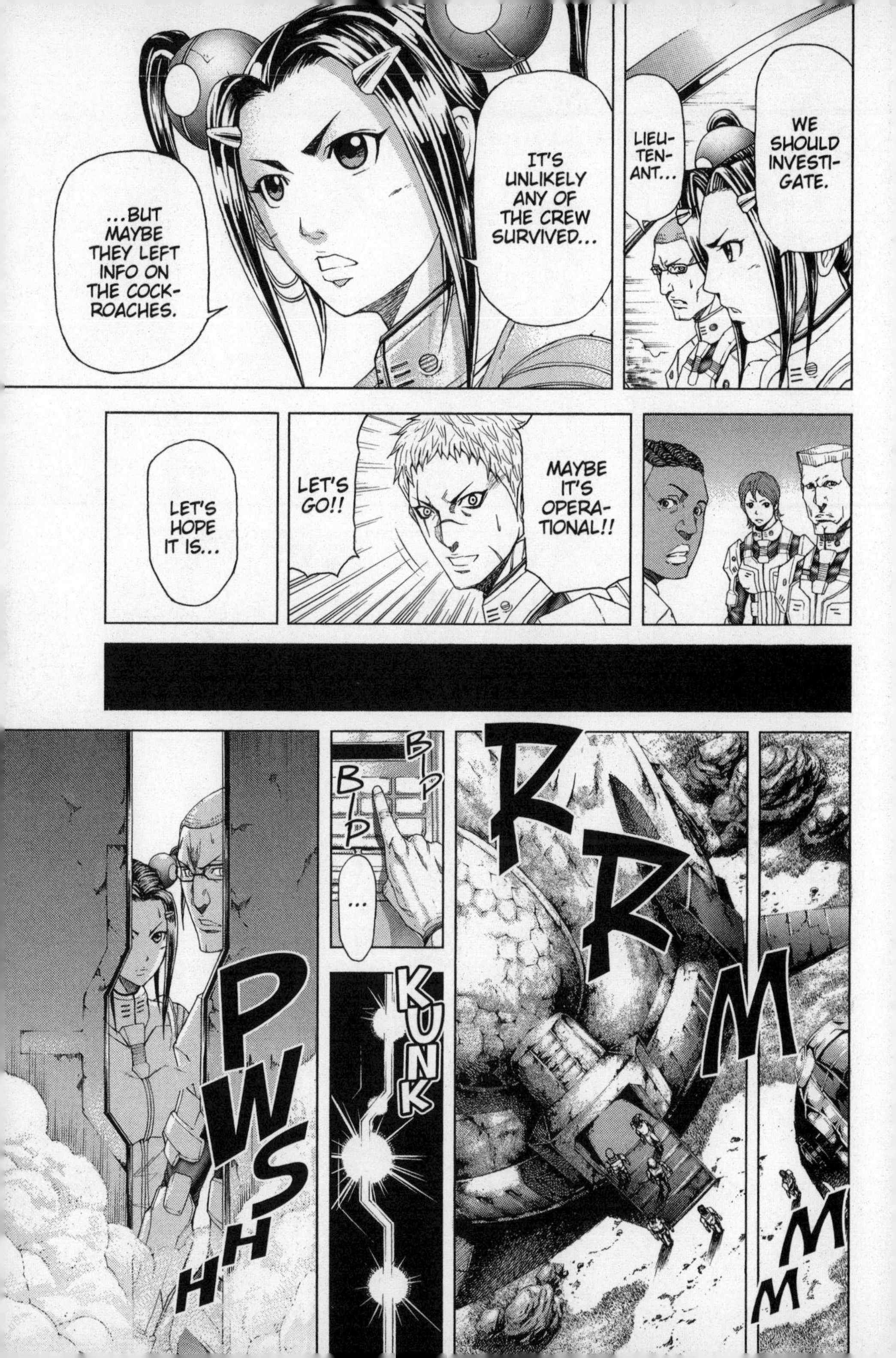
WE SHOULD INVESTIGATE.
LIEUTENANT...
IT'S UNLIKELY ANY OF THE CREW SURVIVED...
...BUT MAYBE THEY LEFT INFO ON THE COCKROACHES.
MAYBE IT'S OPERATIONAL!!
LET'S GO!!
LET'S HOPE IT IS...
RRMMMM
BIP BIP
...
KUNK
PWSHHH

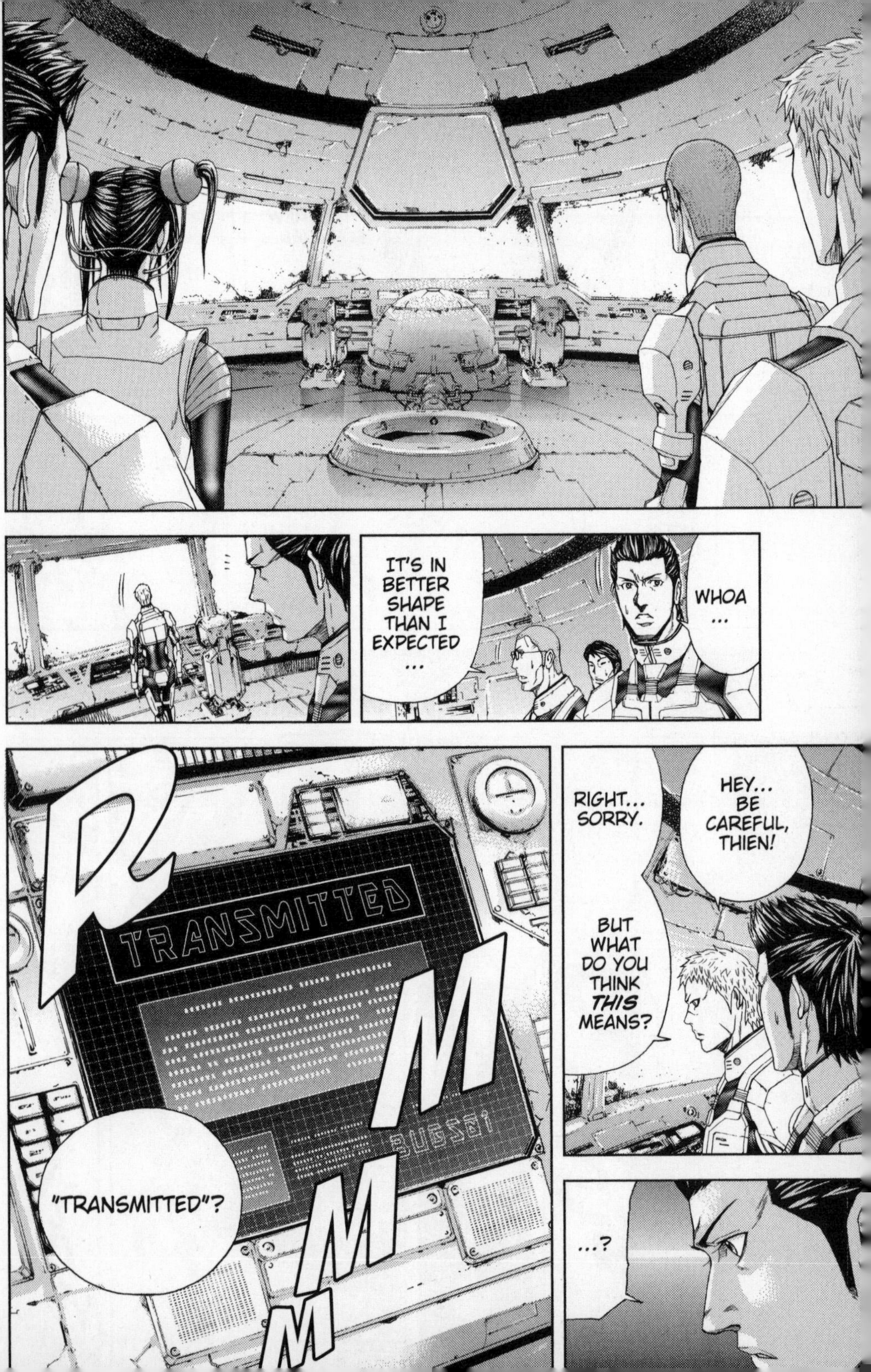
WHOA...
IT'S IN BETTER SHAPE THAN I EXPECTED...
HEY... BE CAREFUL, THIEN!
RIGHT... SORRY.
BUT WHAT DO YOU THINK *THIS* MEANS?
...?
RMMM
TRANSMITTED
"TRANSMITTED"?

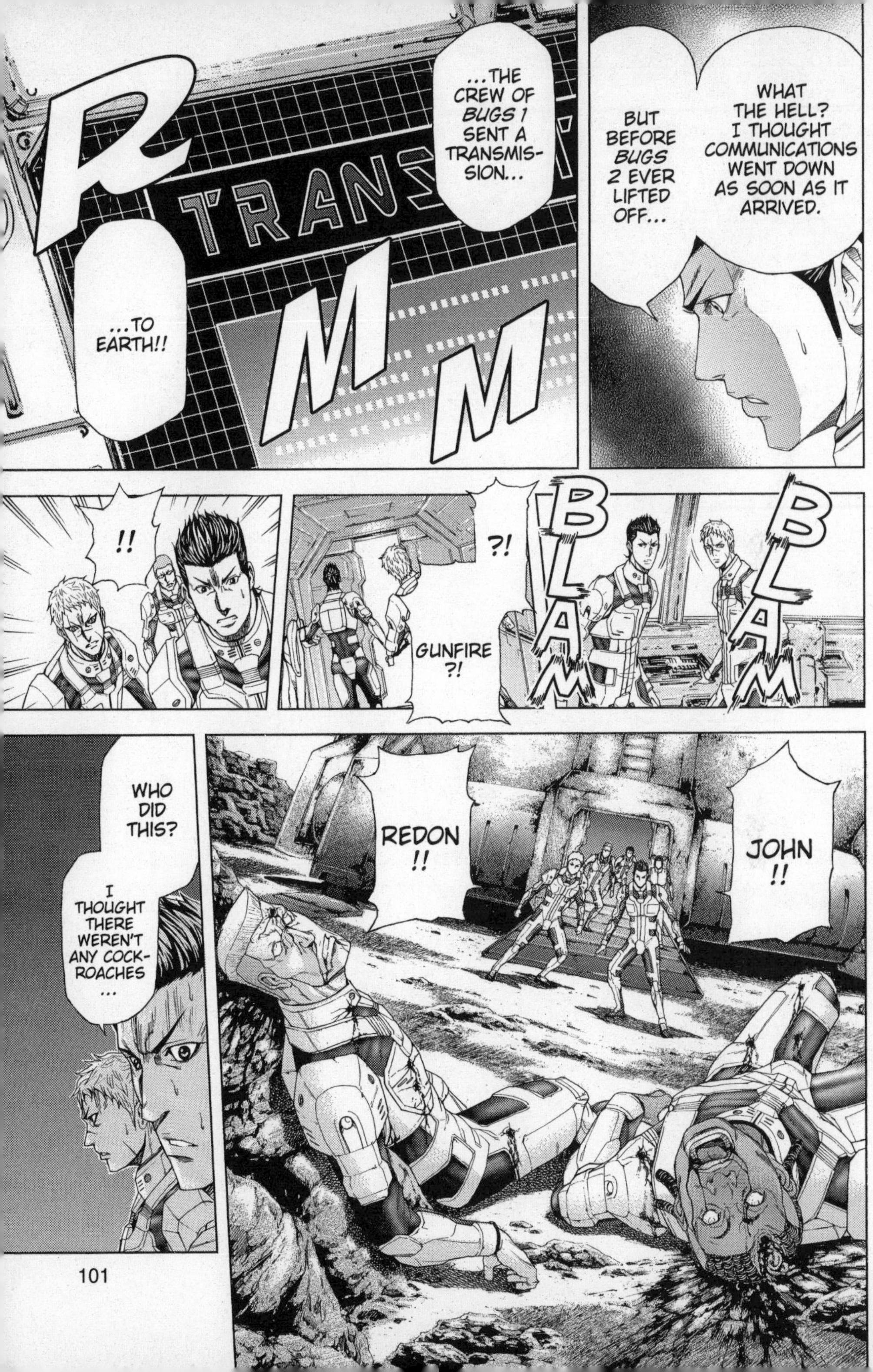
WHAT THE HELL? I THOUGHT COMMUNICATIONS WENT DOWN AS SOON AS IT ARRIVED.
BUT BEFORE *BUGS 2* EVER LIFTED OFF...
...THE CREW OF *BUGS 1* SENT A TRANSMISSION...
R
TRANS
M
M
...TO EARTH!!
B L A M
B L A M
?!
GUNFIRE ?!
!!
JOHN !!
REDON !!
WHO DID THIS?
I THOUGHT THERE WEREN'T ANY COCKROACHES...

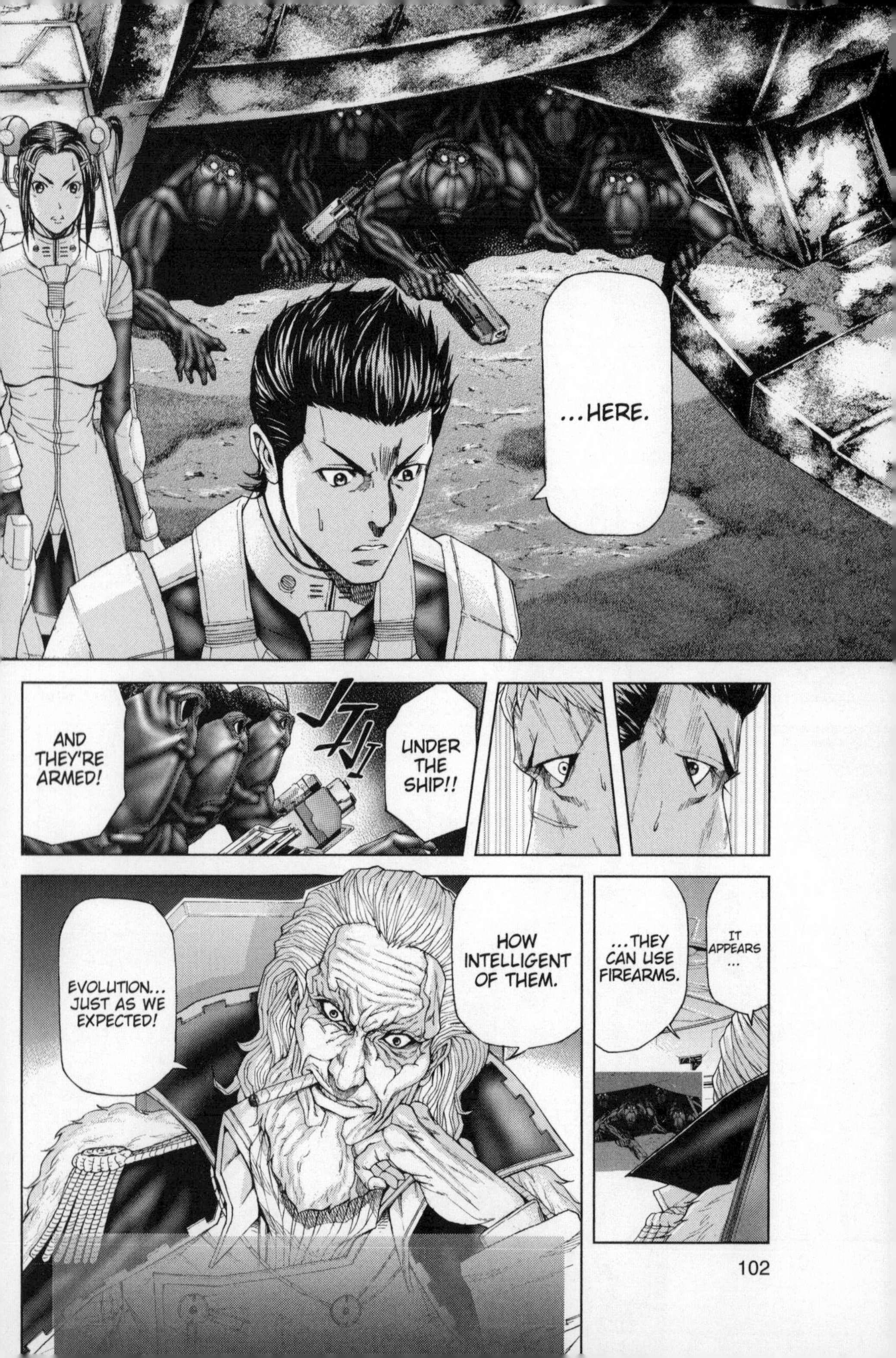
...HERE.
UNDER THE SHIP!!
AND THEY'RE ARMED!
IT APPEARS ...
...THEY CAN USE FIREARMS.
HOW INTELLIGENT OF THEM.
EVOLUTION... JUST AS WE EXPECTED!

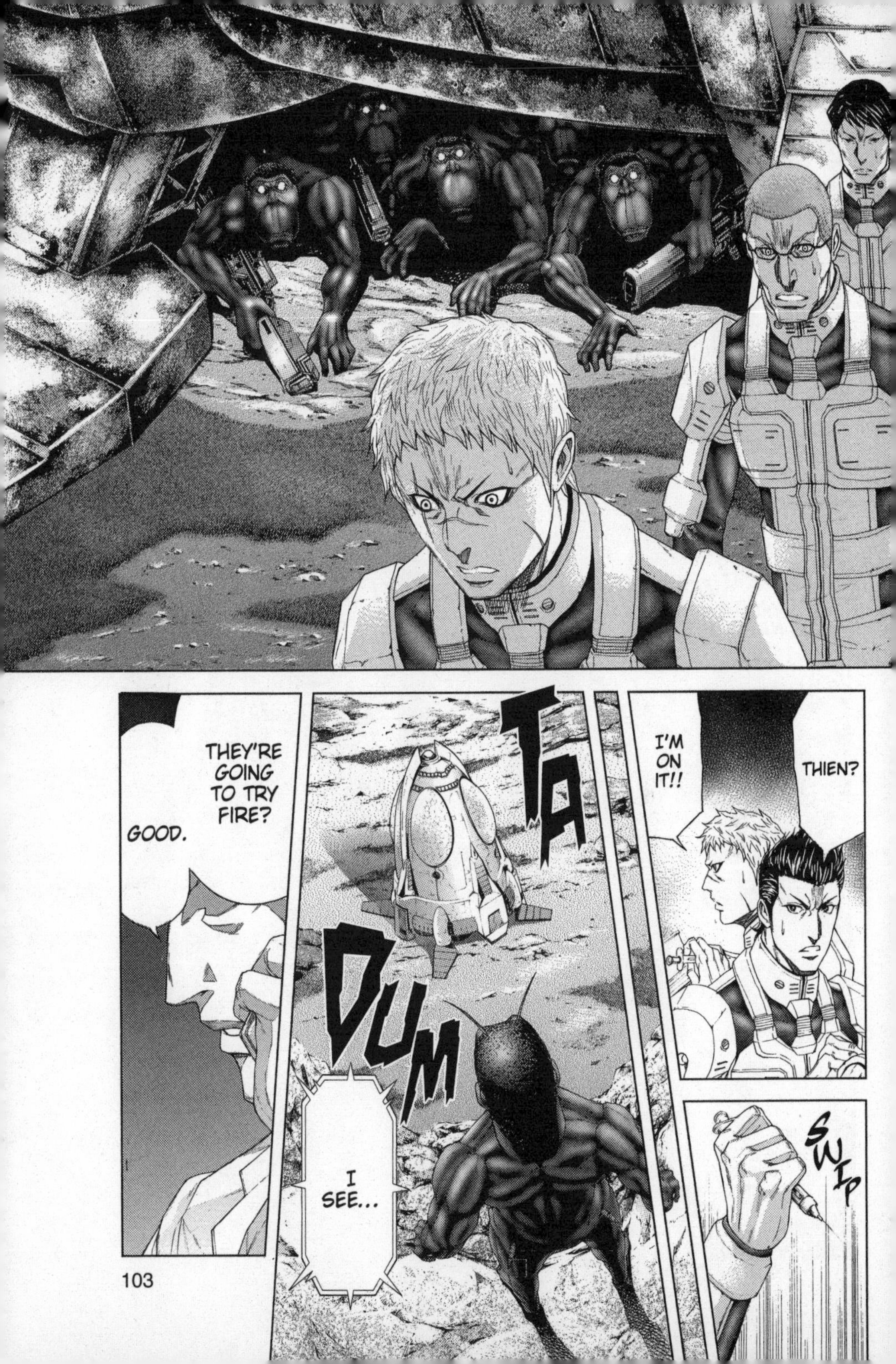
THIEN?
I'M ON IT!!
SWIP
TA
DUM
I SEE...
THEY'RE GOING TO TRY FIRE?
GOOD.

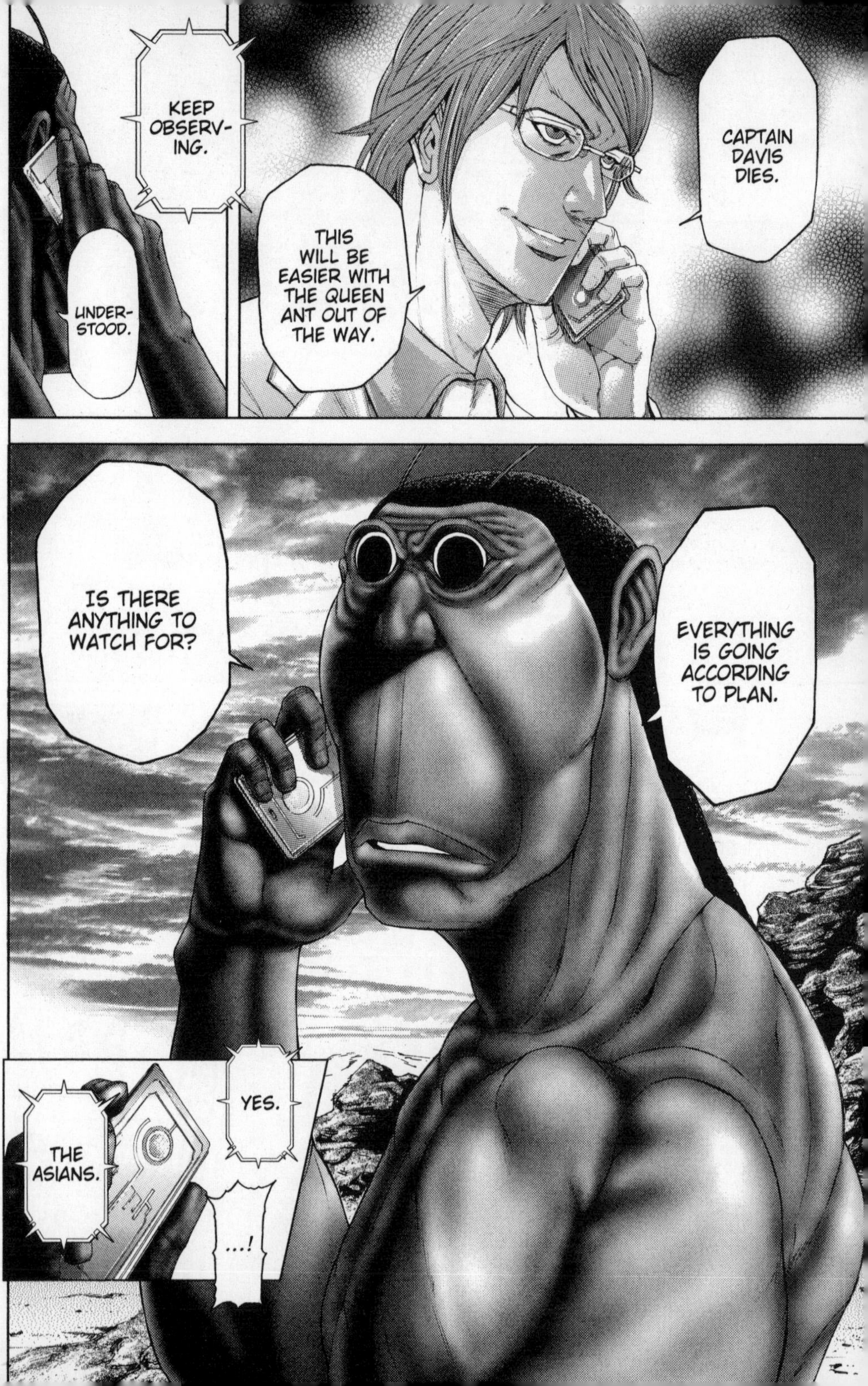
CAPTAIN DAVIS DIES.
THIS WILL BE EASIER WITH THE QUEEN ANT OUT OF THE WAY.
KEEP OBSERVING.
UNDERSTOOD.
EVERYTHING IS GOING ACCORDING TO PLAN.
IS THERE ANYTHING TO WATCH FOR?
YES.
THE ASIANS.
...!

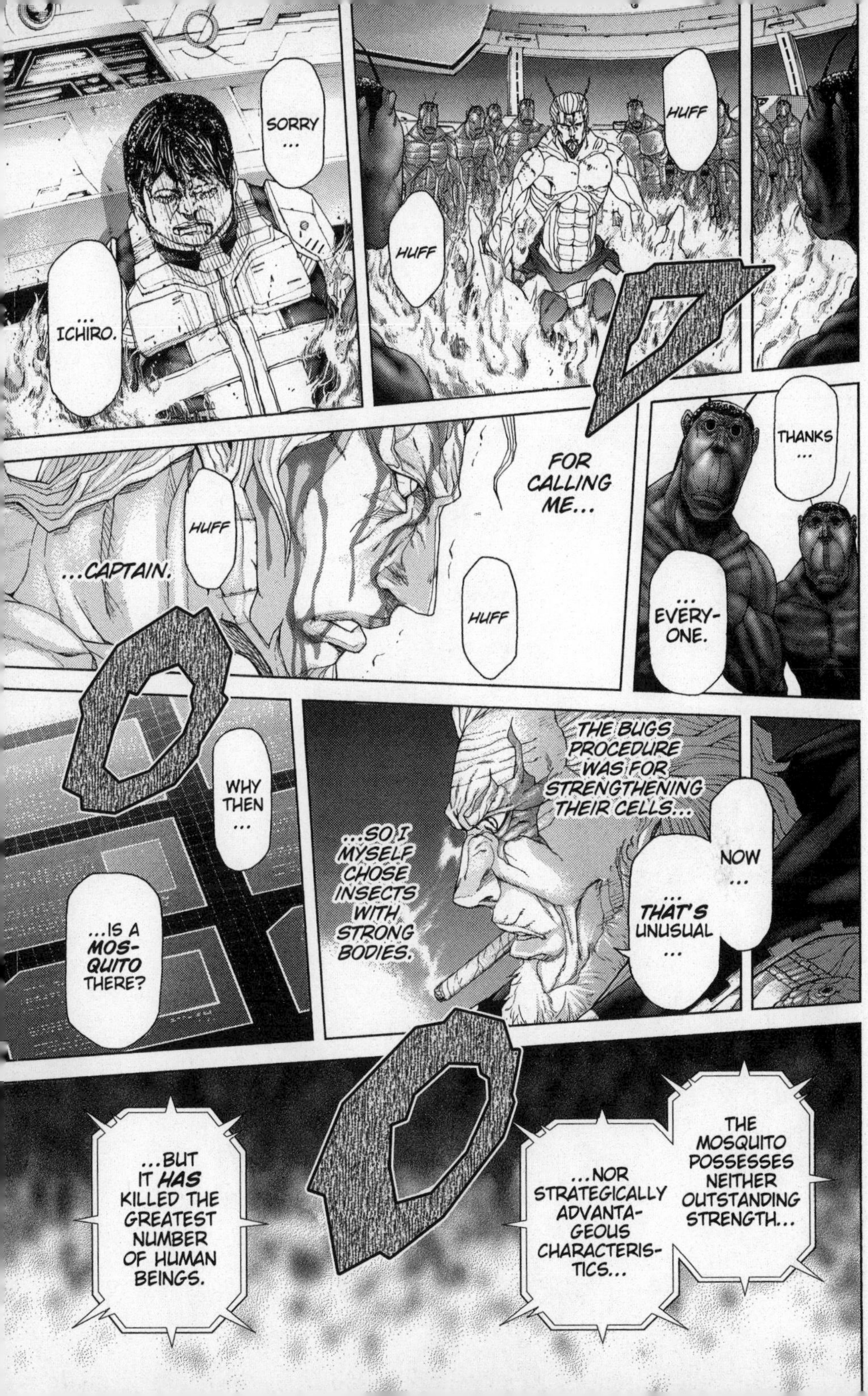
HUFF
HUFF
SORRY ...
... ICHIRO.
THANKS ...
... EVERY-ONE.
FOR CALLING ME...
HUFF
HUFF
...CAPTAIN.
THE BUGS PROCEDURE WAS FOR STRENGTHENING THEIR CELLS...
NOW ...
... *THAT'S* UNUSUAL ...
...SO I MYSELF CHOSE INSECTS WITH STRONG BODIES.
WHY THEN ...
...IS A *MOSQUITO* THERE?
THE MOSQUITO POSSESSES NEITHER OUTSTANDING STRENGTH...
...NOR STRATEGICALLY ADVANTAGEOUS CHARACTERISTICS...
...BUT IT *HAS* KILLED THE GREATEST NUMBER OF HUMAN BEINGS.

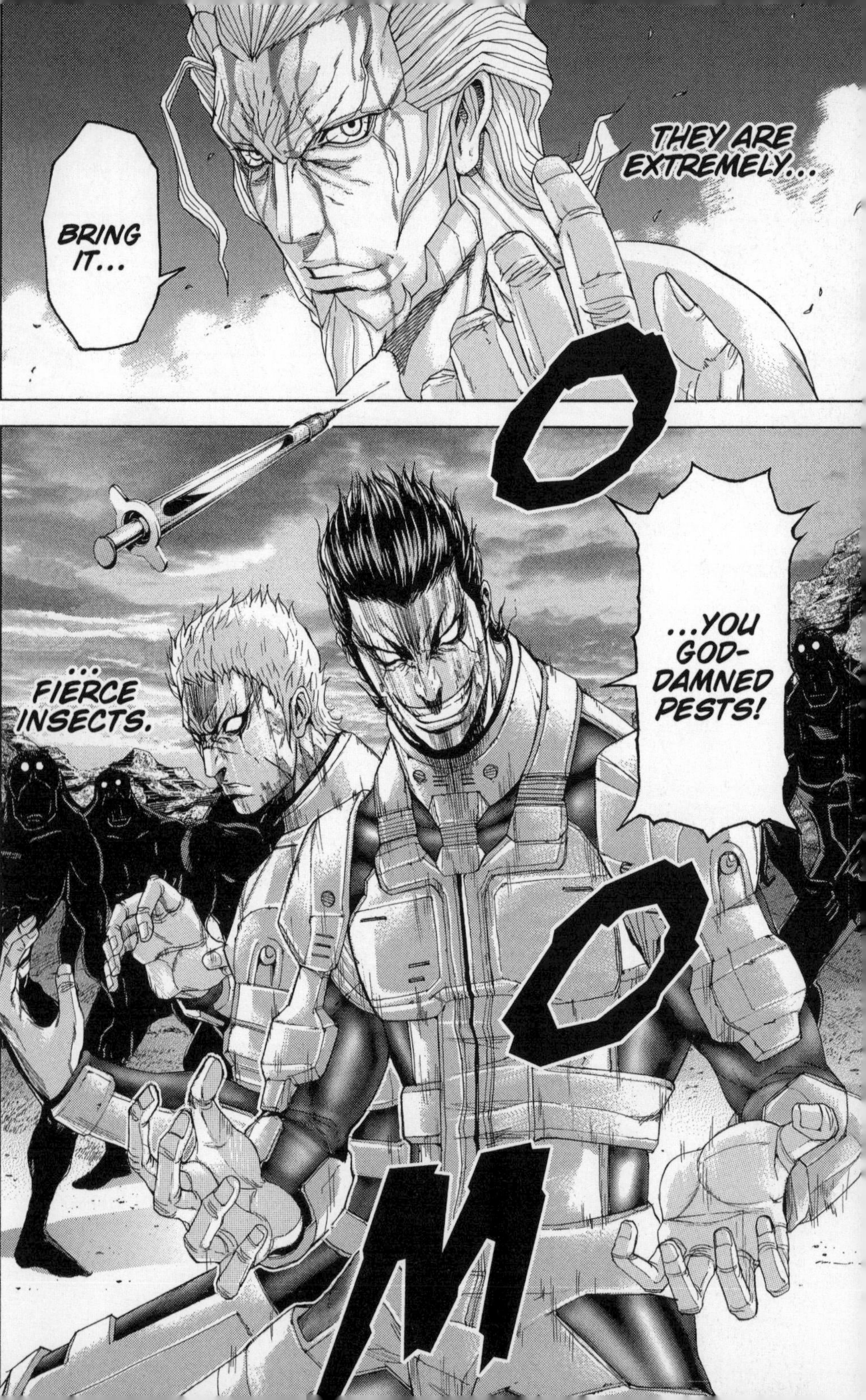
THEY ARE EXTREMELY...
BRING IT...
...YOU GOD-DAMNED PESTS!
...FIERCE INSECTS.
OOM

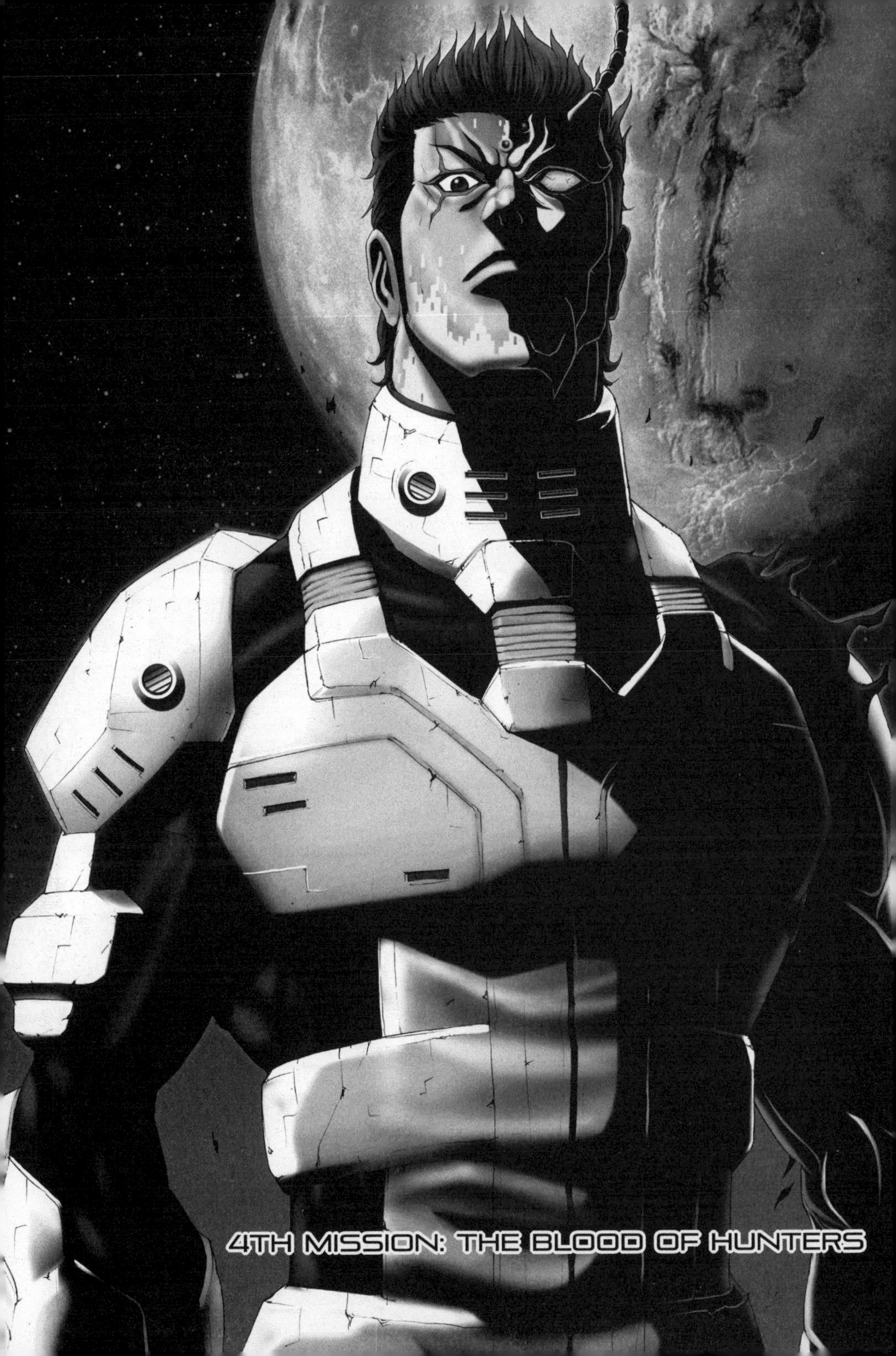
4TH MISSION: THE BLOOD OF HUNTERS

TERRA FORMARS
character

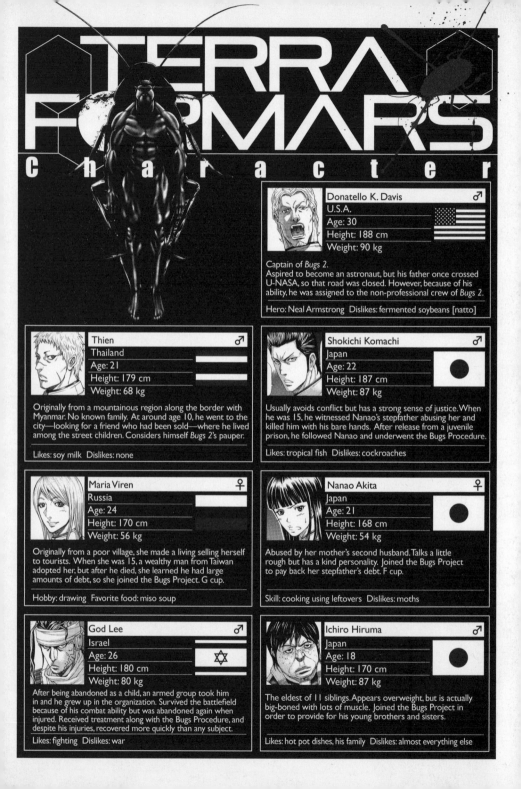

Donatello K. Davis ♂
U.S.A.
Age: 30
Height: 188 cm
Weight: 90 kg

Captain of *Bugs 2*.
Aspired to become an astronaut, but his father once crossed U-NASA, so that road was closed. However, because of his ability, he was assigned to the non-professional crew of *Bugs 2*.

Hero: Neal Armstrong Dislikes: fermented soybeans [natto]

Thien ♂
Thailand
Age: 21
Height: 179 cm
Weight: 68 kg

Originally from a mountainous region along the border with Myanmar. No known family. At around age 10, he went to the city—looking for a friend who had been sold—where he lived among the street children. Considers himself *Bugs 2*'s pauper.

Likes: soy milk Dislikes: none

Shokichi Komachi ♂
Japan
Age: 22
Height: 187 cm
Weight: 87 kg

Usually avoids conflict but has a strong sense of justice. When he was 15, he witnessed Nanao's stepfather abusing her and killed him with his bare hands. After release from a juvenile prison, he followed Nanao and underwent the Bugs Procedure.

Likes: tropical fish Dislikes: cockroaches

Maria Viren ♀
Russia
Age: 24
Height: 170 cm
Weight: 56 kg

Originally from a poor village, she made a living selling herself to tourists. When she was 15, a wealthy man from Taiwan adopted her, but after he died, she learned he had large amounts of debt, so she joined the Bugs Project. G cup.

Hobby: drawing Favorite food: miso soup

Nanao Akita ♀
Japan
Age: 21
Height: 168 cm
Weight: 54 kg

Abused by her mother's second husband. Talks a little rough but has a kind personality. Joined the Bugs Project to pay back her stepfather's debt. F cup.

Skill: cooking using leftovers Dislikes: moths

God Lee ♂
Israel
Age: 26
Height: 180 cm
Weight: 80 kg

After being abandoned as a child, an armed group took him in and he grew up in the organization. Survived the battlefield because of his combat ability but was abandoned again when injured. Received treatment along with the Bugs Procedure, and despite his injuries, recovered more quickly than any subject.

Likes: fighting Dislikes: war

Ichiro Hiruma ♂
Japan
Age: 18
Height: 170 cm
Weight: 87 kg

The eldest of 11 siblings. Appears overweight, but is actually big-boned with lots of muscle. Joined the Bugs Project in order to provide for his young brothers and sisters.

Likes: hot pot dishes, his family Dislikes: almost everything else

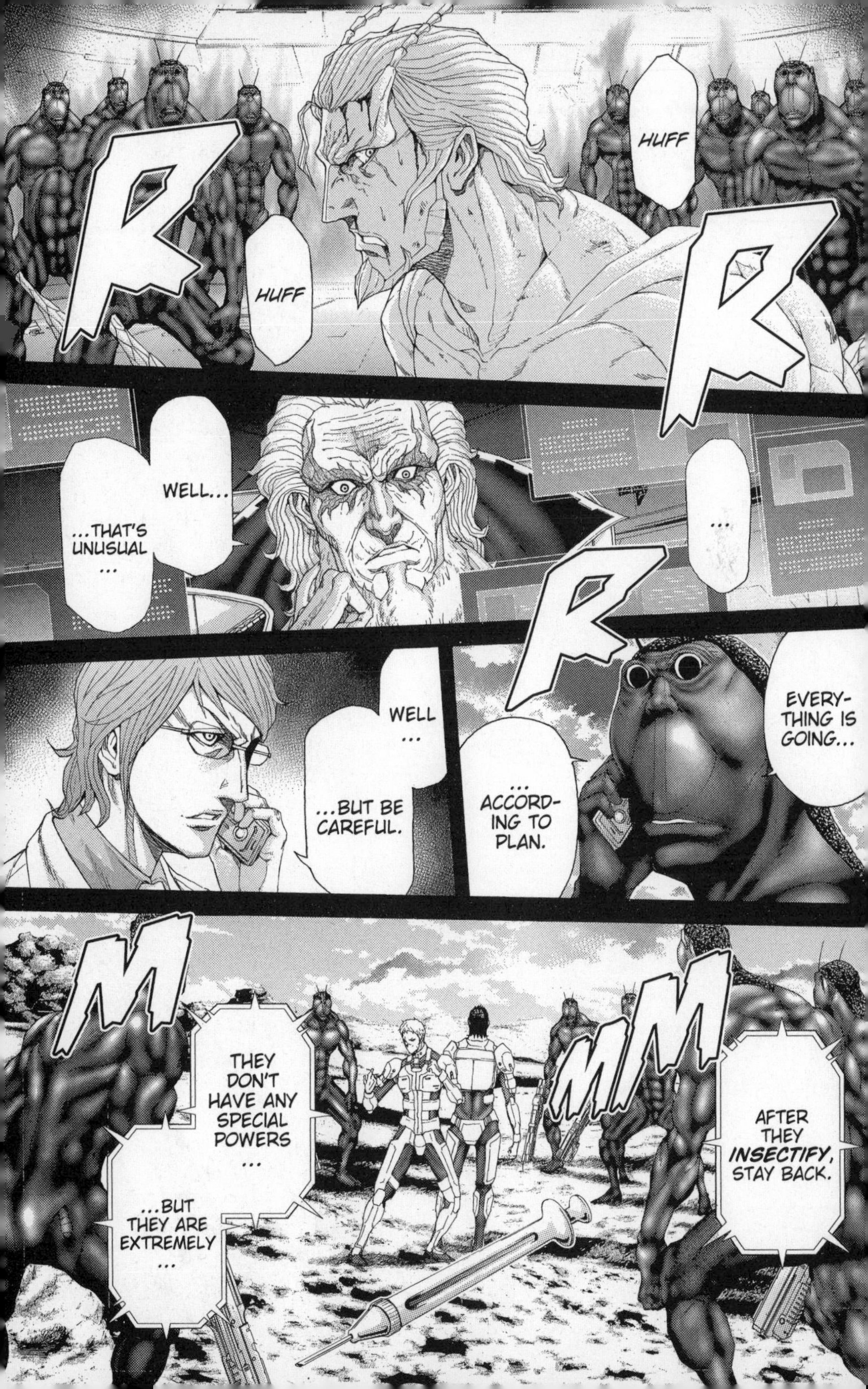
R
HUFF
HUFF
R
...
WELL...
...THAT'S UNUSUAL ...
R
EVERY-THING IS GOING...
... ACCORD-ING TO PLAN.
WELL ...
...BUT BE CAREFUL.
MM
AFTER THEY *INSECTIFY*, STAY BACK.
M
THEY DON'T HAVE ANY SPECIAL POWERS ...
...BUT THEY ARE EXTREMELY ...

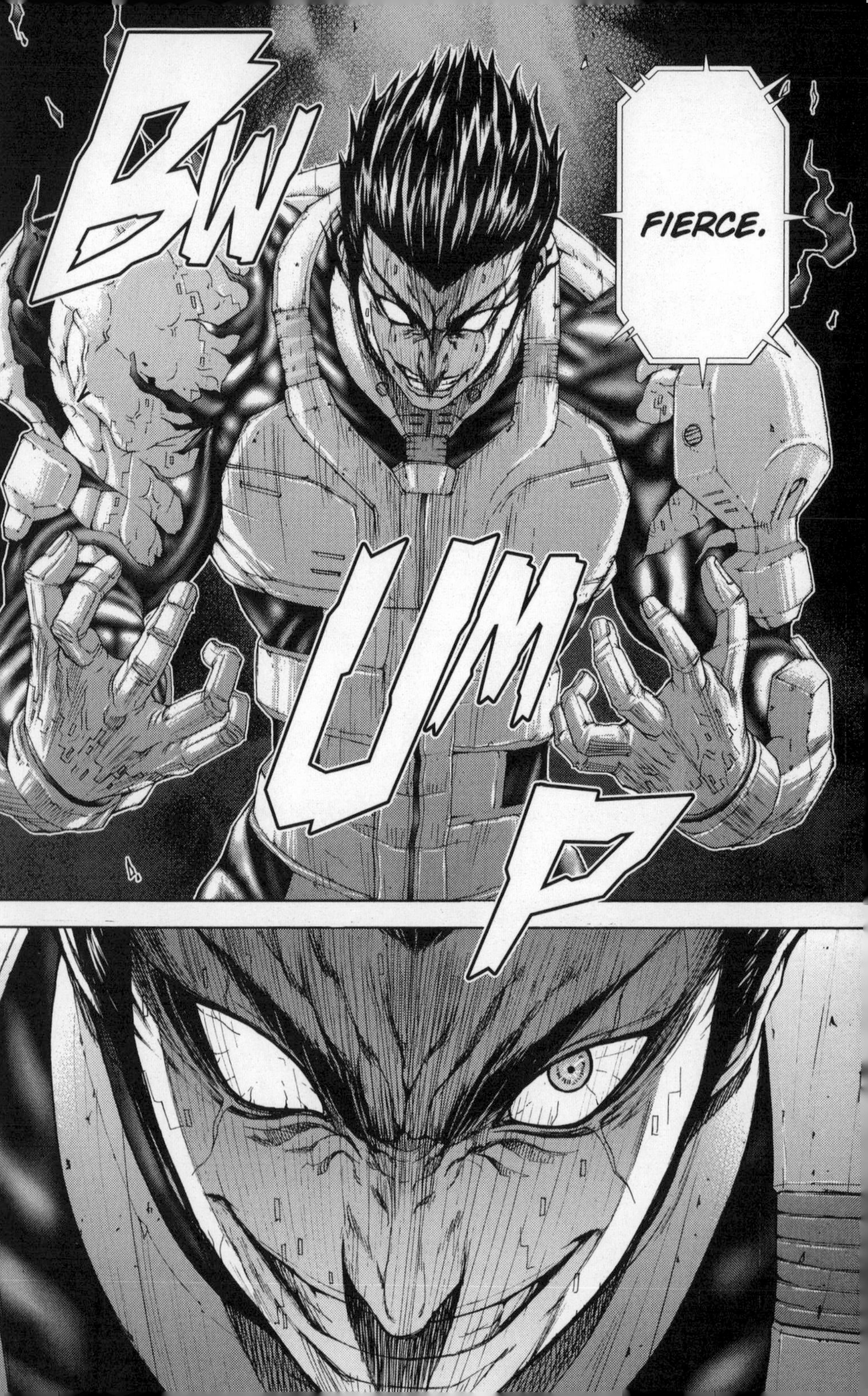
FIERCE.
BUMP

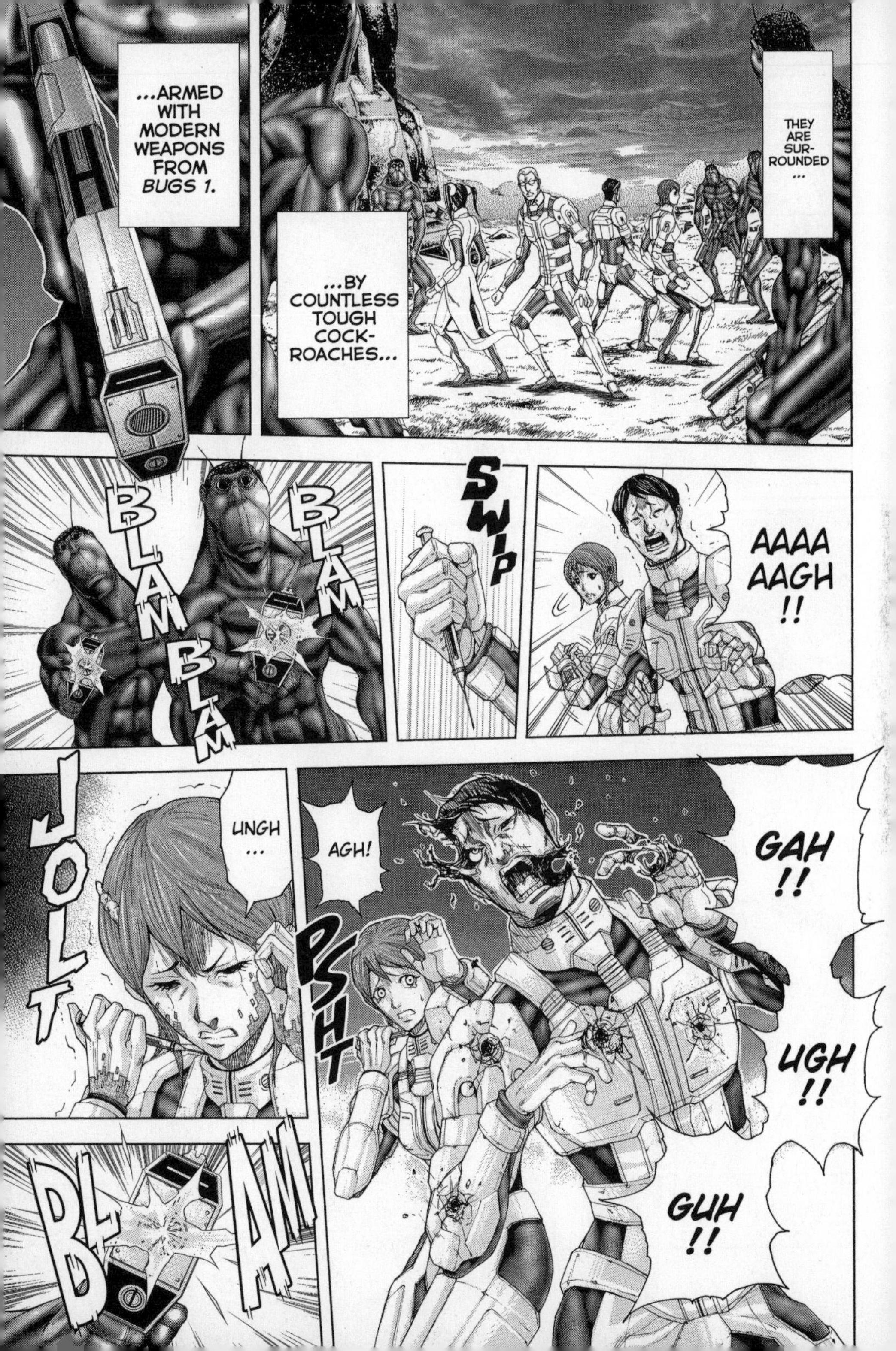
THEY ARE SUR-ROUNDED ...
...BY COUNTLESS TOUGH COCK-ROACHES...
...ARMED WITH MODERN WEAPONS FROM BUGS 1.
AAAA AAGH !!
SWIP
BLAM BLAM
BLAM BLAM
GAH !!
UGH !!
GUH !!
AGH!
PSHT
UNGH ...
JOLT
BLAM

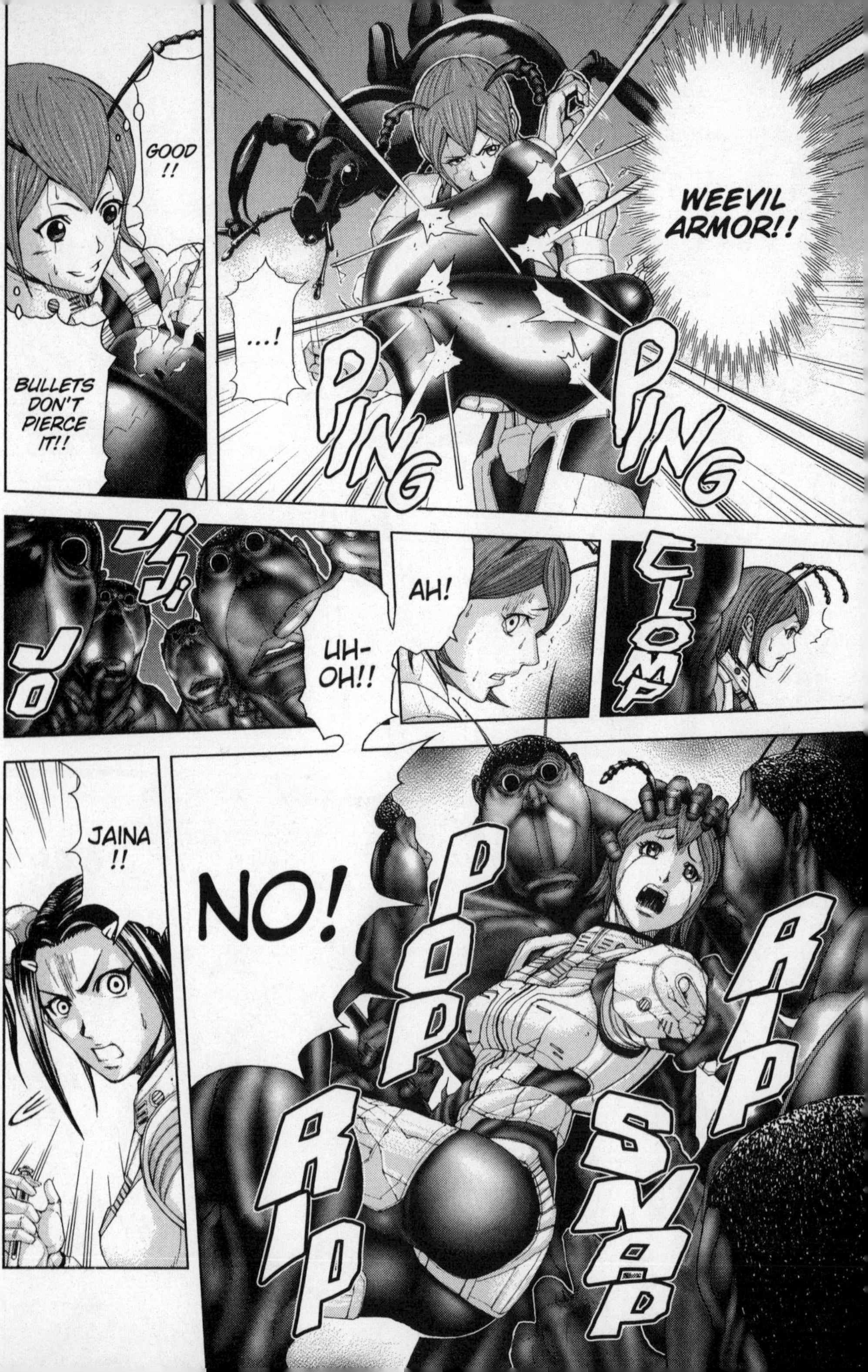
WEEVIL ARMOR!!
...!
PING
PING
GOOD!!
BULLETS DON'T PIERCE IT!!
CLOMP
AH!
UH-OH!!
JIJI
JO
RIP
SNAP
POP
POP
NO!
RIP
JAINA!!

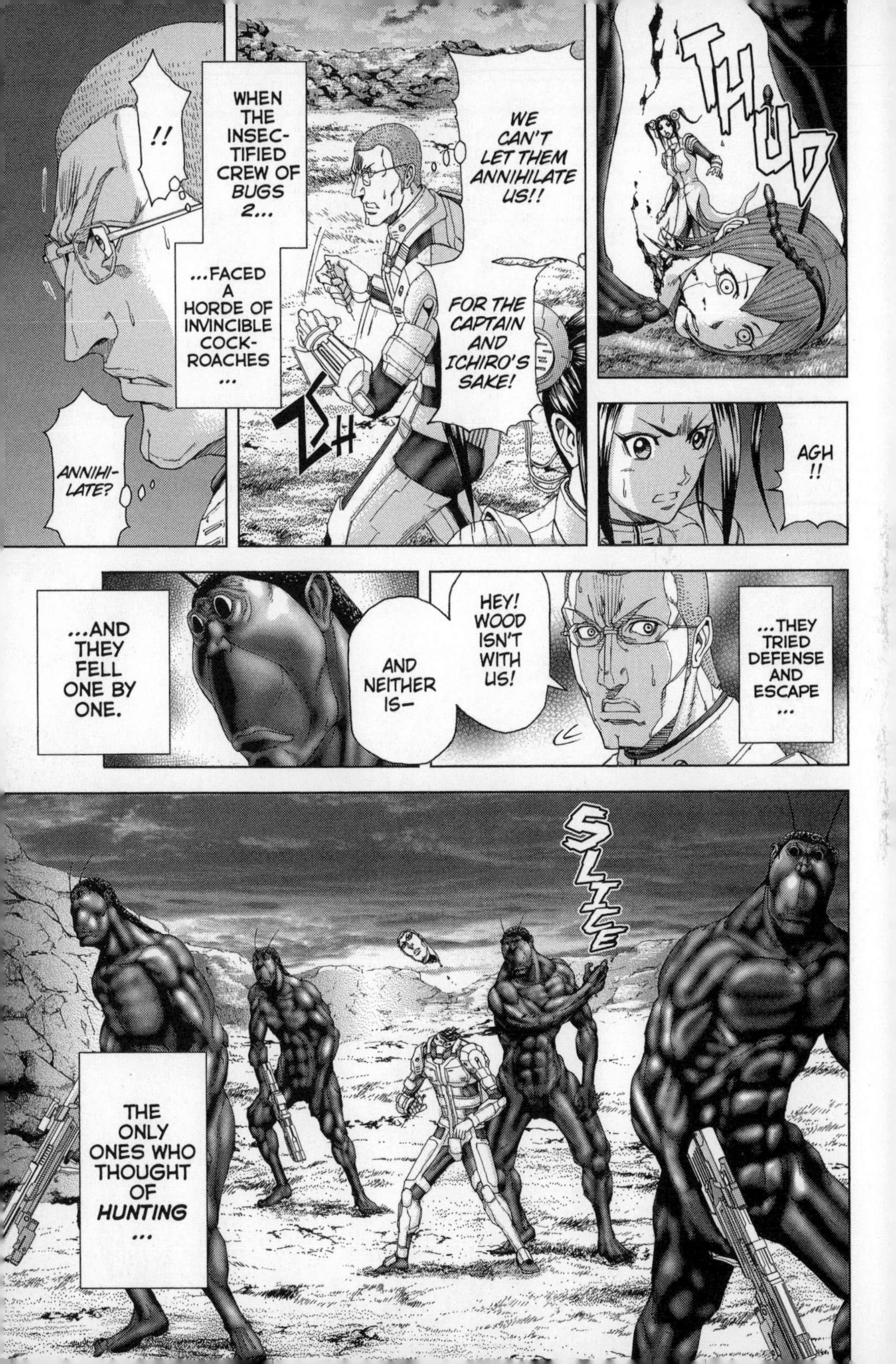
THUD
AGH!!
WE CAN'T LET THEM ANNIHILATE US!!
WHEN THE INSECTIFIED CREW OF BUGS 2...
FOR THE CAPTAIN AND ICHIRO'S SAKE!
...FACED A HORDE OF INVINCIBLE COCKROACHES...
ZSH
!!
ANNIHILATE?
...THEY TRIED DEFENSE AND ESCAPE...
HEY! WOOD ISN'T WITH US!
AND NEITHER IS—
...AND THEY FELL ONE BY ONE.
SLICE
THE ONLY ONES WHO THOUGHT OF HUNTING...

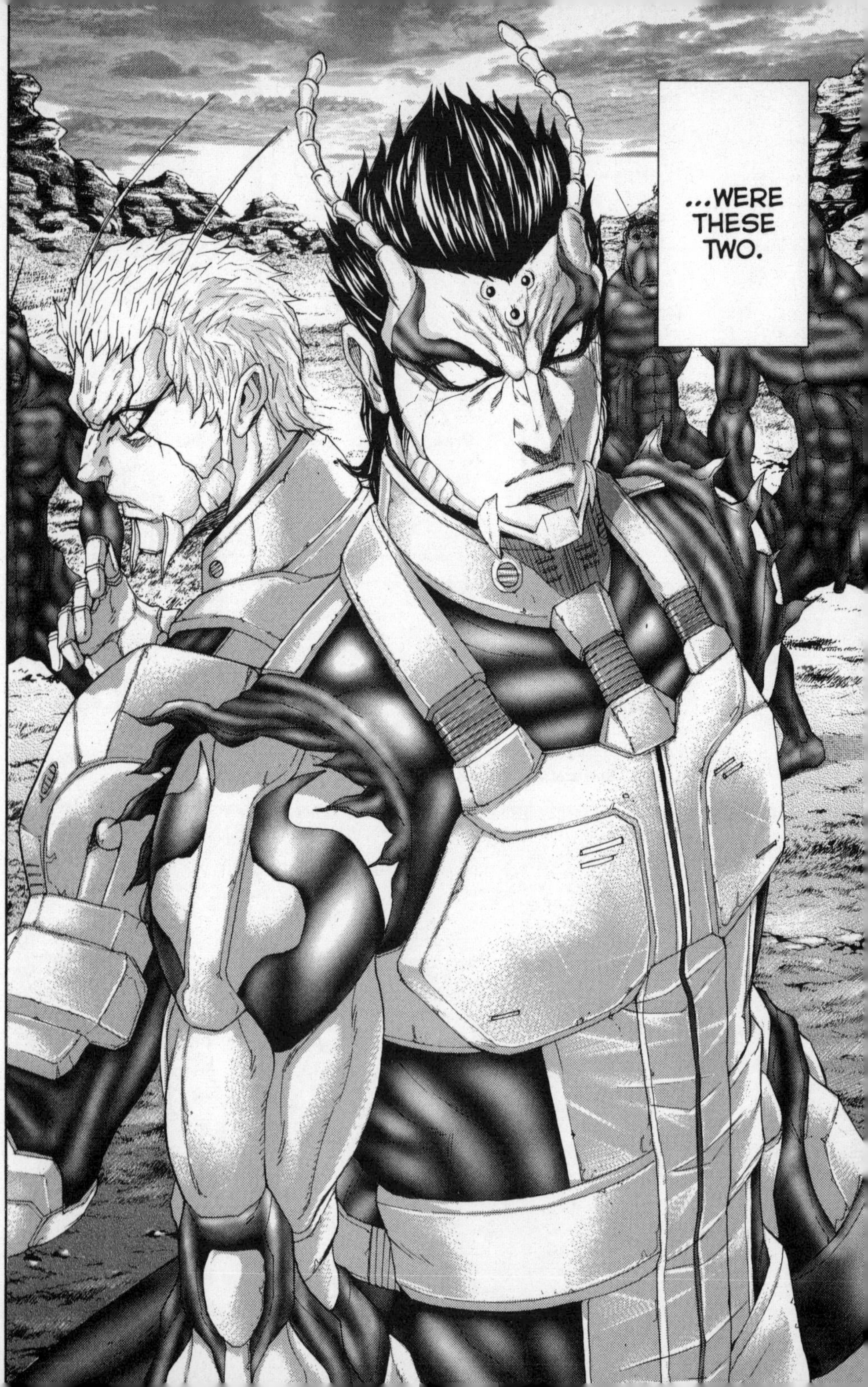
...WERE
THESE
TWO.

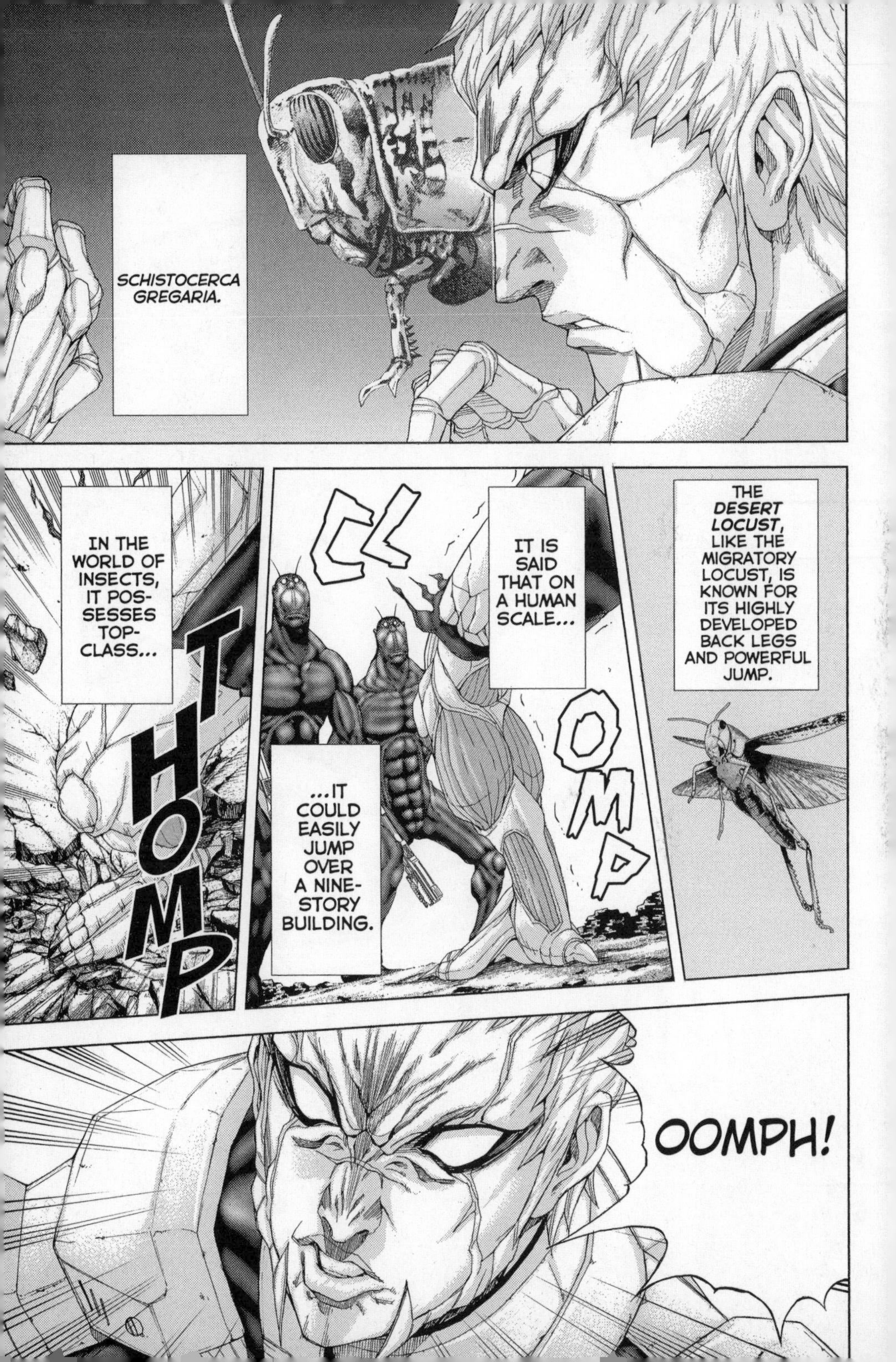
SCHISTOCERCA GREGARIA.
THE *DESERT LOCUST*, LIKE THE MIGRATORY LOCUST, IS KNOWN FOR ITS HIGHLY DEVELOPED BACK LEGS AND POWERFUL JUMP.
IT IS SAID THAT ON A HUMAN SCALE...
CL
OMP
...IT COULD EASILY JUMP OVER A NINE-STORY BUILDING.
IN THE WORLD OF INSECTS, IT POSSESSES TOP-CLASS...
THOMP
OOMPH!

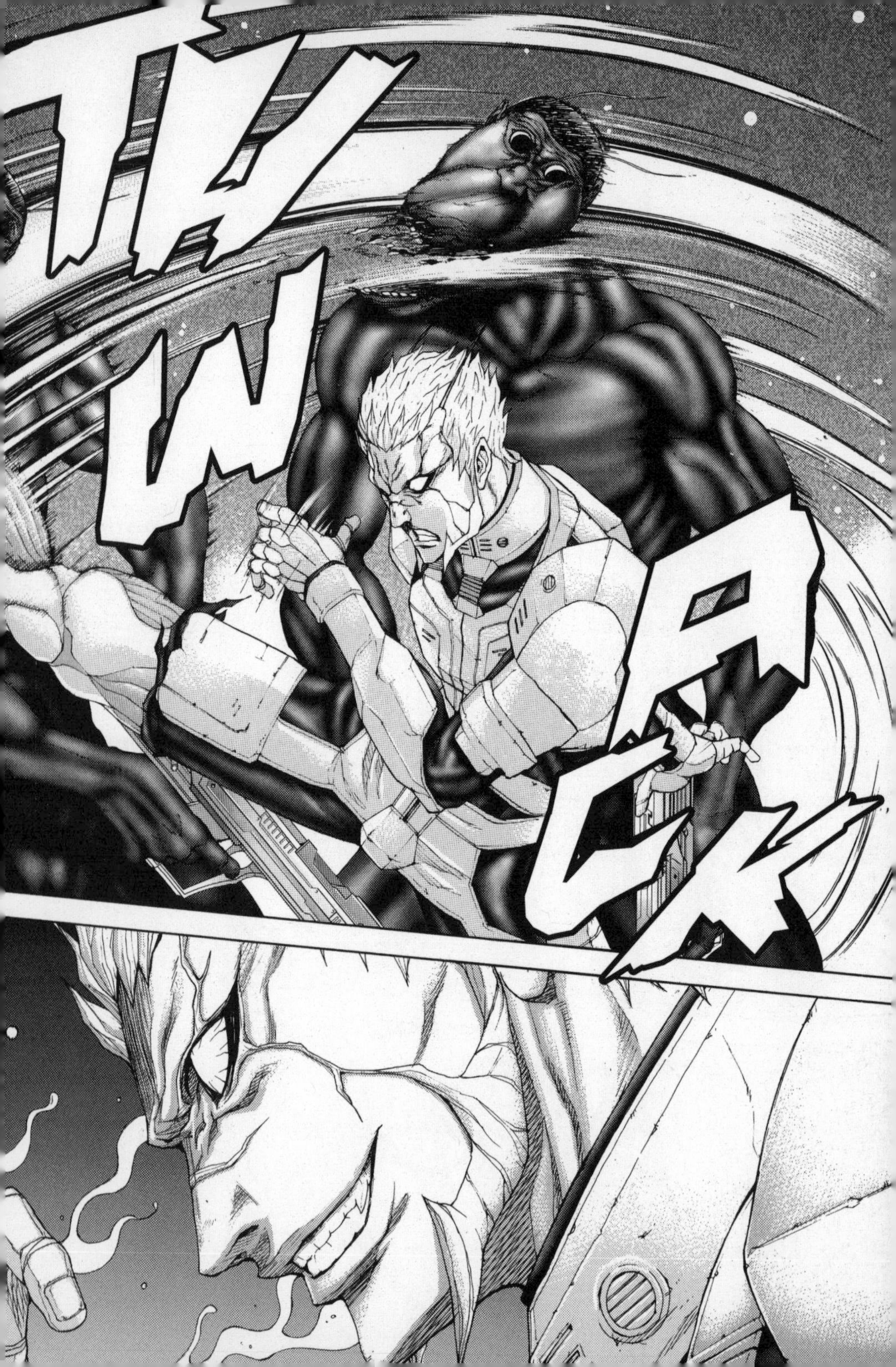
THWACK

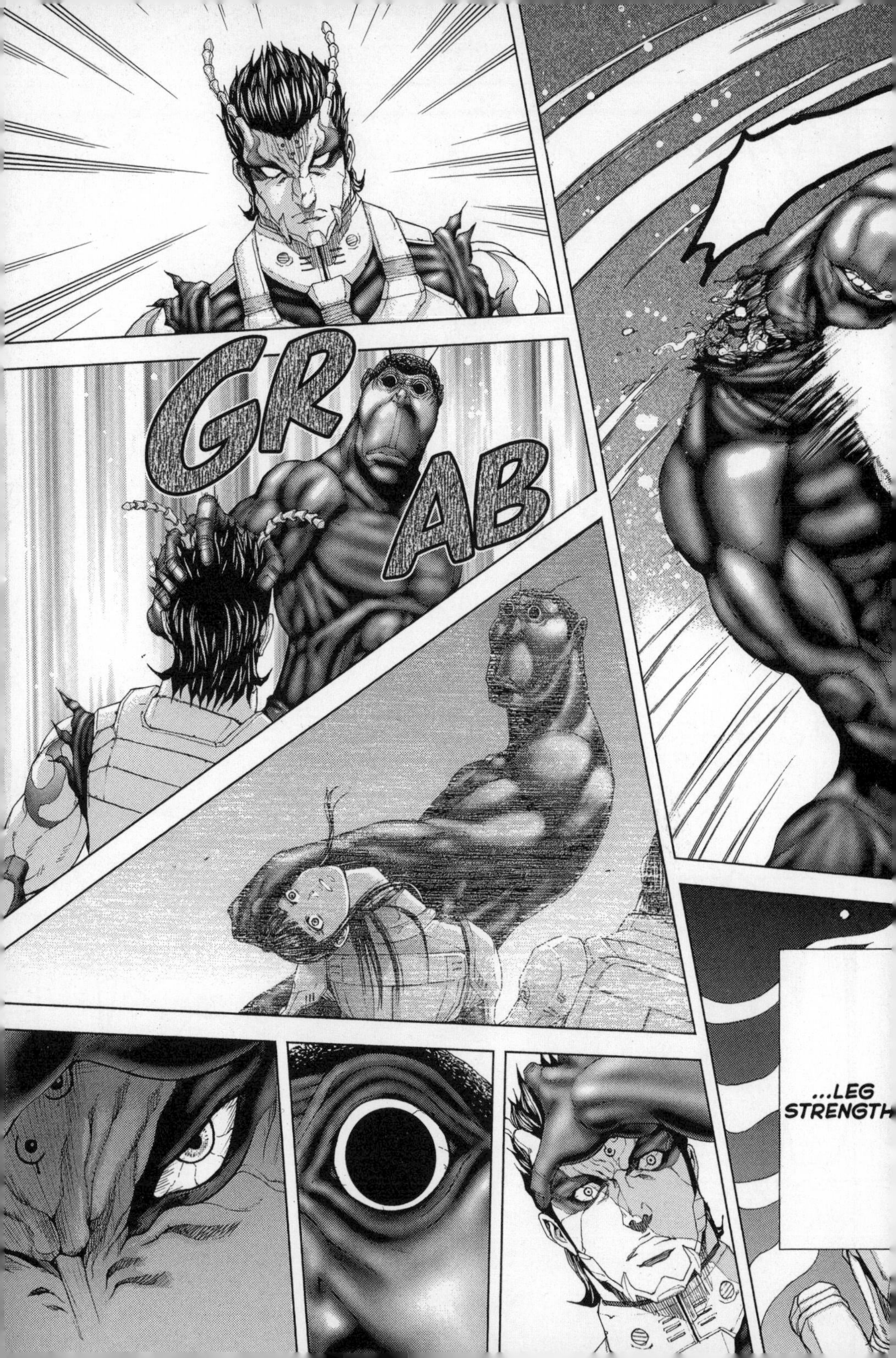
GRAB
...LEG STRENGTH

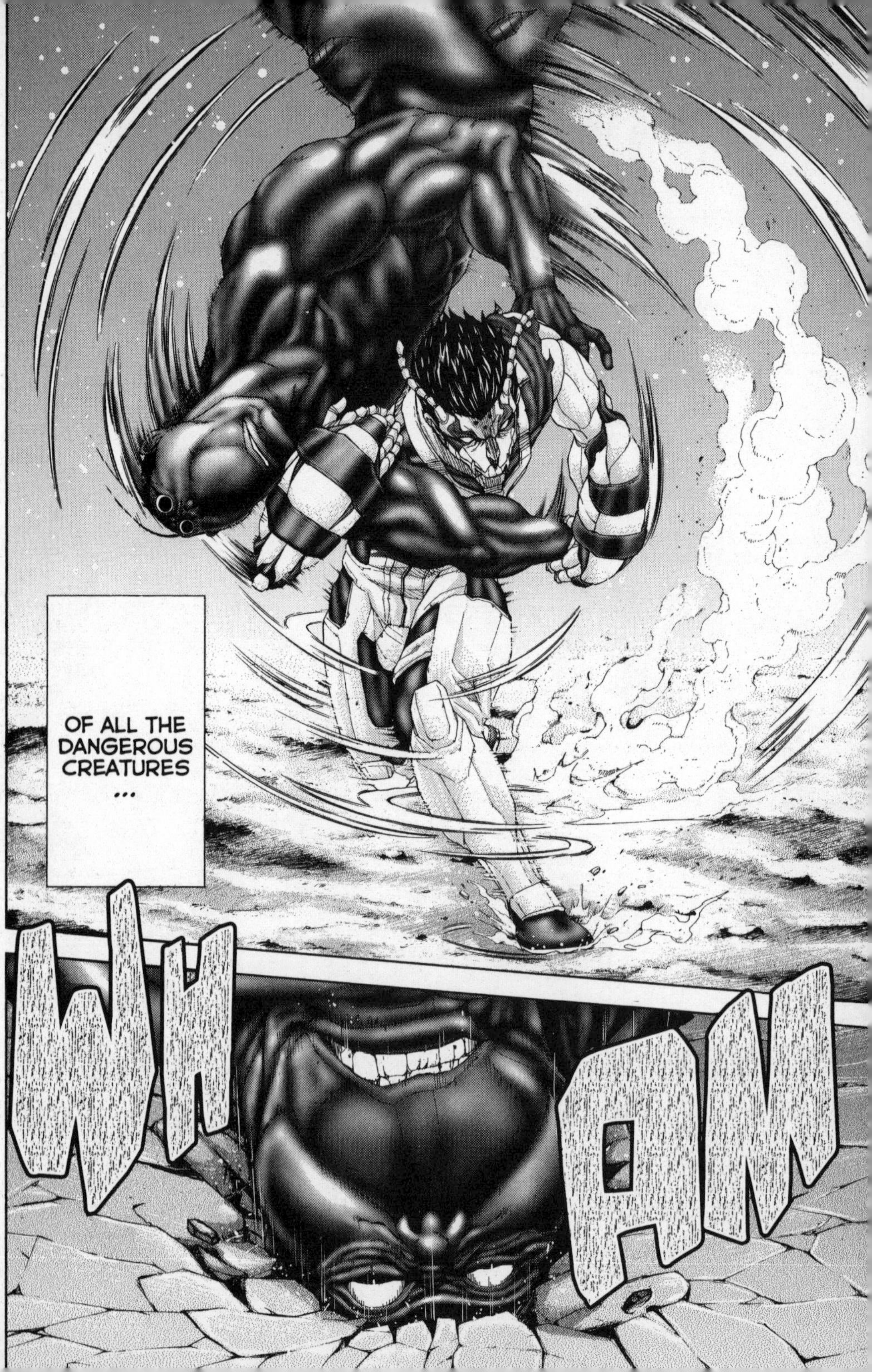
OF ALL THE DANGEROUS CREATURES ...
WHAM

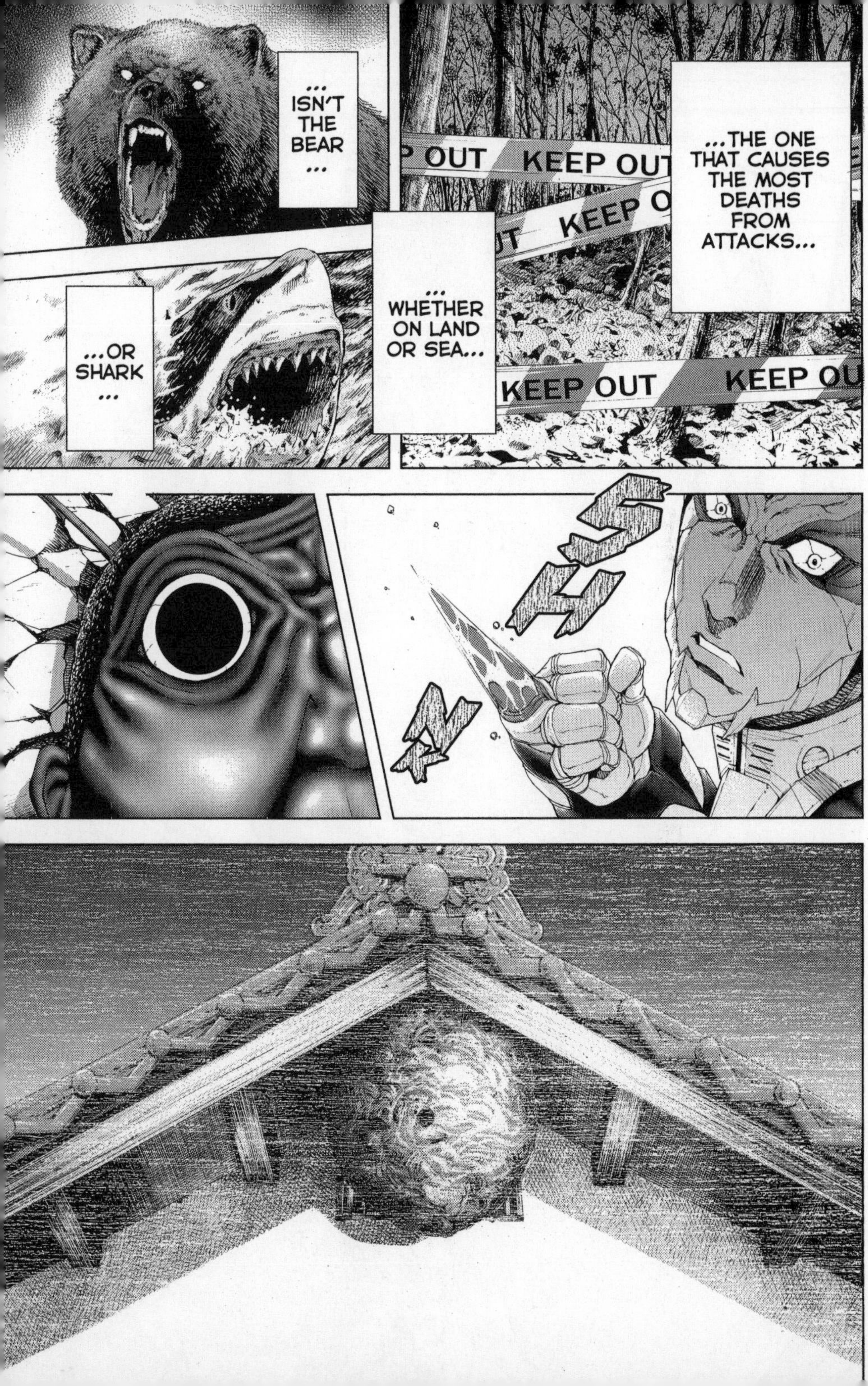
...THE ONE THAT CAUSES THE MOST DEATHS FROM ATTACKS...
KEEP OUT
KEEP OUT
KEEP OUT
KEEP OUT
...WHETHER ON LAND OR SEA...
...ISN'T THE BEAR...
...OR SHARK...

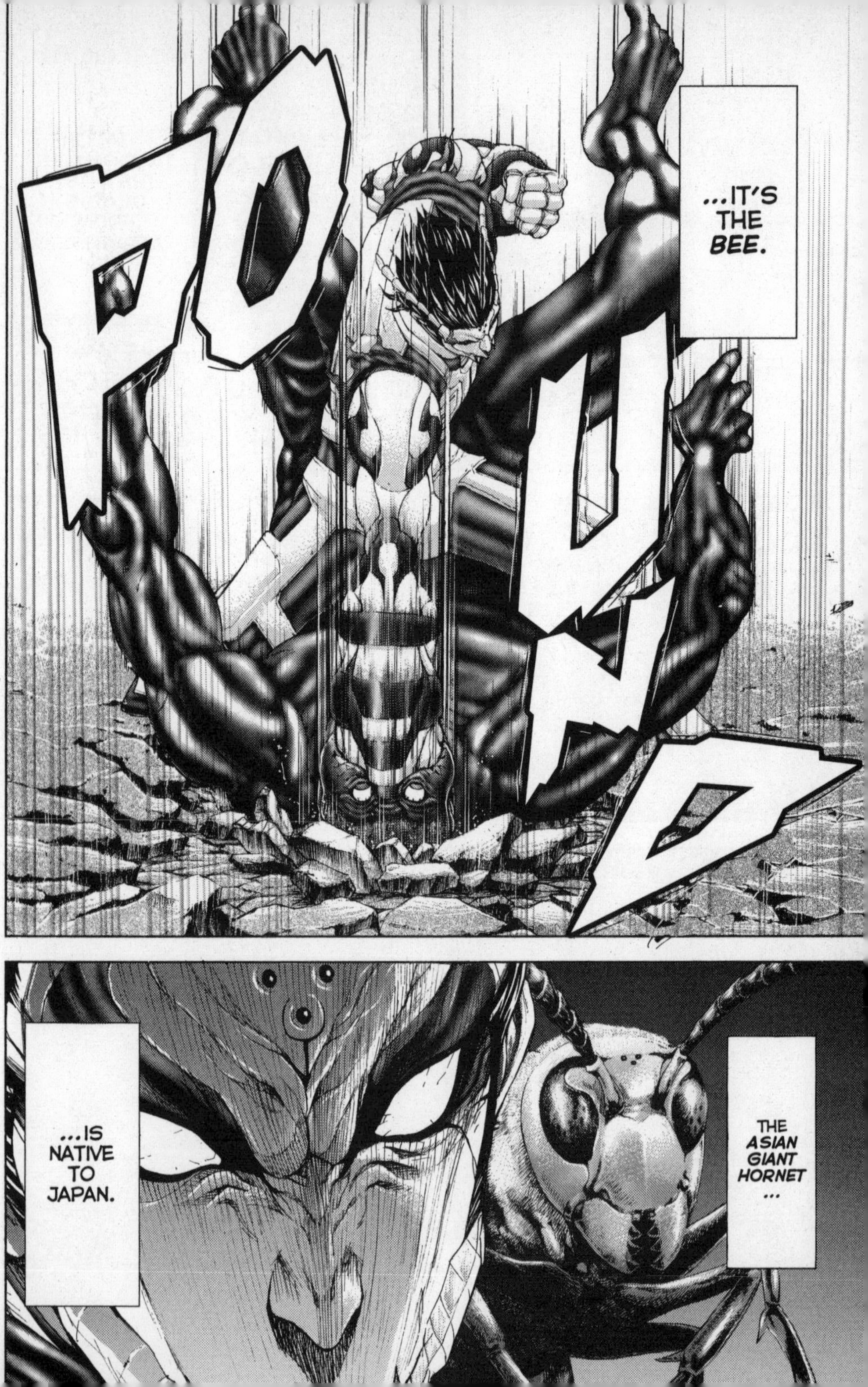
POUND
...IT'S THE BEE.
THE ASIAN GIANT HORNET ...
...IS NATIVE TO JAPAN.

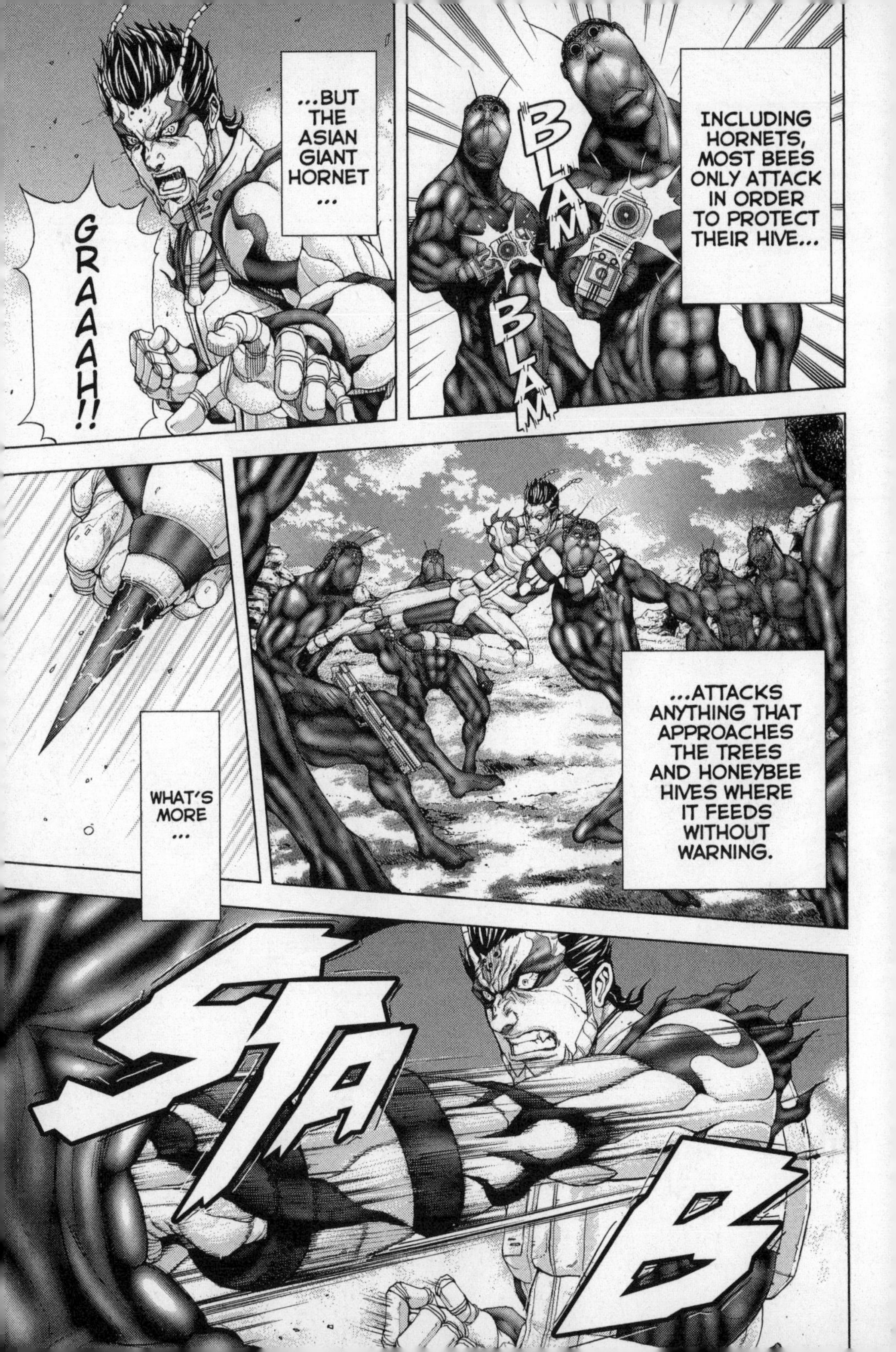
INCLUDING HORNETS, MOST BEES ONLY ATTACK IN ORDER TO PROTECT THEIR HIVE...
BLAM
BLAM
...BUT THE ASIAN GIANT HORNET ...
GRAAAH!!
...ATTACKS ANYTHING THAT APPROACHES THE TREES AND HONEYBEE HIVES WHERE IT FEEDS WITHOUT WARNING.
WHAT'S MORE ...
STAB

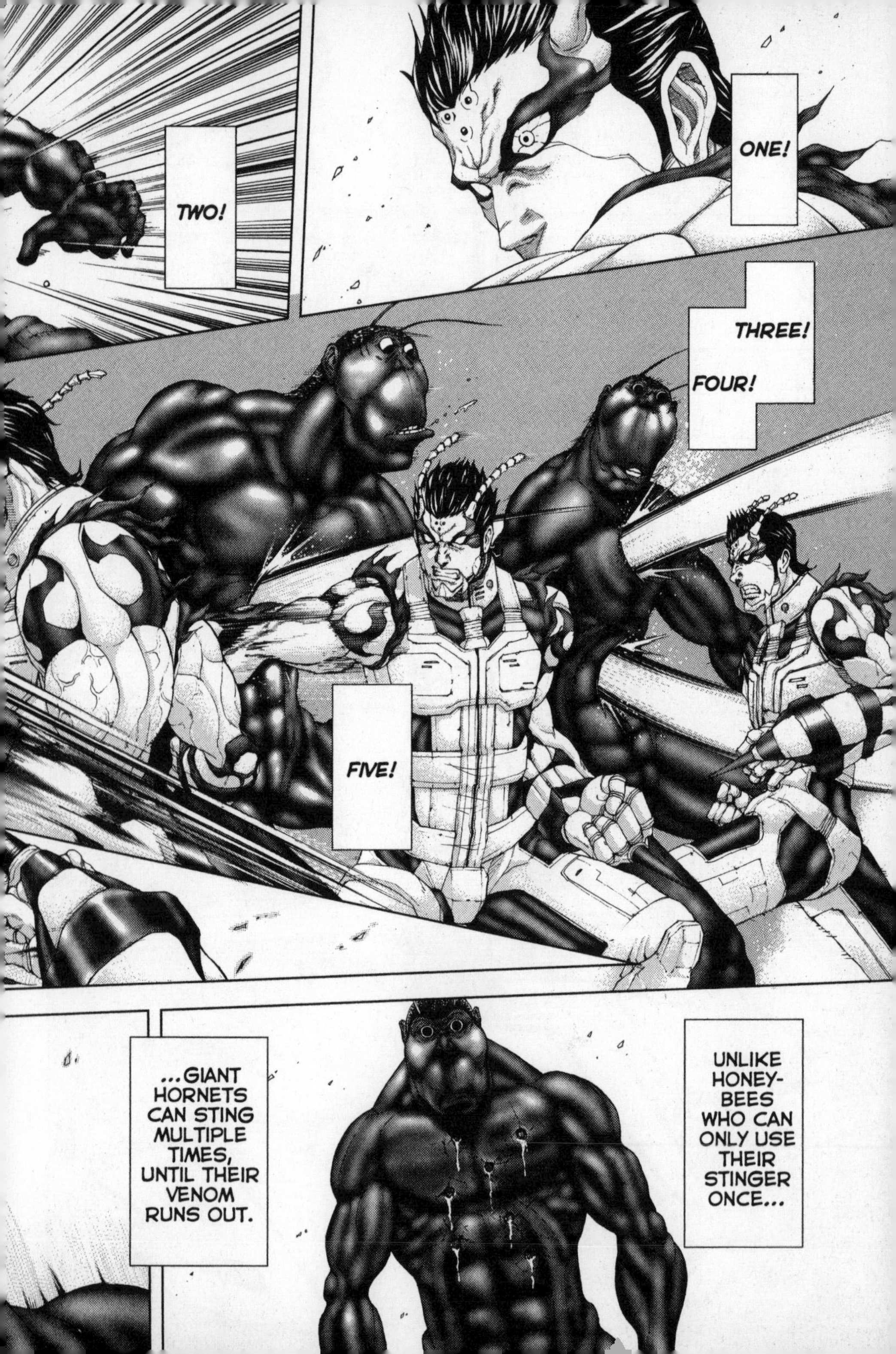
ONE!
TWO!
THREE!
FOUR!
FIVE!
UNLIKE HONEY-BEES WHO CAN ONLY USE THEIR STINGER ONCE...
...GIANT HORNETS CAN STING MULTIPLE TIMES, UNTIL THEIR VENOM RUNS OUT.

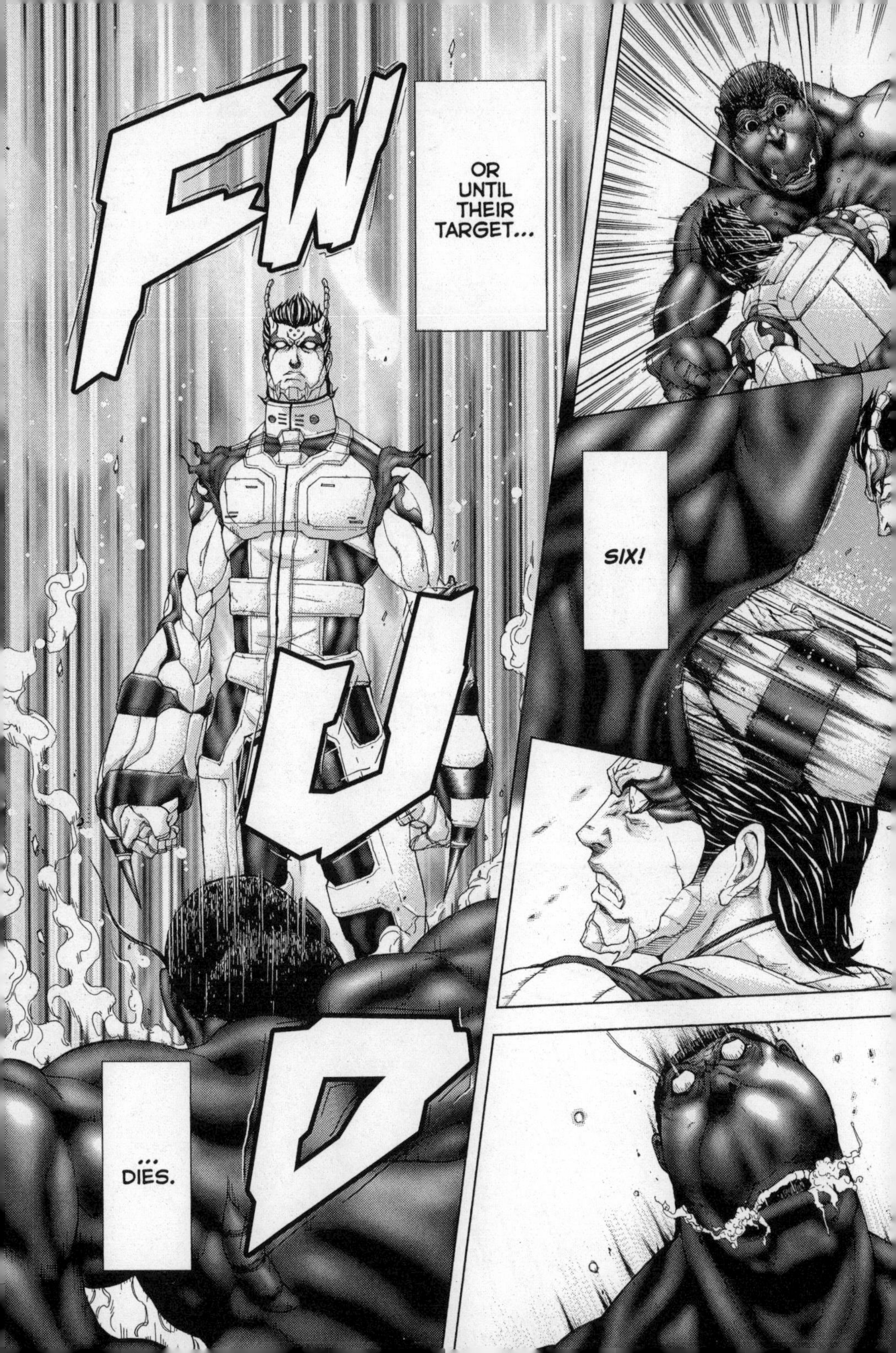
SIX!
OR UNTIL THEIR TARGET...
FWUD
...DIES.

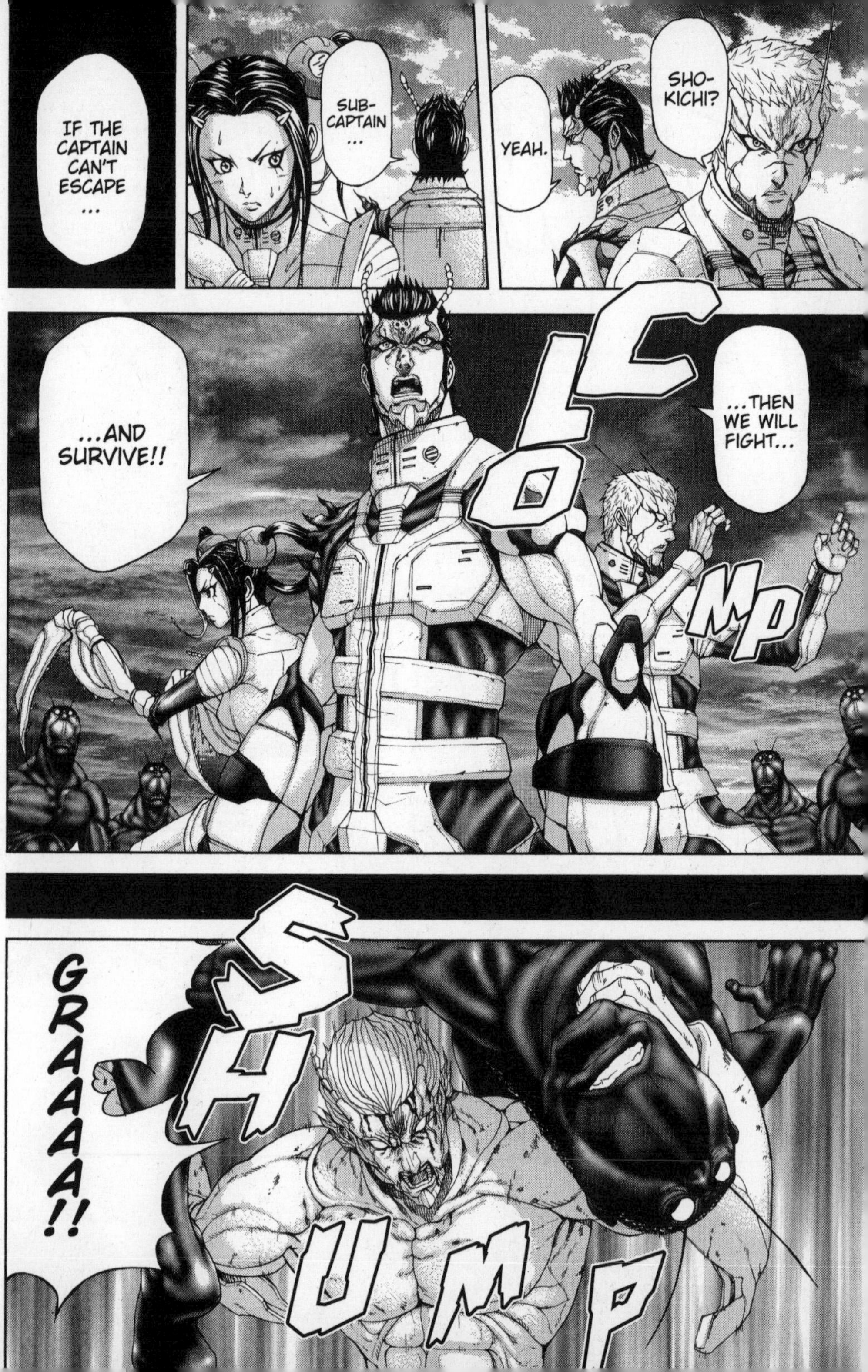
SHO-KICHI?
YEAH.
SUB-CAPTAIN ...
IF THE CAPTAIN CAN'T ESCAPE ...
...THEN WE WILL FIGHT...
...AND SURVIVE!!
CLO
OMP
SH
UMP
GRAAAAA!!

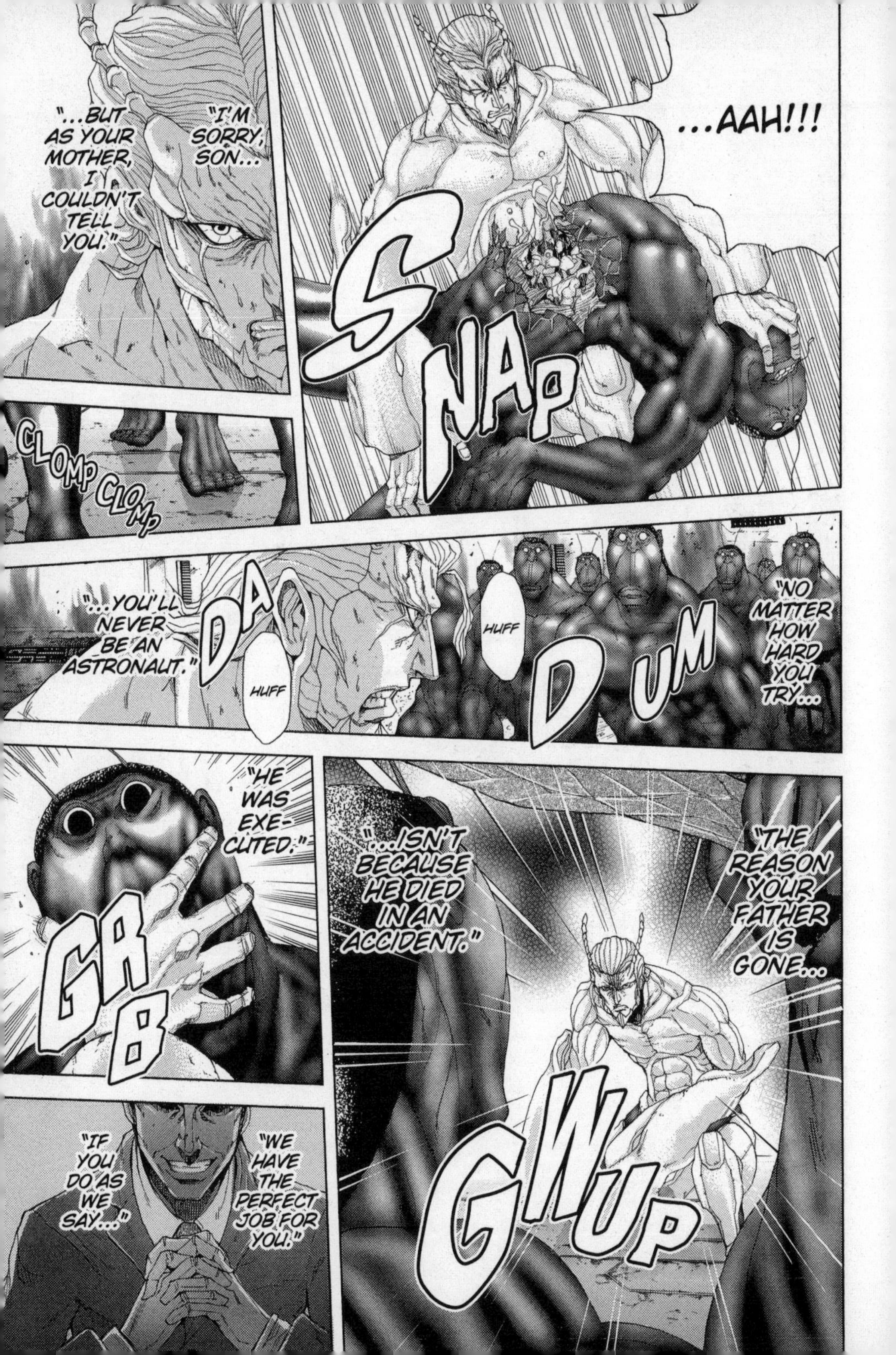
...AAH!!!
SNAP
"I'M SORRY, SON...
"...BUT AS YOUR MOTHER, I COULDN'T TELL YOU."
CLOMP CLOMP
"NO MATTER HOW HARD YOU TRY...
DA DUM
HUFF
HUFF
"...YOU'LL NEVER BE AN ASTRONAUT."
"THE REASON YOUR FATHER IS GONE...
"...ISN'T BECAUSE HE DIED IN AN ACCIDENT."
GWUP
"HE WAS EXE-CUTED."
GR B
"WE HAVE THE PERFECT JOB FOR YOU."
"IF YOU DO AS WE SAY..."

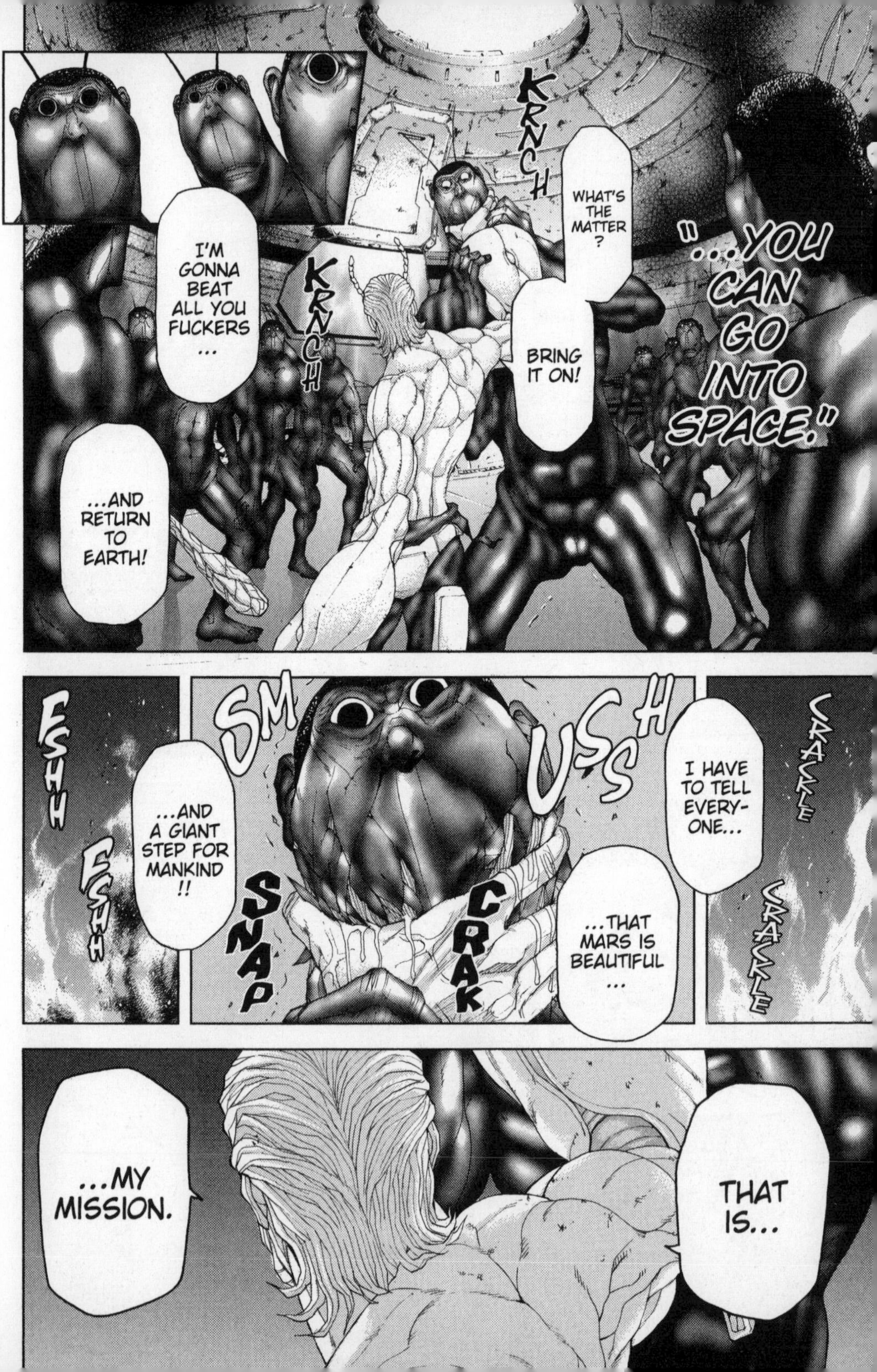
"...YOU CAN GO INTO SPACE."
KRNCH
WHAT'S THE MATTER?
BRING IT ON!
KRNCH
I'M GONNA BEAT ALL YOU FUCKERS...
...AND RETURN TO EARTH!
CRACKLE
CRACKLE
I HAVE TO TELL EVERY-ONE...
...THAT MARS IS BEAUTIFUL...
SMUSSH
CRAK
SNAP
...AND A GIANT STEP FOR MANKIND!!
FSHH
FSHH
THAT IS...
...MY MISSION.

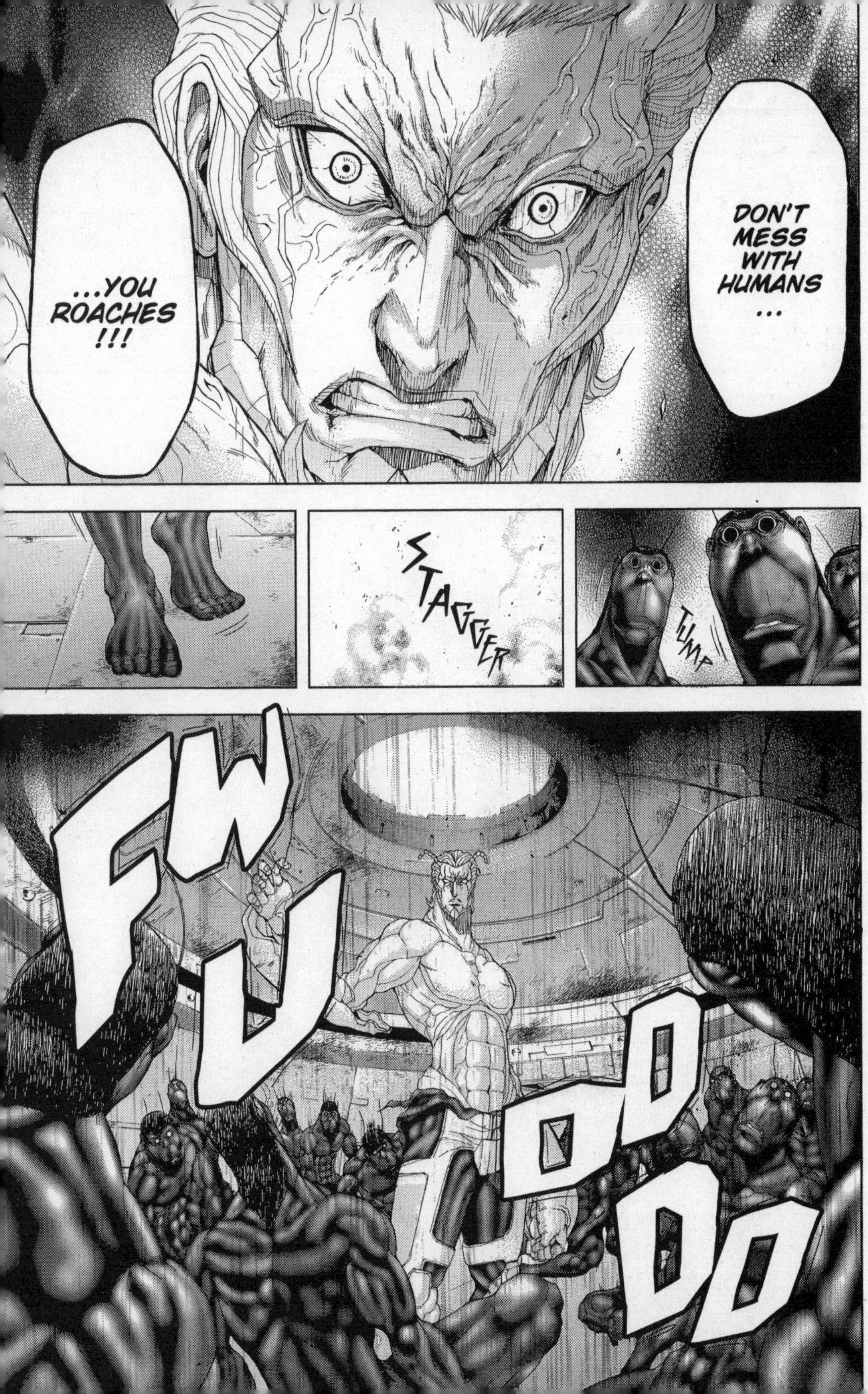
DON'T MESS WITH HUMANS ...
...YOU ROACHES !!!
TUMP
STAGGER
FWU
DODODO

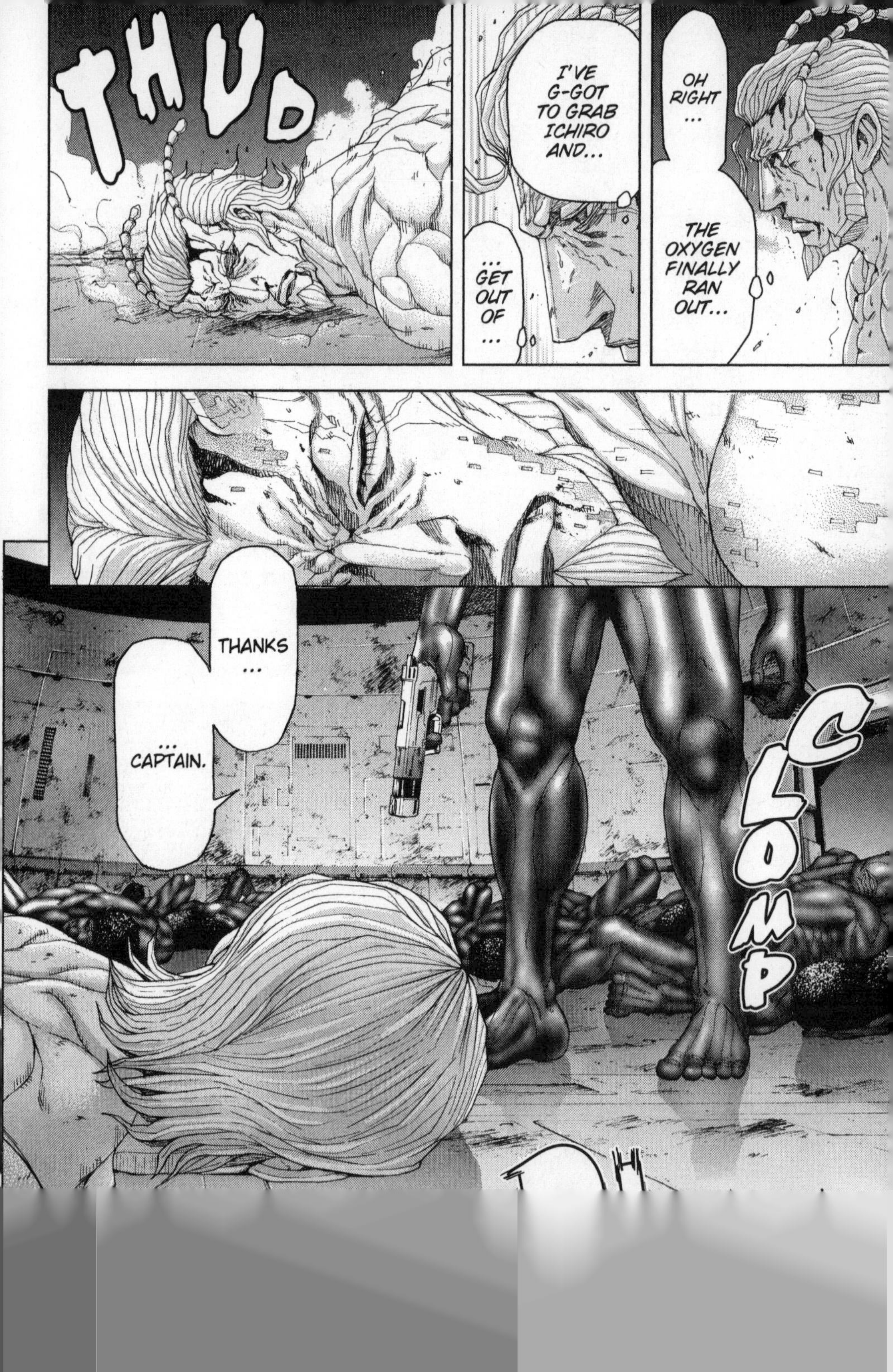
OH RIGHT ...
THE OXYGEN FINALLY RAN OUT...
I'VE G-GOT TO GRAB ICHIRO AND...
...GET OUT OF ...
THUD
CLOMP
THANKS ...
... CAPTAIN.

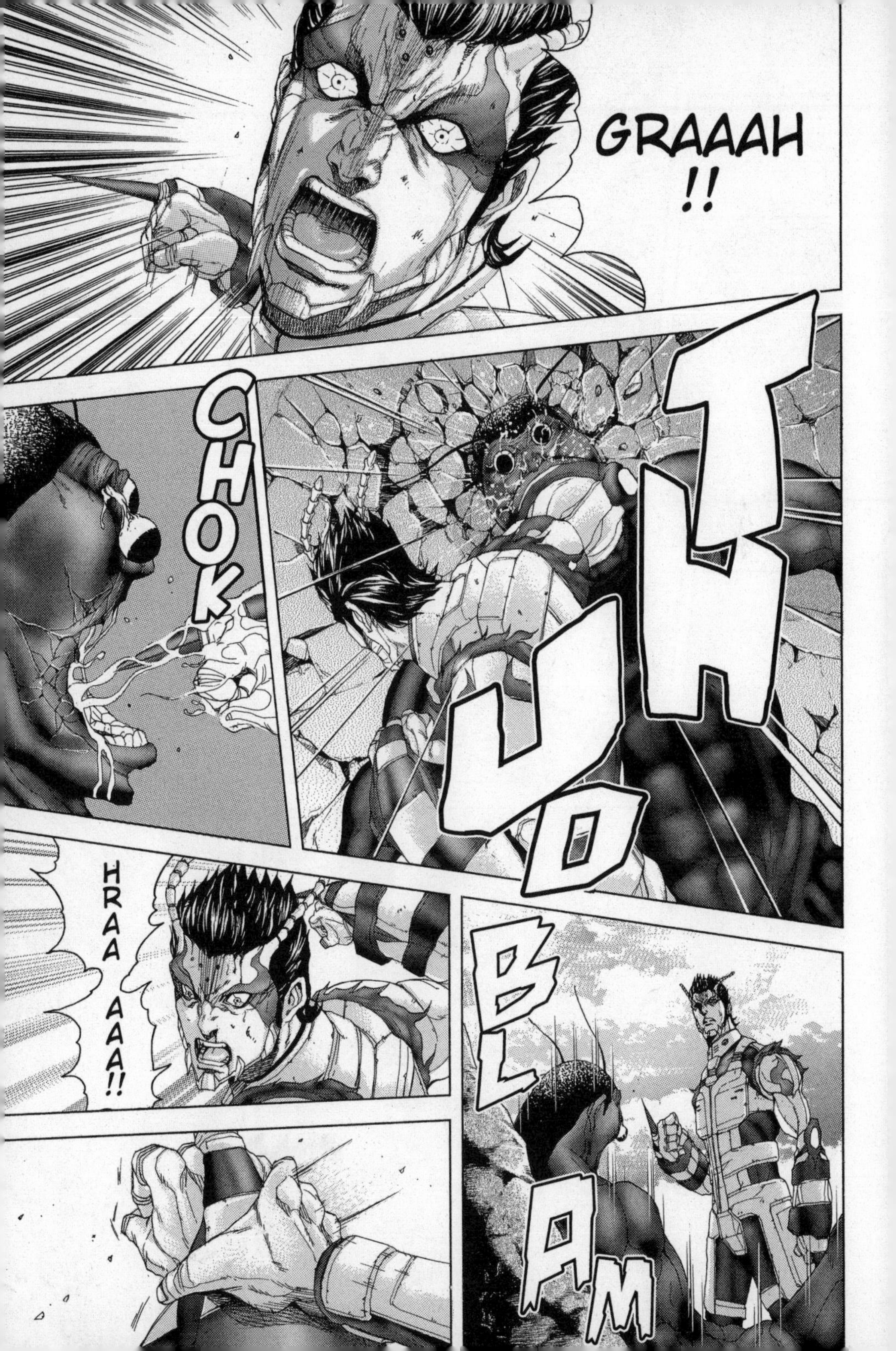
GRAAAH!!
THUD
CHOK
BLAM
HRAAAAA!!

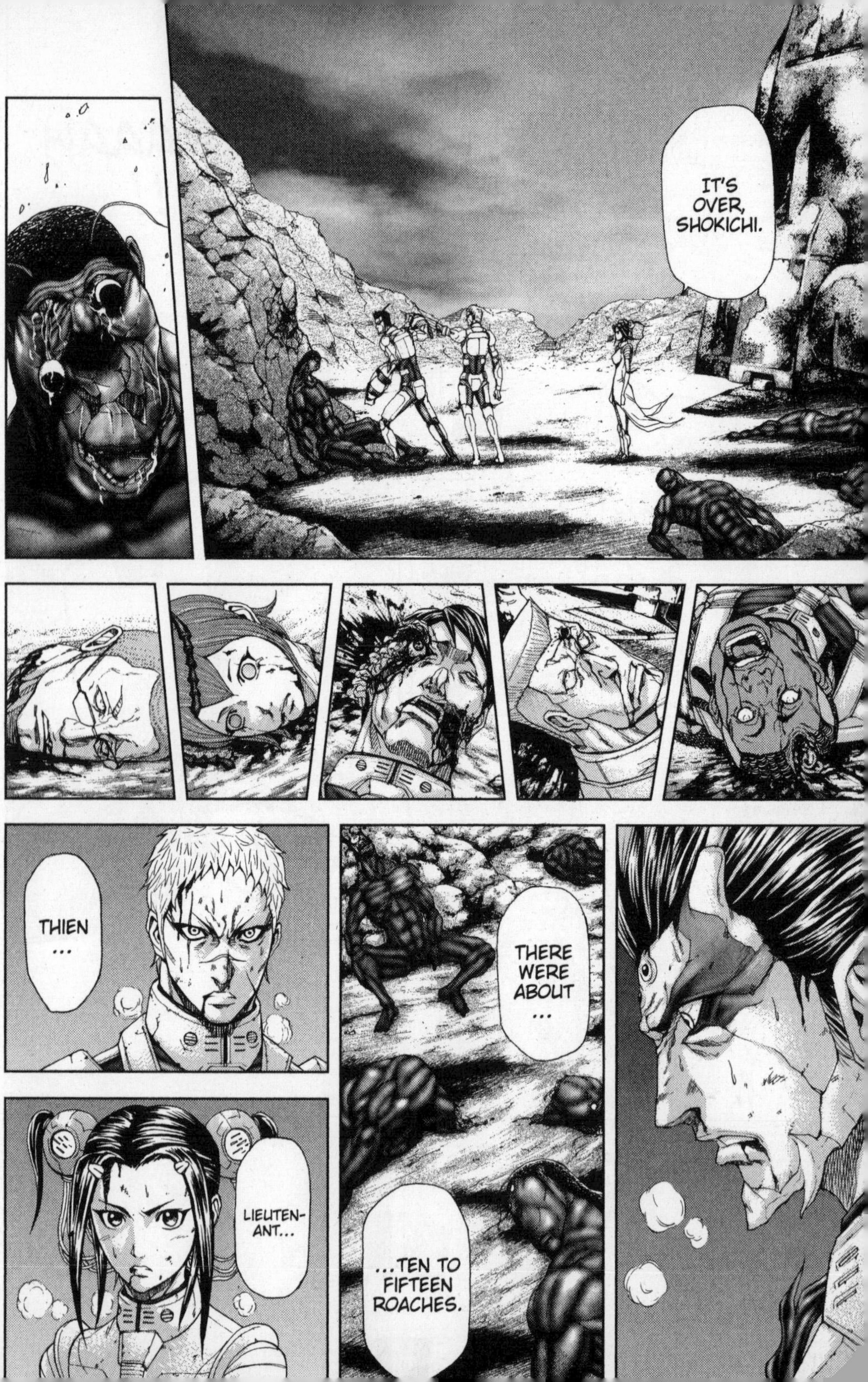
IT'S OVER, SHOKICHI.
THERE WERE ABOUT...
...TEN TO FIFTEEN ROACHES.
THIEN...
LIEUTEN-ANT...

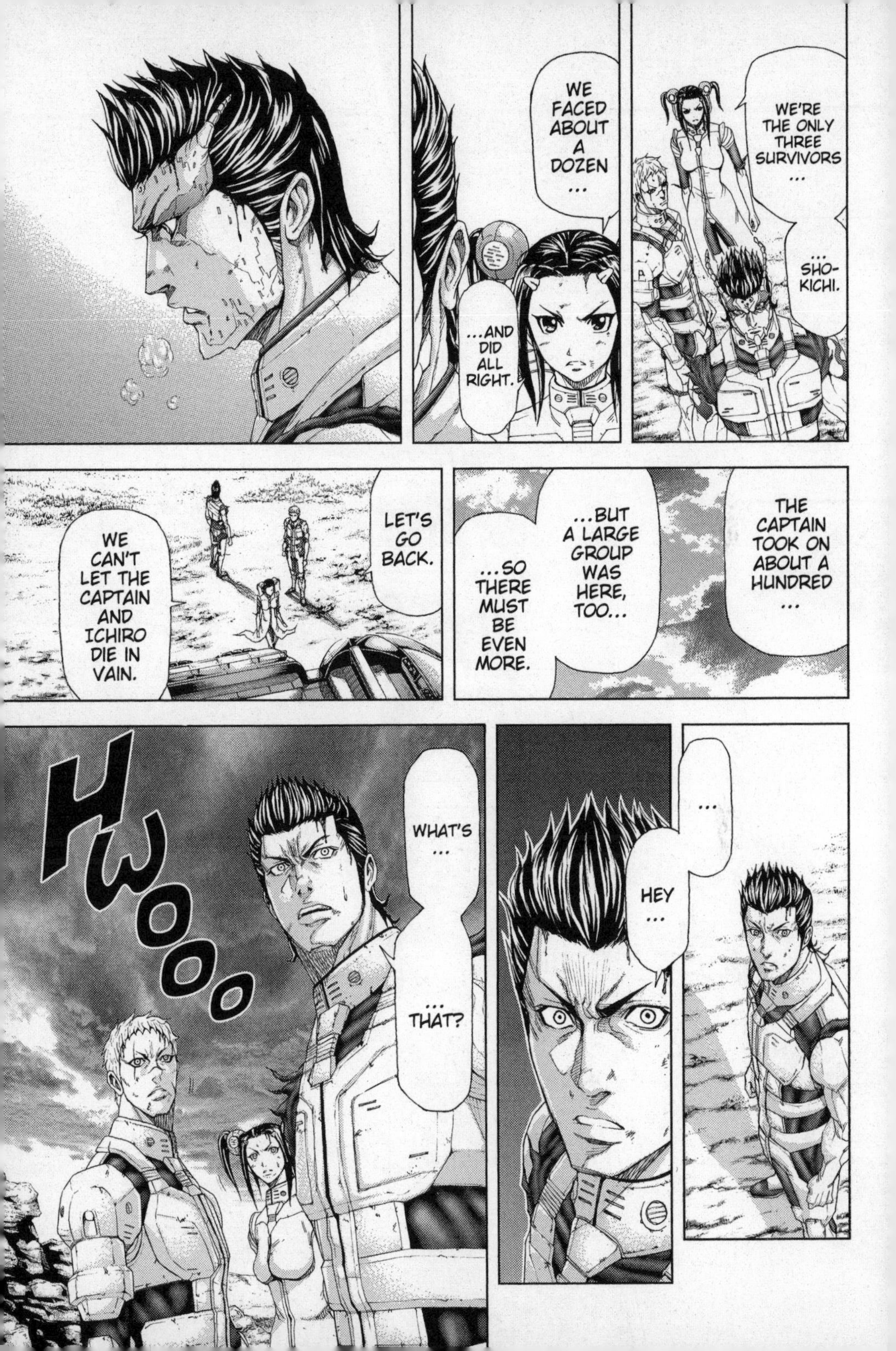

WE'RE THE ONLY THREE SURVIVORS...
...SHO-KICHI.
WE FACED ABOUT A DOZEN...
...AND DID ALL RIGHT.
THE CAPTAIN TOOK ON ABOUT A HUNDRED...
...BUT A LARGE GROUP WAS HERE, TOO...
...SO THERE MUST BE EVEN MORE.
LET'S GO BACK.
WE CAN'T LET THE CAPTAIN AND ICHIRO DIE IN VAIN.
...
HEY...
WHAT'S...
...THAT?
HWOOOO

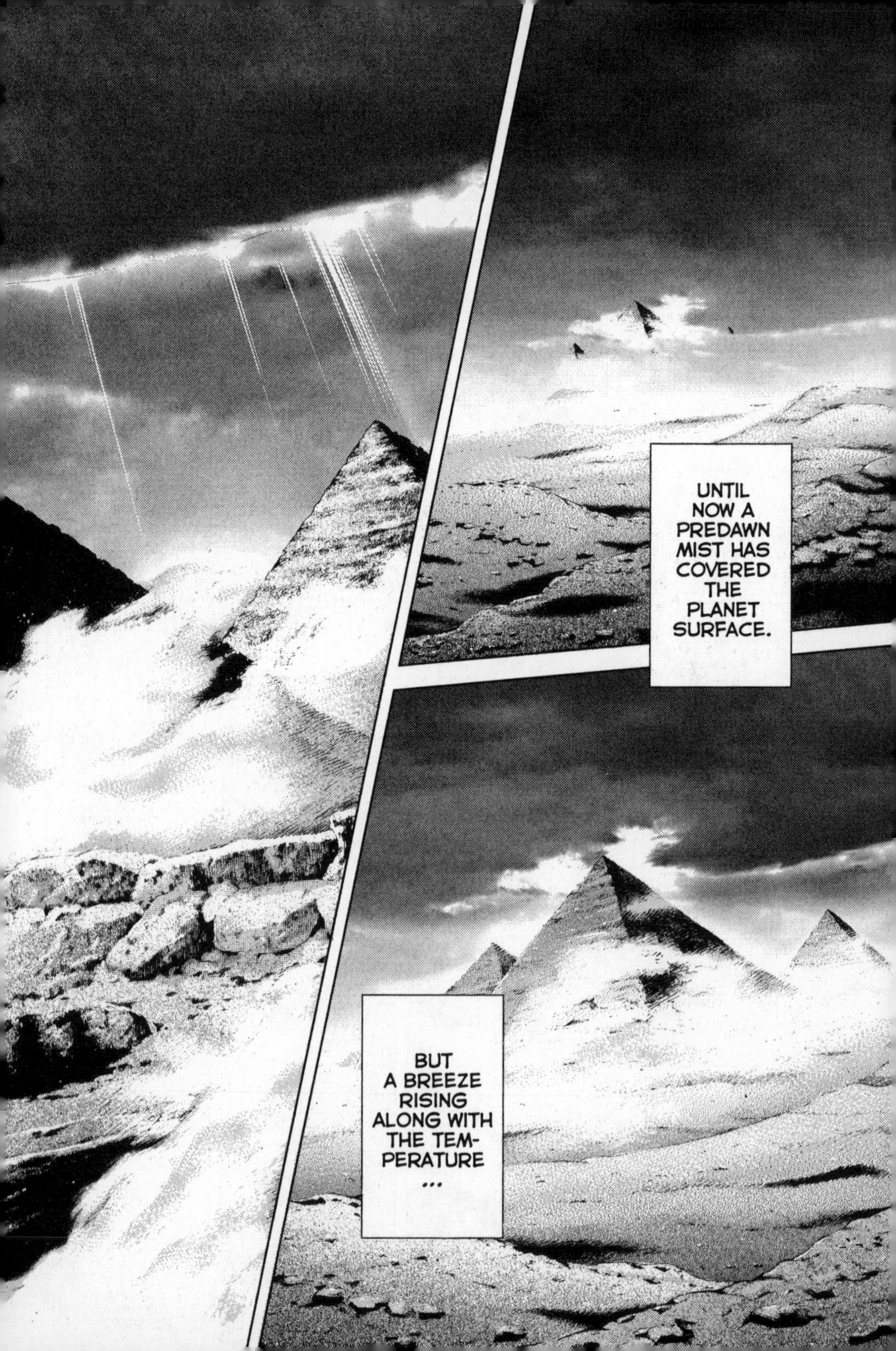
UNTIL NOW A PREDAWN MIST HAS COVERED THE PLANET SURFACE.
BUT A BREEZE RISING ALONG WITH THE TEMPERATURE ...

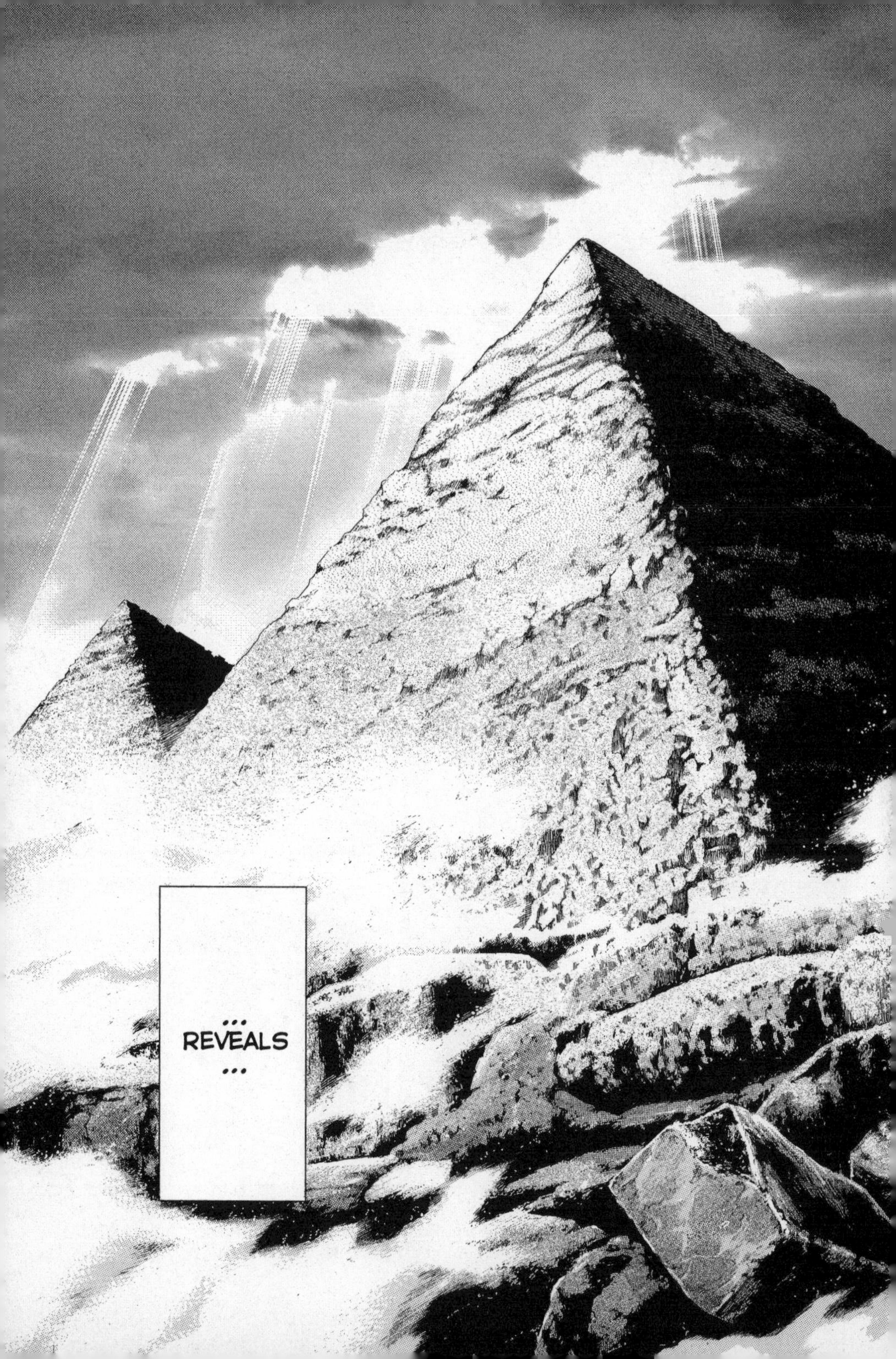
...
REVEALS
...

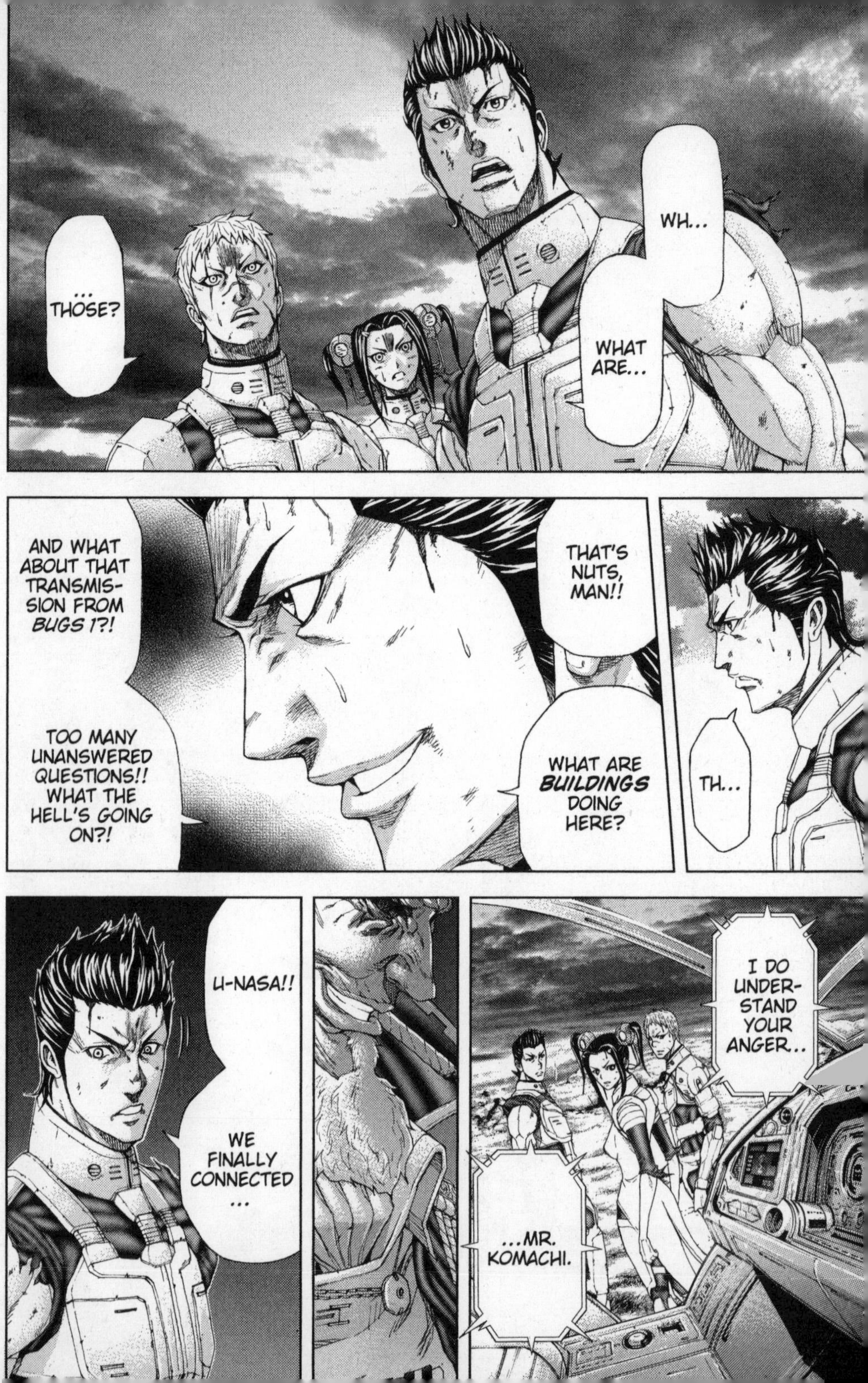
WH...
WHAT ARE...
...THOSE?
TH...
THAT'S NUTS, MAN!!
WHAT ARE *BUILDINGS* DOING HERE?
AND WHAT ABOUT THAT TRANSMISSION FROM *BUGS 1*?!
TOO MANY UNANSWERED QUESTIONS!! WHAT THE HELL'S GOING ON?!
I DO UNDERSTAND YOUR ANGER...
...MR. KOMACHI.
U-NASA!!
WE FINALLY CONNECTED...

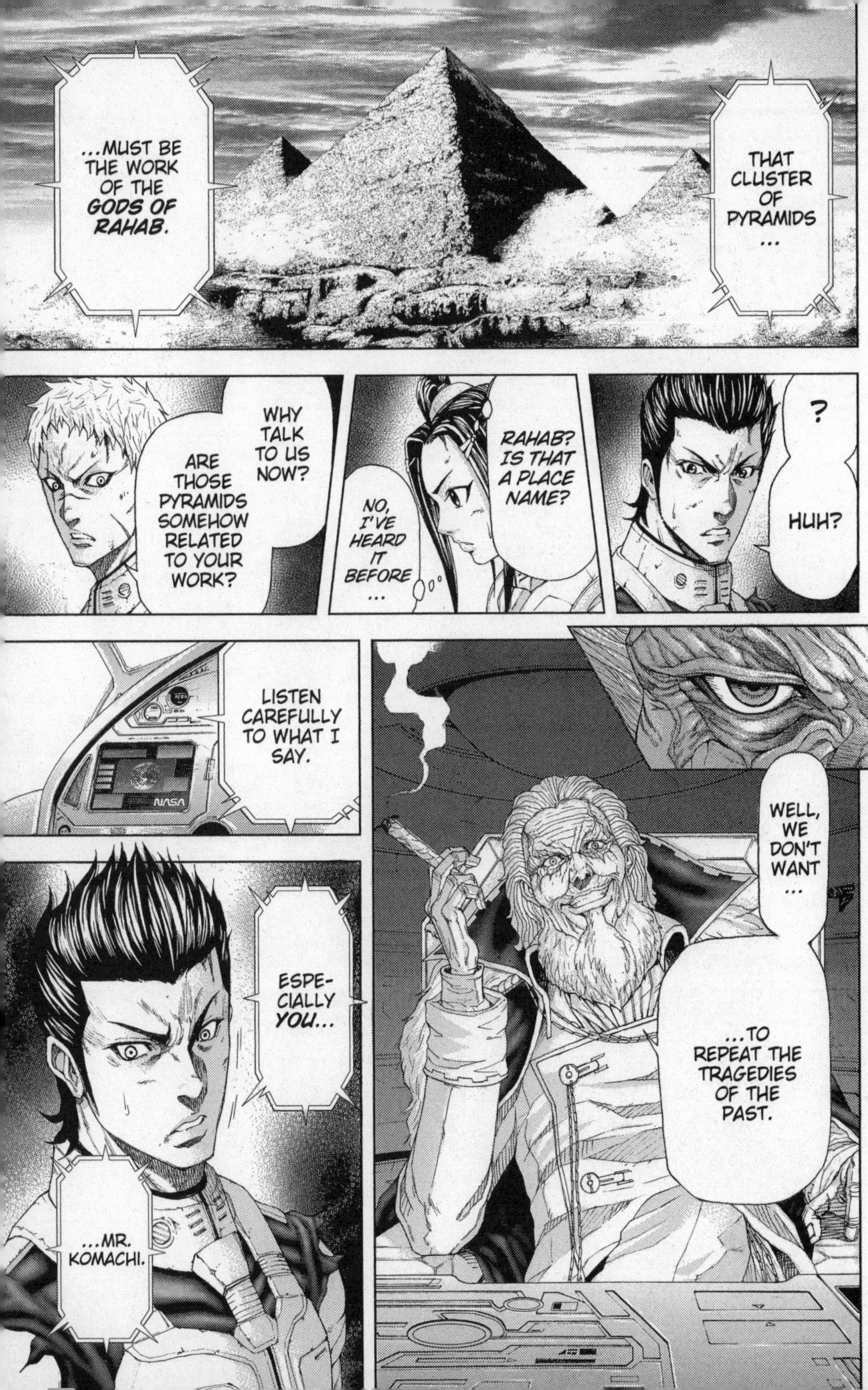
THAT CLUSTER OF PYRAMIDS ...
...MUST BE THE WORK OF THE *GODS OF RAHAB.*
?
HUH?
RAHAB? IS THAT A PLACE NAME?
NO, I'VE HEARD IT BEFORE ...
WHY TALK TO US NOW?
ARE THOSE PYRAMIDS SOMEHOW RELATED TO YOUR WORK?
WELL, WE DON'T WANT ...
...TO REPEAT THE TRAGEDIES OF THE PAST.
LISTEN CAREFULLY TO WHAT I SAY.
ESPE-CIALLY *YOU...*
...MR. KOMACHI.

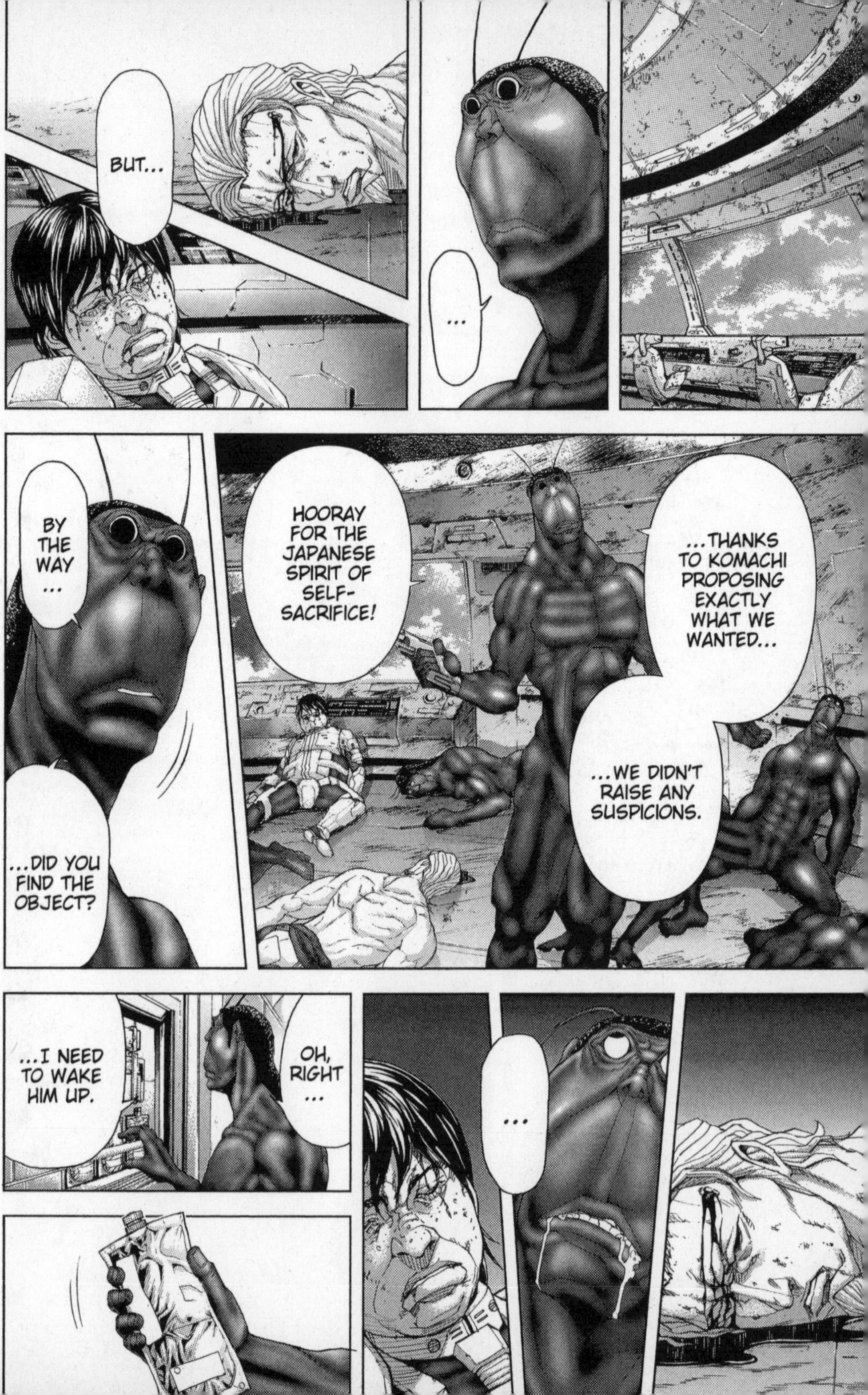
...
BUT...
...THANKS TO KOMACHI PROPOSING EXACTLY WHAT WE WANTED...
HOORAY FOR THE JAPANESE SPIRIT OF SELF-SACRIFICE!
...WE DIDN'T RAISE ANY SUSPICIONS.
BY THE WAY...
...DID YOU FIND THE OBJECT?
...
OH, RIGHT...
...I NEED TO WAKE HIM UP.

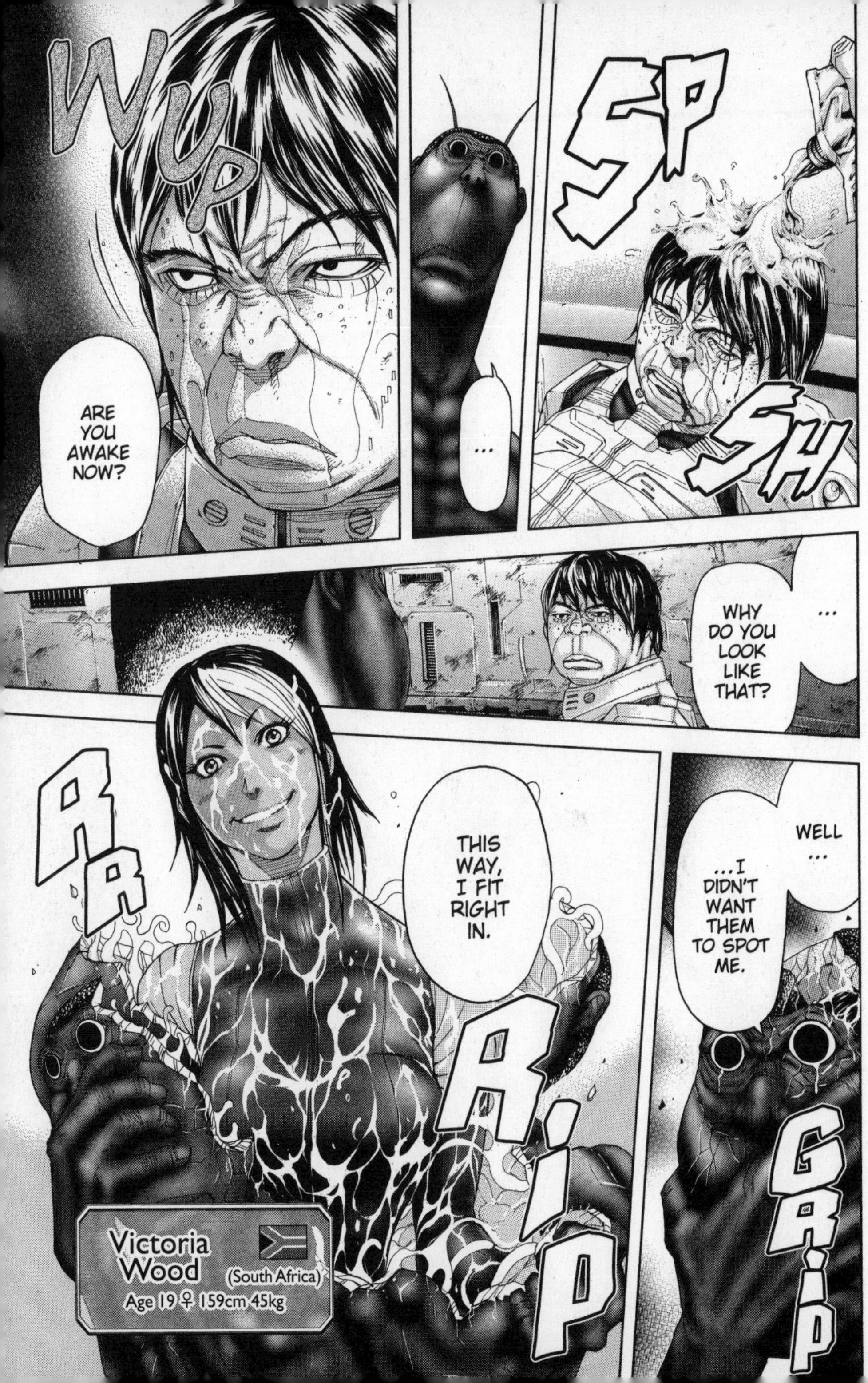
SP
SH
...
WUP
ARE YOU AWAKE NOW?
WHY DO YOU LOOK LIKE THAT? ...
WELL...
...I DIDN'T WANT THEM TO SPOT ME.
GRIP
THIS WAY, I FIT RIGHT IN.
RIP
RR
Victoria Wood (South Africa)
Age 19 ♀ 159cm 45kg

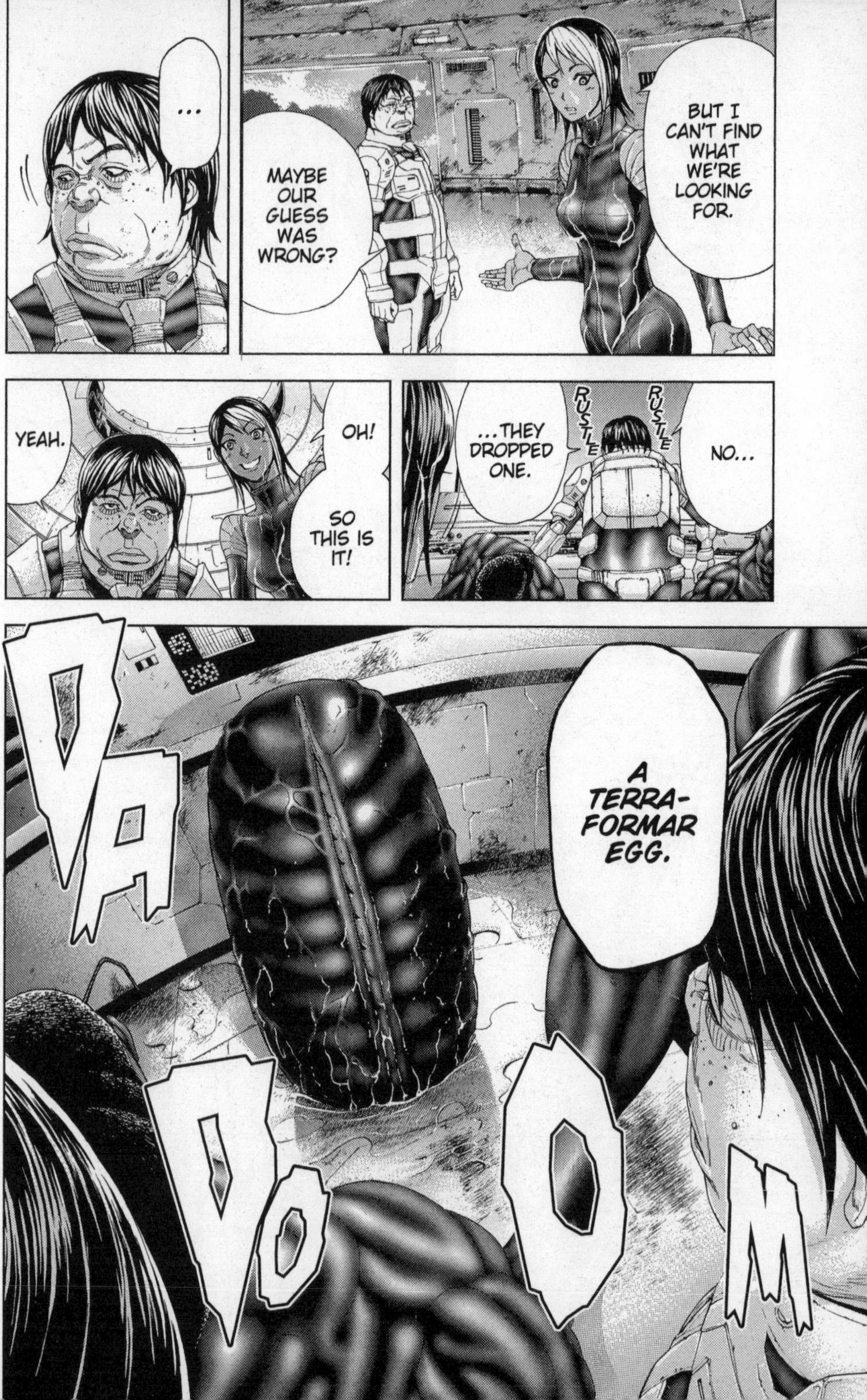
BUT I CAN'T FIND WHAT WE'RE LOOKING FOR.
MAYBE OUR GUESS WAS WRONG?
...
NO...
RUSTLE
RUSTLE
...THEY DROPPED ONE.
OH!
SO THIS IS IT!
YEAH.
A TERRA-FORMAR EGG.
DADOOM

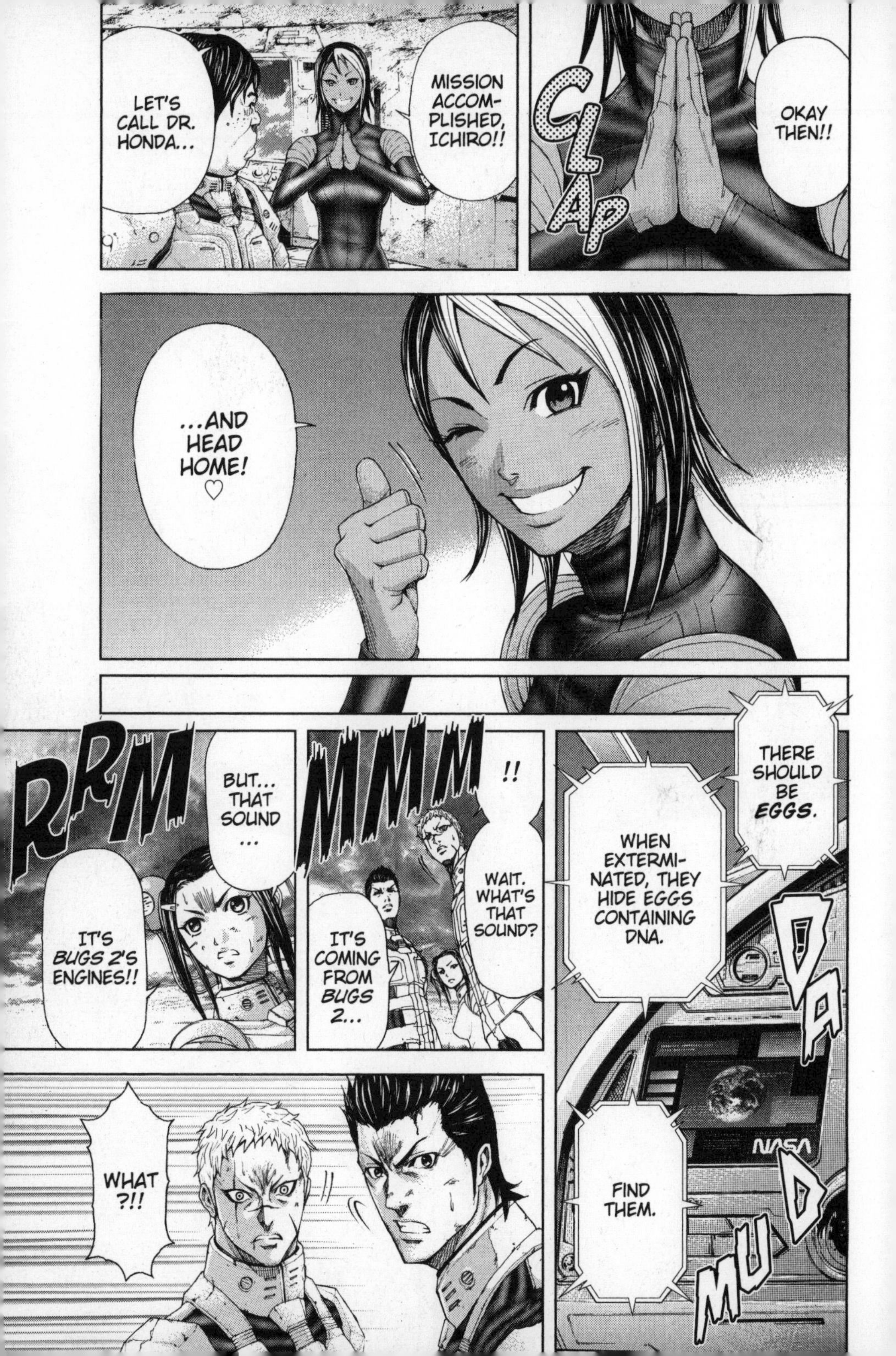
CLAP
OKAY THEN!!
MISSION ACCOM-PLISHED, ICHIRO!!
LET'S CALL DR. HONDA...
...AND HEAD HOME! ♡
THERE SHOULD BE EGGS.
WHEN EXTERMI-NATED, THEY HIDE EGGS CONTAINING DNA.
FIND THEM.
DA
MU D
RRMMMMM
!!
WAIT. WHAT'S THAT SOUND?
IT'S COMING FROM BUGS 2...
BUT... THAT SOUND...
IT'S BUGS 2'S ENGINES!!
WHAT?!!

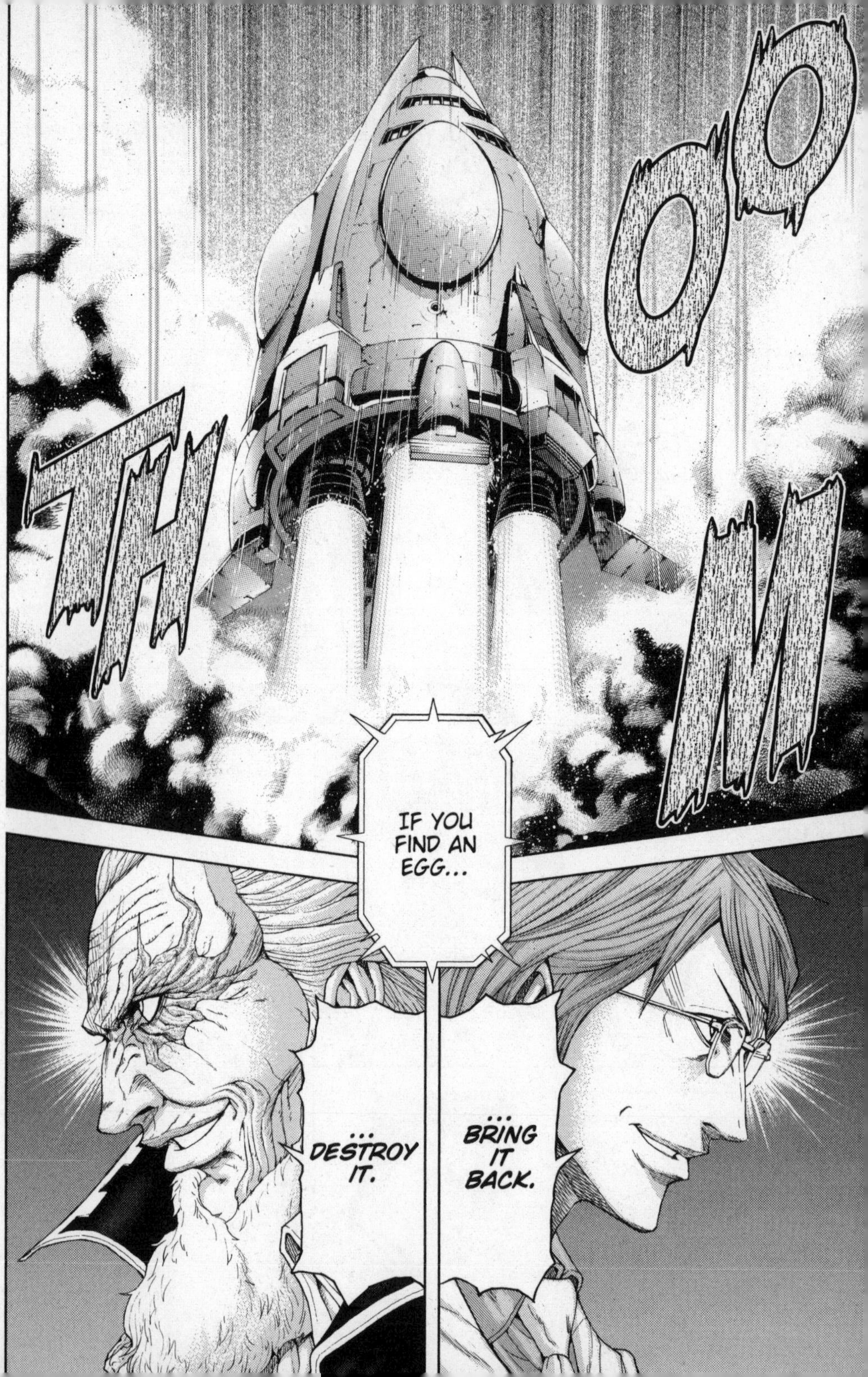
THOOOM
IF YOU FIND AN EGG...
...BRING IT BACK.
...DESTROY IT.

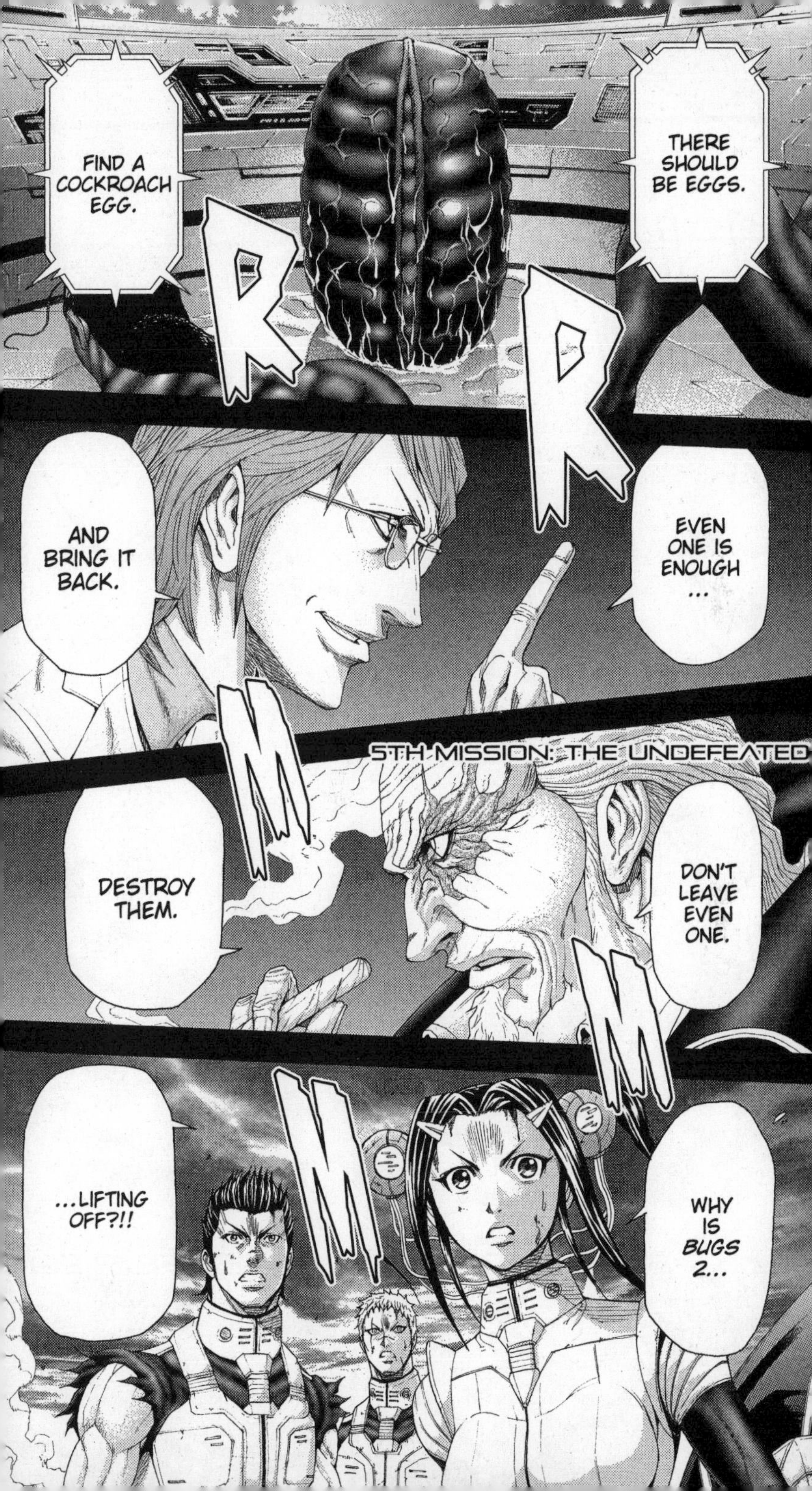
THERE SHOULD BE EGGS.
FIND A COCKROACH EGG.
RRMMM
EVEN ONE IS ENOUGH...
AND BRING IT BACK.
5TH MISSION: THE UNDEFEATED
DON'T LEAVE EVEN ONE.
DESTROY THEM.
WHY IS BUGS 2...
...LIFTING OFF?!!

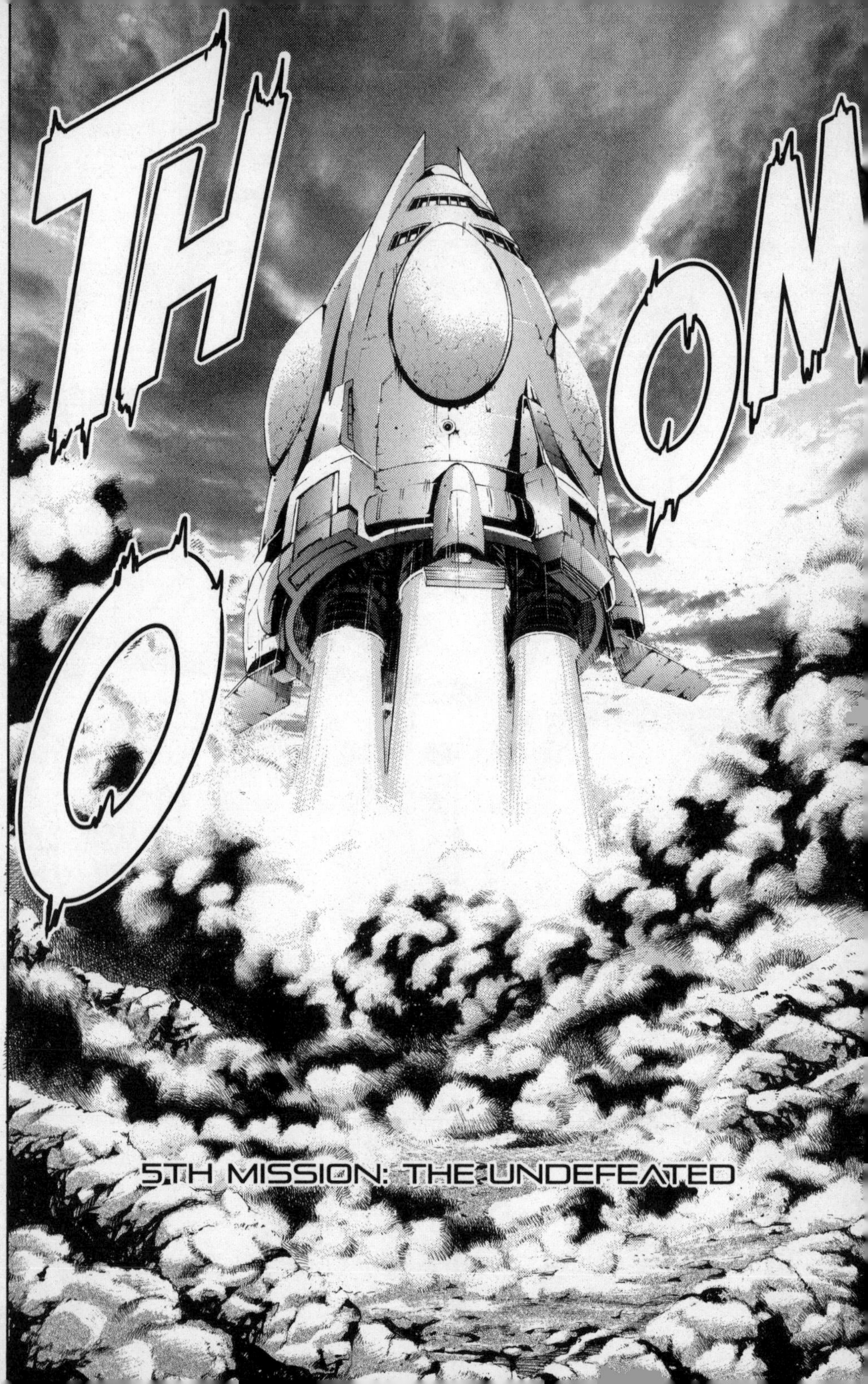
THOOM
5TH MISSION: THE UNDEFEATED

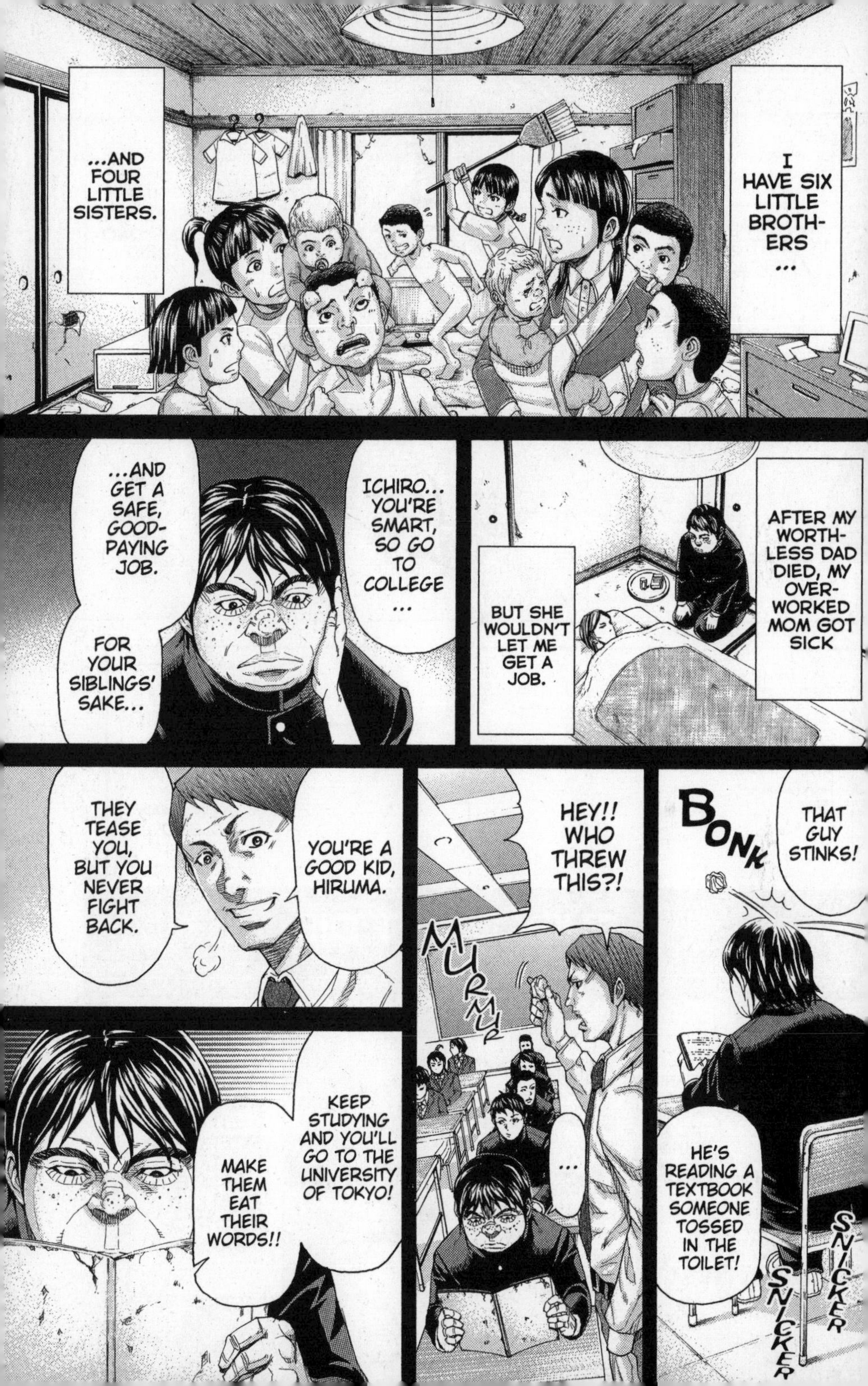
I HAVE SIX LITTLE BROTHERS...
...AND FOUR LITTLE SISTERS.
AFTER MY WORTHLESS DAD DIED, MY OVERWORKED MOM GOT SICK
BUT SHE WOULDN'T LET ME GET A JOB.
ICHIRO... YOU'RE SMART, SO GO TO COLLEGE...
...AND GET A SAFE, GOOD-PAYING JOB.
FOR YOUR SIBLINGS' SAKE...
THAT GUY STINKS!
BONK
HE'S READING A TEXTBOOK SOMEONE TOSSED IN THE TOILET!
SNICKER
SNICKER
HEY!! WHO THREW THIS?!
MURMUR
...
YOU'RE A GOOD KID, HIRUMA.
THEY TEASE YOU, BUT YOU NEVER FIGHT BACK.
KEEP STUDYING AND YOU'LL GO TO THE UNIVERSITY OF TOKYO!
MAKE THEM EAT THEIR WORDS!!

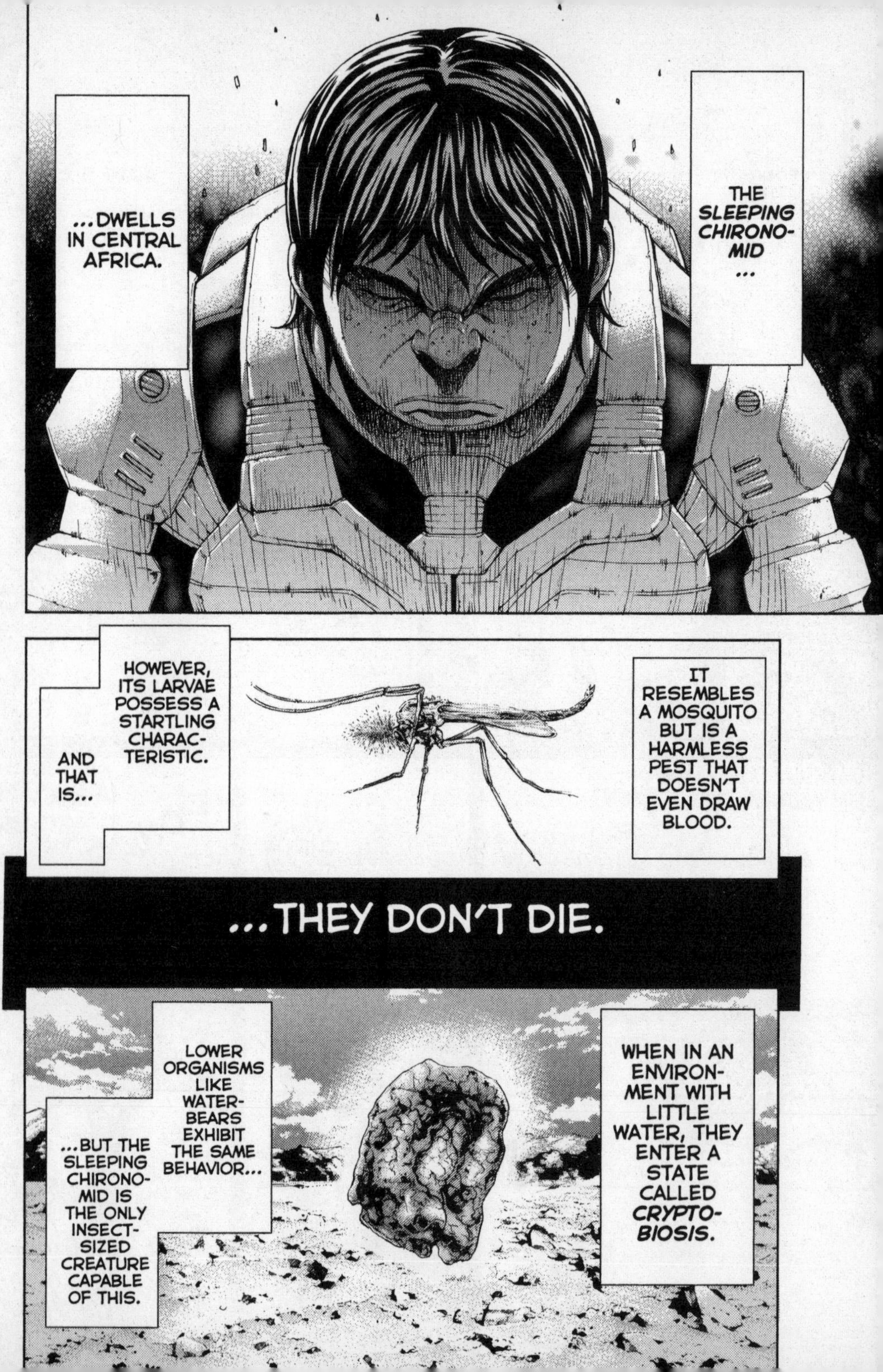
THE SLEEPING CHIRONOMID...
...DWELLS IN CENTRAL AFRICA.
IT RESEMBLES A MOSQUITO BUT IS A HARMLESS PEST THAT DOESN'T EVEN DRAW BLOOD.
HOWEVER, ITS LARVAE POSSESS A STARTLING CHARACTERISTIC.
AND THAT IS...
...THEY DON'T DIE.
WHEN IN AN ENVIRONMENT WITH LITTLE WATER, THEY ENTER A STATE CALLED CRYPTOBIOSIS.
LOWER ORGANISMS LIKE WATERBEARS EXHIBIT THE SAME BEHAVIOR...
...BUT THE SLEEPING CHIRONOMID IS THE ONLY INSECT-SIZED CREATURE CAPABLE OF THIS.

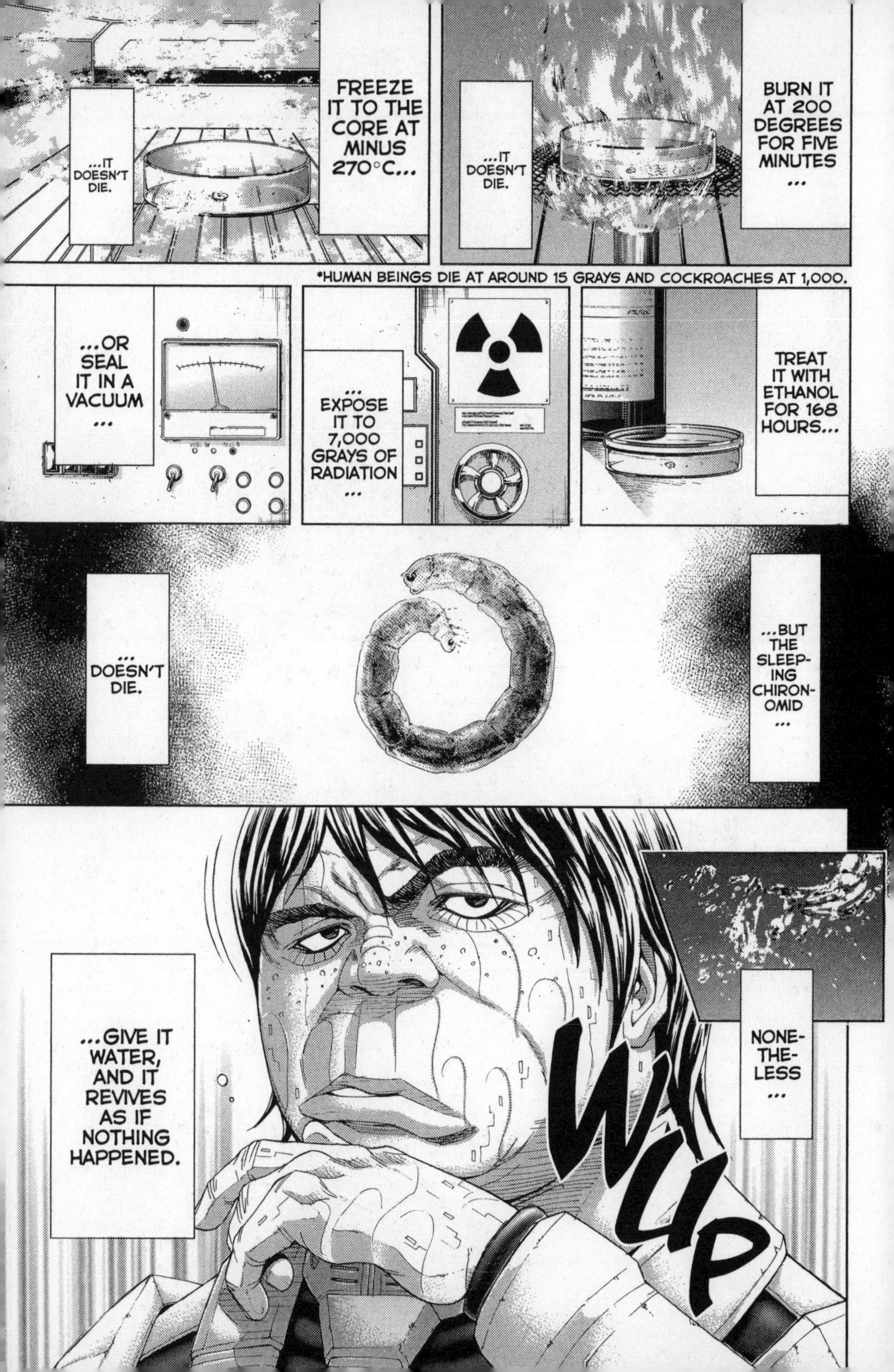
BURN IT AT 200 DEGREES FOR FIVE MINUTES ...
...IT DOESN'T DIE.
FREEZE IT TO THE CORE AT MINUS 270°C...
...IT DOESN'T DIE.
*HUMAN BEINGS DIE AT AROUND 15 GRAYS AND COCKROACHES AT 1,000.
TREAT IT WITH ETHANOL FOR 168 HOURS...
... EXPOSE IT TO 7,000 GRAYS OF RADIATION ...
...OR SEAL IT IN A VACUUM ...
...BUT THE SLEEP-ING CHIRON-OMID ...
... DOESN'T DIE.
NONE-THE-LESS ...
WUP
...GIVE IT WATER, AND IT REVIVES AS IF NOTHING HAPPENED.

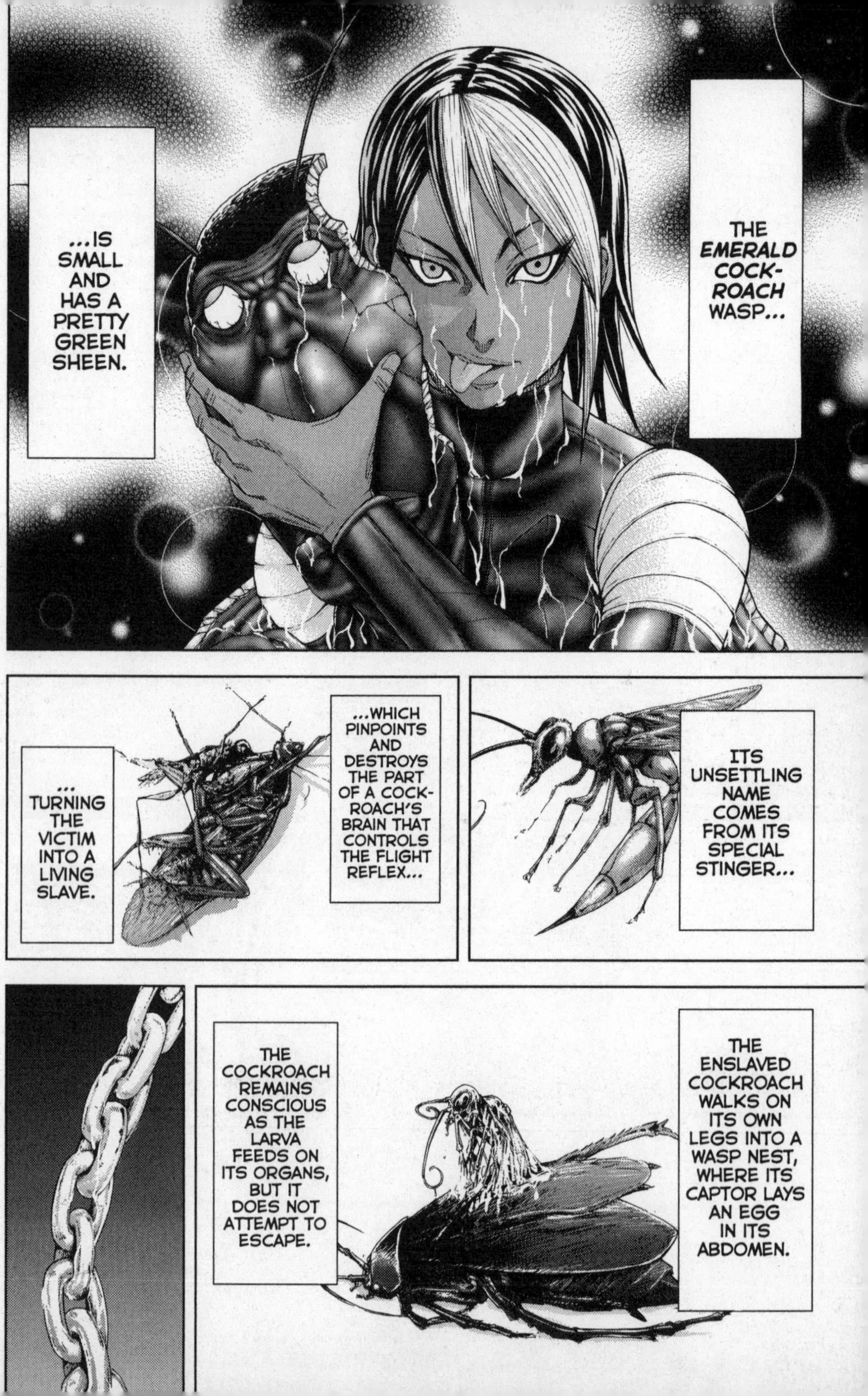
THE *EMERALD COCKROACH* WASP...
...IS SMALL AND HAS A PRETTY GREEN SHEEN.
ITS UNSETTLING NAME COMES FROM ITS SPECIAL STINGER...
...WHICH PINPOINTS AND DESTROYS THE PART OF A COCKROACH'S BRAIN THAT CONTROLS THE FLIGHT REFLEX...
...TURNING THE VICTIM INTO A LIVING SLAVE.
THE ENSLAVED COCKROACH WALKS ON ITS OWN LEGS INTO A WASP NEST, WHERE ITS CAPTOR LAYS AN EGG IN ITS ABDOMEN.
THE COCKROACH REMAINS CONSCIOUS AS THE LARVA FEEDS ON ITS ORGANS, BUT IT DOES NOT ATTEMPT TO ESCAPE.

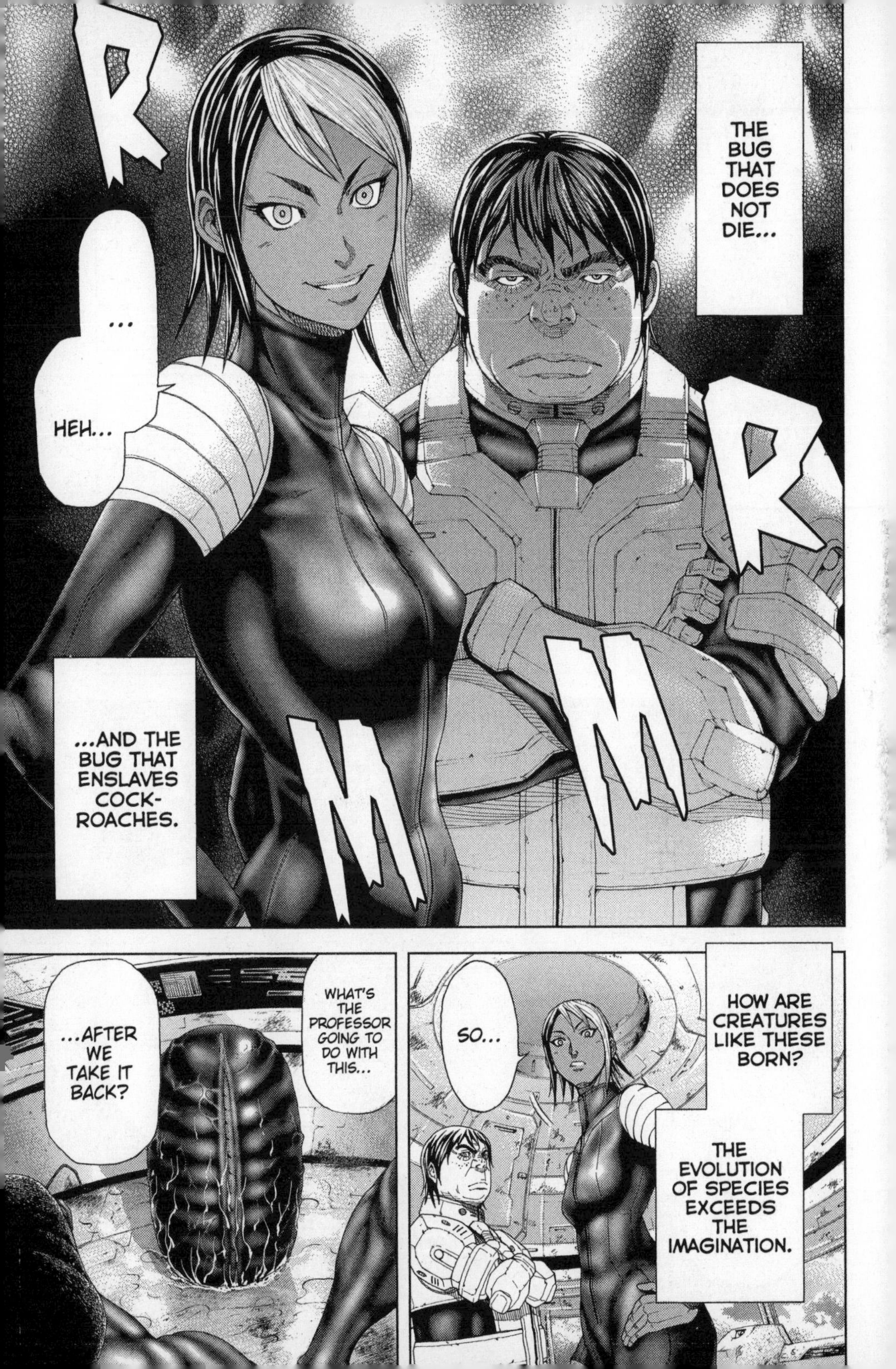
THE BUG THAT DOES NOT DIE...
RRMM
...
HEH...
...AND THE BUG THAT ENSLAVES COCK-ROACHES.
HOW ARE CREATURES LIKE THESE BORN?
THE EVOLUTION OF SPECIES EXCEEDS THE IMAGINATION.
SO...
WHAT'S THE PROFESSOR GOING TO DO WITH THIS...
...AFTER WE TAKE IT BACK?

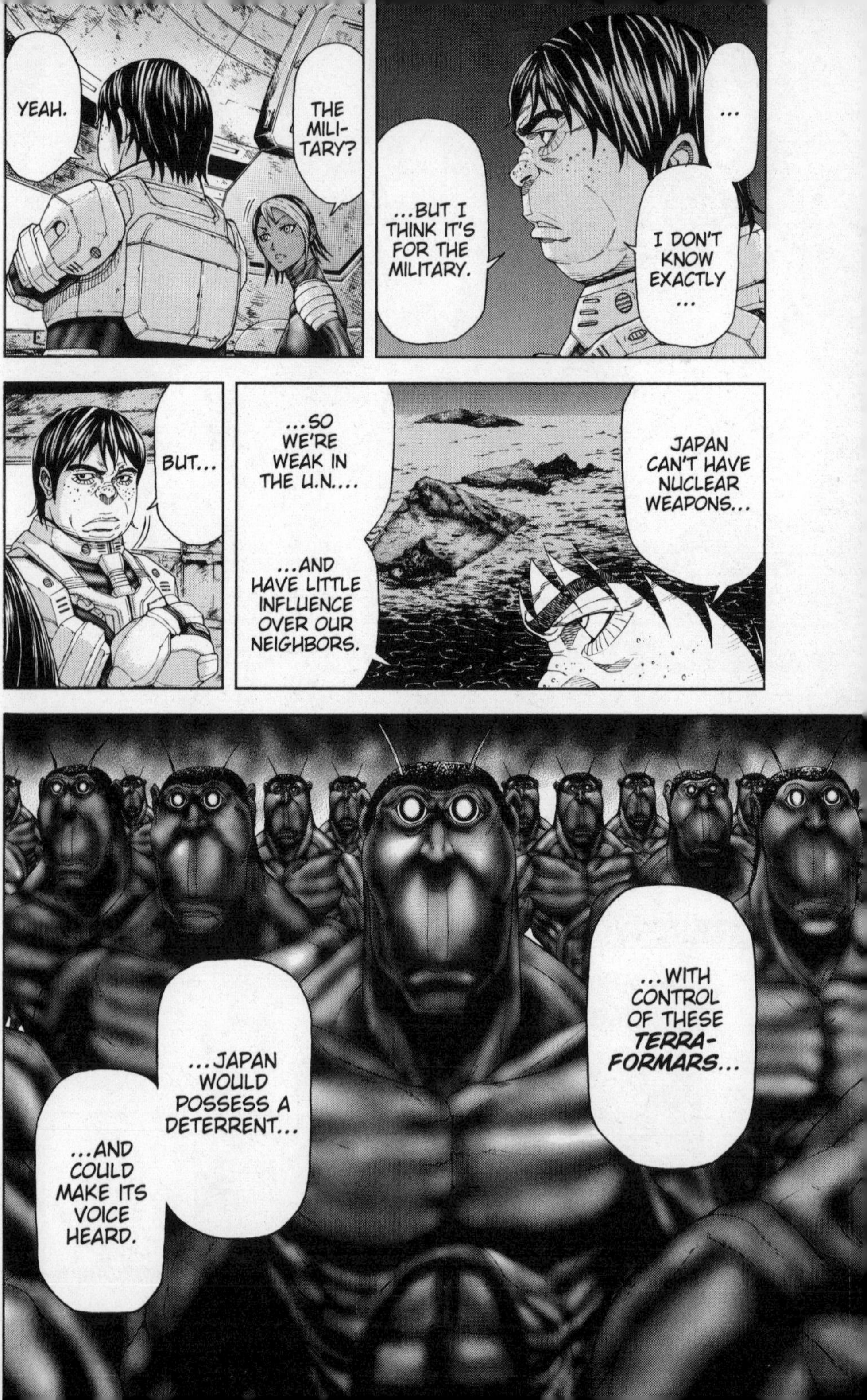
...
I DON'T KNOW EXACTLY ...
...BUT I THINK IT'S FOR THE MILITARY.
THE MILI-TARY?
YEAH.
JAPAN CAN'T HAVE NUCLEAR WEAPONS...
...SO WE'RE WEAK IN THE U.N....
...AND HAVE LITTLE INFLUENCE OVER OUR NEIGHBORS.
BUT...
...WITH CONTROL OF THESE *TERRA-FORMARS*...
...JAPAN WOULD POSSESS A DETERRENT...
...AND COULD MAKE ITS VOICE HEARD.

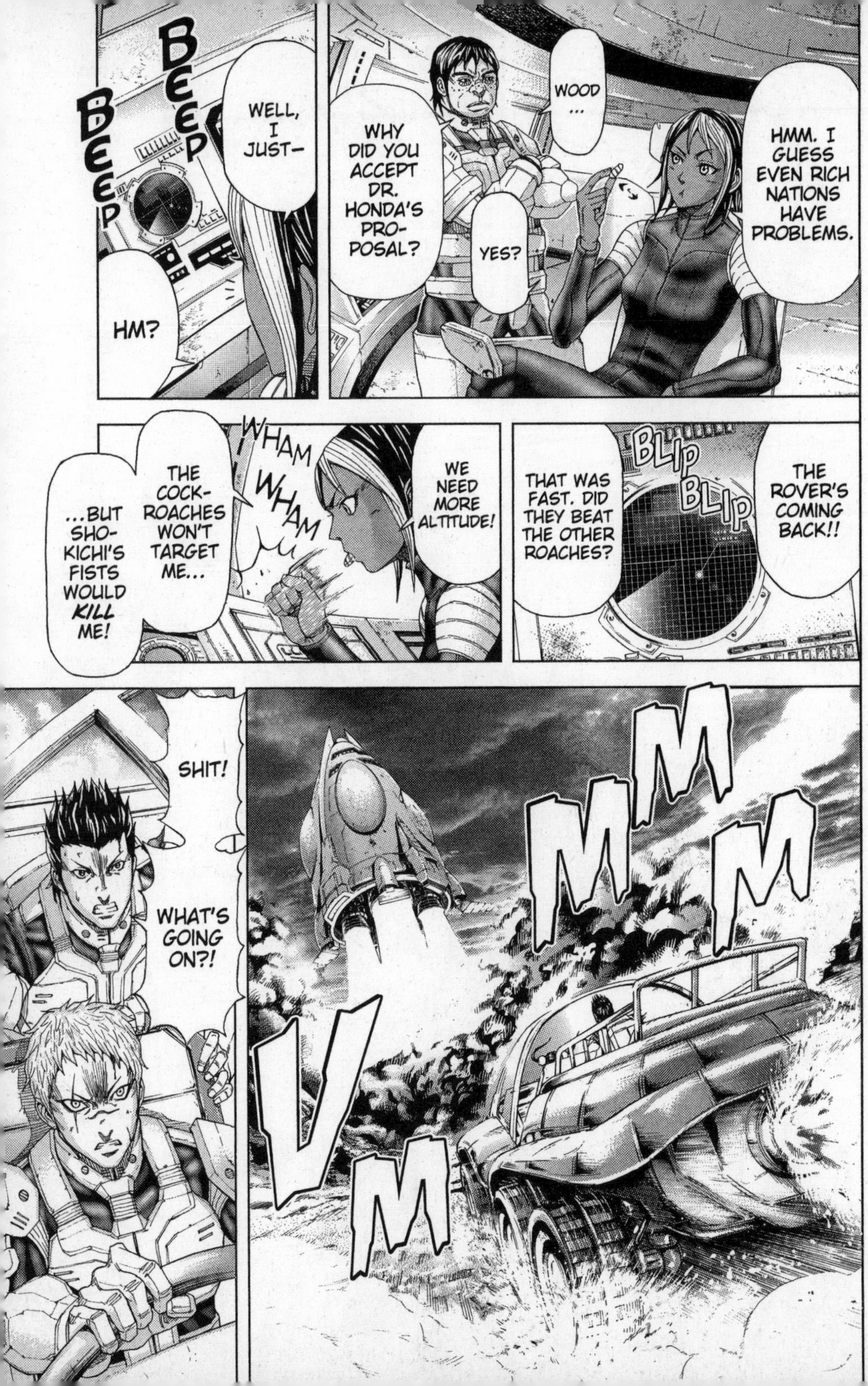
HMM. I GUESS EVEN RICH NATIONS HAVE PROBLEMS.
WOOD ...
YES?
WHY DID YOU ACCEPT DR. HONDA'S PRO-POSAL?
WELL, I JUST—
BEEP BEEP
BEEP BEEP
HM?
THE ROVER'S COMING BACK!!
BLIP BLIP
THAT WAS FAST. DID THEY BEAT THE OTHER ROACHES?
WE NEED MORE ALTITUDE!
WHAM WHAM
THE COCK-ROACHES WON'T TARGET ME...
...BUT SHO-KICHI'S FISTS WOULD *KILL* ME!
MMMM
VM
SHIT!
WHAT'S GOING ON?!

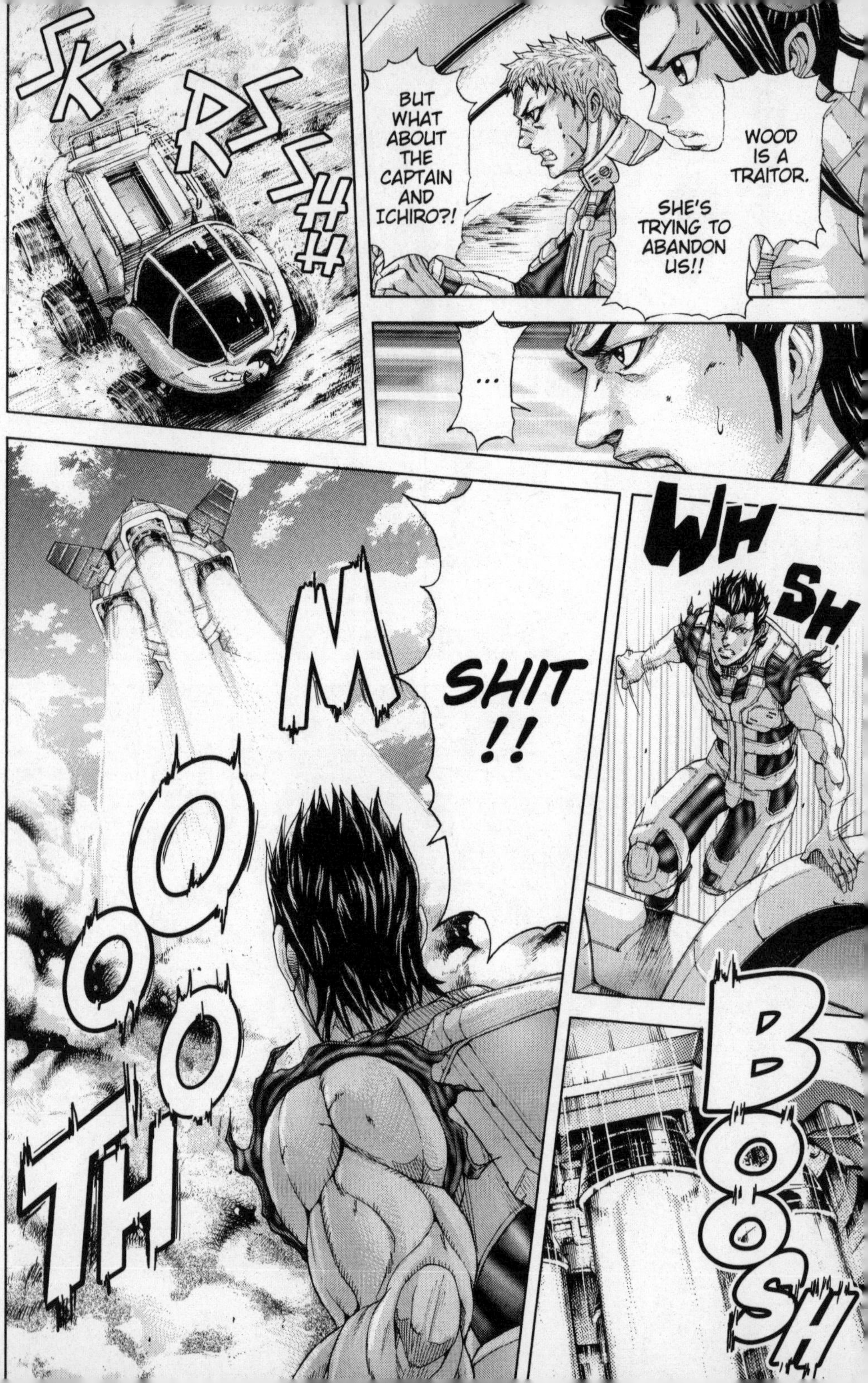
WOOD IS A TRAITOR.
SHE'S TRYING TO ABANDON US!!
BUT WHAT ABOUT THE CAPTAIN AND ICHIRO?!
...
SKRSSHH
WHSH
BOOSH
MOOOTH
SHIT!!

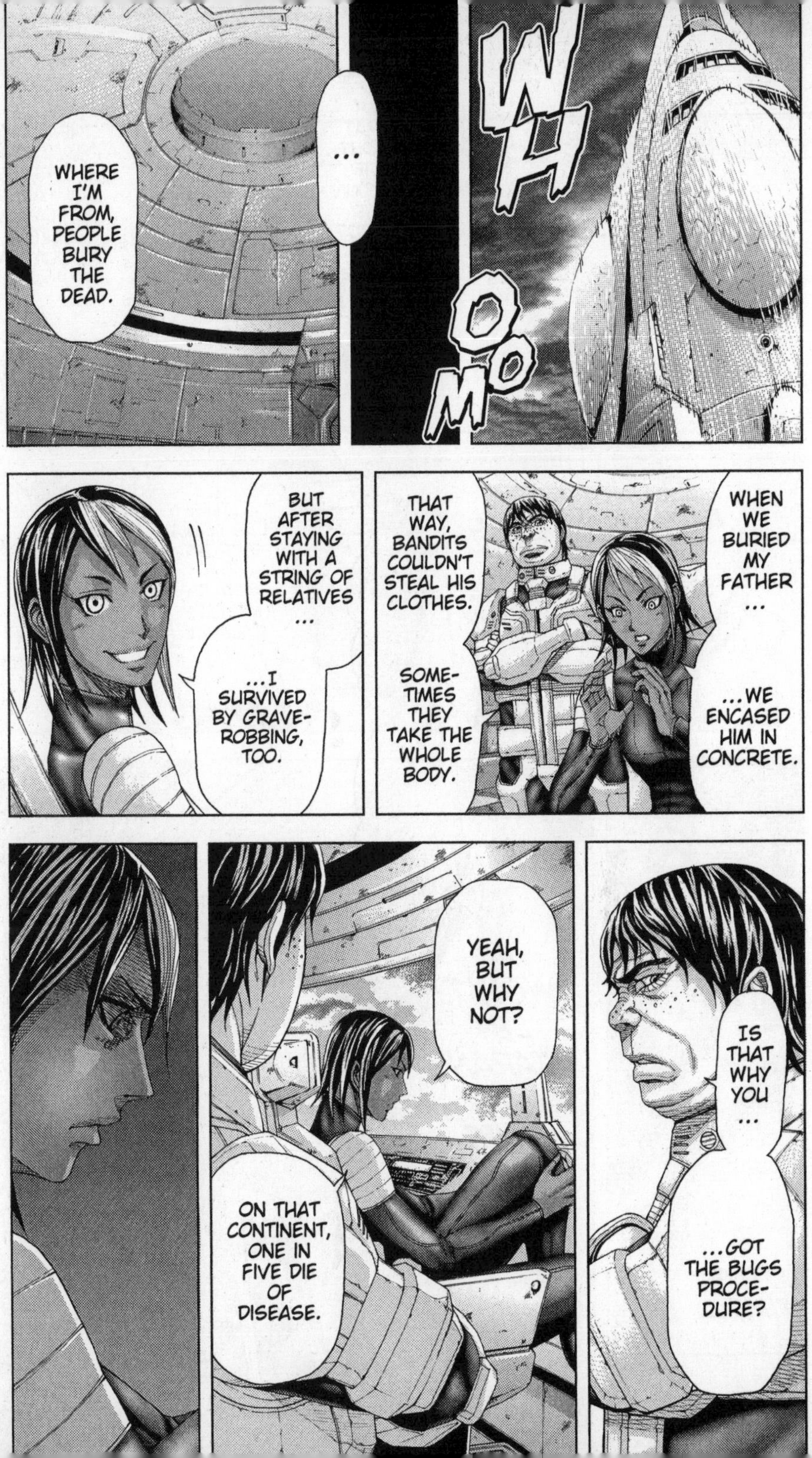
WHOOM
...
WHERE I'M FROM, PEOPLE BURY THE DEAD.
WHEN WE BURIED MY FATHER...
...WE ENCASED HIM IN CONCRETE.
THAT WAY, BANDITS COULDN'T STEAL HIS CLOTHES.
SOMETIMES THEY TAKE THE WHOLE BODY.
BUT AFTER STAYING WITH A STRING OF RELATIVES...
...I SURVIVED BY GRAVE-ROBBING, TOO.
IS THAT WHY YOU...
...GOT THE BUGS PROCEDURE?
YEAH, BUT WHY NOT?
ON THAT CONTINENT, ONE IN FIVE DIE OF DISEASE.

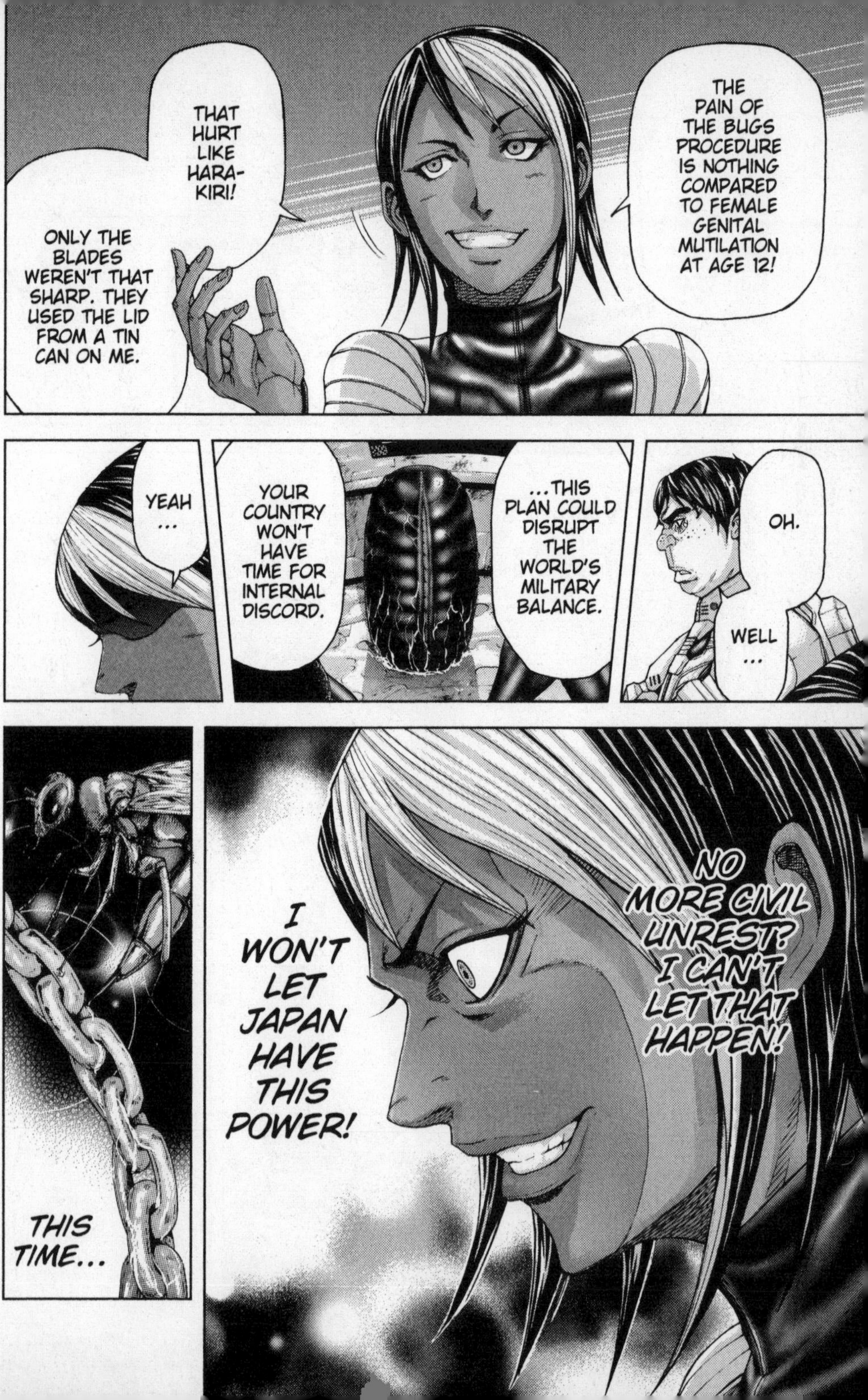
THE PAIN OF THE BUGS PROCEDURE IS NOTHING COMPARED TO FEMALE GENITAL MUTILATION AT AGE 12!
THAT HURT LIKE HARA-KIRI!
ONLY THE BLADES WEREN'T THAT SHARP. THEY USED THE LID FROM A TIN CAN ON ME.
OH.
WELL...
...THIS PLAN COULD DISRUPT THE WORLD'S MILITARY BALANCE.
YOUR COUNTRY WON'T HAVE TIME FOR INTERNAL DISCORD.
YEAH...
NO MORE CIVIL UNREST? I CAN'T LET THAT HAPPEN!
I WON'T LET JAPAN HAVE THIS POWER!
THIS TIME...

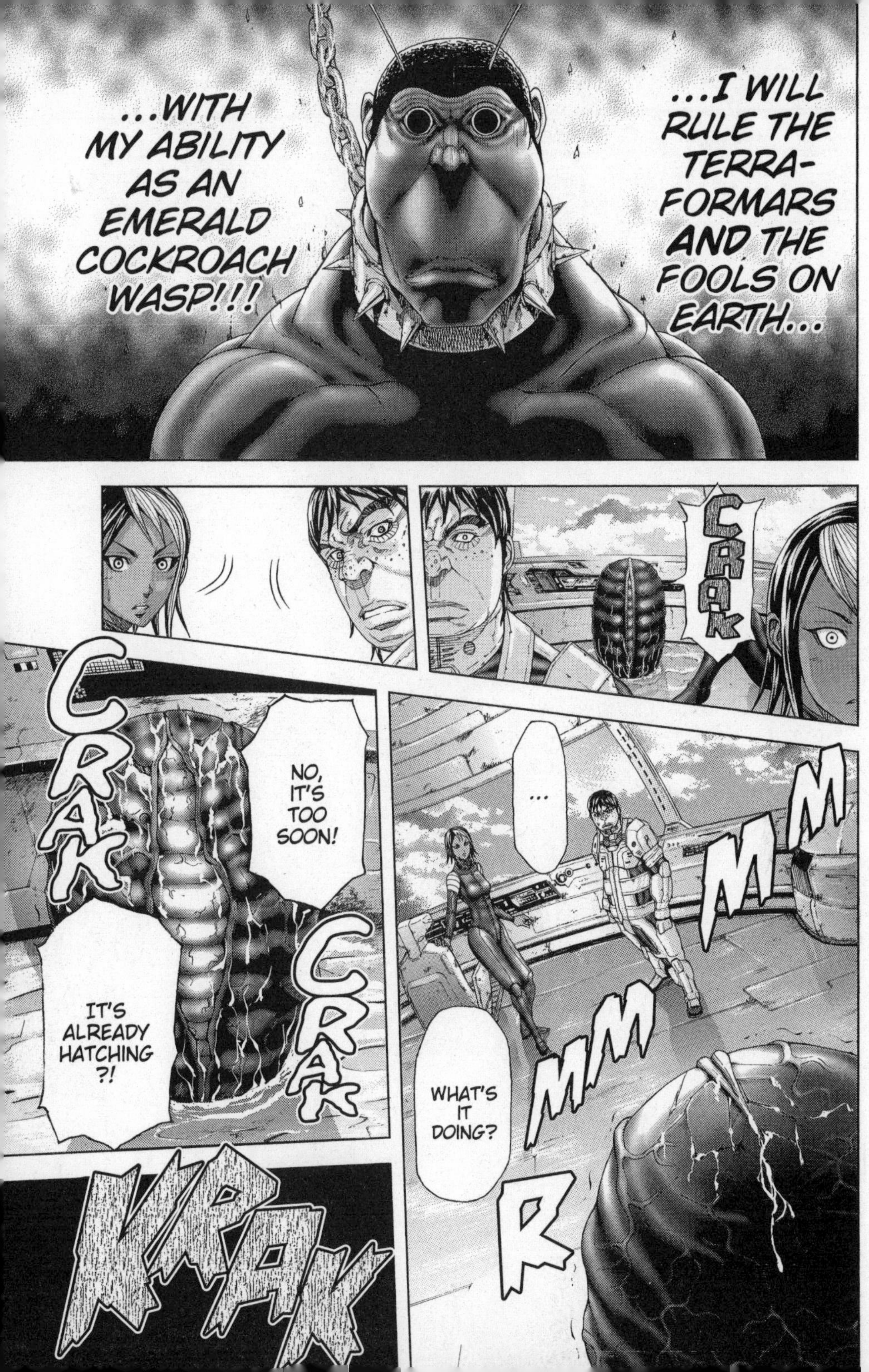
...I WILL RULE THE TERRA-FORMARS AND THE FOOLS ON EARTH...
...WITH MY ABILITY AS AN EMERALD COCKROACH WASP!!!
CRAK
...
MMMMMR
WHAT'S IT DOING?
CRAK
NO, IT'S TOO SOON!
CRAK
IT'S ALREADY HATCHING?!
VRAK

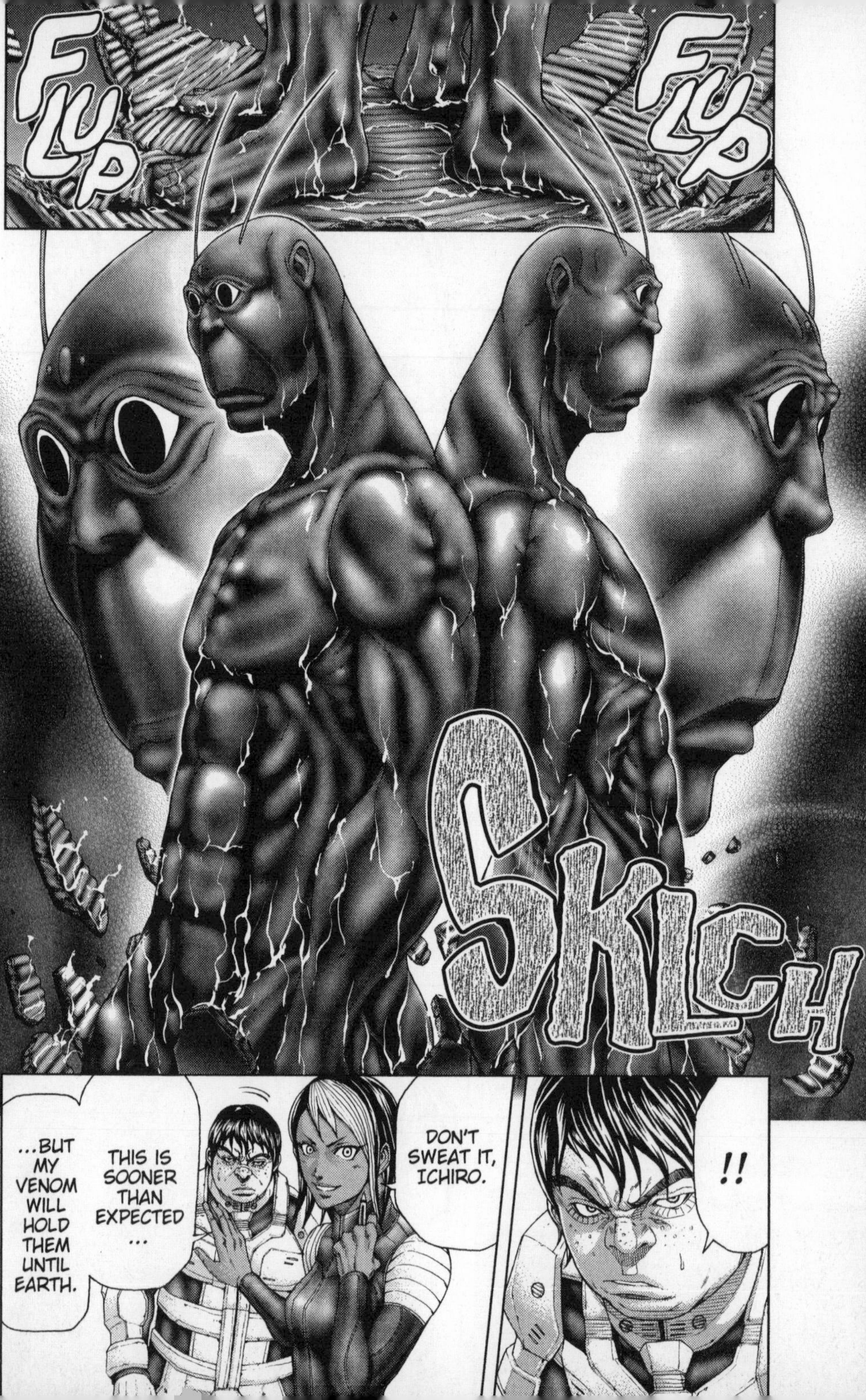
FLUP
FLUP
SKLCH
!!
DON'T SWEAT IT, ICHIRO.
THIS IS SOONER THAN EXPECTED ...
...BUT MY VENOM WILL HOLD THEM UNTIL EARTH.

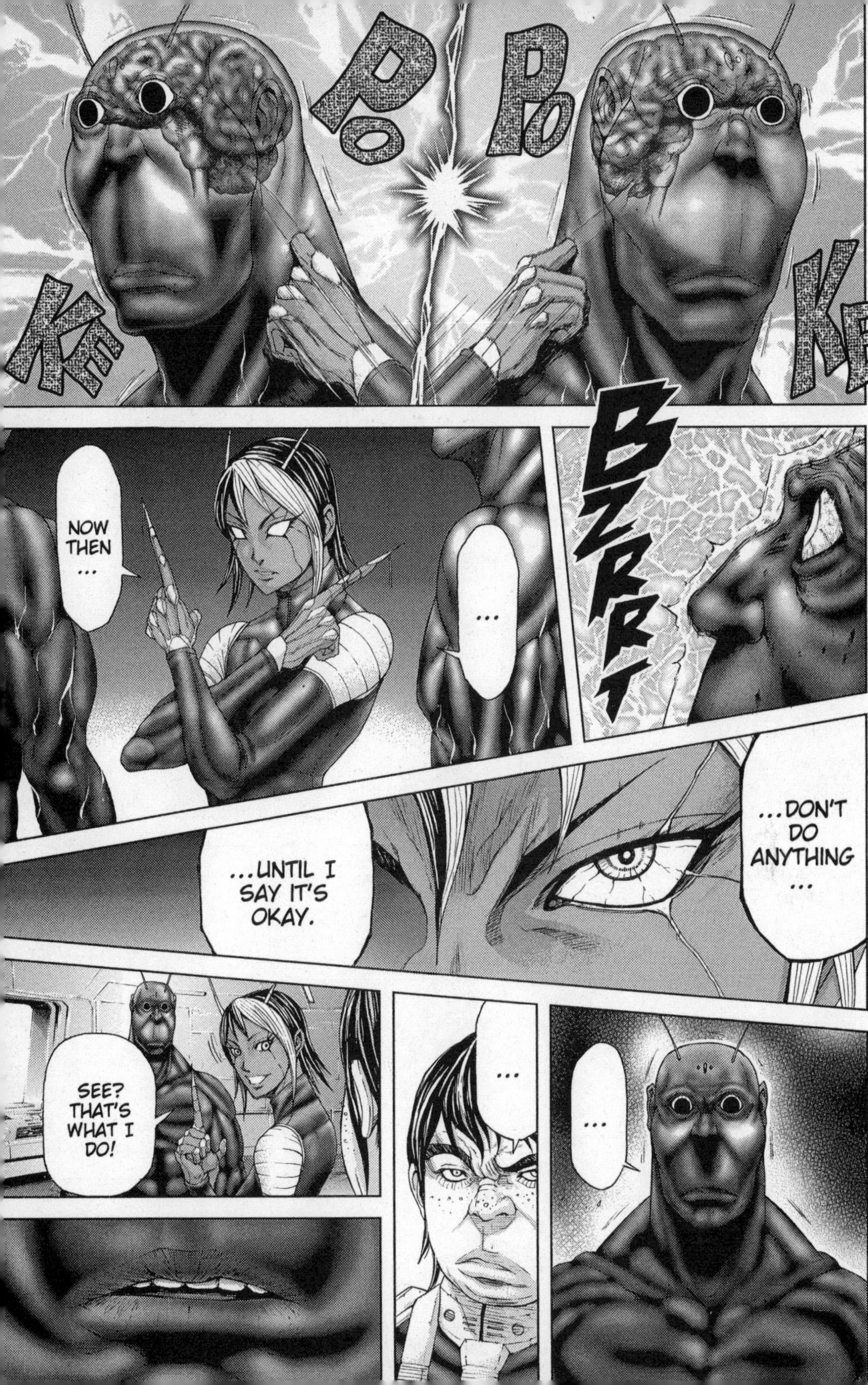
PO
KE
PO
KE
BZZRT
...
NOW THEN ...
...DON'T DO ANYTHING ...
...UNTIL I SAY IT'S OKAY.
...
...
...
SEE? THAT'S WHAT I DO!

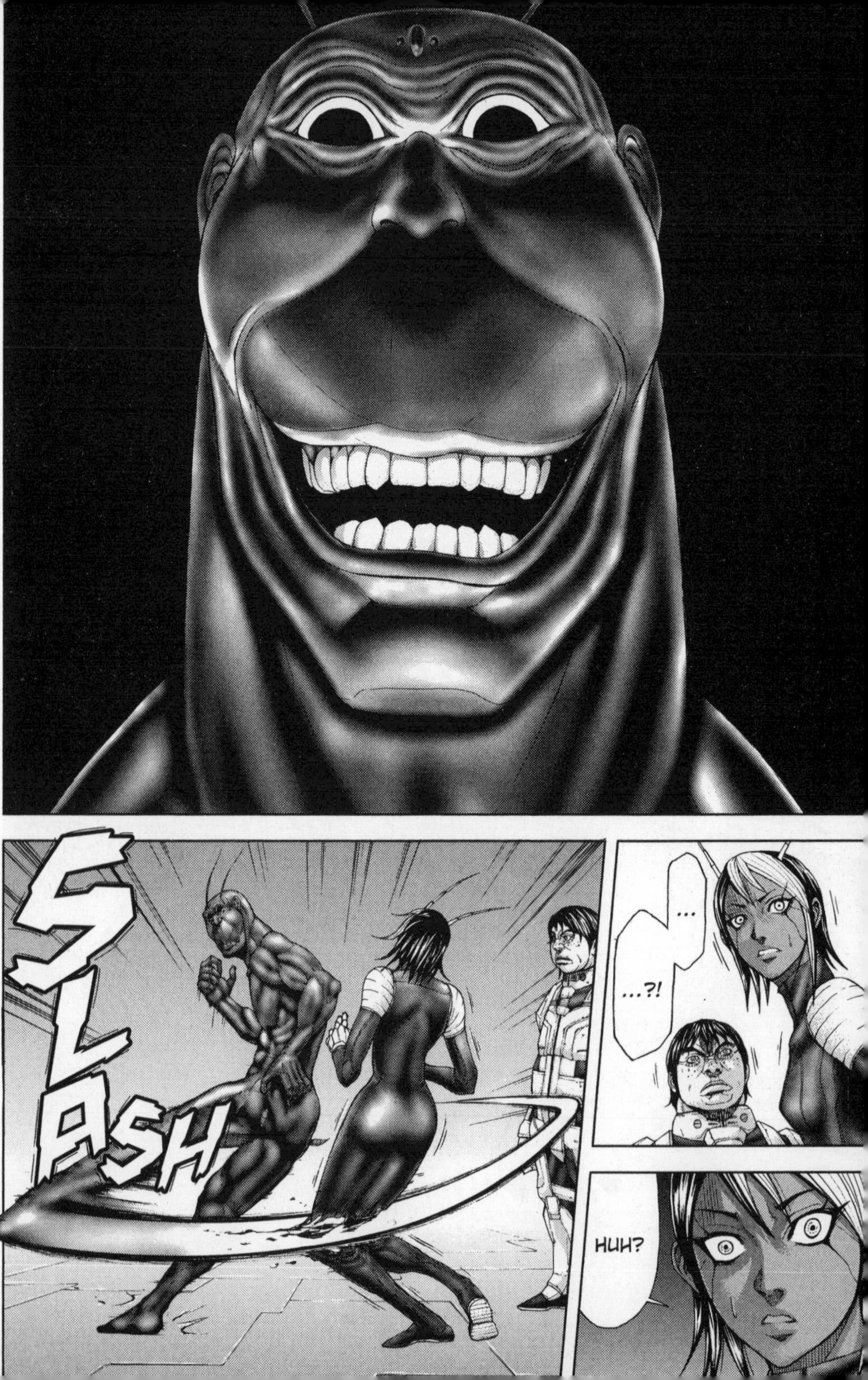
...
...?!
HUH?
SLASH

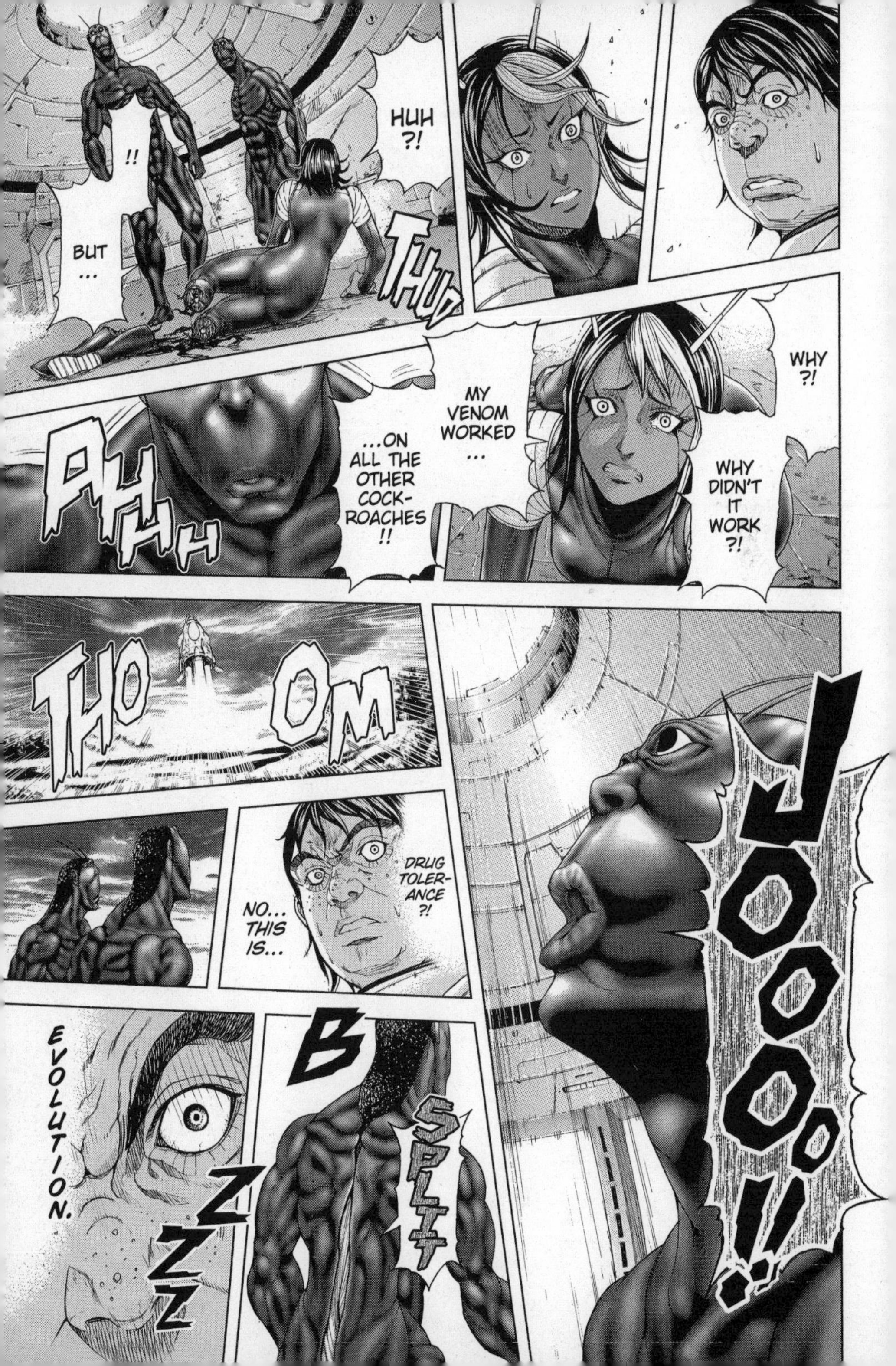
HUH ?!
!!
BUT ...
THUD
WHY ?!
WHY DIDN'T IT WORK ?!
MY VENOM WORKED ...
...ON ALL THE OTHER COCK-ROACHES !!
PHHH
JOOOO!!
THOOM
DRUG TOLER-ANCE ?!
NO... THIS IS...
B
SPLIT
ZZZ
EVOLUTION.

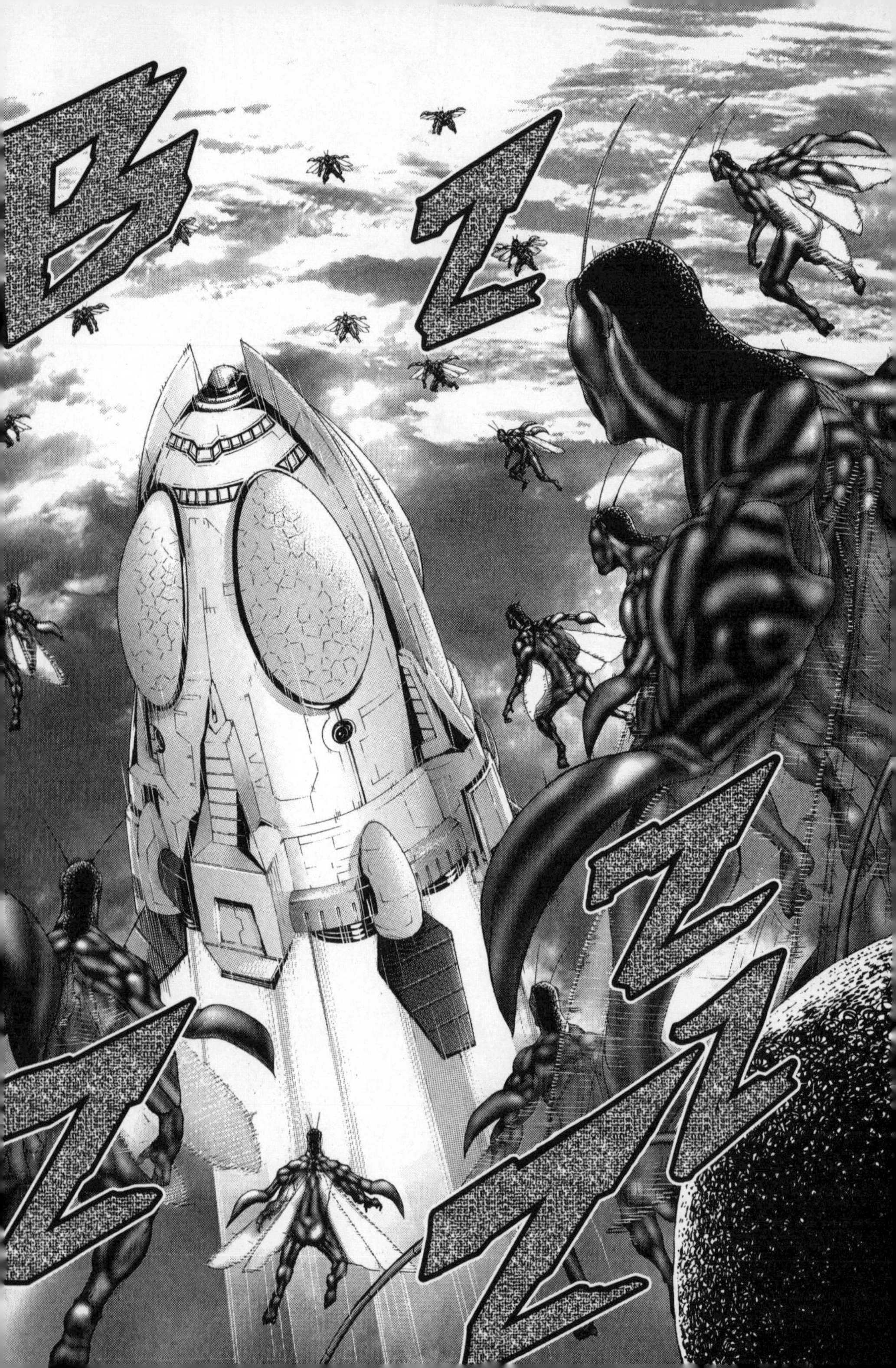
BZ
ZZZ
ZZ

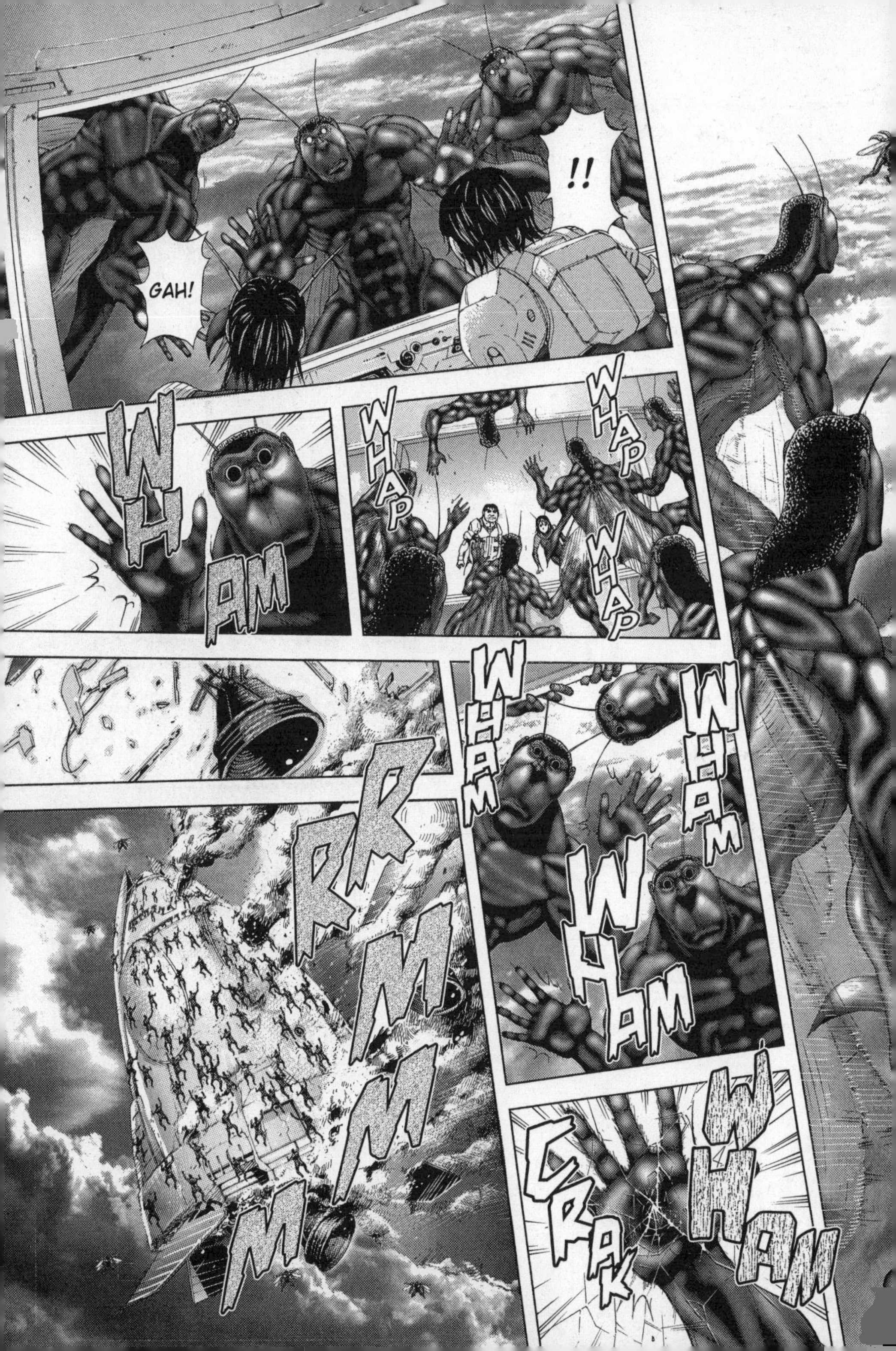
!!
GAH!
WHAP
WHAP
WHAP
WHAM
WHAM
WHAM
WHAM
RRMMM
WHAM
CRAK

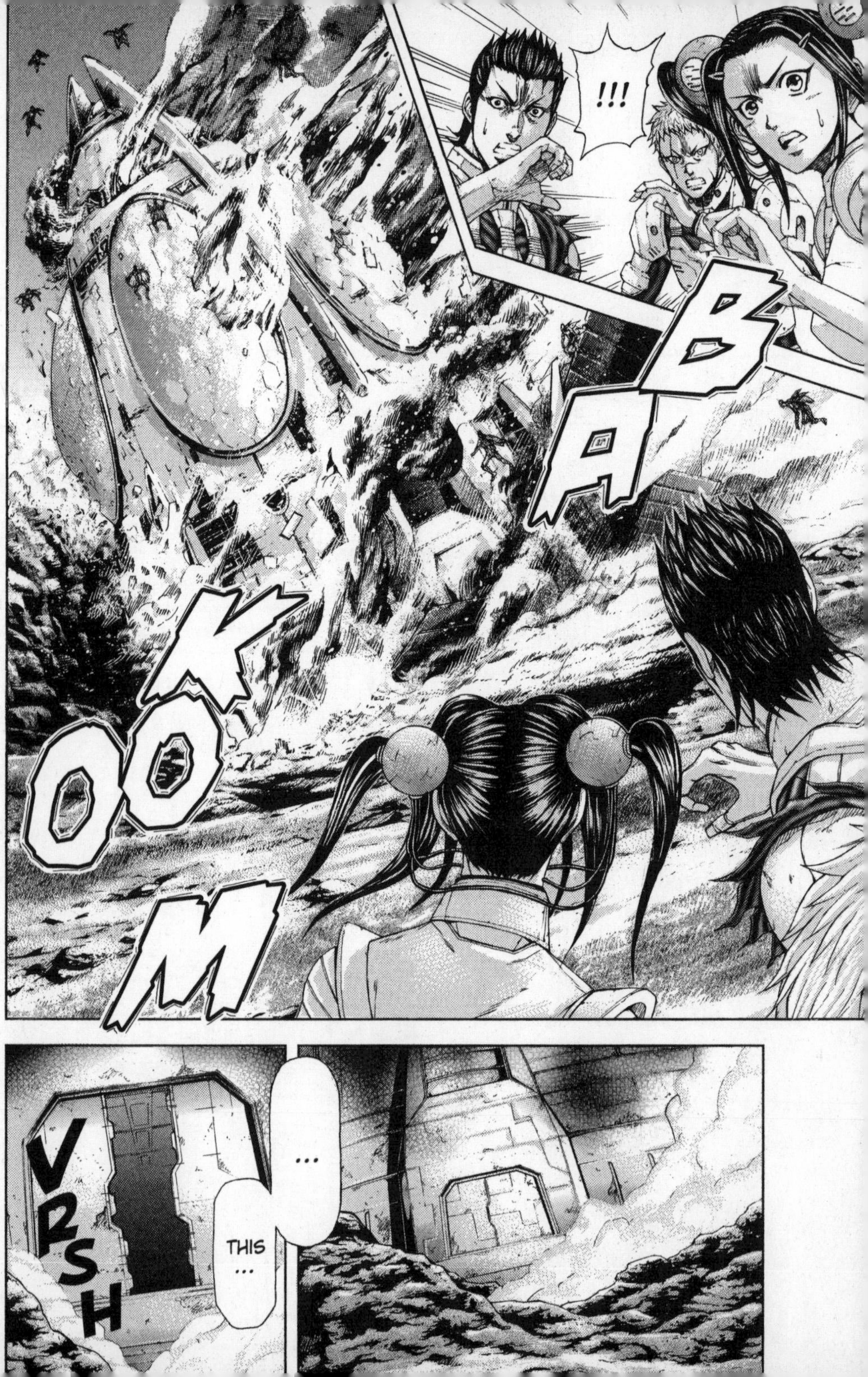
!!!
BAM
KOOOM
...
THIS ...
VRSH

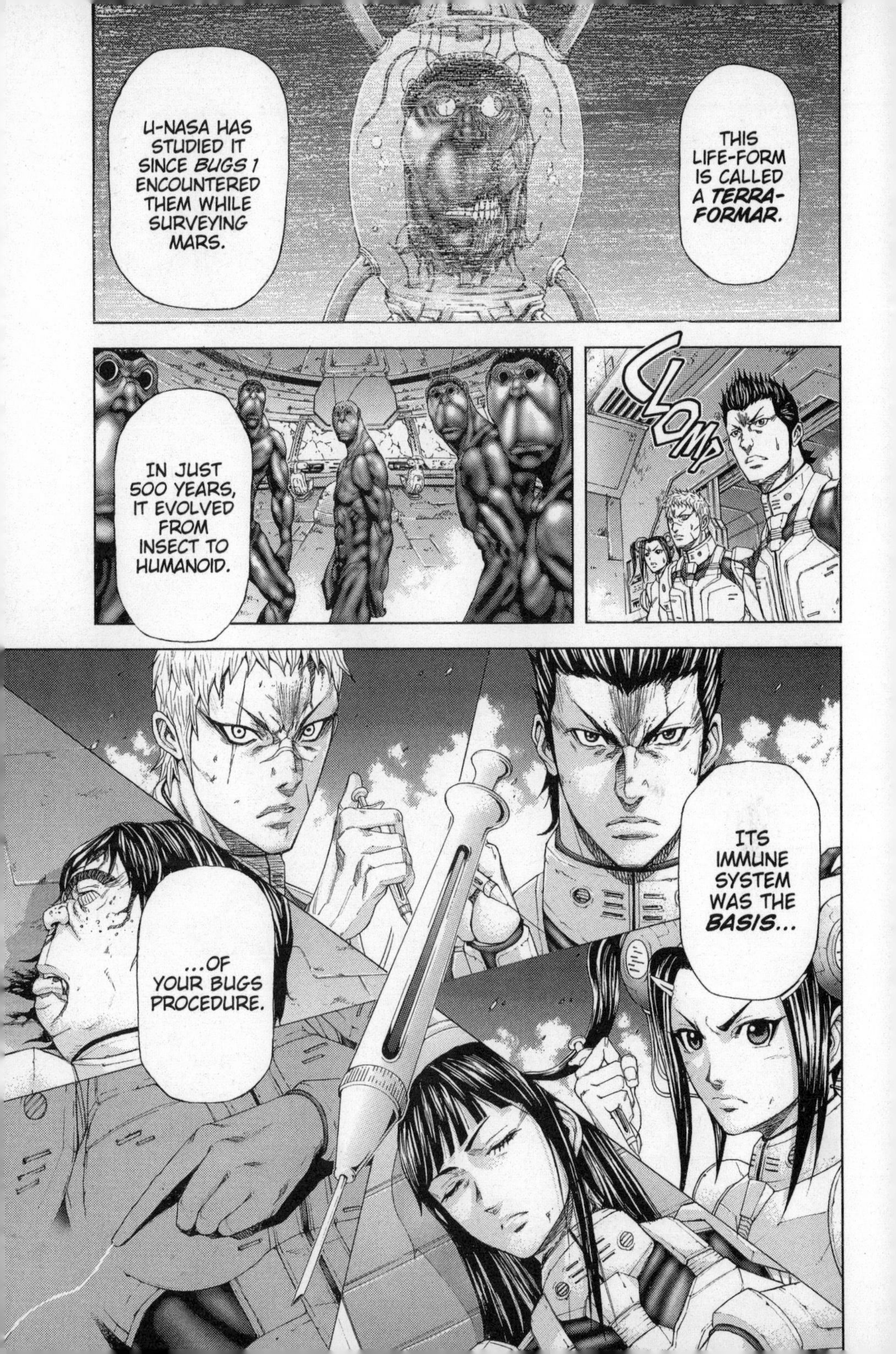
THIS LIFE-FORM IS CALLED A TERRA-FORMAR.
U-NASA HAS STUDIED IT SINCE BUGS 1 ENCOUNTERED THEM WHILE SURVEYING MARS.
CLOMP
IN JUST 500 YEARS, IT EVOLVED FROM INSECT TO HUMANOID.
ITS IMMUNE SYSTEM WAS THE BASIS...
...OF YOUR BUGS PROCEDURE.

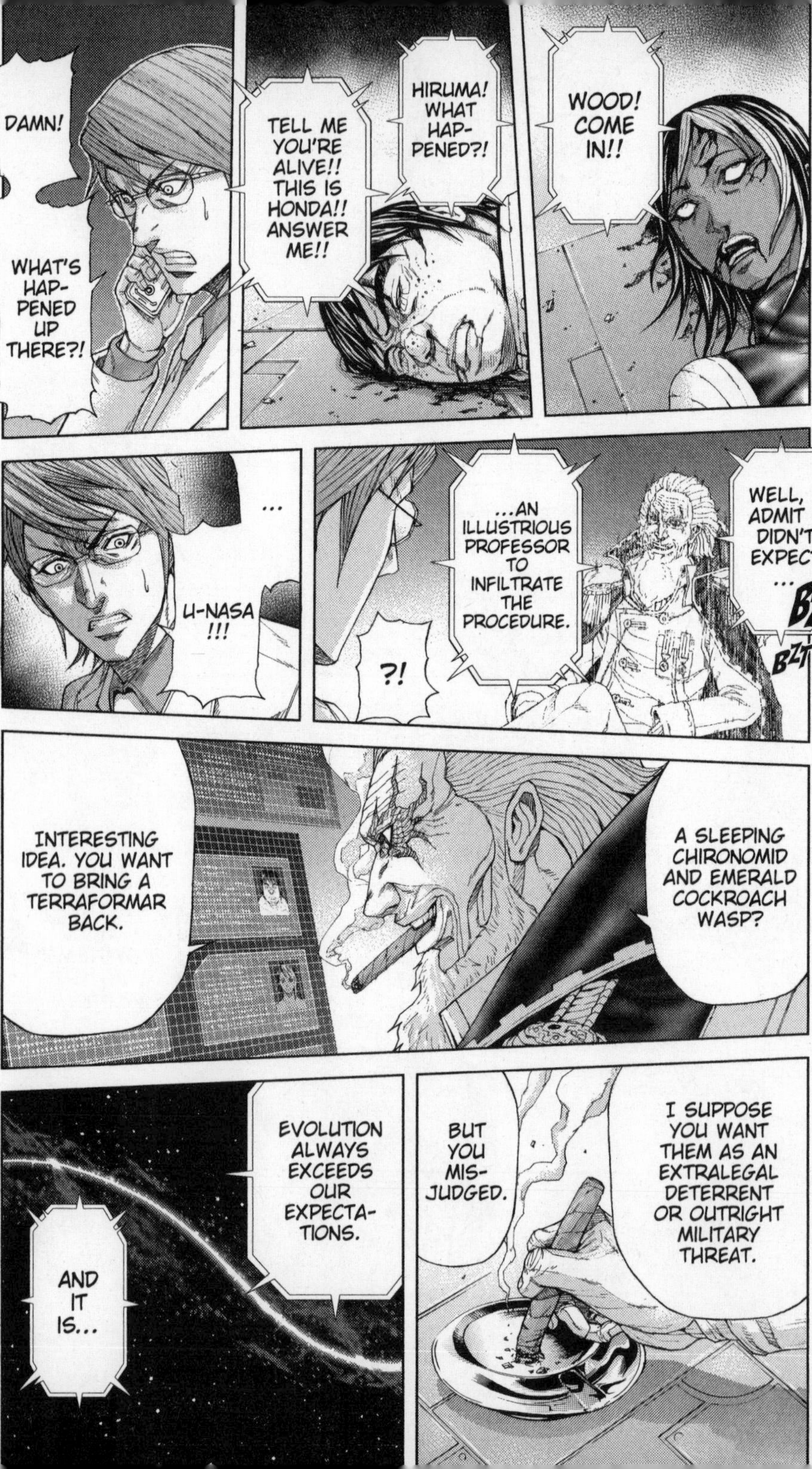
WOOD! COME IN!!
HIRUMA! WHAT HAP-PENED?!
TELL ME YOU'RE ALIVE!! THIS IS HONDA!! ANSWER ME!!
DAMN!
WHAT'S HAP-PENED UP THERE?!
WELL, I ADMIT I DIDN'T EXPECT ...
BZT
BZT
...AN ILLUSTRIOUS PROFESSOR TO INFILTRATE THE PROCEDURE.
?!
...
U-NASA !!!
A SLEEPING CHIRONOMID AND EMERALD COCKROACH WASP?
INTERESTING IDEA. YOU WANT TO BRING A TERRAFORMAR BACK.
I SUPPOSE YOU WANT THEM AS AN EXTRALEGAL DETERRENT OR OUTRIGHT MILITARY THREAT.
BUT YOU MIS-JUDGED.
EVOLUTION ALWAYS EXCEEDS OUR EXPECTA-TIONS.
AND IT IS...

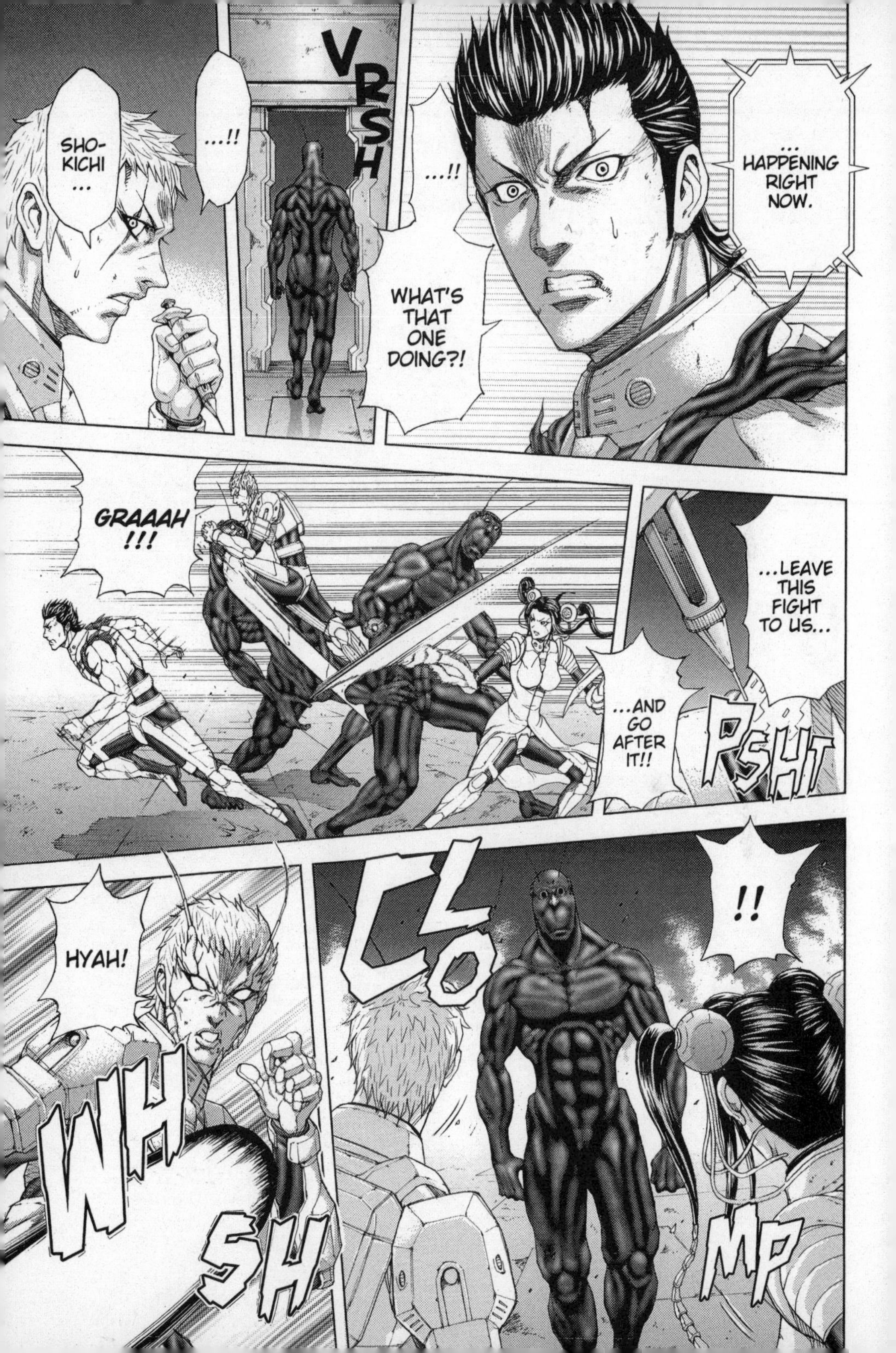

...HAPPENING RIGHT NOW.
...!!
WHAT'S THAT ONE DOING?!
VRSH
...!!
SHO-KICHI...
...LEAVE THIS FIGHT TO US...
...AND GO AFTER IT!!
PSHT
GRAAAH!!!
!!
CLO
MP
HYAH!
WHSH

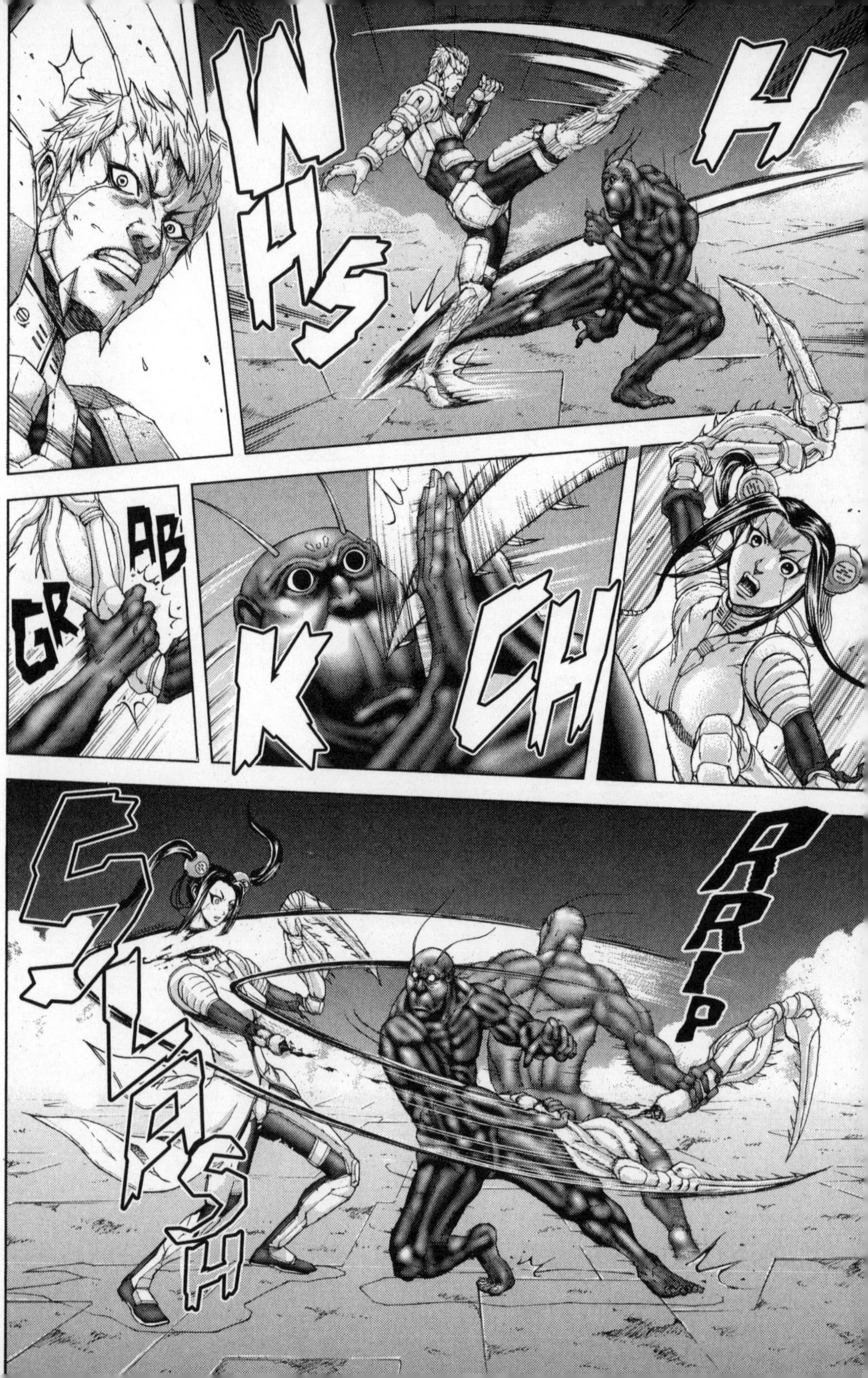
H
WHS
KCH
GRAB
RRIP
SLASH

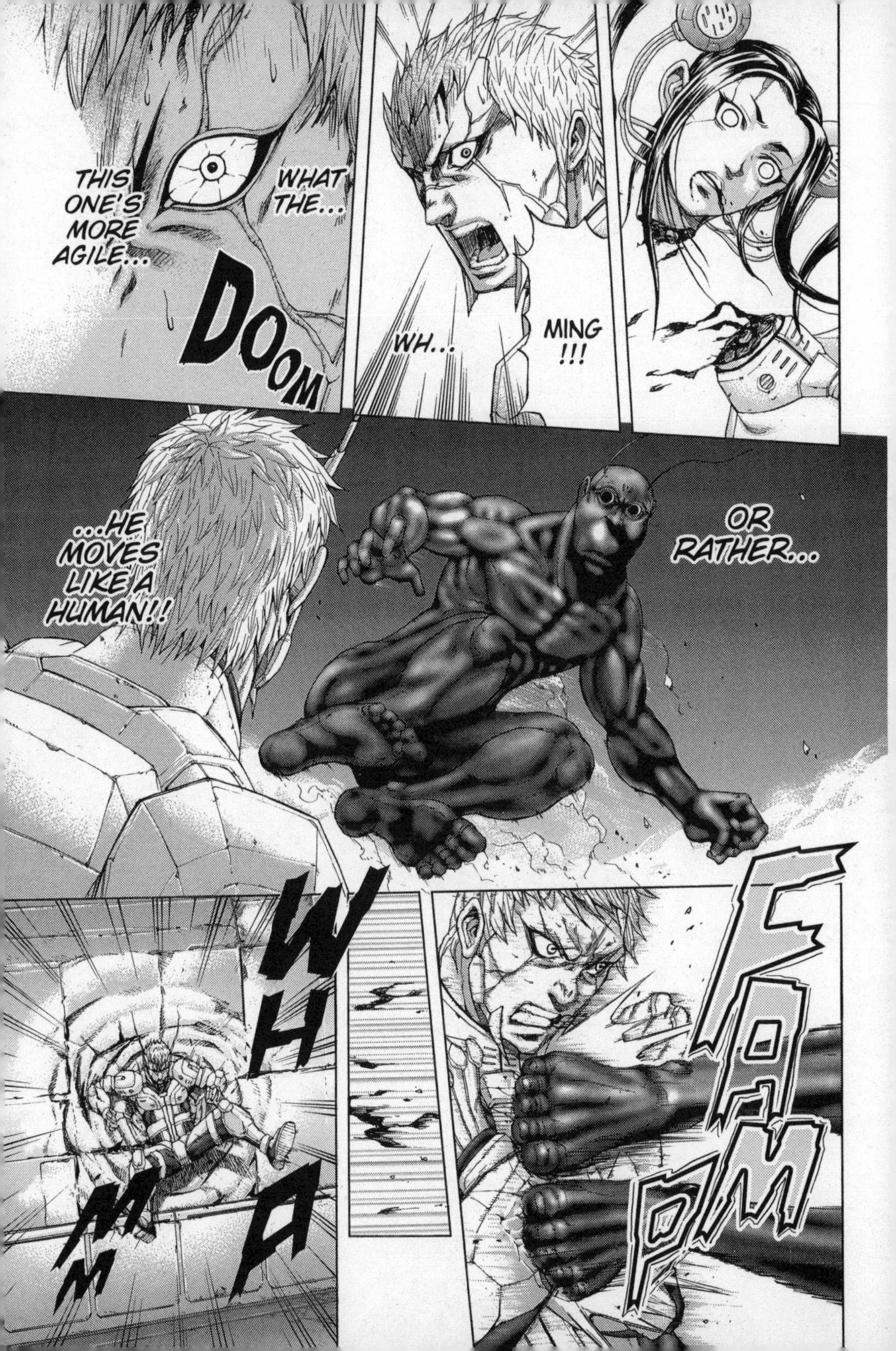
MING !!!
WH...
WHAT THE...
THIS ONE'S MORE AGILE...
DOOM
OR RATHER...
...HE MOVES LIKE A HUMAN!!
FAMP
WHAMM

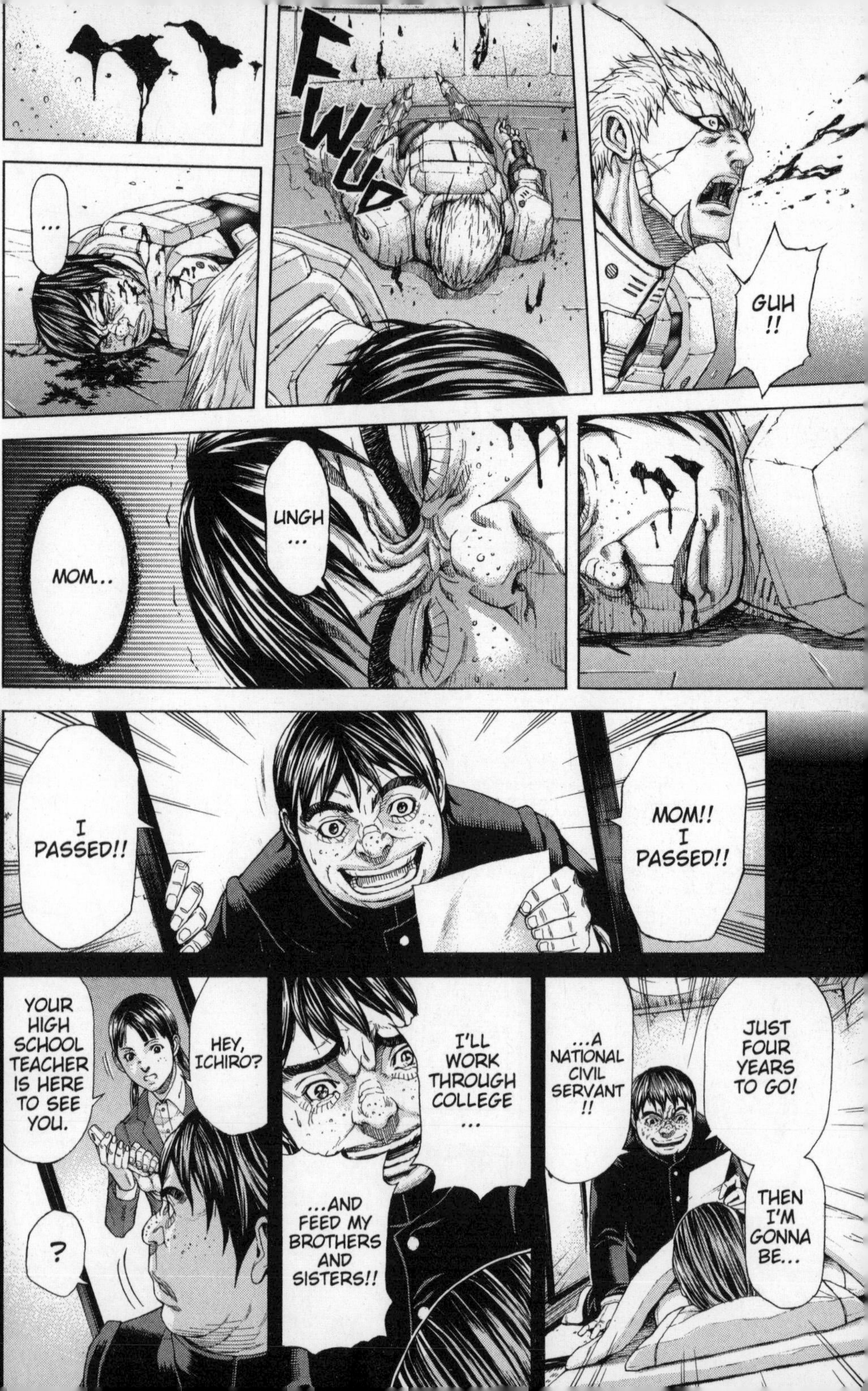
GUH !!
FWUD
...
UNGH ...
MOM...
MOM!! I PASSED!!
I PASSED!!
JUST FOUR YEARS TO GO!
THEN I'M GONNA BE...
...A NATIONAL CIVIL SERVANT !!
I'LL WORK THROUGH COLLEGE ...
...AND FEED MY BROTHERS AND SISTERS!!
HEY, ICHIRO?
YOUR HIGH SCHOOL TEACHER IS HERE TO SEE YOU.
?

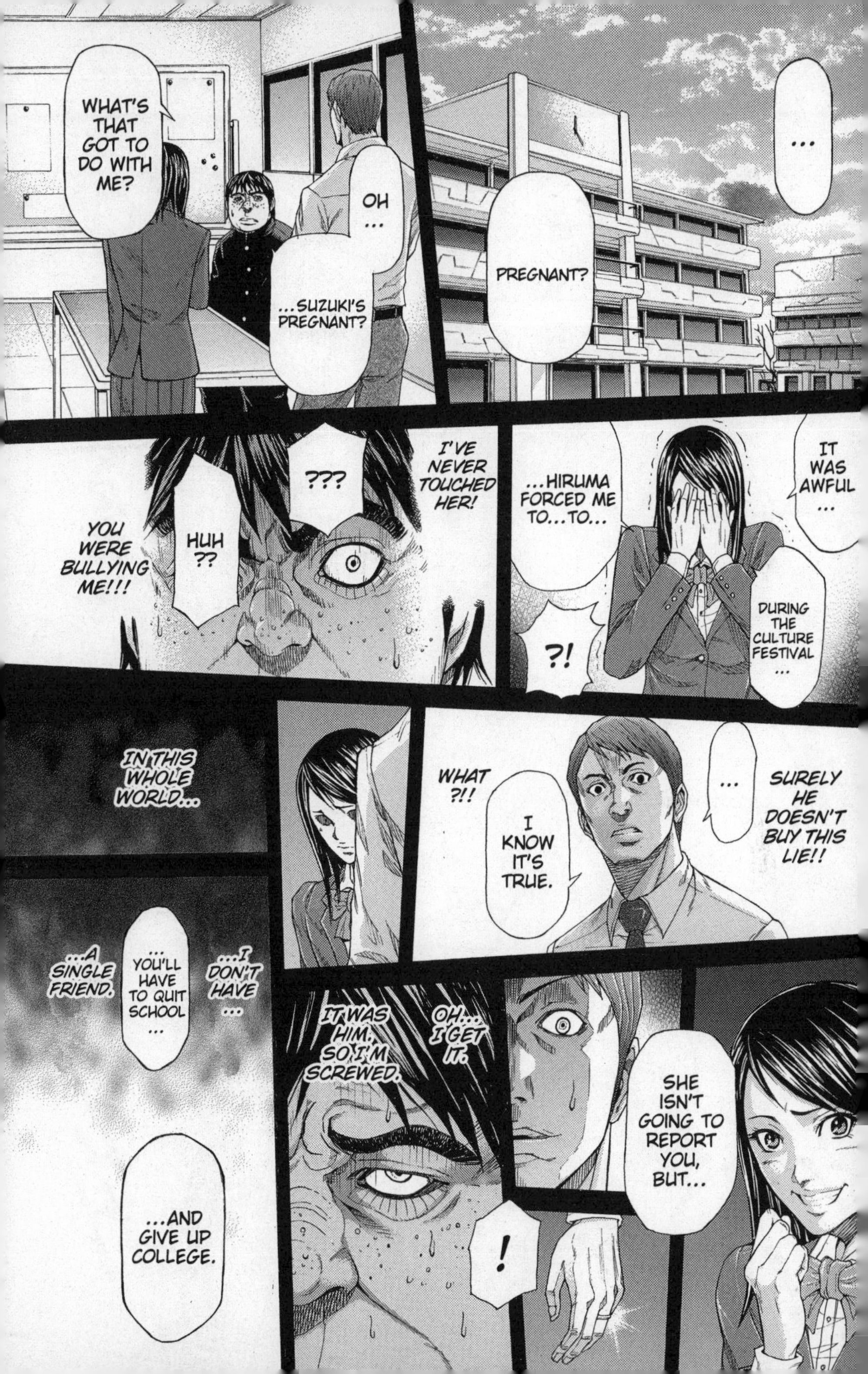
...
PREGNANT?
OH ...
...SUZUKI'S PREGNANT?
WHAT'S THAT GOT TO DO WITH ME?
IT WAS AWFUL ...
DURING THE CULTURE FESTIVAL ...
...HIRUMA FORCED ME TO...TO...
?!
I'VE NEVER TOUCHED HER!
???
HUH ??
YOU WERE BULLYING ME!!!
...
SURELY HE DOESN'T BUY THIS LIE!!
WHAT ?!!
I KNOW IT'S TRUE.
SHE ISN'T GOING TO REPORT YOU, BUT...
OH... I GET IT.
IT WAS HIM. SO I'M SCREWED.
!
IN THIS WHOLE WORLD...
...I DON'T HAVE ...
... YOU'LL HAVE TO QUIT SCHOOL ...
...A SINGLE FRIEND.
...AND GIVE UP COLLEGE.

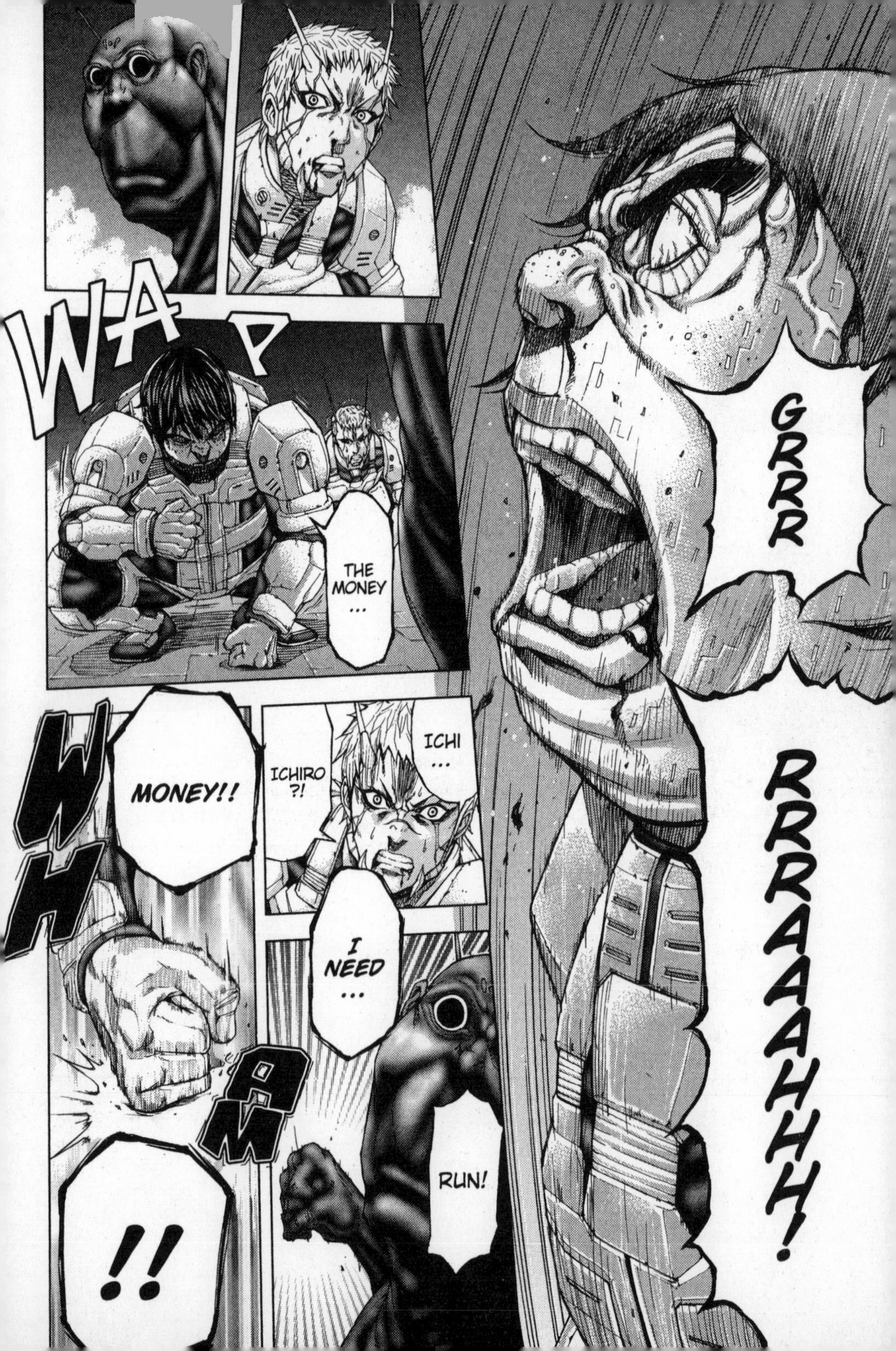
GRRR
RRRAAAHHH!
WAP
THE MONEY ...
ICHI ...
ICHIRO ?!
MONEY!!
WHAM
I NEED ...
RUN!
!!

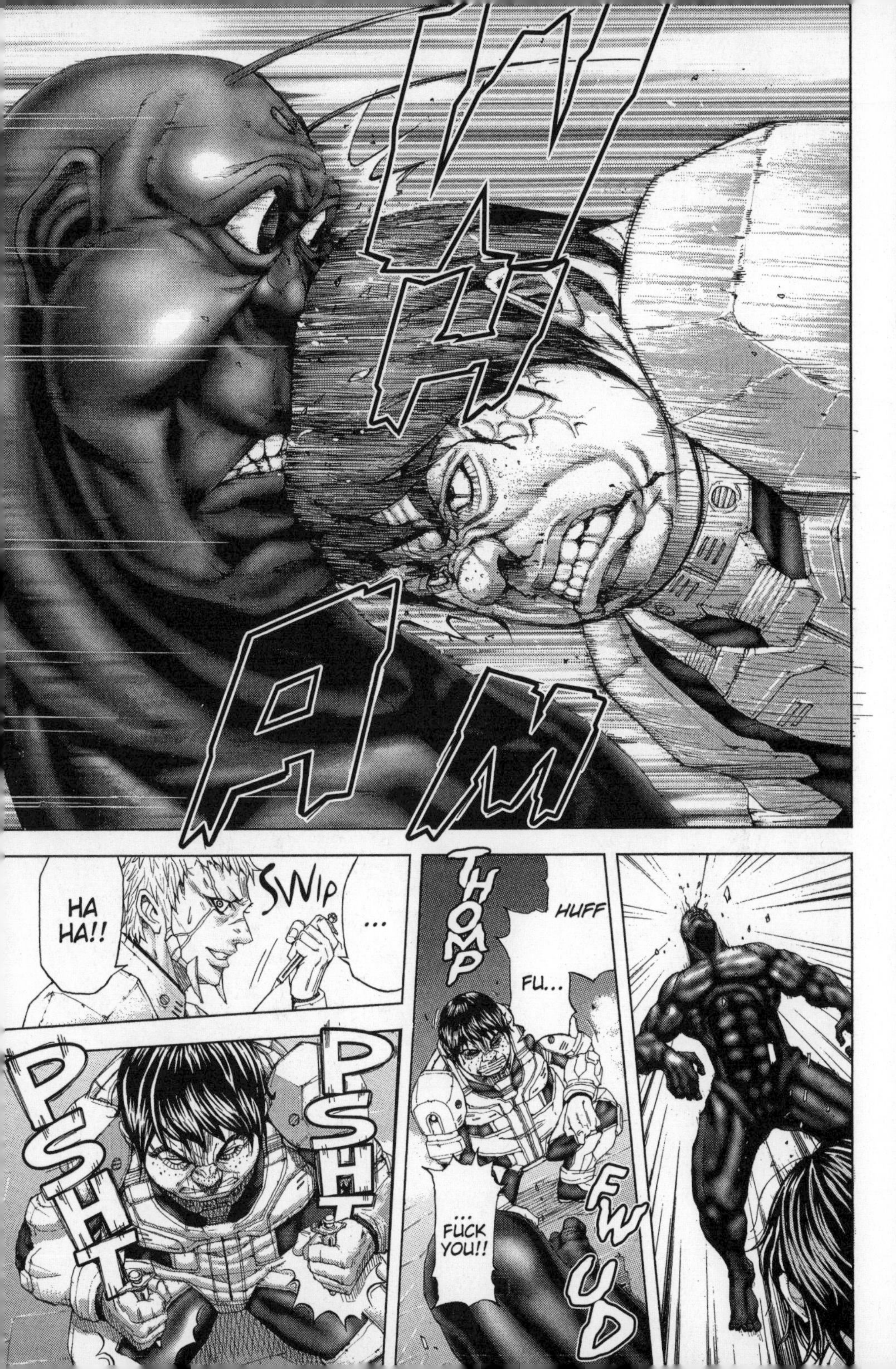
WHAM
FWUD
THOMP
HUFF
FU...
... FÜCK YOU!!
...
SWIP
HA HA!!
PSHT
PSHT

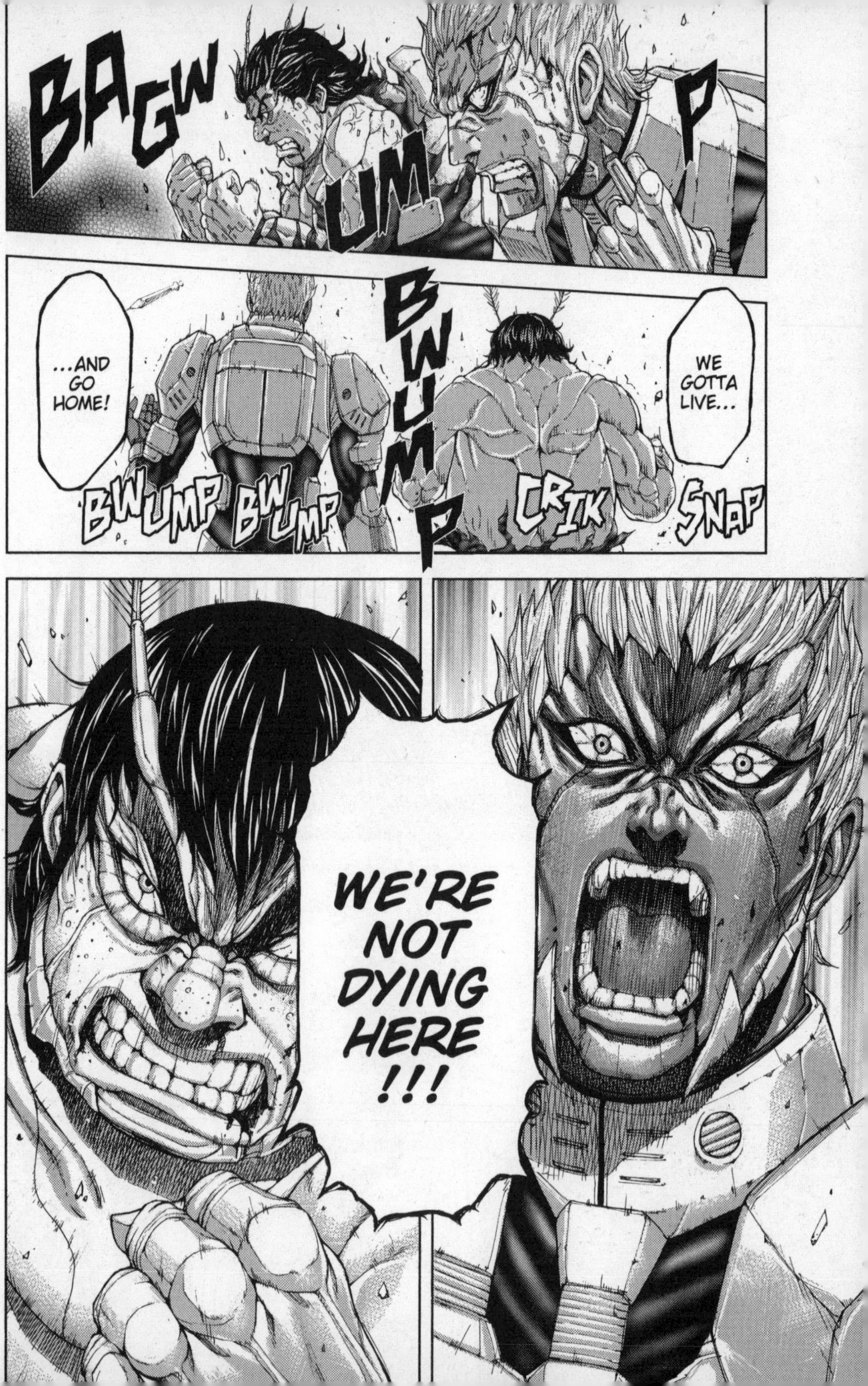
BAGWUMP
WE GOTTA LIVE...
...AND GO HOME!
BWUMP
SNAP
CRIK
BWUMP
BWUMP
WE'RE NOT DYING HERE!!!

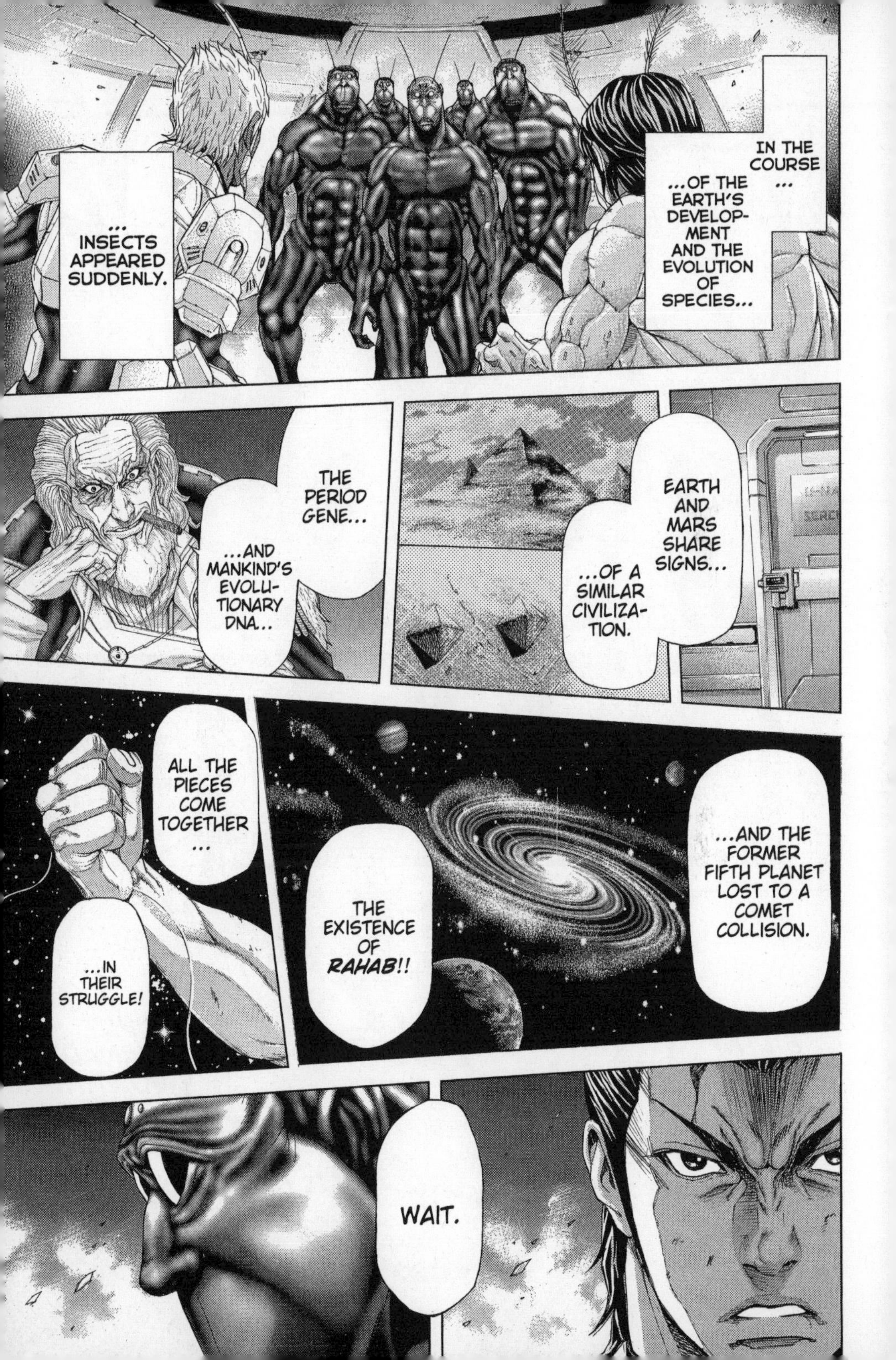
IN THE COURSE ...
...OF THE EARTH'S DEVELOPMENT AND THE EVOLUTION OF SPECIES...
... INSECTS APPEARED SUDDENLY.
EARTH AND MARS SHARE SIGNS...
...OF A SIMILAR CIVILIZATION.
THE PERIOD GENE...
...AND MANKIND'S EVOLUTIONARY DNA...
...AND THE FORMER FIFTH PLANET LOST TO A COMET COLLISION.
THE EXISTENCE OF RAHAB!!
ALL THE PIECES COME TOGETHER ...
...IN THEIR STRUGGLE!
WAIT.

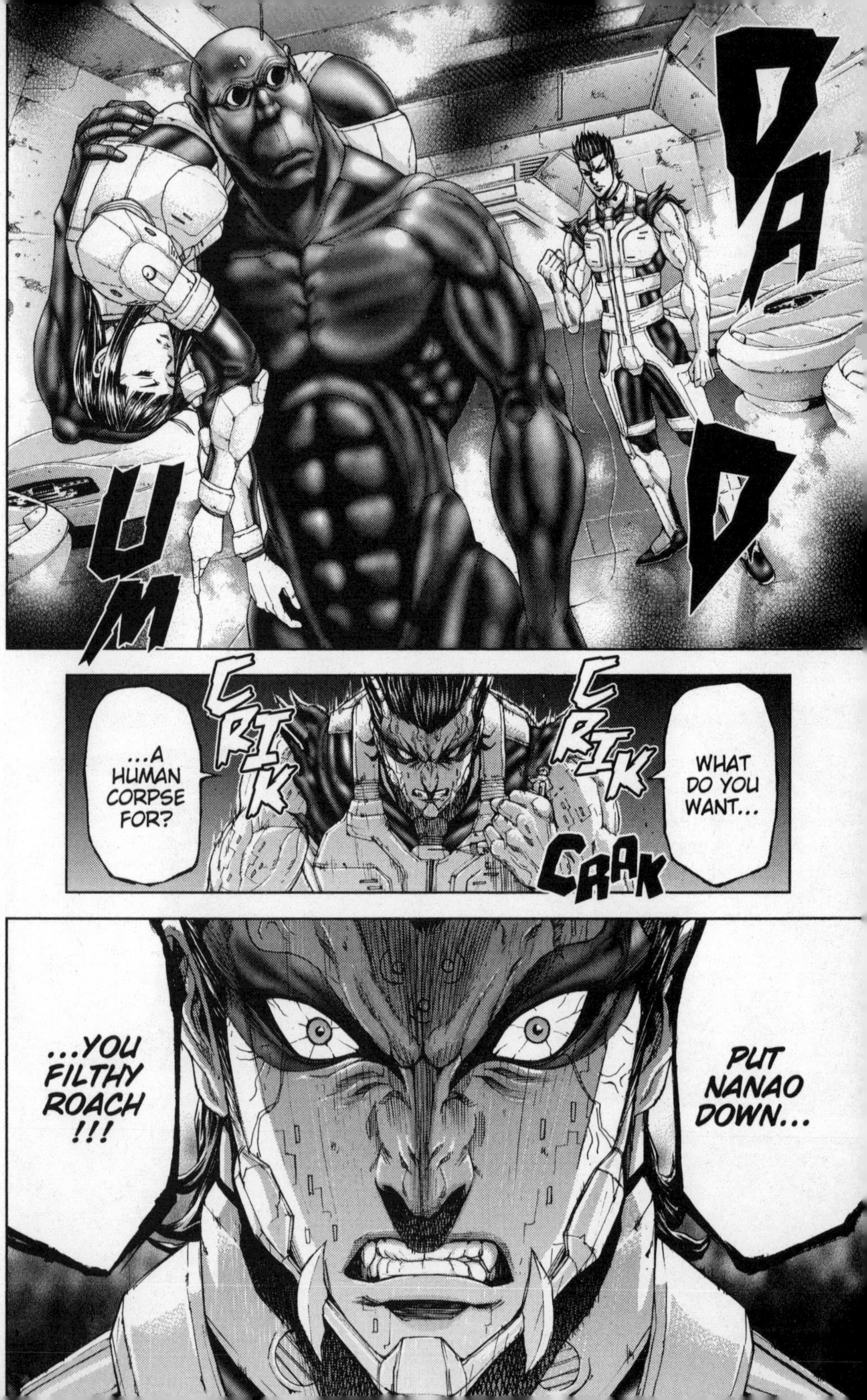
DA
D
UM
WHAT DO YOU WANT...
CRIK
CRAK
CRIK
...A HUMAN CORPSE FOR?
PUT NANAO DOWN...
...YOU FILTHY ROACH!!!

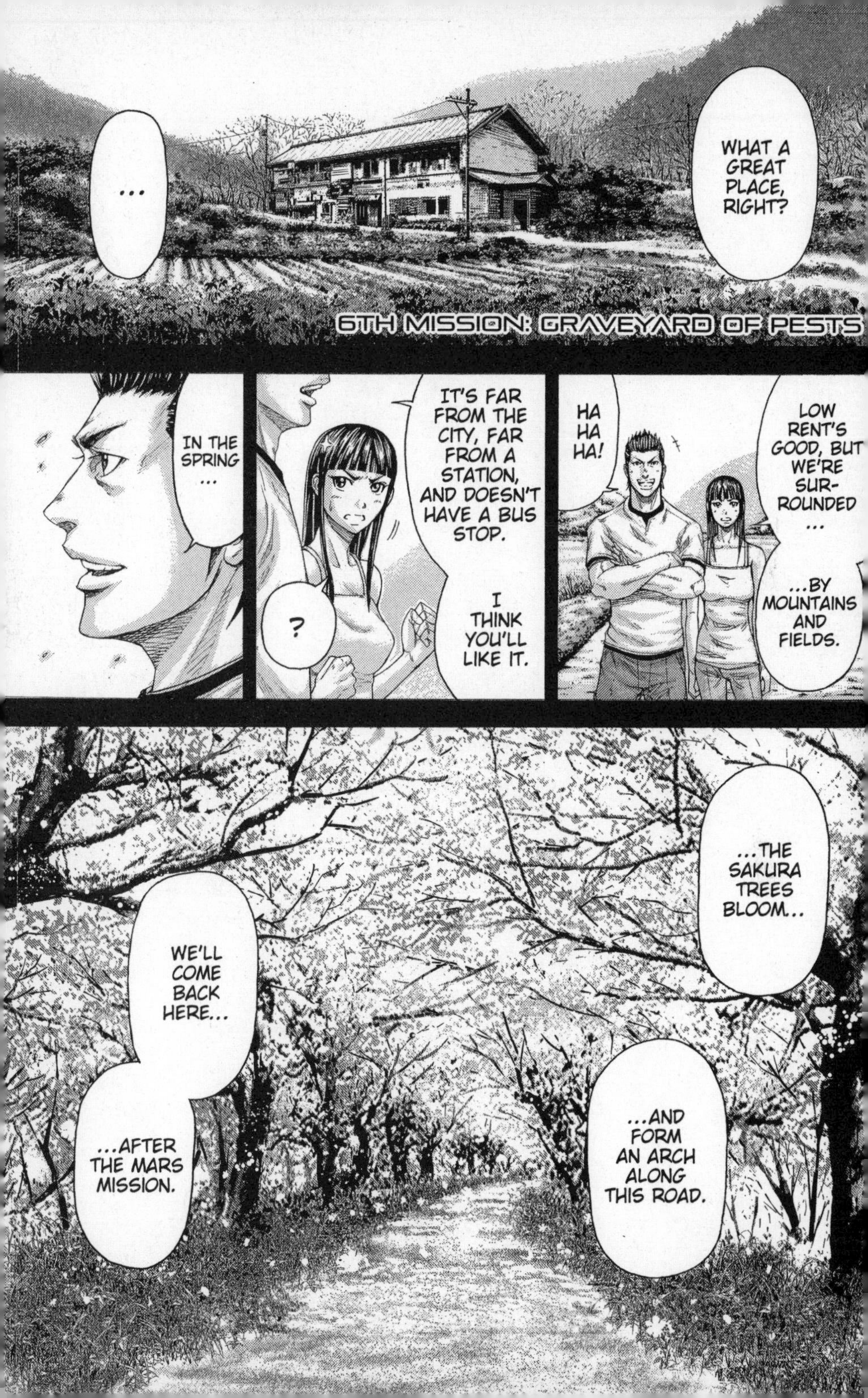
WHAT A GREAT PLACE, RIGHT?
...
6TH MISSION: GRAVEYARD OF PESTS
LOW RENT'S GOOD, BUT WE'RE SUR-ROUNDED...
...BY MOUNTAINS AND FIELDS.
HA HA HA!
IT'S FAR FROM THE CITY, FAR FROM A STATION, AND DOESN'T HAVE A BUS STOP.
I THINK YOU'LL LIKE IT.
?
IN THE SPRING...
...THE SAKURA TREES BLOOM...
...AND FORM AN ARCH ALONG THIS ROAD.
WE'LL COME BACK HERE...
...AFTER THE MARS MISSION.

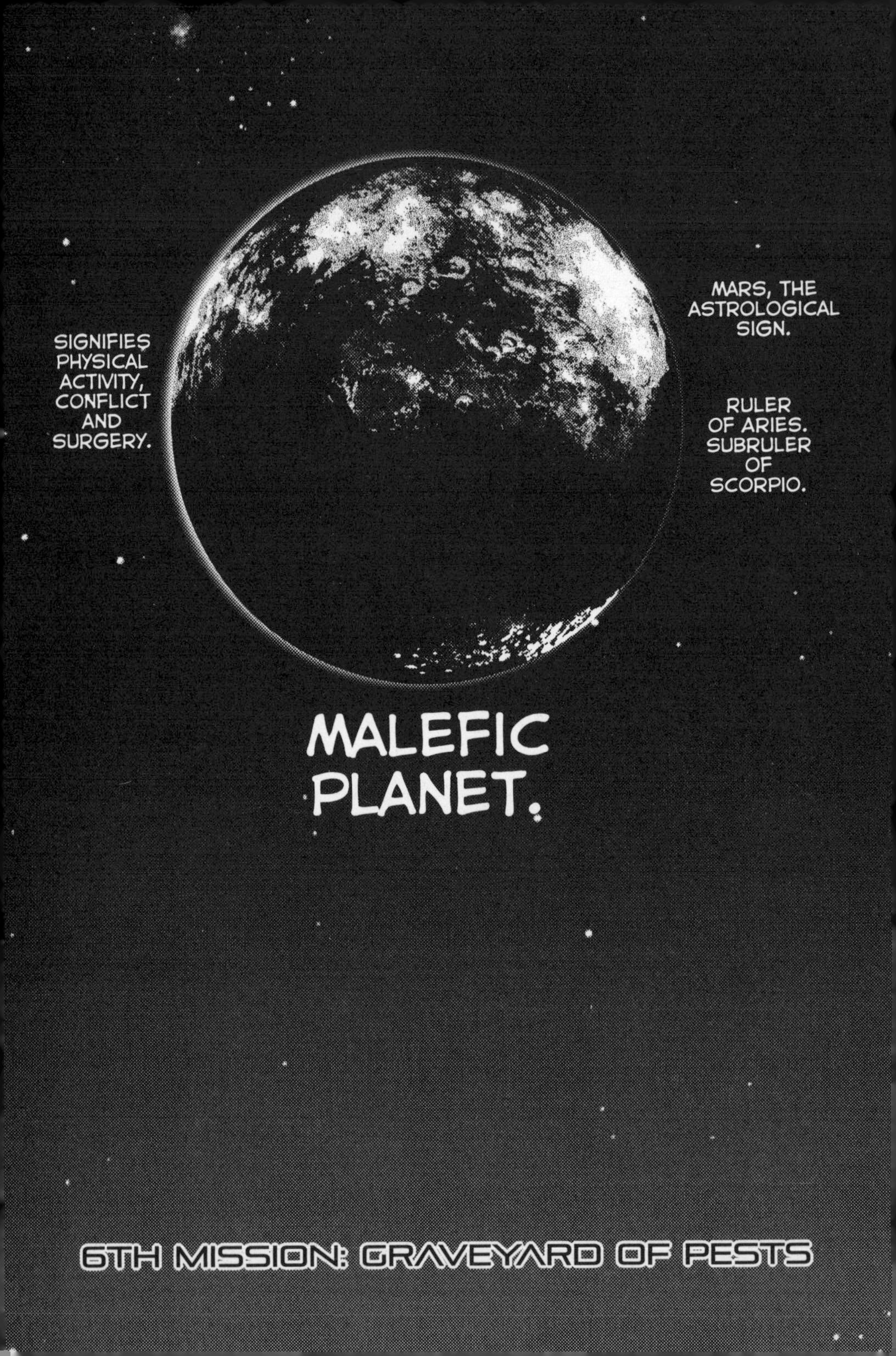
MARS, THE ASTROLOGICAL SIGN.
RULER OF ARIES. SUBRULER OF SCORPIO.
SIGNIFIES PHYSICAL ACTIVITY, CONFLICT AND SURGERY.
MALEFIC PLANET.
6TH MISSION: GRAVEYARD OF PESTS

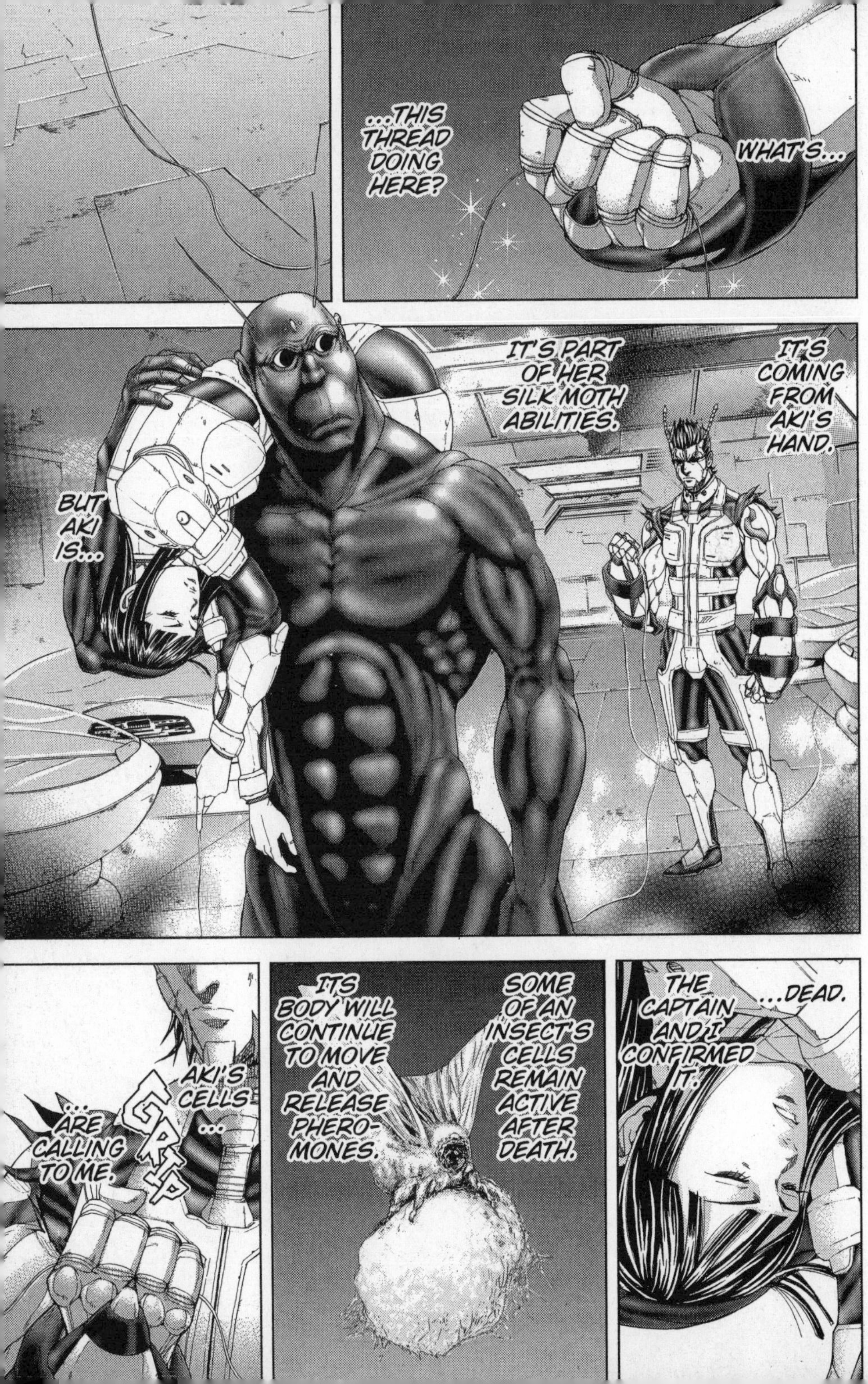
WHAT'S...
...THIS THREAD DOING HERE?
IT'S COMING FROM AKI'S HAND.
IT'S PART OF HER SILK MOTH ABILITIES.
BUT AKI IS...
...DEAD.
THE CAPTAIN AND I CONFIRMED IT.
SOME OF AN INSECT'S CELLS REMAIN ACTIVE AFTER DEATH.
ITS BODY WILL CONTINUE TO MOVE AND RELEASE PHERO-MONES.
AKI'S CELLS...
GRIP
...ARE CALLING TO ME.

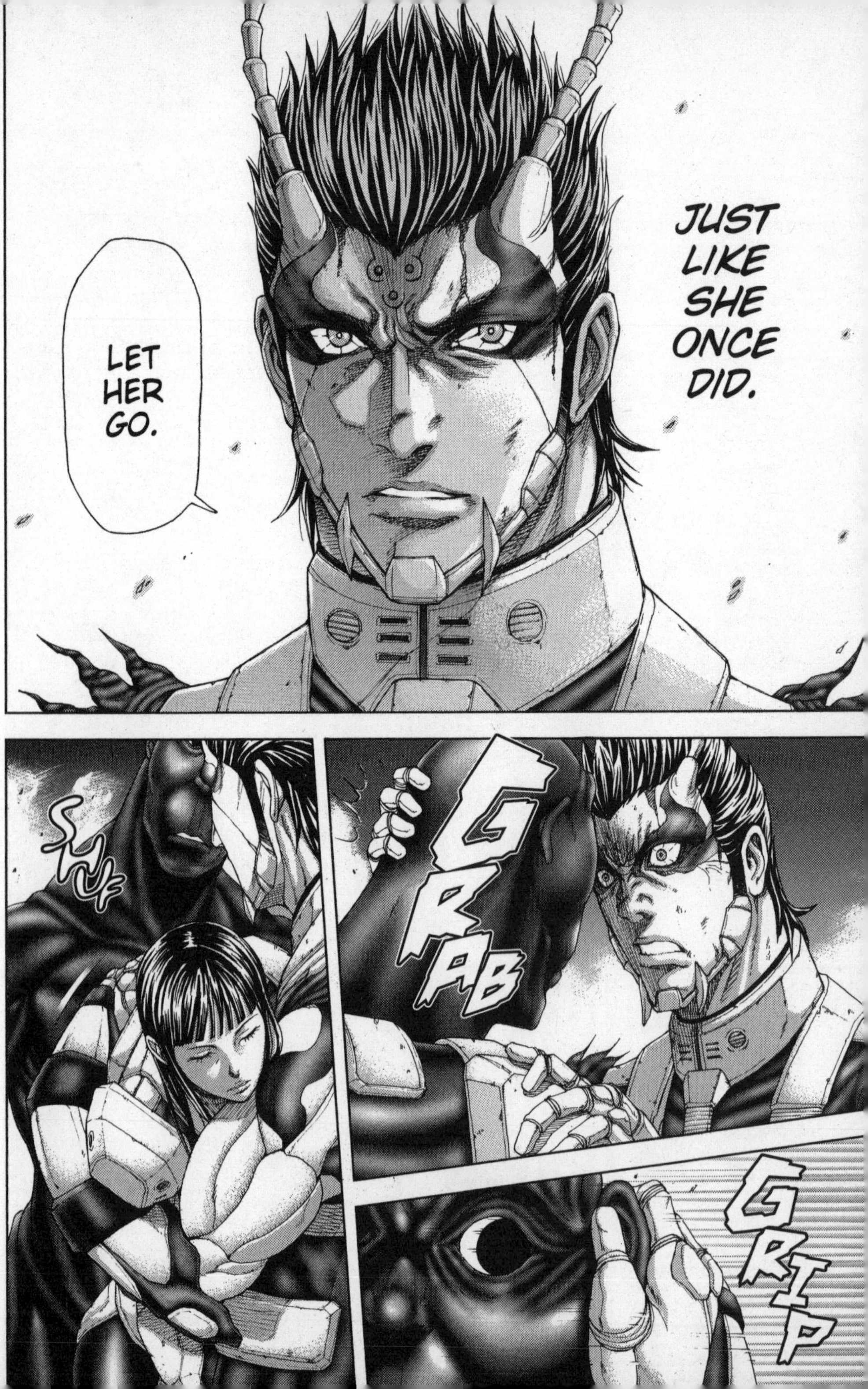
JUST LIKE SHE ONCE DID.
LET HER GO.
GRAB
SHUF
GRIP

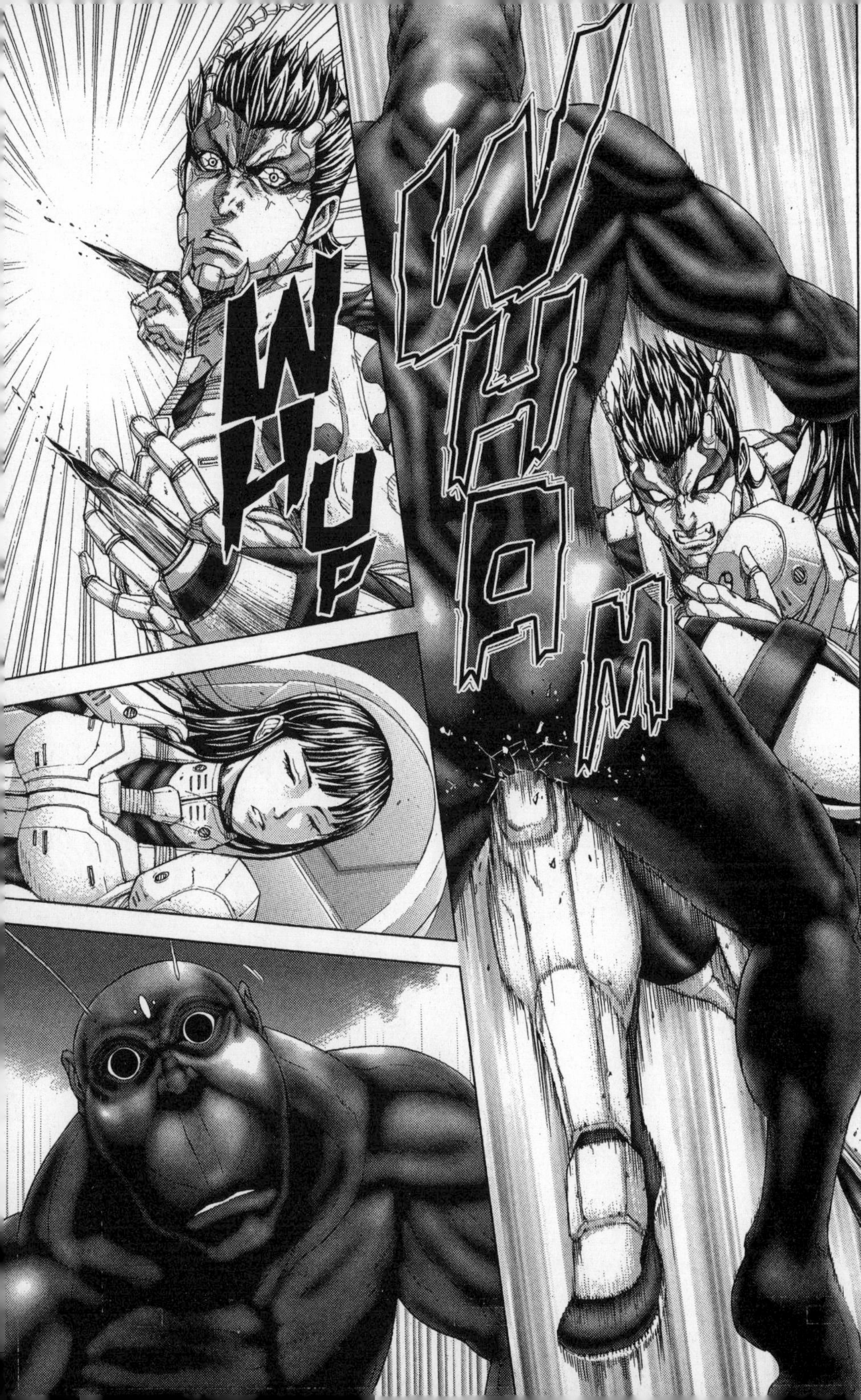
WHAM
WHUP

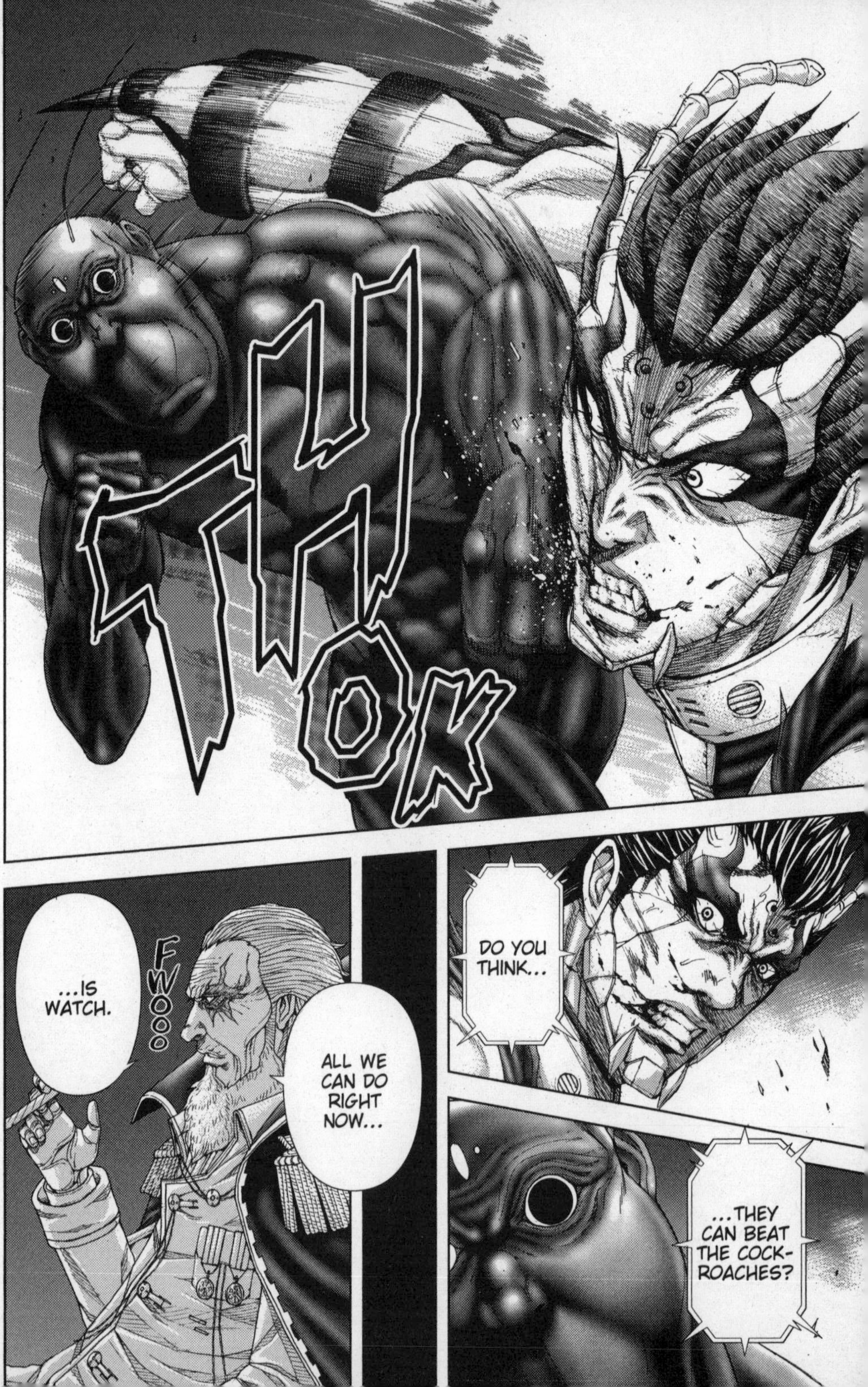
THOK
DO YOU THINK...
...THEY CAN BEAT THE COCK-ROACHES?
ALL WE CAN DO RIGHT NOW...
...IS WATCH.
FWOOO

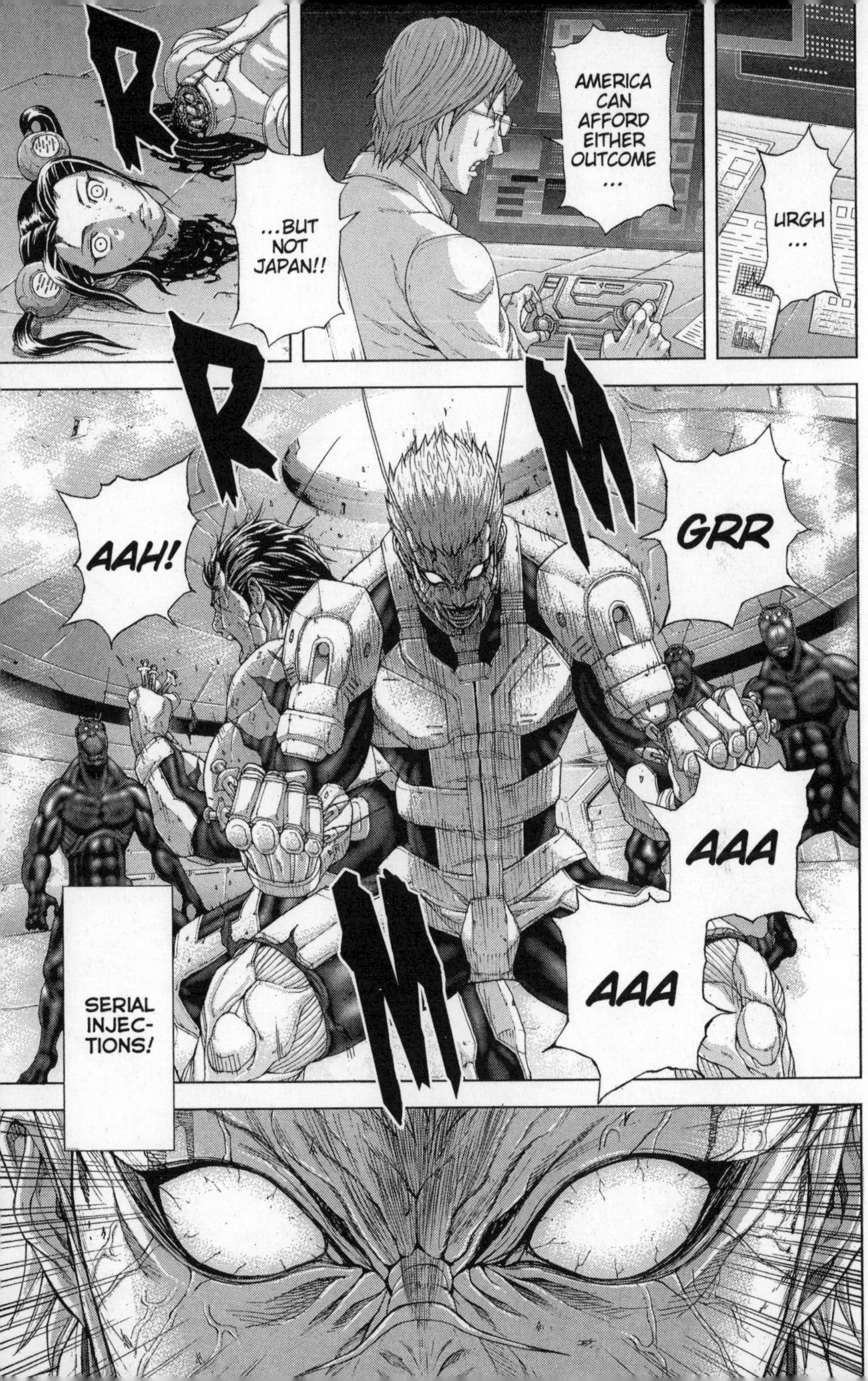
URGH ...
AMERICA CAN AFFORD EITHER OUTCOME ...
...BUT NOT JAPAN!!
R
R
M
M
GRR
AAA
AAA
AAH!
SERIAL INJEC-TIONS!

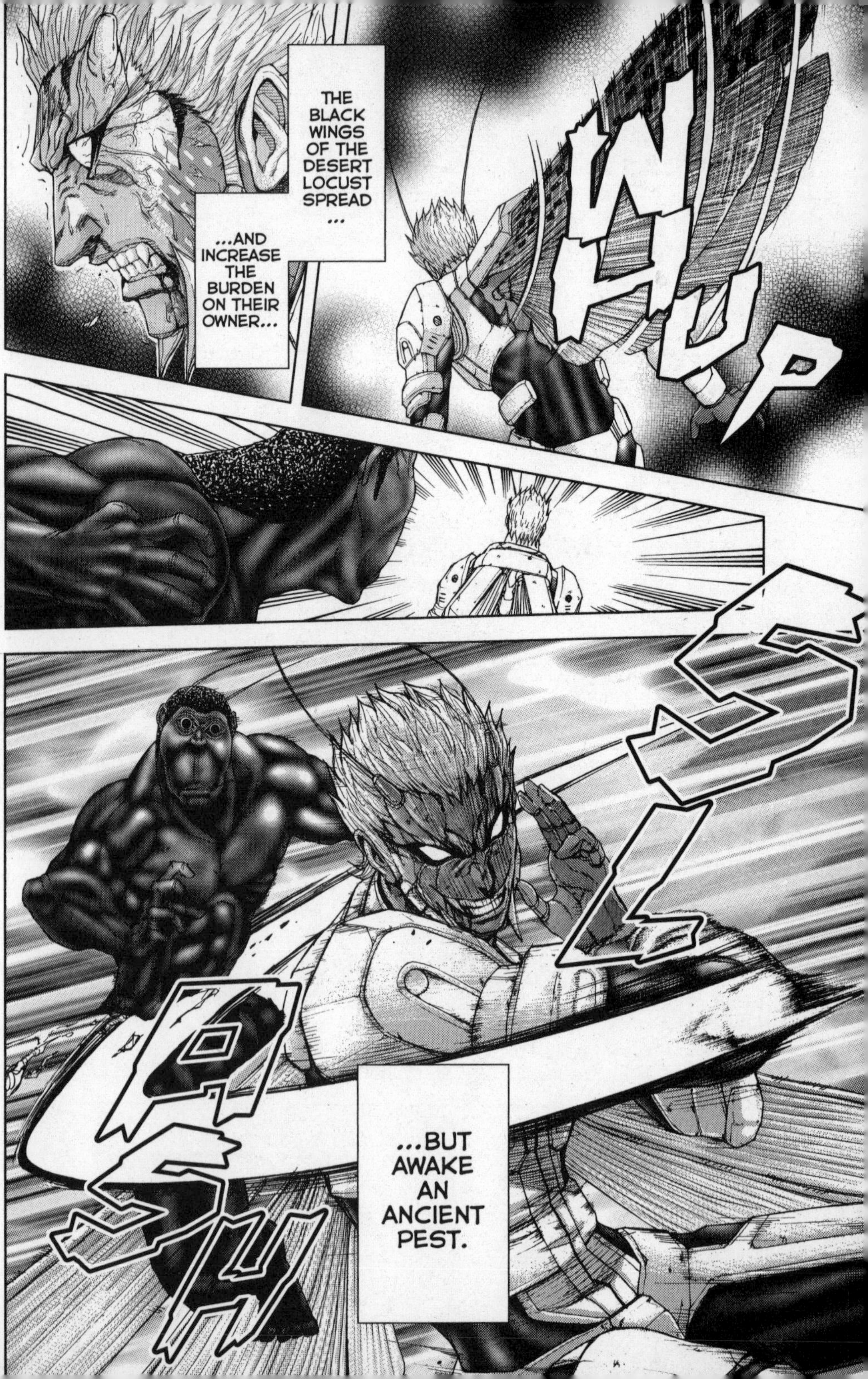
WHUP
THE BLACK WINGS OF THE DESERT LOCUST SPREAD...
...AND INCREASE THE BURDEN ON THEIR OWNER...
...BUT AWAKE AN ANCIENT PEST.

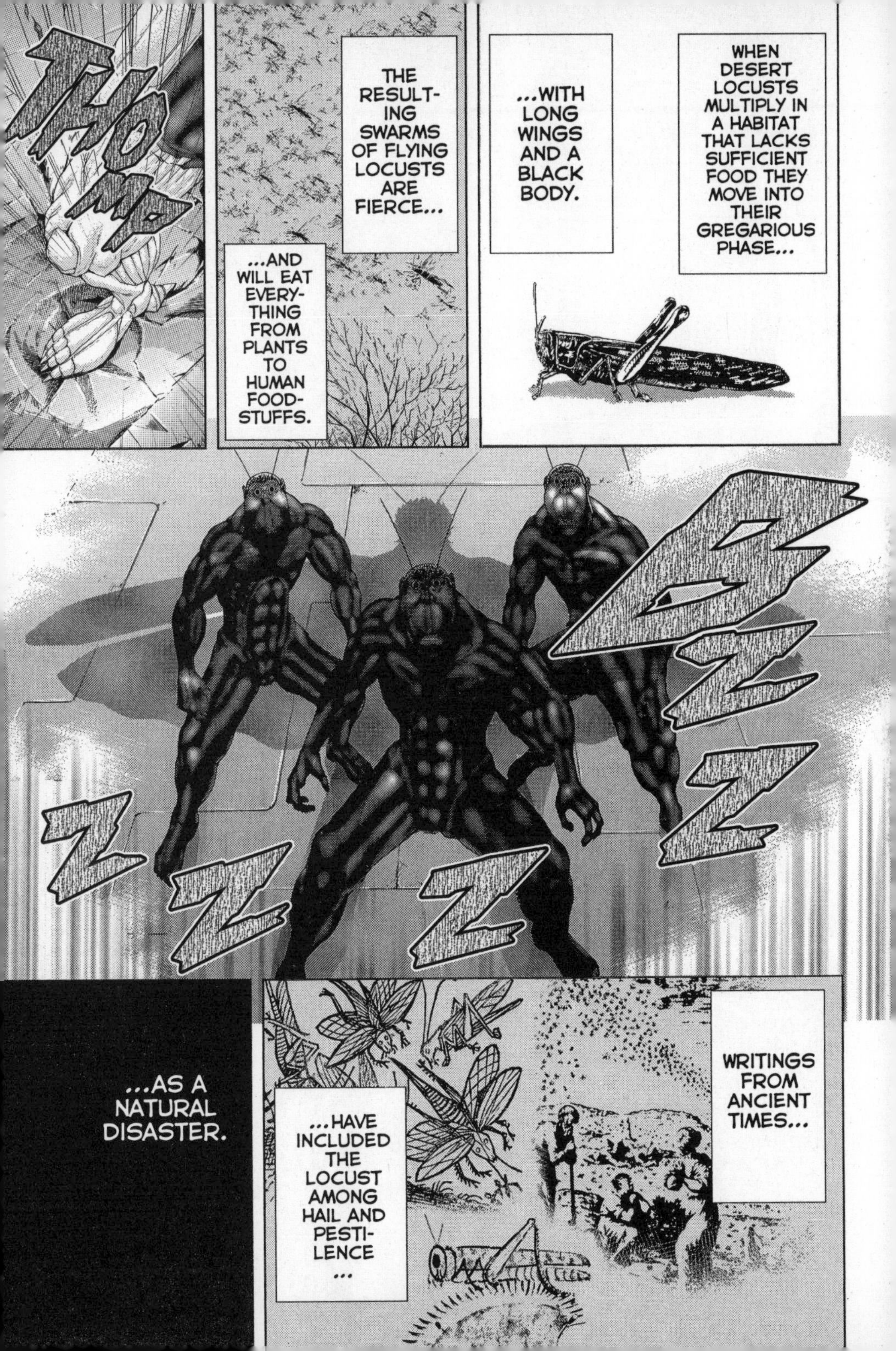
WHEN DESERT LOCUSTS MULTIPLY IN A HABITAT THAT LACKS SUFFICIENT FOOD THEY MOVE INTO THEIR GREGARIOUS PHASE...
...WITH LONG WINGS AND A BLACK BODY.
THE RESULTING SWARMS OF FLYING LOCUSTS ARE FIERCE...
...AND WILL EAT EVERYTHING FROM PLANTS TO HUMAN FOODSTUFFS.
THOMP
BZZZZZ
WRITINGS FROM ANCIENT TIMES...
...HAVE INCLUDED THE LOCUST AMONG HAIL AND PESTILENCE...
...AS A NATURAL DISASTER.

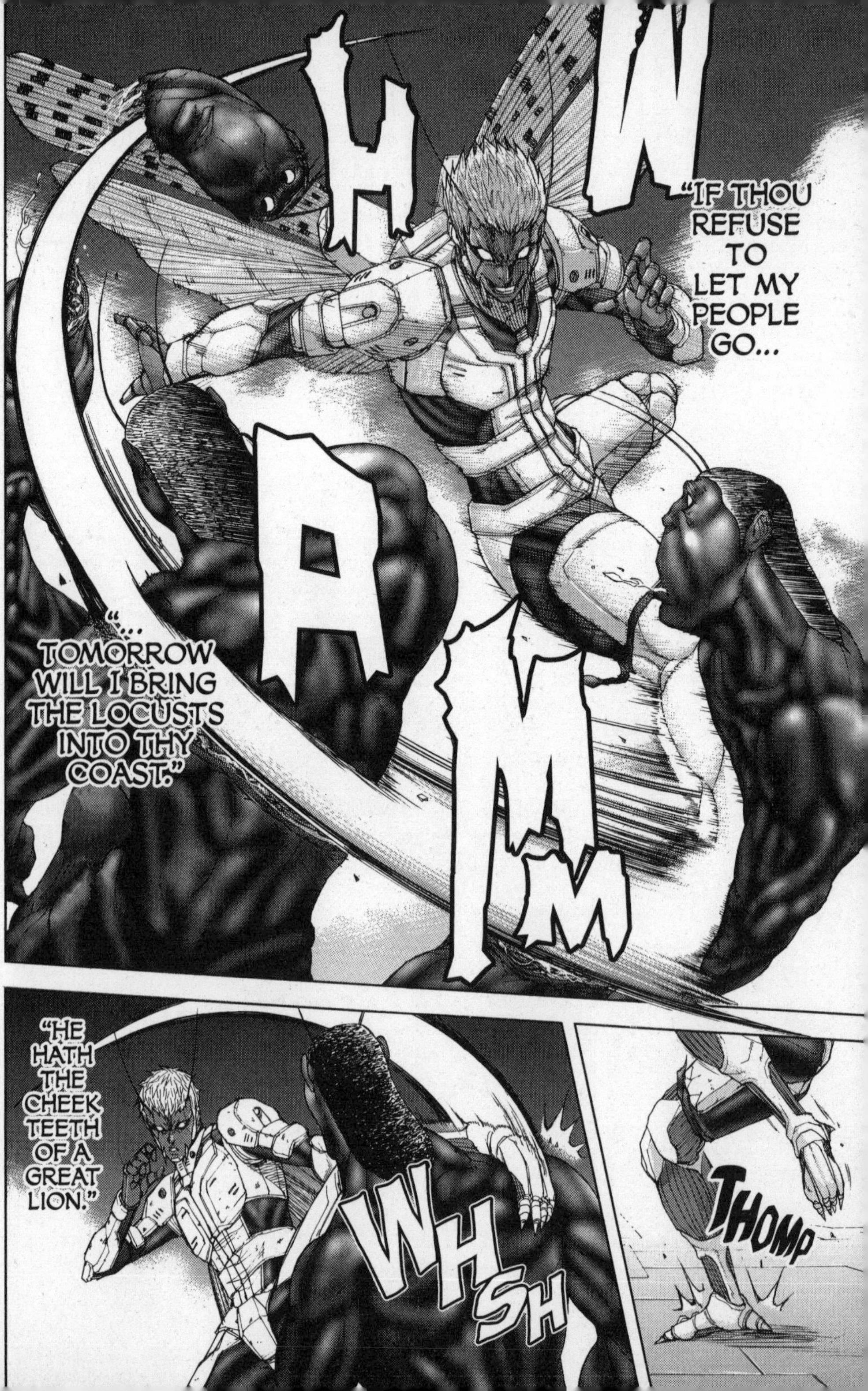
"IF THOU REFUSE TO LET MY PEOPLE GO...
WHAMM
"...TOMORROW WILL I BRING THE LOCUSTS INTO THY COAST."
THOMP
"HE HATH THE CHEEK TEETH OF A GREAT LION."
WHSH

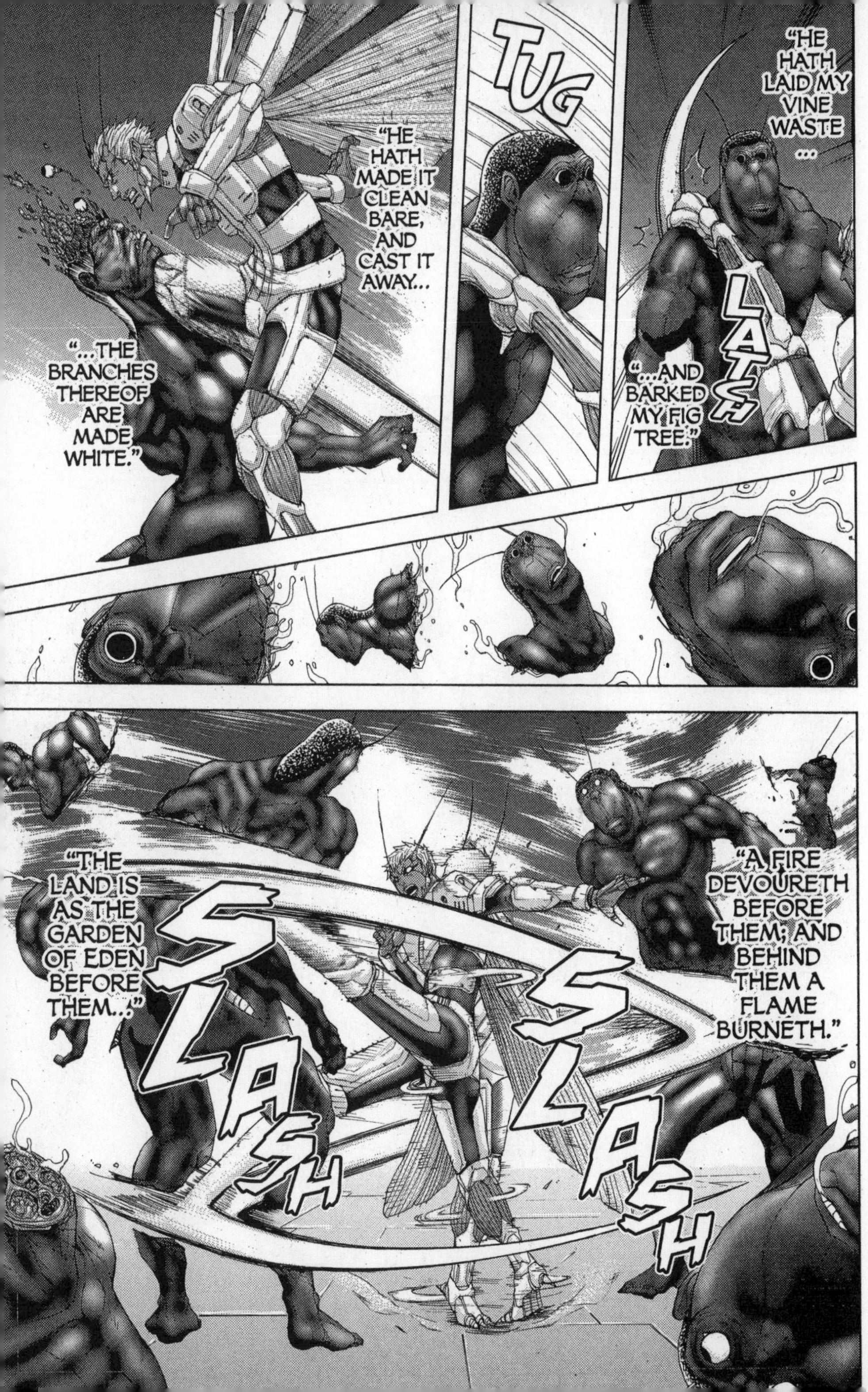
"HE HATH LAID MY VINE WASTE ...
LATCH
"...AND BARKED MY FIG TREE."
TUG
"HE HATH MADE IT CLEAN BARE, AND CAST IT AWAY...
"...THE BRANCHES THEREOF ARE MADE WHITE."
"A FIRE DEVOURETH BEFORE THEM; AND BEHIND THEM A FLAME BURNETH."
SLASH
"THE LAND IS AS THE GARDEN OF EDEN BEFORE THEM..."
SLASH

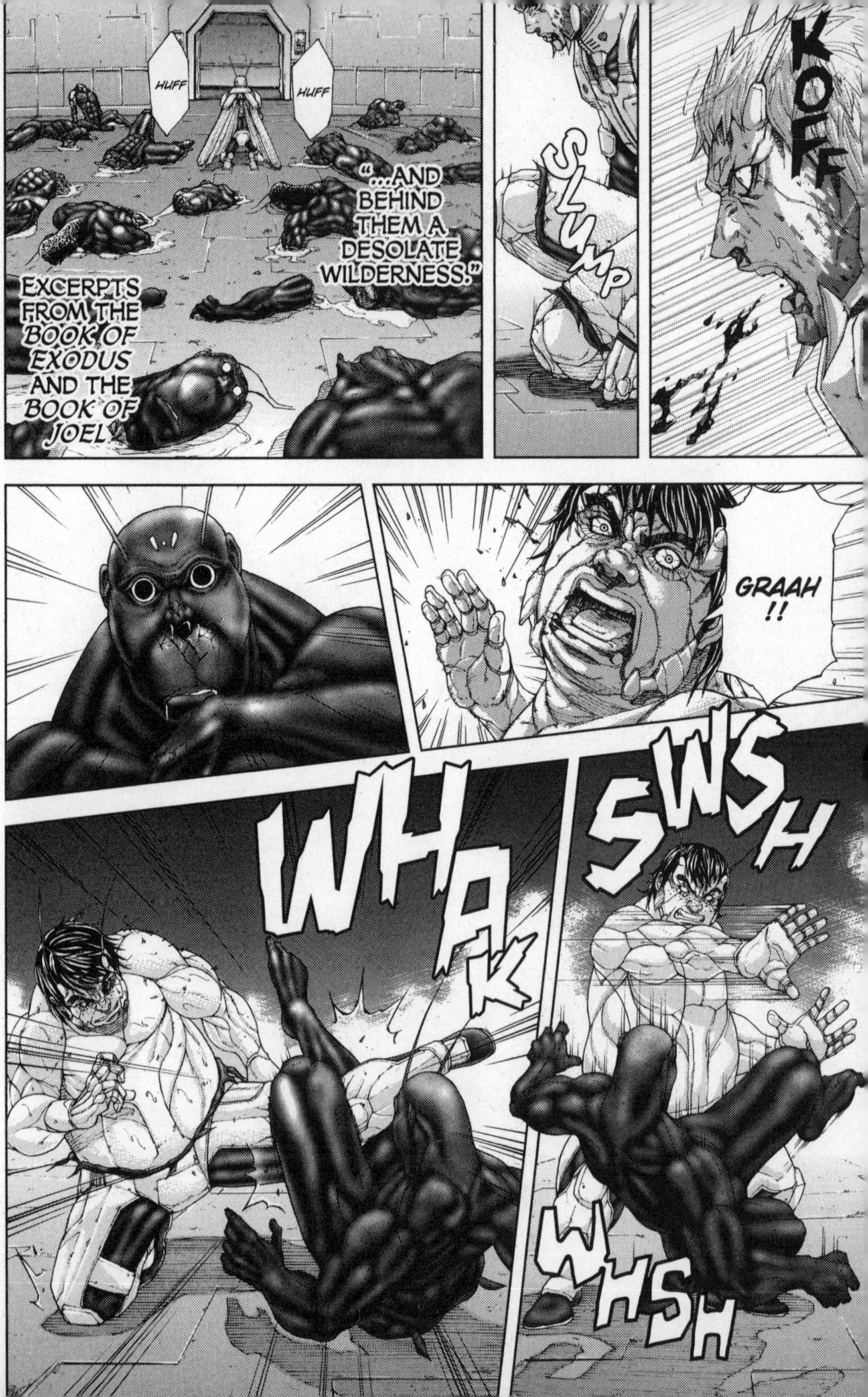
KOFF
SLUMP
HUFF
HUFF
"...AND BEHIND THEM A DESOLATE WILDERNESS."
EXCERPTS FROM THE BOOK OF EXODUS AND THE BOOK OF JOEL
GRAAH !!
SWSH
WHSH
WHAK

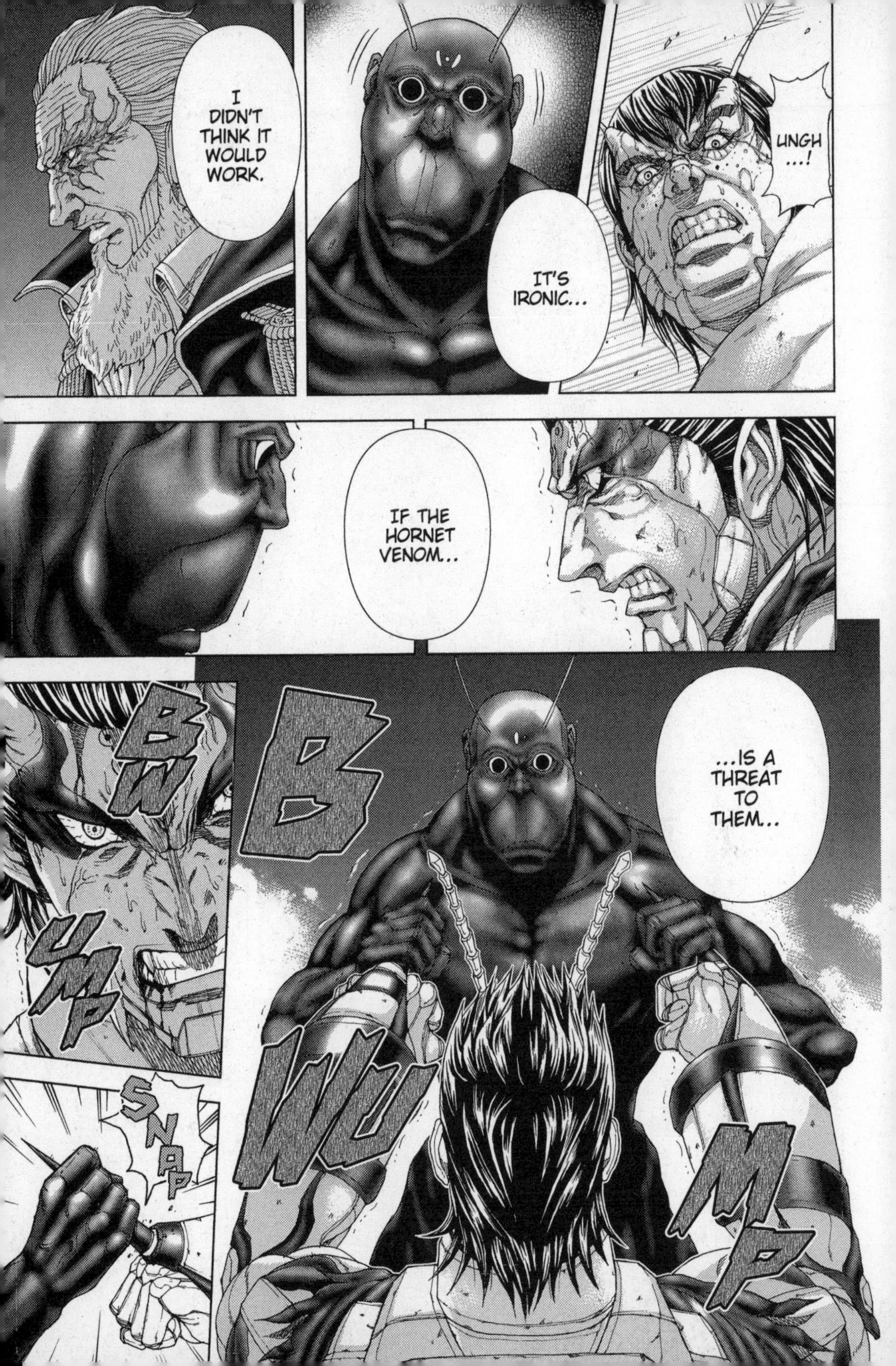
UNGH ...!
IT'S IRONIC...
I DIDN'T THINK IT WOULD WORK.
IF THE HORNET VENOM...
...IS A THREAT TO THEM...
BWUMP
BWUMP
SNAP

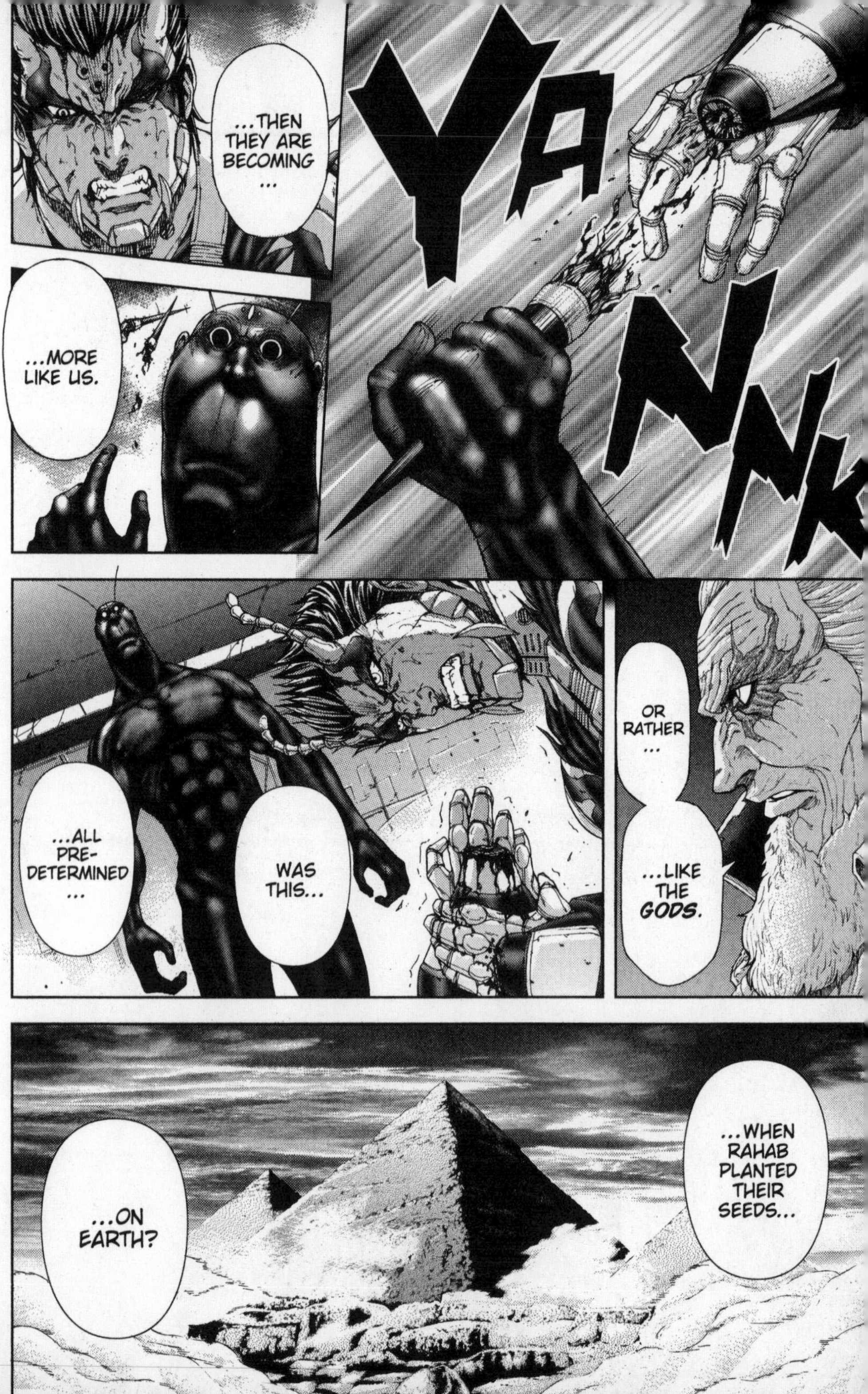
YANNNK
...THEN THEY ARE BECOMING...
...MORE LIKE US.
OR RATHER...
...LIKE THE *GODS*.
WAS THIS...
...ALL PRE-DETERMINED...
...WHEN RAHAB PLANTED THEIR SEEDS...
...ON EARTH?

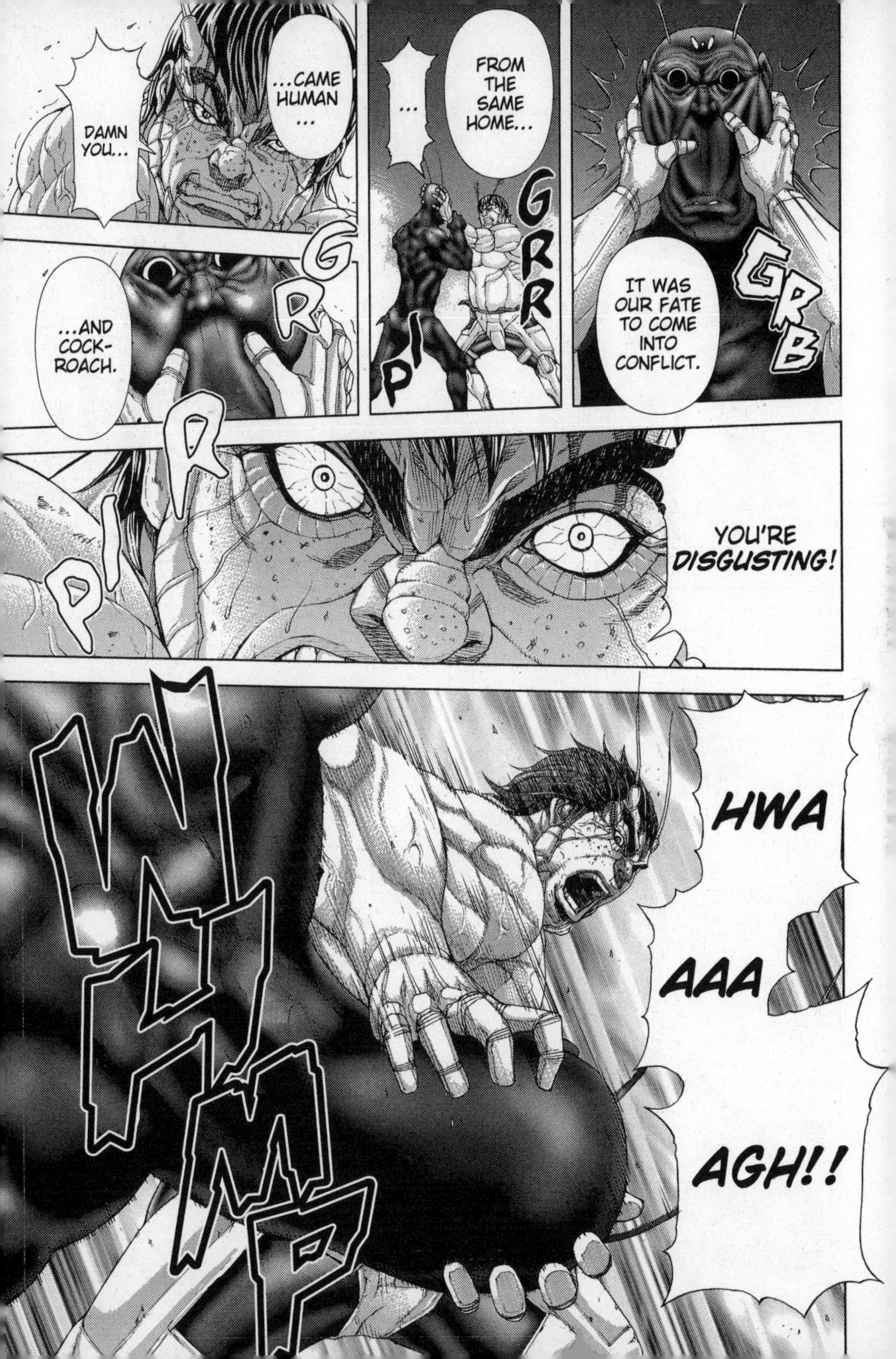

IT WAS OUR FATE TO COME INTO CONFLICT.
GRB
FROM THE SAME HOME...
...
GRR
PI
...CAME HUMAN...
DAMN YOU...
GR
...AND COCK-ROACH.
PIR
YOU'RE DISGUSTING!
HWA
AAA
AGH!!
WHUMP

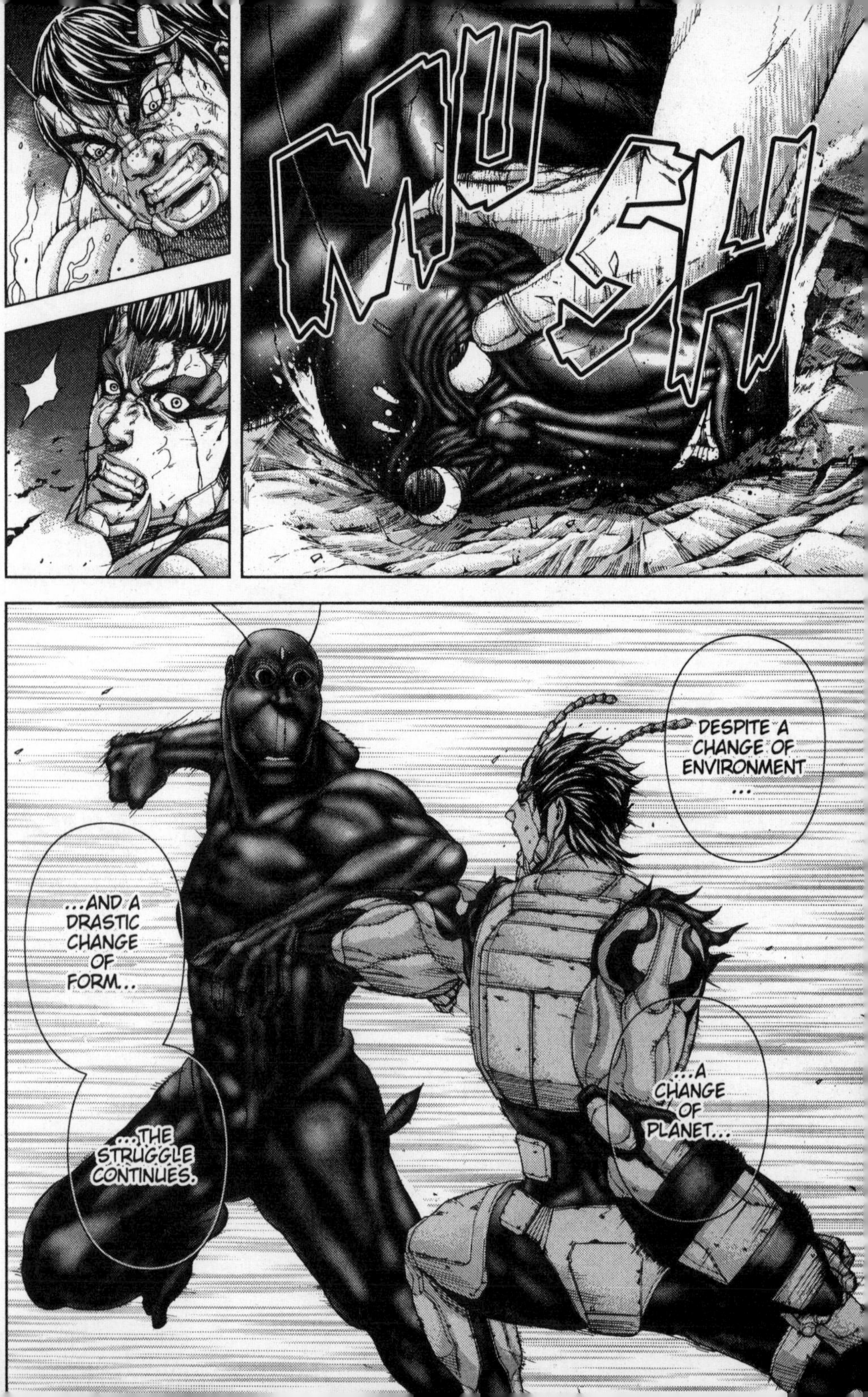
MUSH
DESPITE A CHANGE OF ENVIRONMENT...
...A CHANGE OF PLANET...
...AND A DRASTIC CHANGE OF FORM...
...THE STRUGGLE CONTINUES.

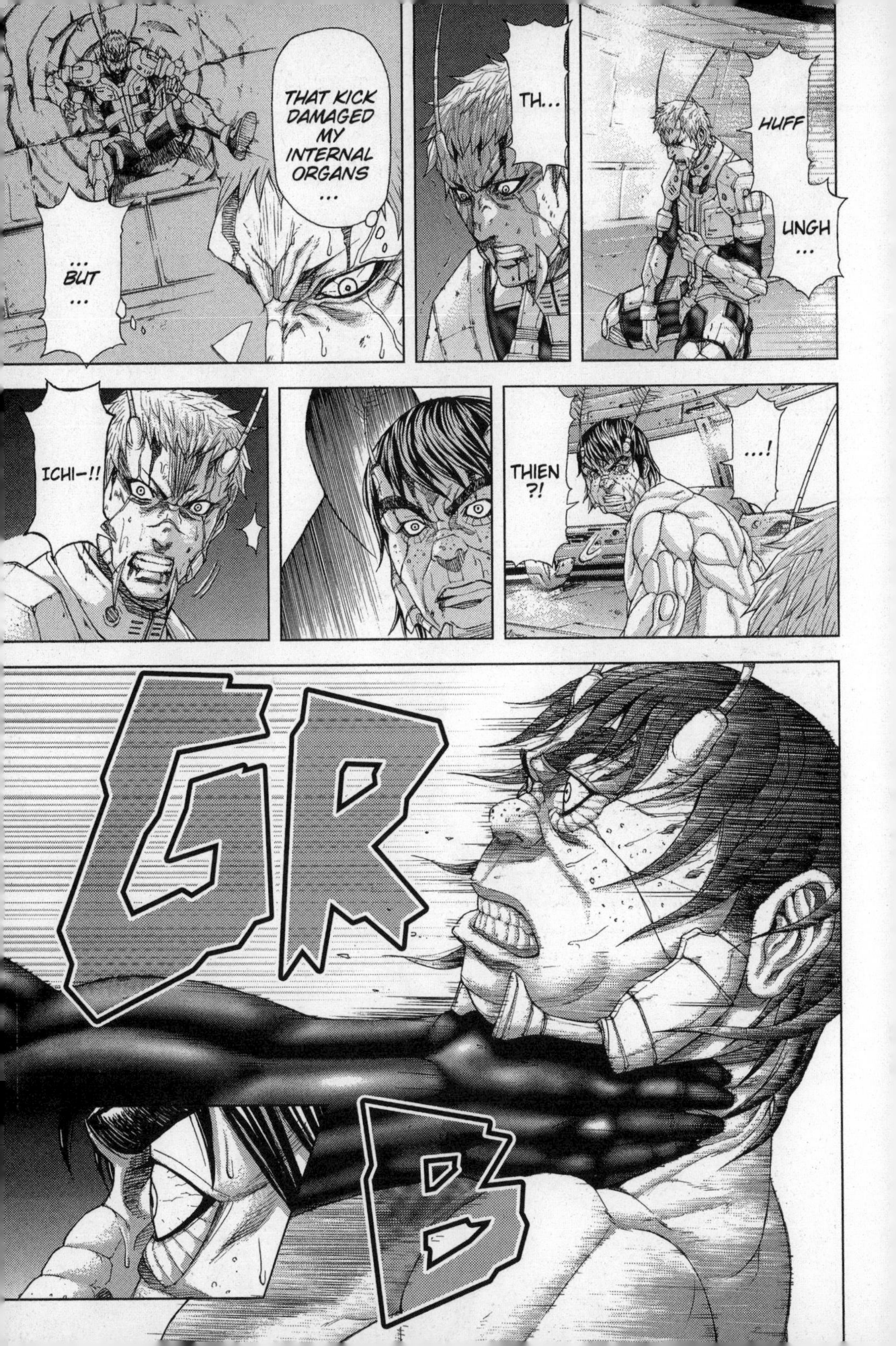
HUFF
UNGH ...
TH...
THAT KICK DAMAGED MY INTERNAL ORGANS ...
... BUT ...
...!
THIEN ?!
ICHI-!!
GR
B

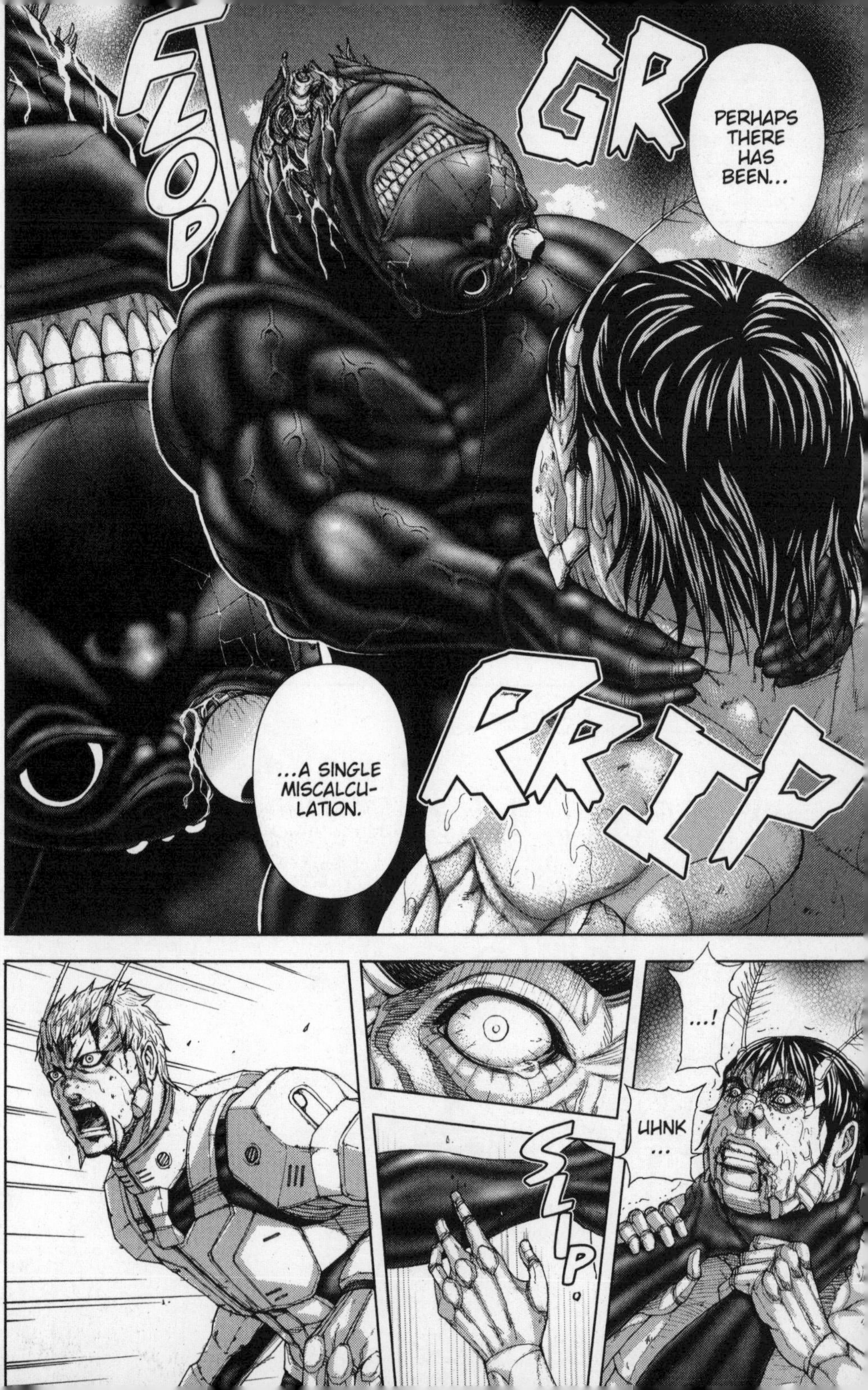
GR
PERHAPS THERE HAS BEEN...
FLOP
...A SINGLE MISCALCU-LATION.
RRIP
...!
UHNK...
SLIP

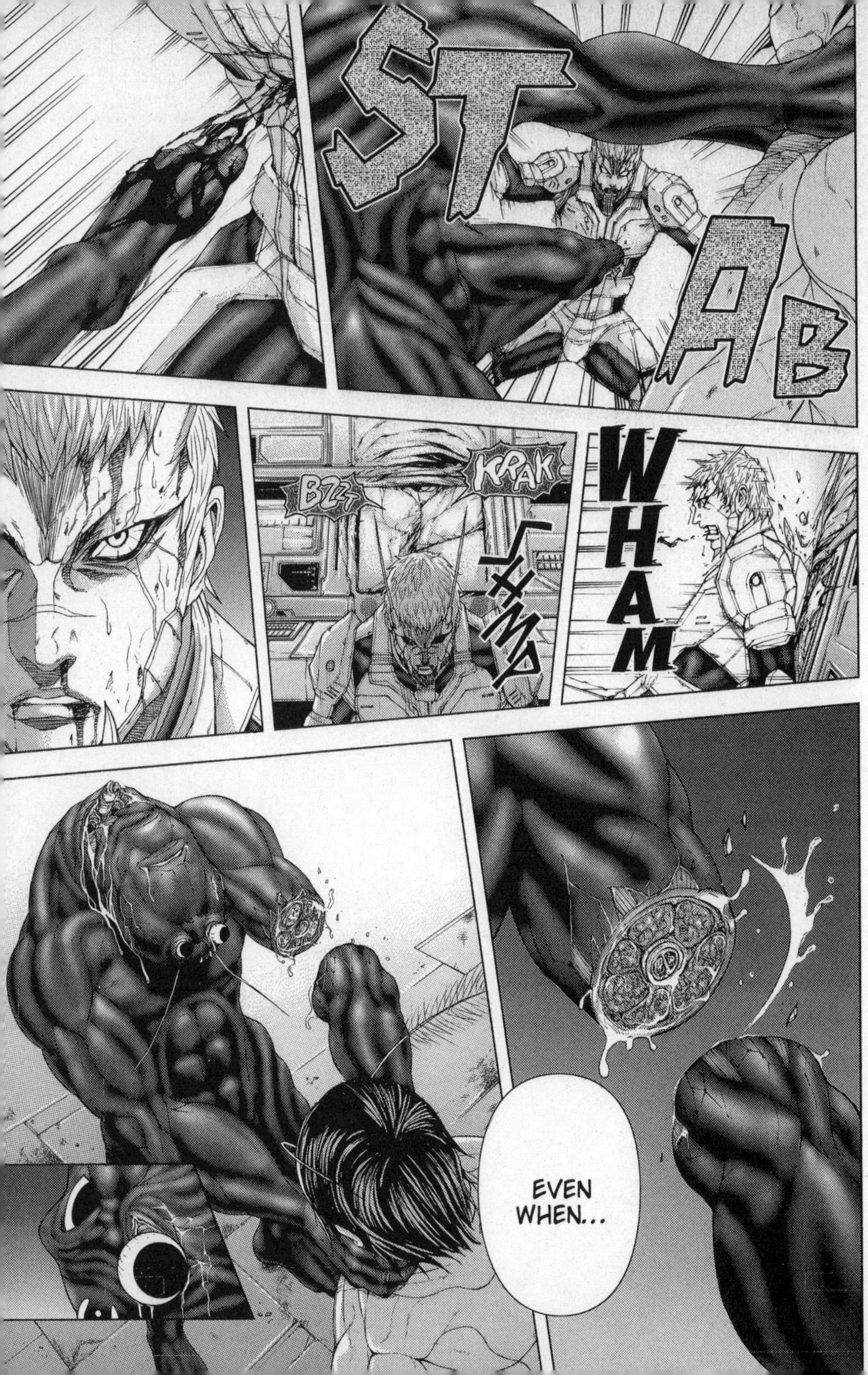

STAB
WHAM
KRAK
BZZT
SHMP
EVEN WHEN...

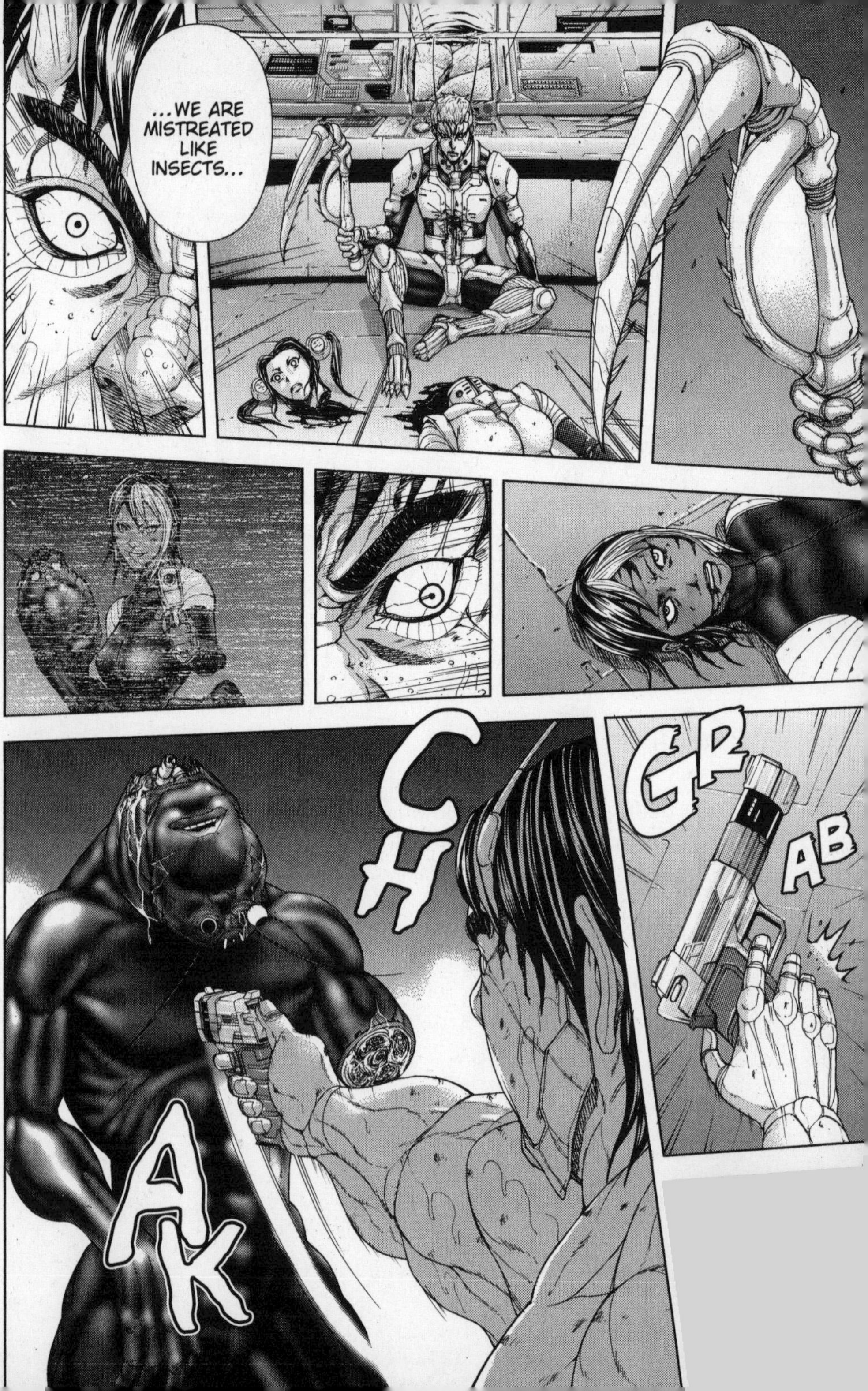
...WE ARE MISTREATED LIKE INSECTS...
GRAB
CHAK

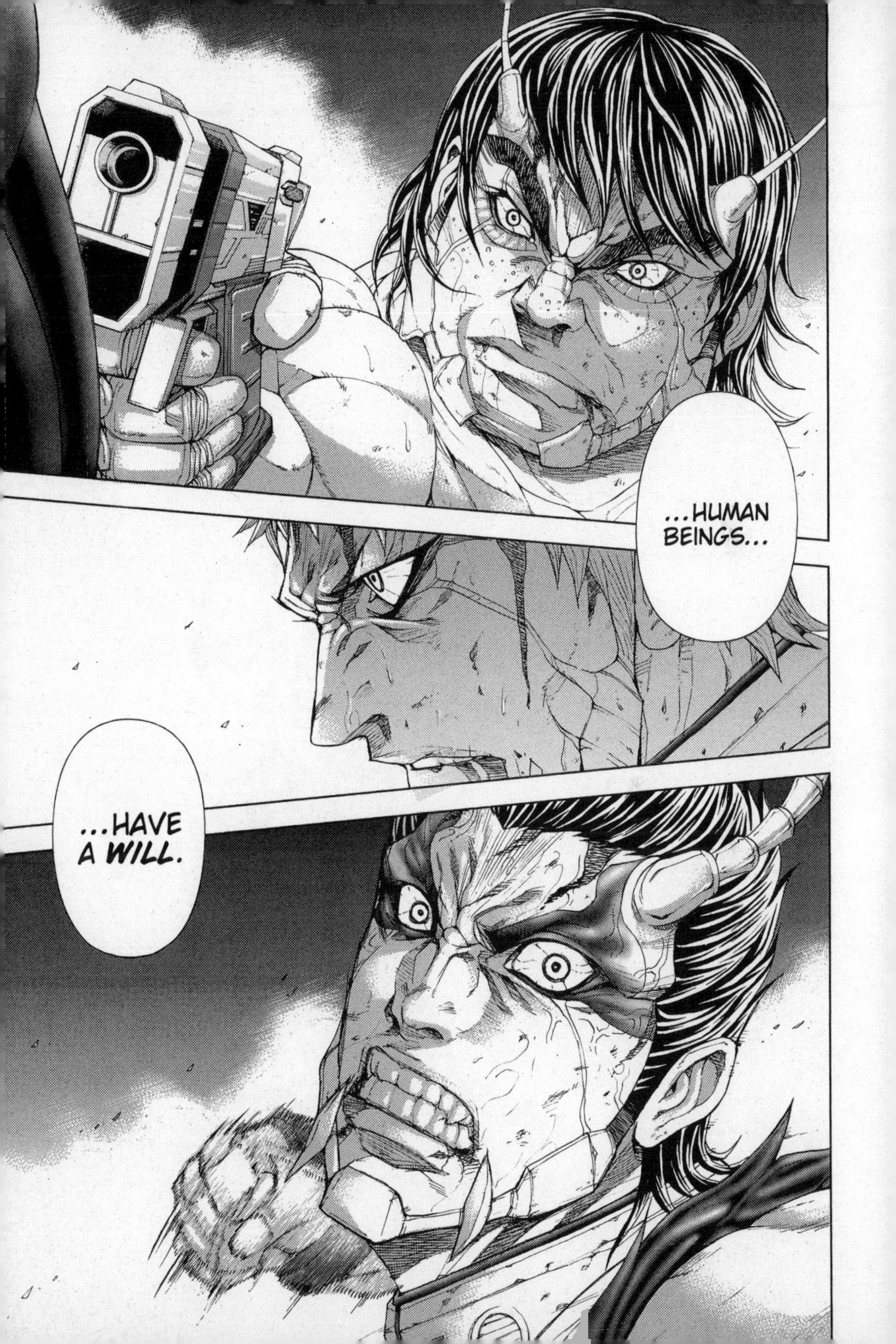
...HUMAN BEINGS...
...HAVE A WILL.

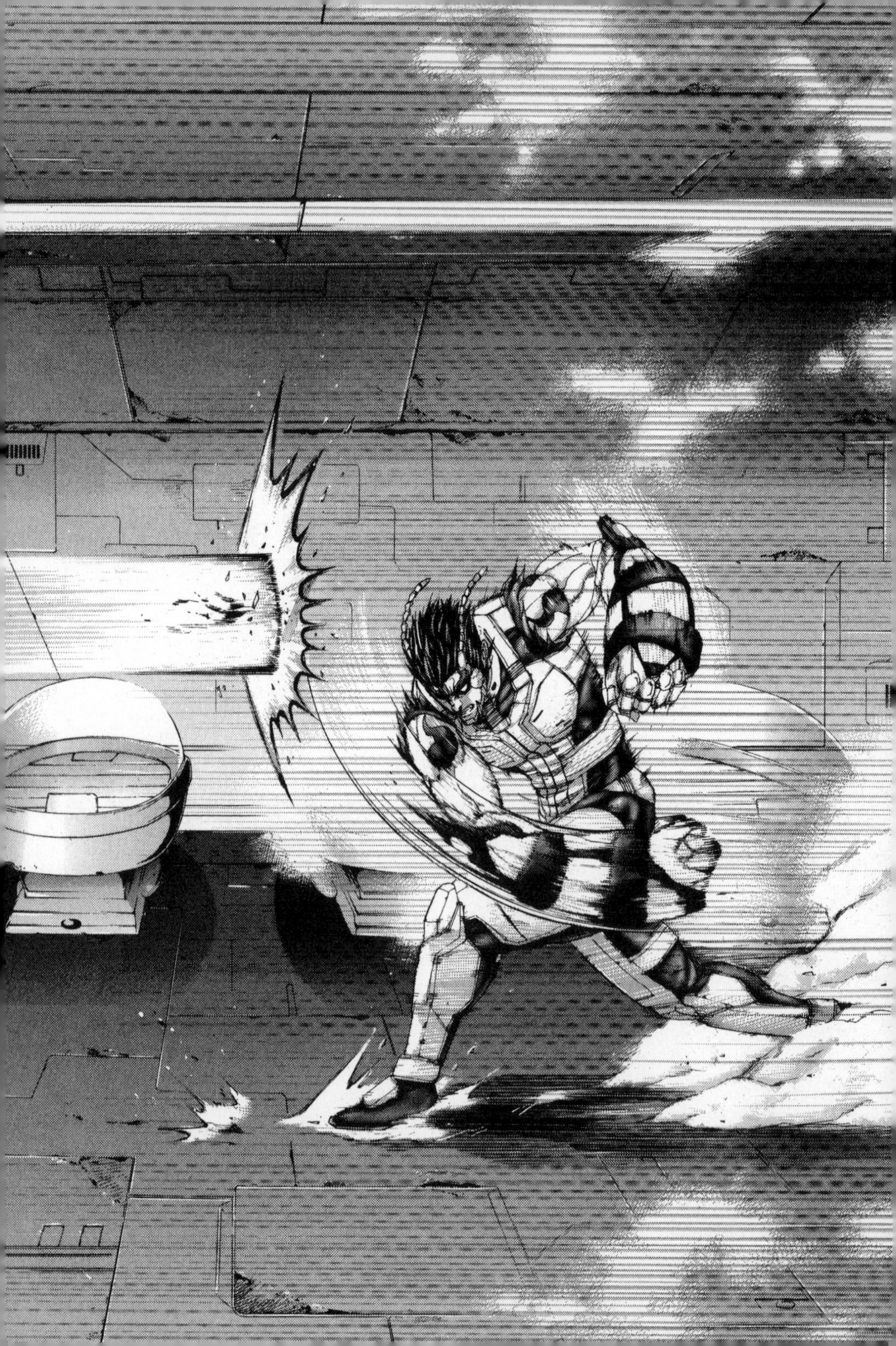

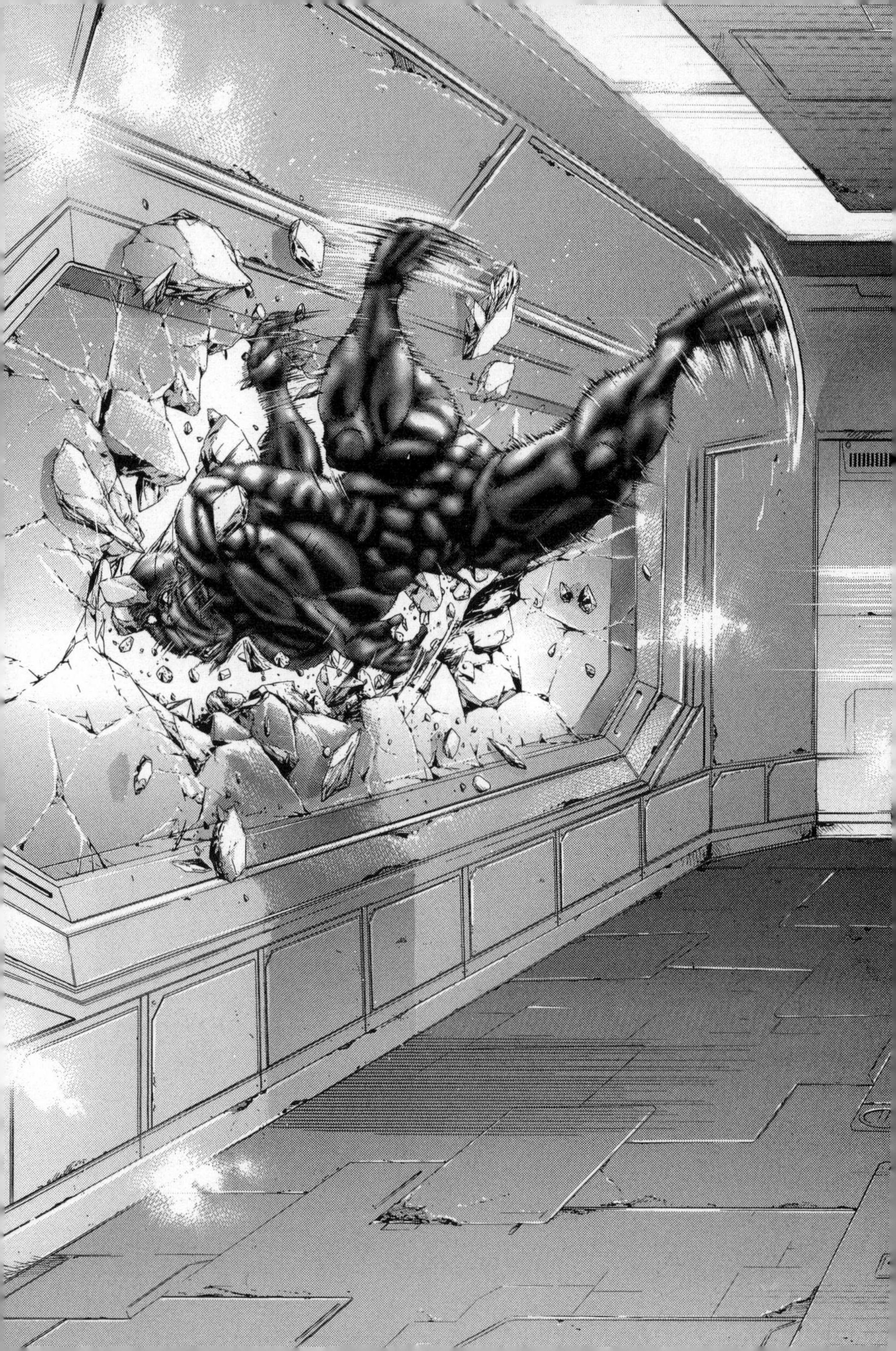

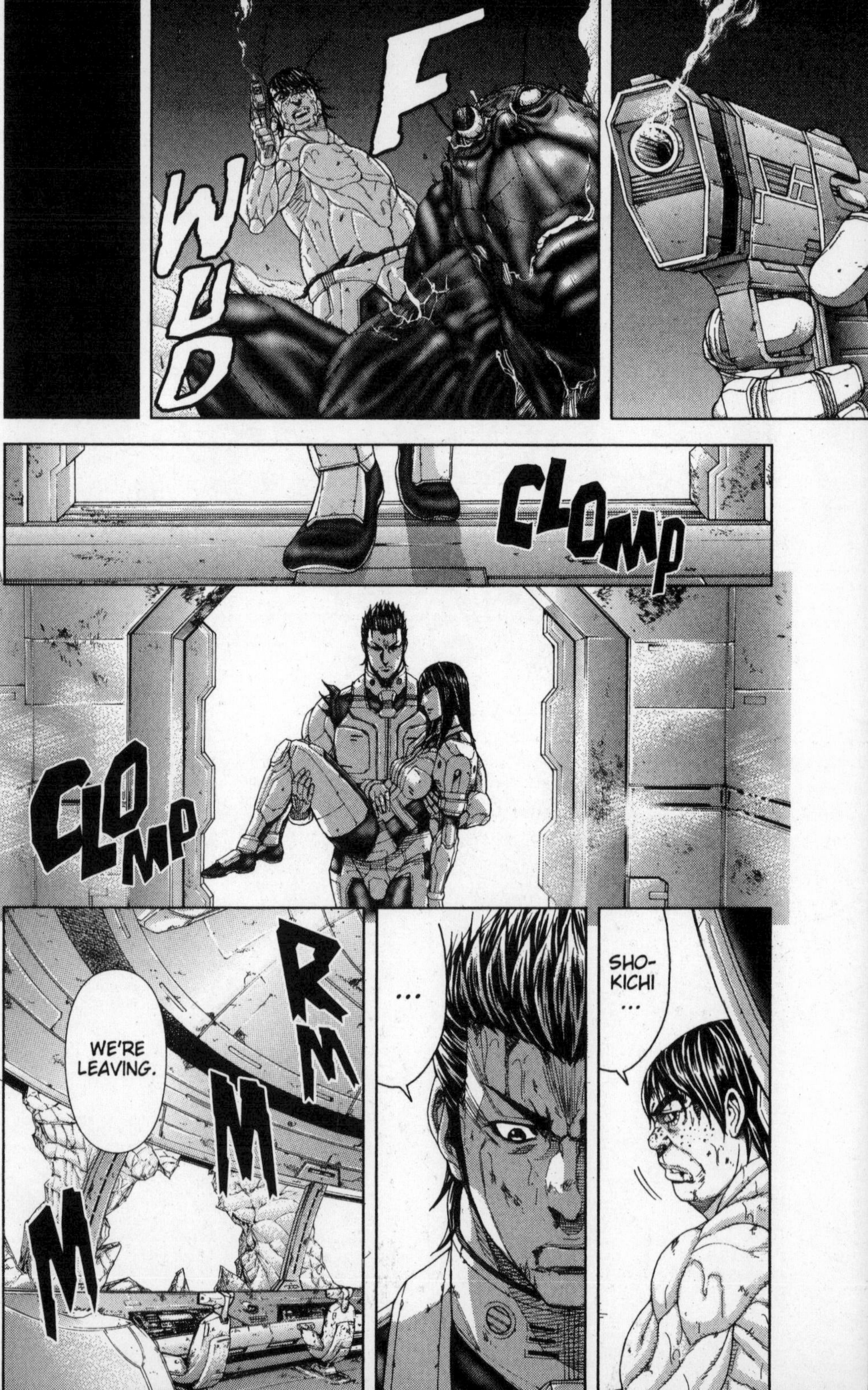
F
WUD
CLOMP
CLOMP
SHO-KICHI ...
...
RMMM
WE'RE LEAVING.

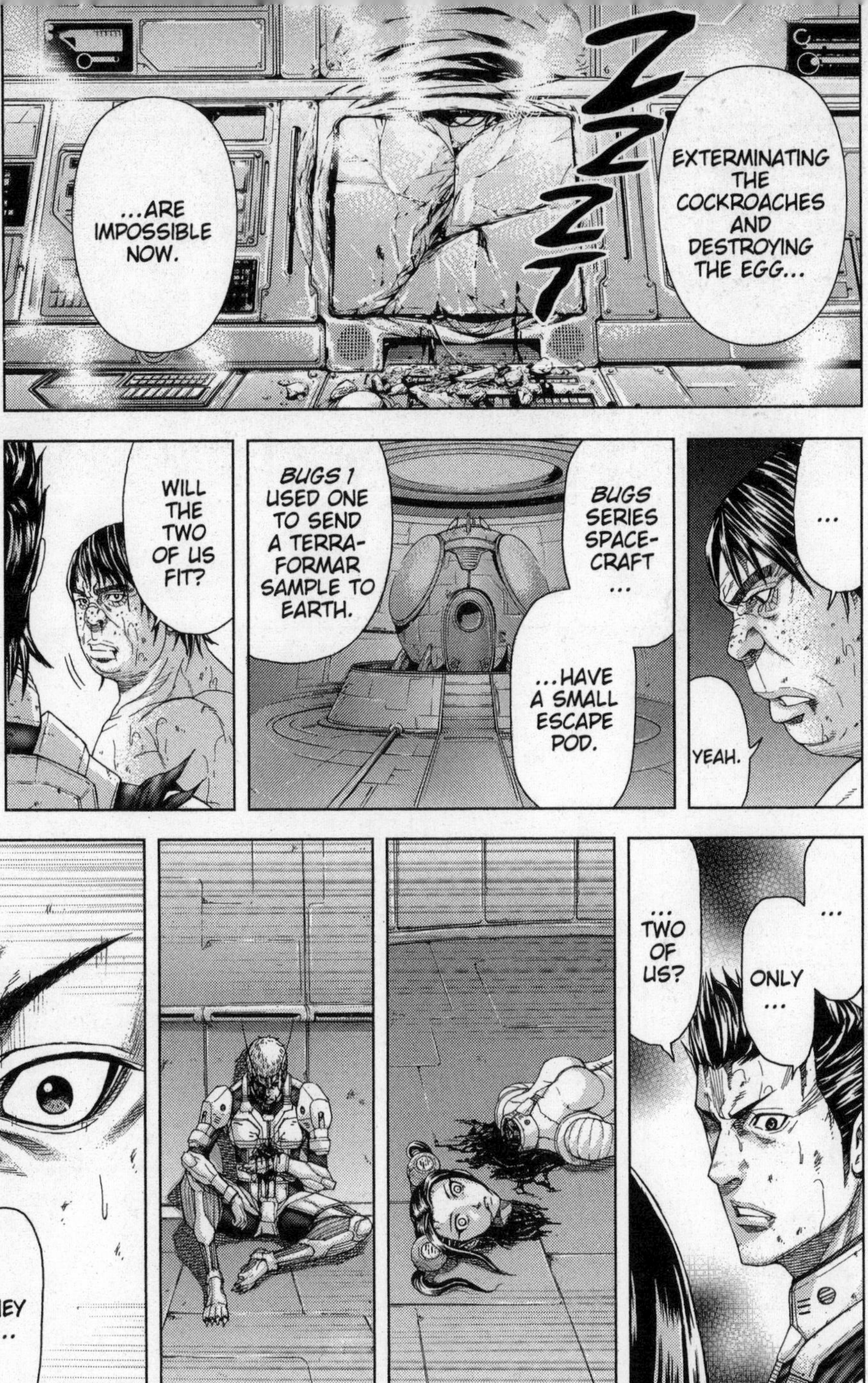
EXTERMINATING THE COCKROACHES AND DESTROYING THE EGG...
ZZZT
...ARE IMPOSSIBLE NOW.
...
YEAH.
BUGS SERIES SPACE-CRAFT ...
...HAVE A SMALL ESCAPE POD.
BUGS 1 USED ONE TO SEND A TERRA-FORMAR SAMPLE TO EARTH.
WILL THE TWO OF US FIT?
... ONLY ...
... TWO OF US?
HEY ...

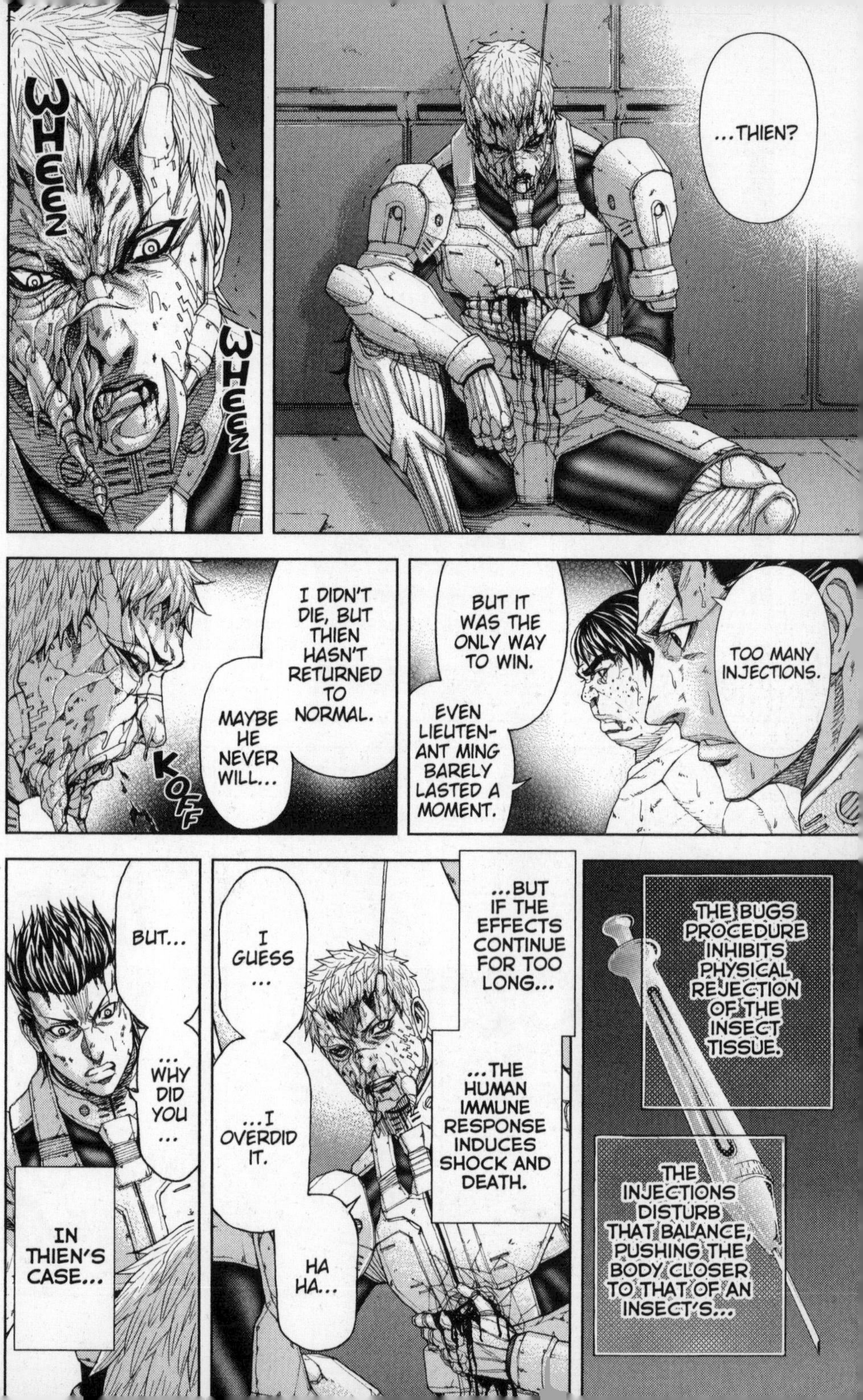
...THIEN?
WHEEZ
WHEEZ
TOO MANY INJECTIONS.
BUT IT WAS THE ONLY WAY TO WIN.
EVEN LIEUTEN-ANT MING BARELY LASTED A MOMENT.
I DIDN'T DIE, BUT THIEN HASN'T RETURNED TO NORMAL.
MAYBE HE NEVER WILL...
KOFF
THE BUGS PROCEDURE INHIBITS PHYSICAL REJECTION OF THE INSECT TISSUE.
THE INJECTIONS DISTURB THAT BALANCE, PUSHING THE BODY CLOSER TO THAT OF AN INSECT'S...
...BUT IF THE EFFECTS CONTINUE FOR TOO LONG...
...THE HUMAN IMMUNE RESPONSE INDUCES SHOCK AND DEATH.
I GUESS...
...I OVERDID IT.
HA HA...
BUT...
...WHY DID YOU...
IN THIEN'S CASE...

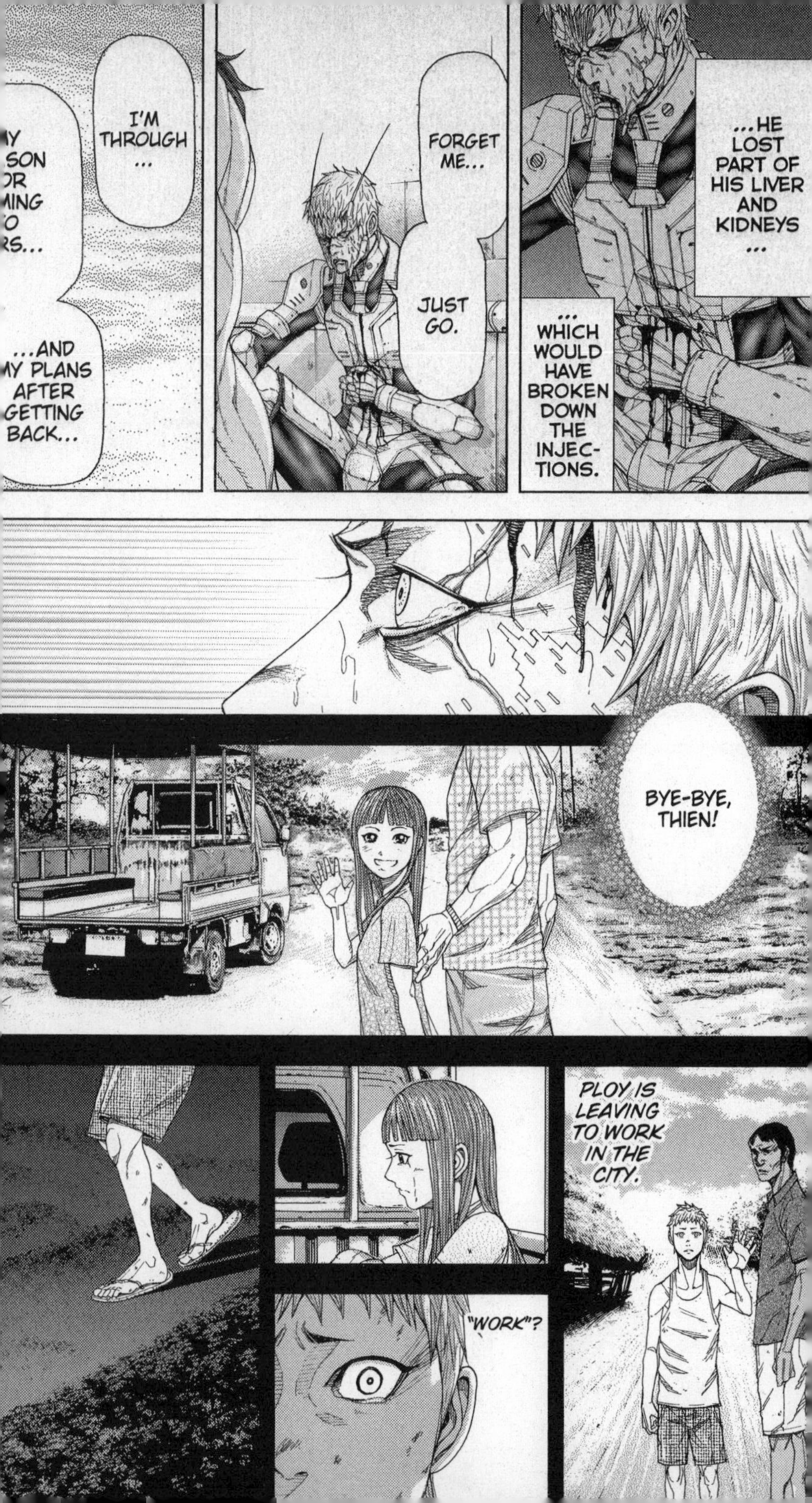
...HE LOST PART OF HIS LIVER AND KIDNEYS ...
...WHICH WOULD HAVE BROKEN DOWN THE INJECTIONS.
FORGET ME...
JUST GO.
I'M THROUGH ...
...AND MY PLANS AFTER GETTING BACK...
BYE-BYE, THIEN!
PLOY IS LEAVING TO WORK IN THE CITY.
"WORK"?

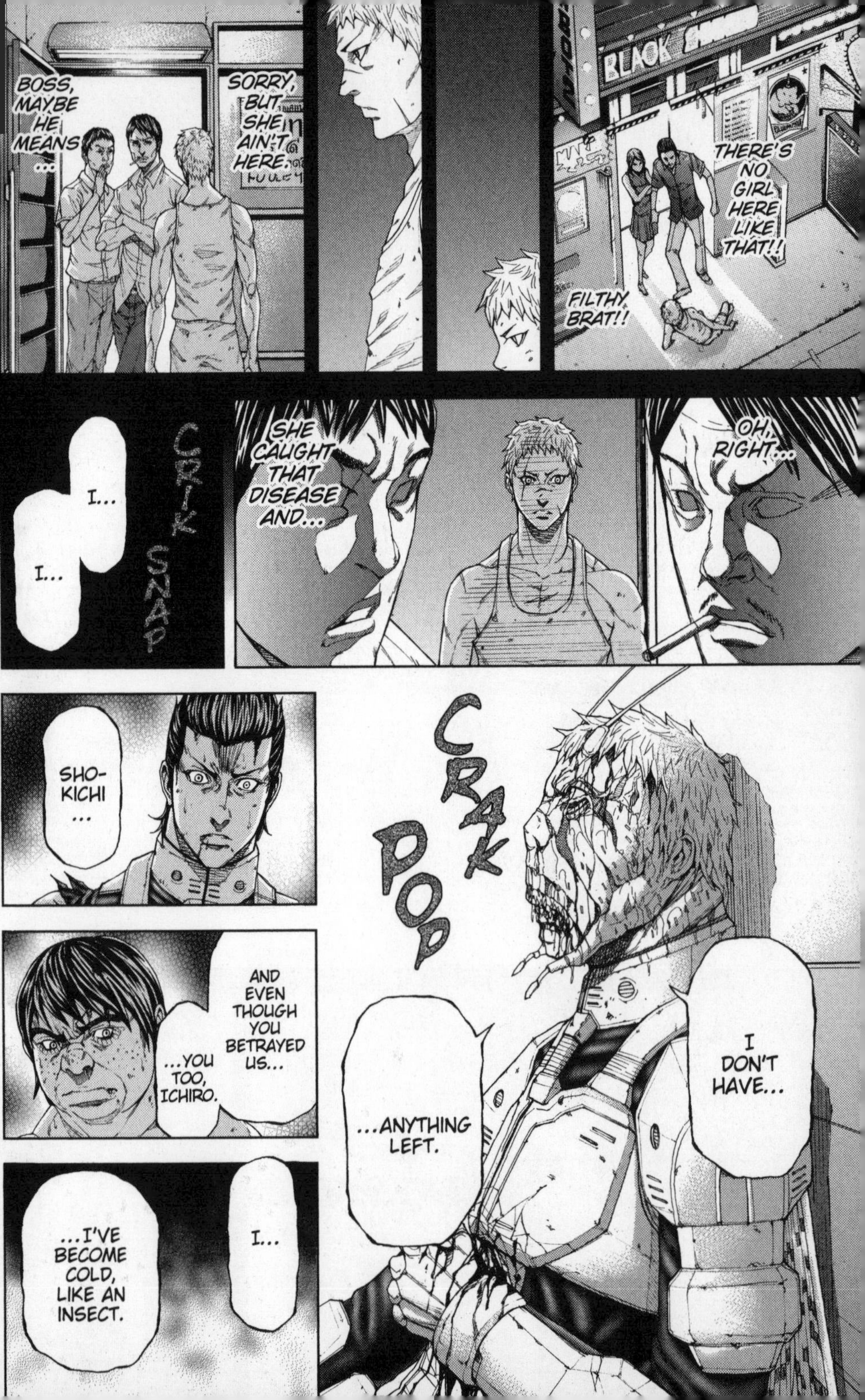
BLACK
THERE'S NO GIRL HERE LIKE THAT!!
FILTHY BRAT!!
SORRY, BUT SHE AIN'T HERE.
BOSS, MAYBE HE MEANS...
OH, RIGHT...
SHE CAUGHT THAT DISEASE AND...
CRIK SNAP
I... I...
CRAK POP
I DON'T HAVE...
...ANYTHING LEFT.
SHO-KICHI...
AND EVEN THOUGH YOU BETRAYED US...
...YOU TOO, ICHIRO.
I...
...I'VE BECOME COLD, LIKE AN INSECT.

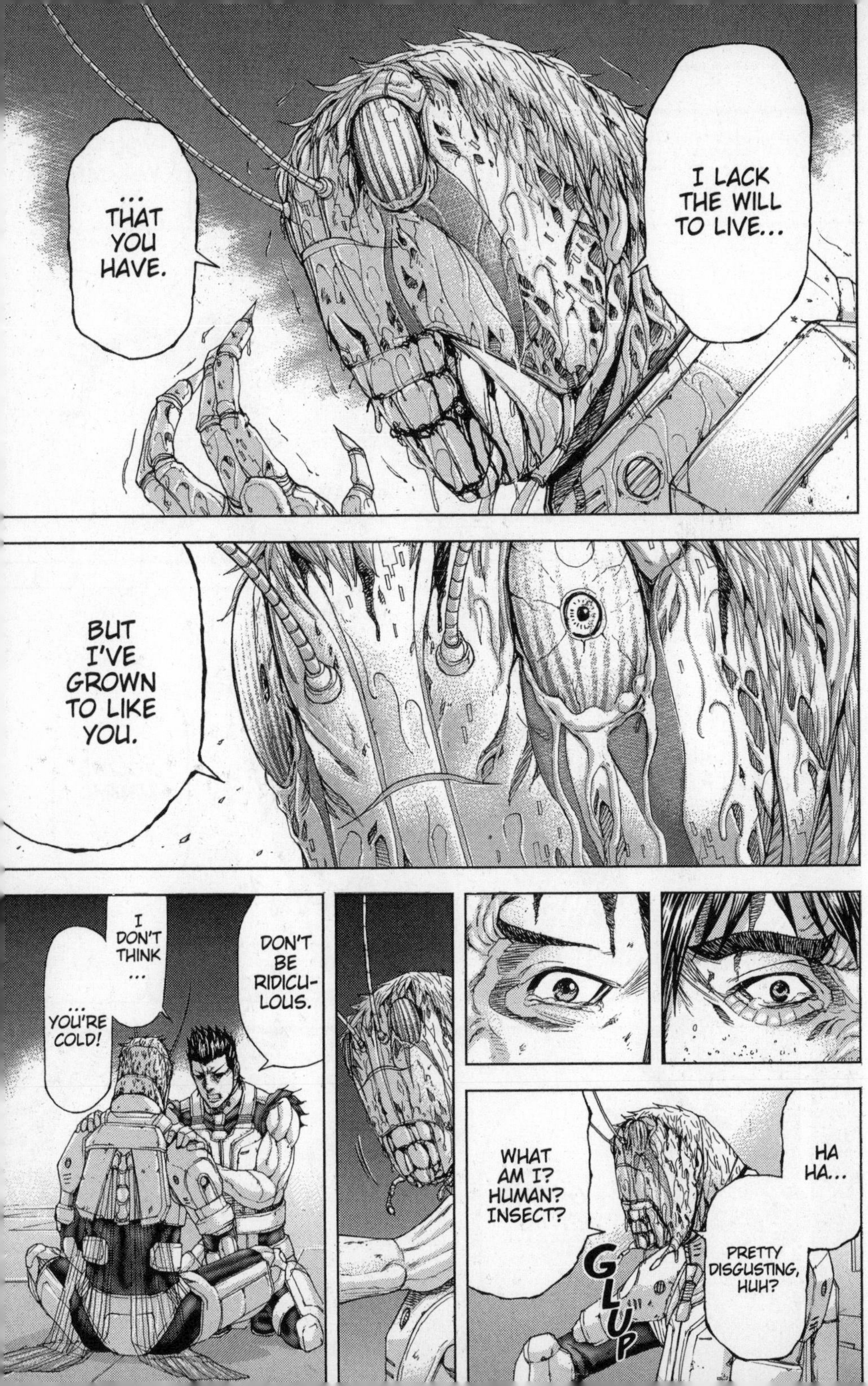
I LACK THE WILL TO LIVE...
...THAT YOU HAVE.
BUT I'VE GROWN TO LIKE YOU.
HA HA...
WHAT AM I? HUMAN? INSECT?
PRETTY DISGUSTING, HUH?
GLUP
DON'T BE RIDICULOUS.
I DON'T THINK...
...YOU'RE COLD!

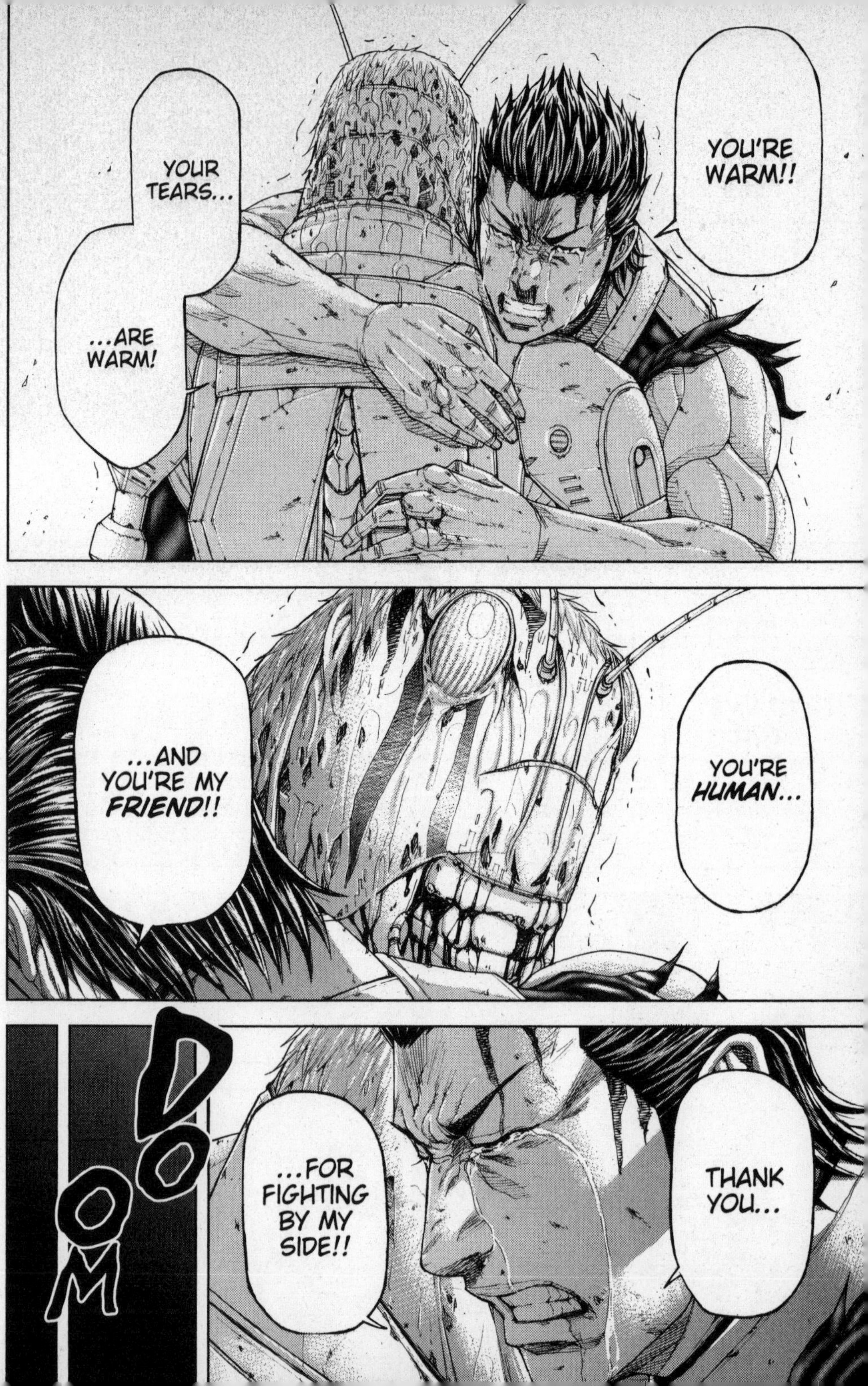
YOU'RE WARM!!
YOUR TEARS...
...ARE WARM!
YOU'RE *HUMAN*...
...AND YOU'RE MY *FRIEND*!!
THANK YOU...
...FOR FIGHTING BY MY SIDE!!
DOOOM

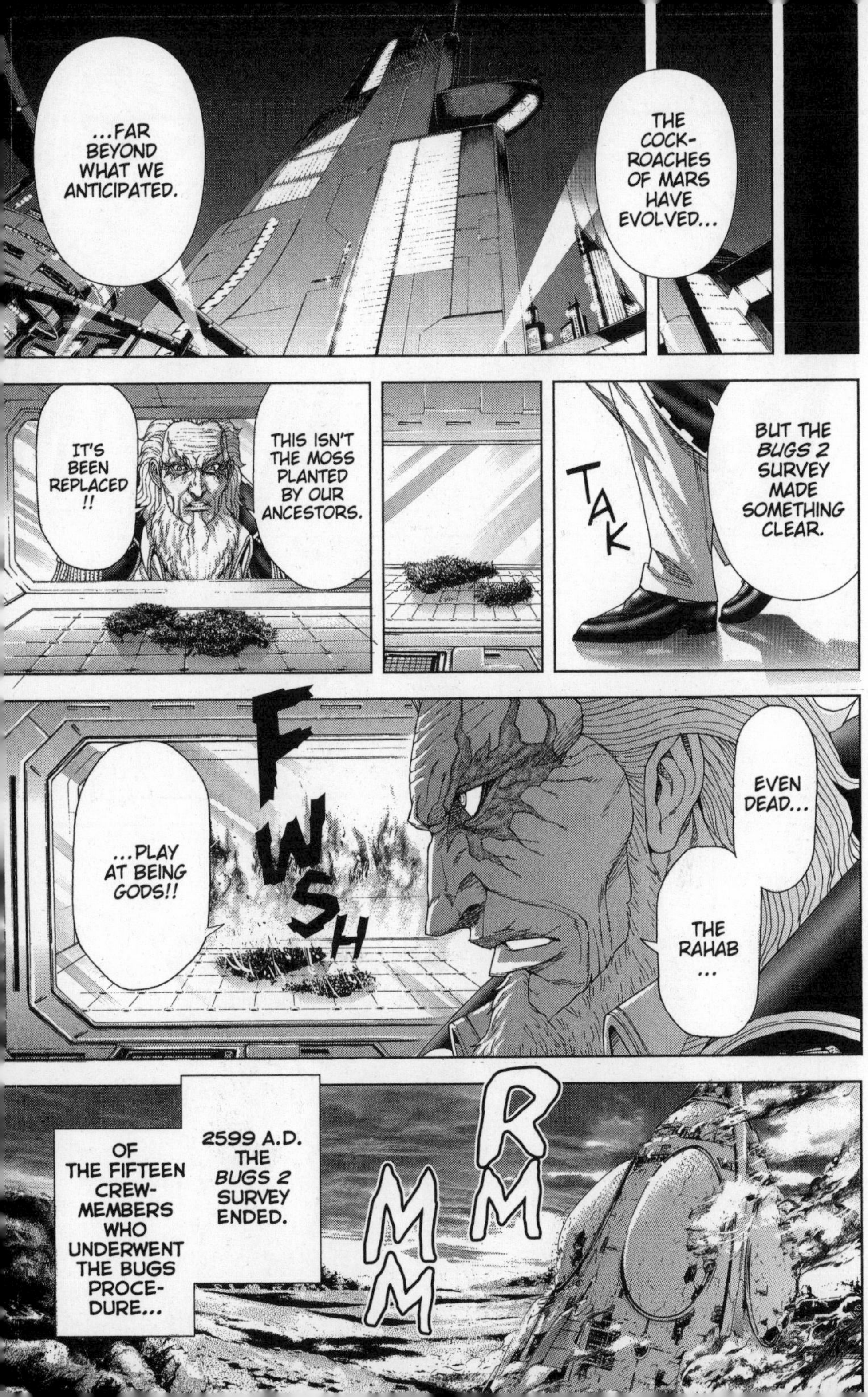
THE COCK-ROACHES OF MARS HAVE EVOLVED...
...FAR BEYOND WHAT WE ANTICIPATED.
TAK
BUT THE *BUGS 2* SURVEY MADE SOMETHING CLEAR.
THIS ISN'T THE MOSS PLANTED BY OUR ANCESTORS.
IT'S BEEN REPLACED!!
EVEN DEAD...
THE RAHAB...
FWSH
...PLAY AT BEING GODS!!
RMMMM
2599 A.D. THE *BUGS 2* SURVEY ENDED.
OF THE FIFTEEN CREW-MEMBERS WHO UNDERWENT THE BUGS PROCEDURE...

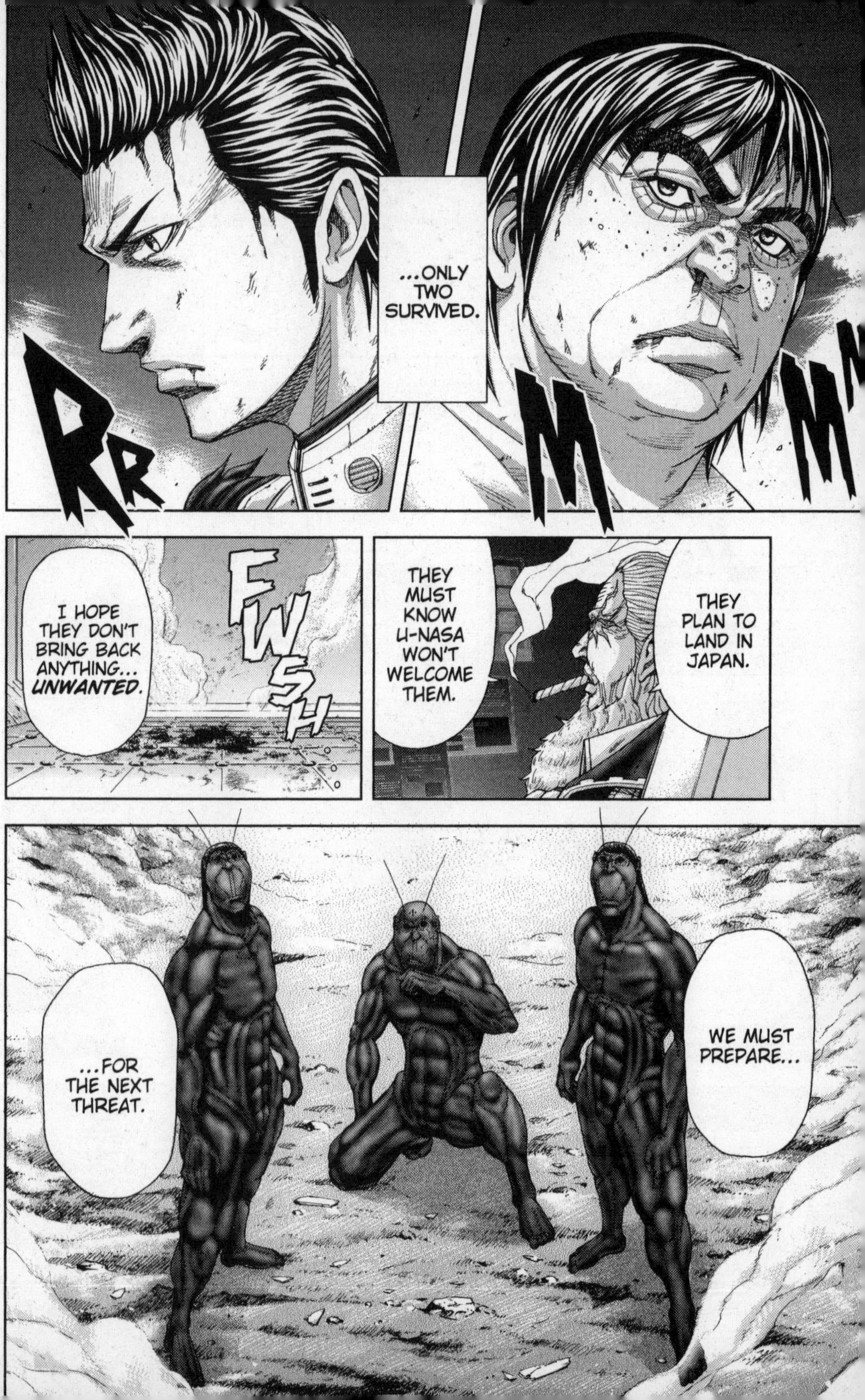
...ONLY TWO SURVIVED.
RRMM
THEY PLAN TO LAND IN JAPAN.
THEY MUST KNOW U-NASA WON'T WELCOME THEM.
FWSH
I HOPE THEY DON'T BRING BACK ANYTHING... *UNWANTED*.
WE MUST PREPARE...
...FOR THE NEXT THREAT.

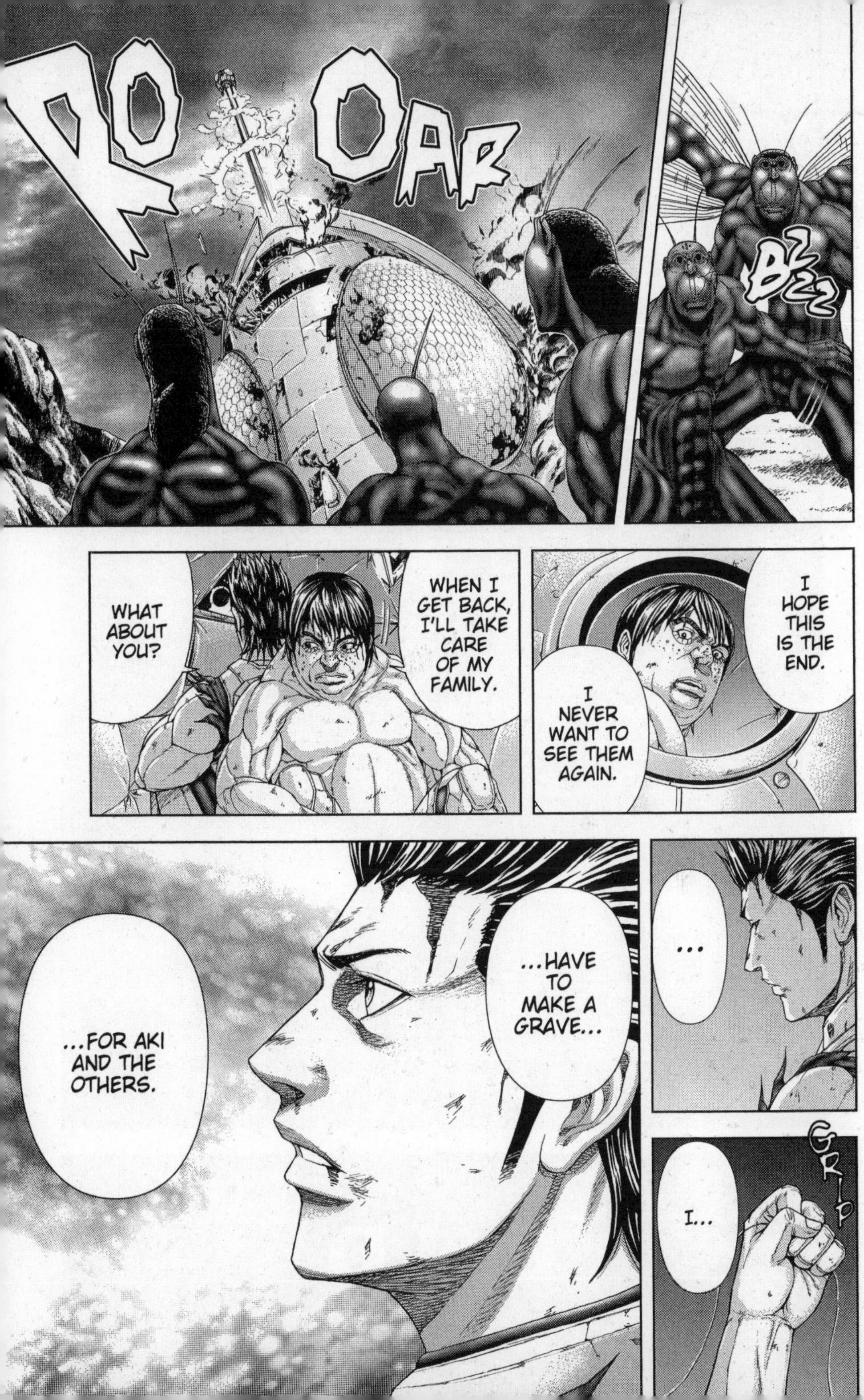
BZZZ
ROOAR
I HOPE THIS IS THE END.
I NEVER WANT TO SEE THEM AGAIN.
WHEN I GET BACK, I'LL TAKE CARE OF MY FAMILY.
WHAT ABOUT YOU?
...
I...
GRIP
...HAVE TO MAKE A GRAVE...
...FOR AKI AND THE OTHERS.

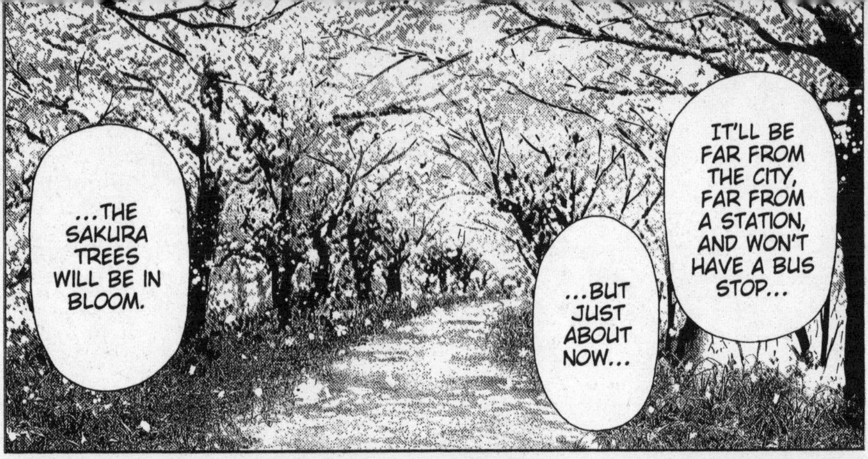
IT'LL BE FAR FROM THE CITY, FAR FROM A STATION, AND WON'T HAVE A BUS STOP...
...BUT JUST ABOUT NOW...
...THE SAKURA TREES WILL BE IN BLOOM.

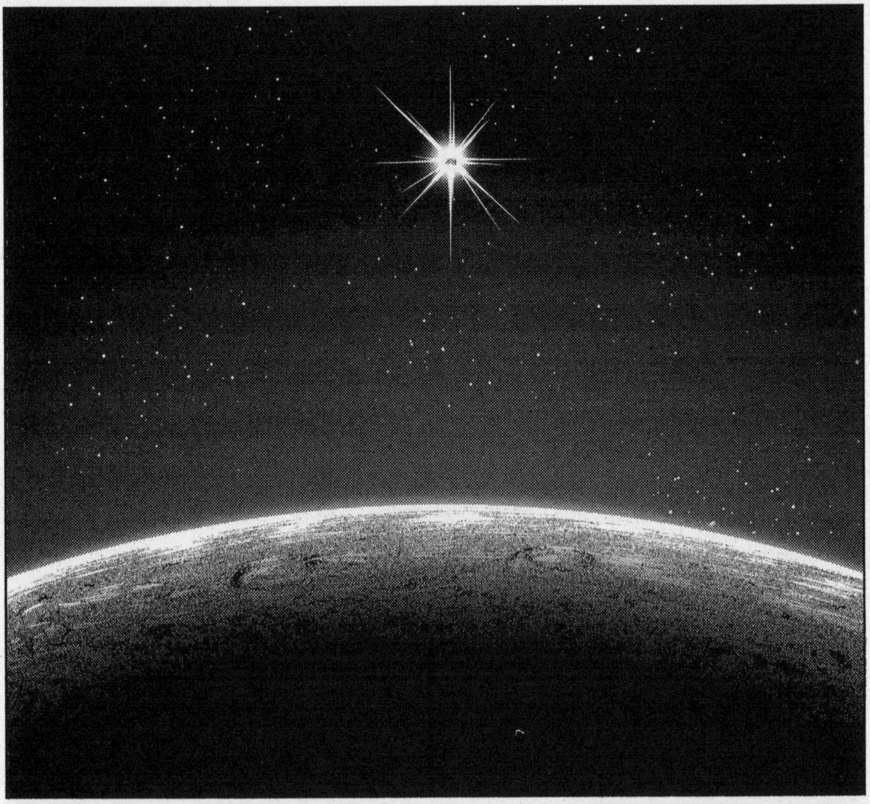

TERRA FORMARS

STORY
YU SASUGA
ART
KENICHI TACHIBANA

STAFF
YORIKI ONO
KAZUO IZUMI
TAKAYUKI TASAKA

EDITOR
MASATO SHINDO (WEEKLY YOUNG JUMP)

REFERENCES
John Minnery
"How to Kill Vol.1"
〈1973〉

Natalie Angier
"The Beauty of the Beastly"
〈1995〉

Richard Schweid
"The Cockroach Papers: A Compendium of History and Lore"
〈1999〉

Armand Marie Leroi
"Mutants on Genetic Variety and the Human Body"
〈2003〉

ANOTHER STORY
TERRA FORMARS ONE
http://youngjump.jp/

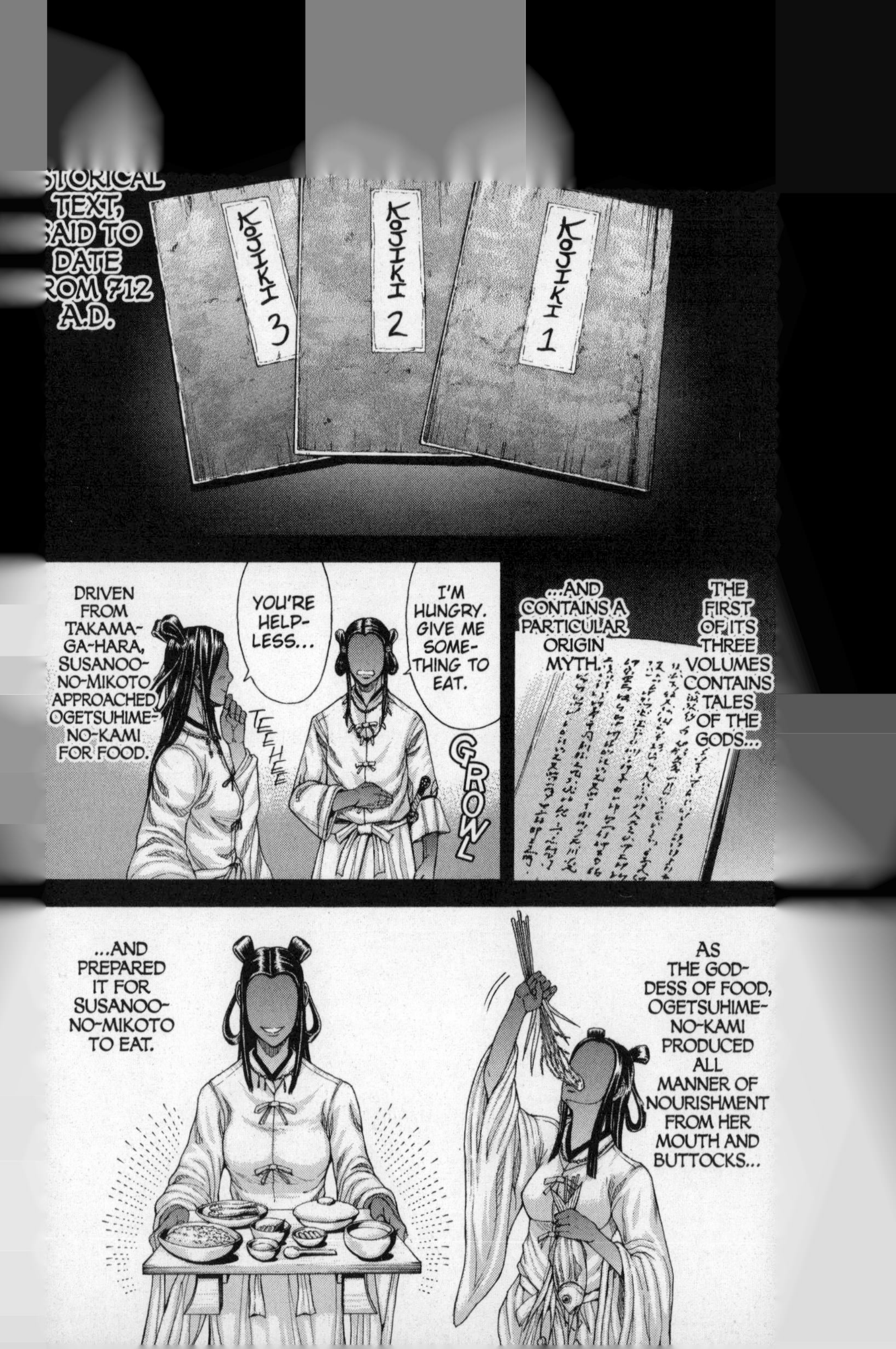
STORICAL TEXT, SAID TO DATE ROM 712 A.D.
KOJIKI 3
KOJIKI 2
KOJIKI 1
THE FIRST OF ITS THREE VOLUMES CONTAINS TALES OF THE GODS...
...AND CONTAINS A PARTICULAR ORIGIN MYTH.
I'M HUNGRY. GIVE ME SOME-THING TO EAT.
GROWL
YOU'RE HELP-LESS...
TEEHEE
DRIVEN FROM TAKAMA-GA-HARA, SUSANOO-NO-MIKOTO APPROACHED OGETSUHIME-NO-KAMI FOR FOOD.
AS THE GOD-DESS OF FOOD, OGETSUHIME-NO-KAMI PRODUCED ALL MANNER OF NOURISHMENT FROM HER MOUTH AND BUTTOCKS...
...AND PREPARED IT FOR SUSANOO-NO-MIKOTO TO EAT.

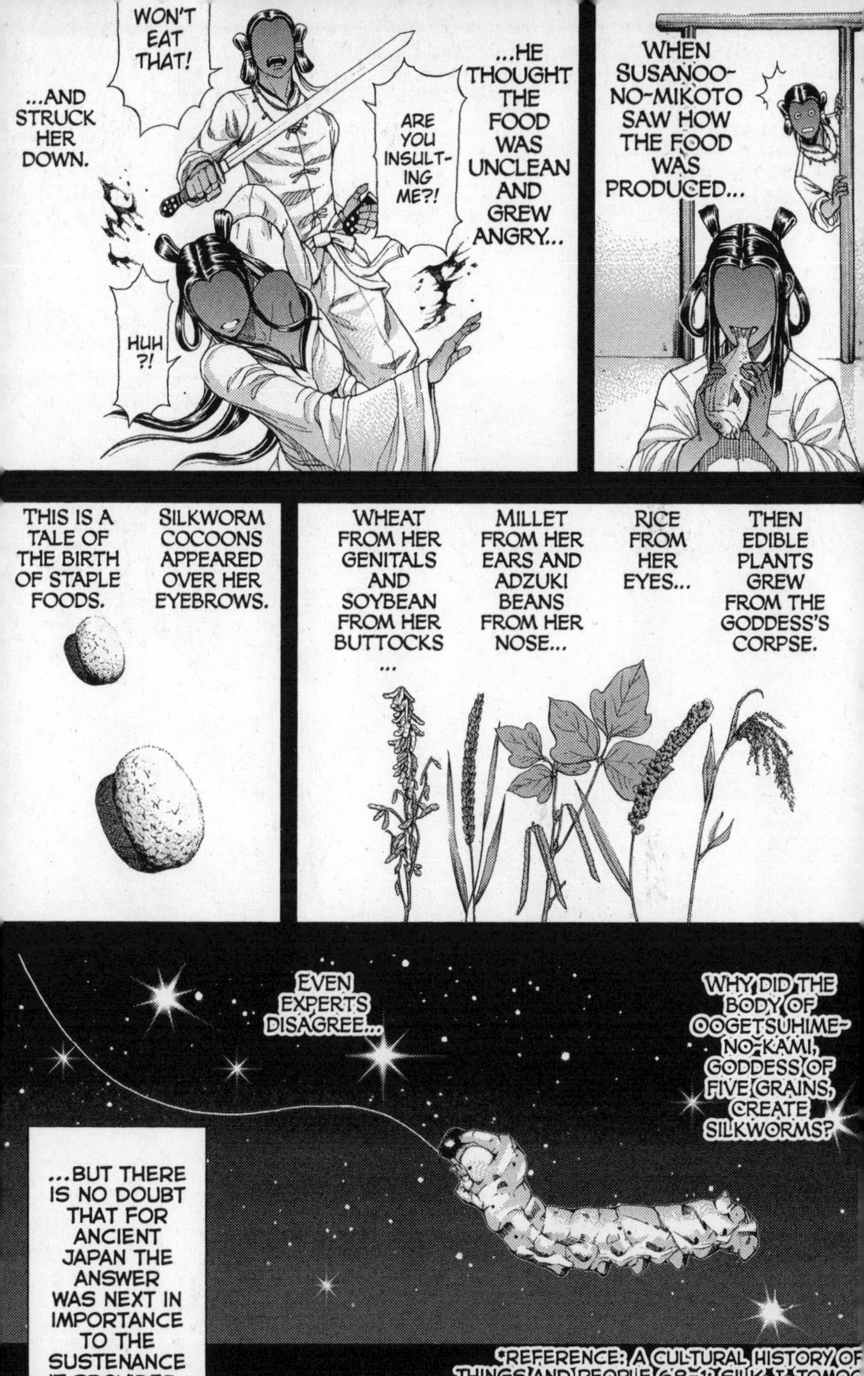
WHEN SUSANOO-NO-MIKOTO SAW HOW THE FOOD WAS PRODUCED...
...HE THOUGHT THE FOOD WAS UNCLEAN AND GREW ANGRY...
ARE YOU INSULTING ME?!
WON'T EAT THAT!
...AND STRUCK HER DOWN.
HUH?!
THEN EDIBLE PLANTS GREW FROM THE GODDESS'S CORPSE.
RICE FROM HER EYES...
MILLET FROM HER EARS AND ADZUKI BEANS FROM HER NOSE...
WHEAT FROM HER GENITALS AND SOYBEAN FROM HER BUTTOCKS...
SILKWORM COCOONS APPEARED OVER HER EYEBROWS.
THIS IS A TALE OF THE BIRTH OF STAPLE FOODS.
WHY DID THE BODY OF OOGETSUHIME-NO-KAMI, GODDESS OF FIVE GRAINS, CREATE SILKWORMS?
EVEN EXPERTS DISAGREE...
...BUT THERE IS NO DOUBT THAT FOR ANCIENT JAPAN THE ANSWER WAS NEXT IN IMPORTANCE TO THE SUSTENANCE IT PROVIDED.
*REFERENCE: A CULTURAL HISTORY OF
THINGS AND PEOPLE 68-1: SILK, I, TOMO

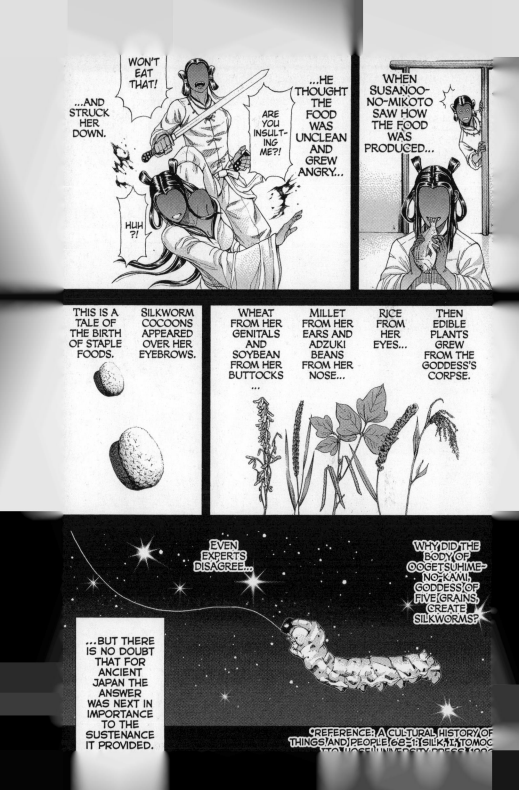

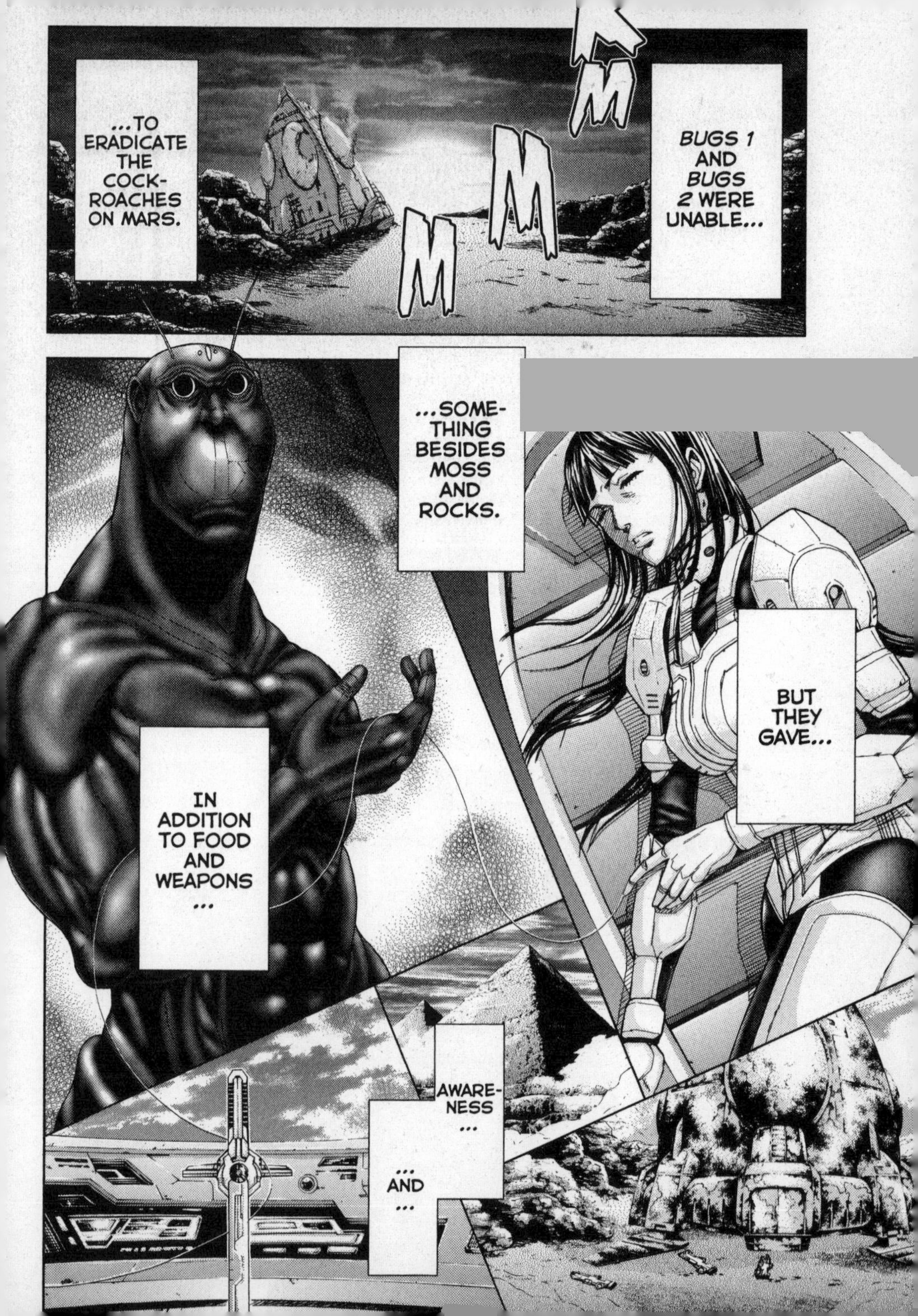
BUGS 1 AND BUGS 2 WERE UNABLE...
MMM
...TO ERADICATE THE COCK-ROACHES ON MARS.
BUT THEY GAVE...
IN ADDITION TO FOOD AND WEAPONS...
...SOME-THING BESIDES MOSS AND ROCKS.
AWARE-NESS...
...AND...

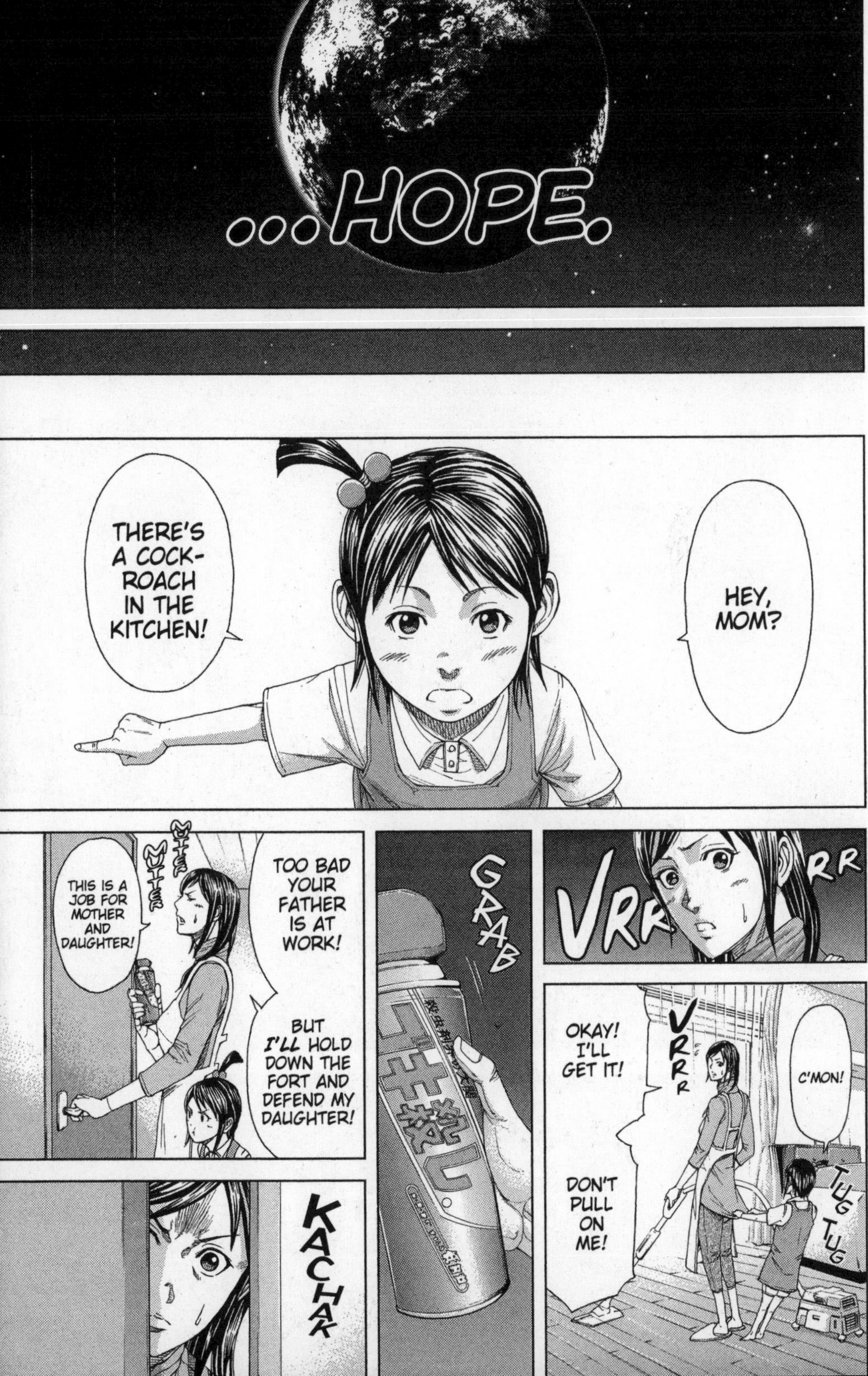
...HOPE.
HEY, MOM?
THERE'S A COCKROACH IN THE KITCHEN!
VRRRR
C'MON!
OKAY! I'LL GET IT!
VRRR
DON'T PULL ON ME!
TUG TUG
GRAB
TOO BAD YOUR FATHER IS AT WORK!
BUT I'LL HOLD DOWN THE FORT AND DEFEND MY DAUGHTER!
MUTTER MUTTER
THIS IS A JOB FOR MOTHER AND DAUGHTER!
KACHAK

TO THE NEXT DIMENSION

TERRA FORMARS 1 (END)

TERRA FORMARS

Character

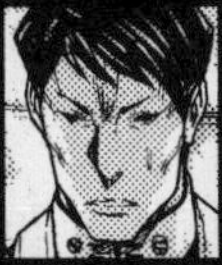

Yang Fuwan ♂
China
Age: 24
Height: 180 cm
Weight: 70 kg

As a second son, he was treated differently from his older brother, almost like a servant. He joined the Bugs Project to earn enough money to cut ties with his family.

Favorite classical text: Fist of the North Star Best dish: Fried rice

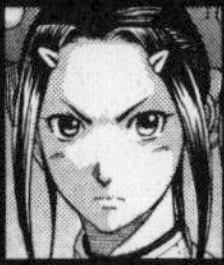

Zhang Ming-Ming ♀
China
Age: 27
Height: 170 cm
Weight: 56 kg

Second-in-command of *Bugs 2*.
Originally, she worked as a spy to steal America's Bugs Procedure technology, but she was captured and subjected to the Bugs Procedure herself, after negotiations with China. D Cup.

Likes: Doraemon Dislikes: Dirty restrooms

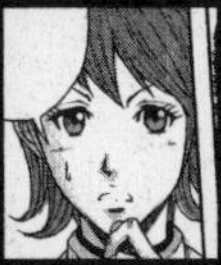

Jaina Eisenstein ♀
Kazakhstan
Age: 19
Height: 161 cm
Weight: 49 kg

Born in a small village, she entered university early. The government was to pay for her study in the U.S., but her family and village stole the funds. After graduation, all she had left was debt, so she underwent the Bugs Procedure. C Cup.

Favorite food: vegetables Dislikes: really big things

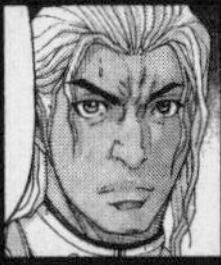

Tejas Viji ♂
India
Age: 26
Height: 175 cm
Weight: 65 kg

The son of the owner of a small IT company in India. Reluctant to take over the company, he procrastinated, but then the economy sank. He joined the Bugs Project after his parents committed suicide and left him in debt.

Hobbies: Playing bass Favorite animal: Giant water bugs

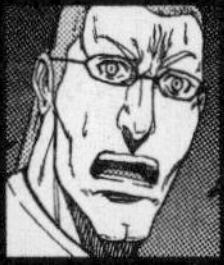

Toshio Bright ♂
England
Age: 22
Height: 170 cm
Weight: 55 kg

Japanese-English. Expected to become a genius manga author in Japan, but his strong personality got him in trouble and the industry shunned him. His savings ran out, so he underwent the Bugs Procedure.

Dislikes: Rice cakes

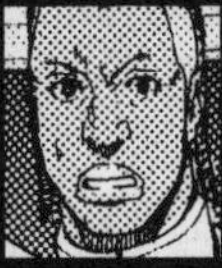

John Welsalk ♂
Australia
Age: 24
Height: 180 cm
Weight: 88 kg

Lived with his grandmother and raised sheep, but all their livestock died of disease. His dream is to take his grandmother traveling overseas.

Favorite food: fried silkworm Dislikes: banks

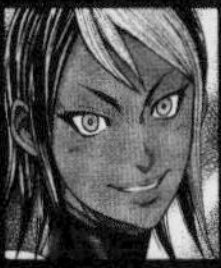

Victoria Wood ♀
South Africa
Age: 19
Height: 159 cm
Weight: 45 kg

Born in a South African farming village. After her father died from an infectious disease when she was 13, relatives took her in along with her siblings. They were poor, but because of FGM, she hesitated to prostitute herself and resorted to theft. A Cup.

Likes: watching rugby Dislikes: pushy older women

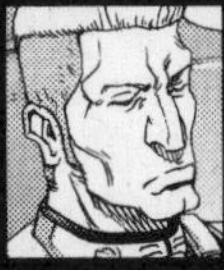

Redon Burgsmuller ♂
U.S.A.
Age: 26
Height: 170 cm
Weight: 80 kg

German-American. Dropped out of college and started a number of businesses, but they all failed. Unable to escape his debts, he underwent the Bugs Procedure.

Likes: Japanese hentai games Dislikes: normal porn

TERRA FORMARS

Volume 1
VIZ Signature Edition

Story by YU SASUGA
Art by KENICHI TACHIBANA

TERRA FORMARS © 2011 by Ken-ichi Tachibana, Yu Sasuga/SHUEISHA Inc.
All rights reserved.
First published in Japan in 2011 by SHUEISHA Inc., Tokyo.
English translation rights arranged by SHUEISHA Inc.

Translation & English Adaptation/John Werry
Touch-up Art & Lettering/Annaliese Christman
Design/Izumi Evers
Editor/Mike Montesa

Printed in the U.S.A.

Published by VIZ Media, LLC
P.O. Box 77010
San Francisco, CA 94107

10 9 8 7 6 5 4 3 2 1
First printing, July 2014

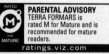

www.viz.com

A RACE TO SAVE A WORLD BEYOND HOPE

BIOMEGA

STORY & ART BY
TSUTOMU NIHEI

WELCOME TO EARTH'S FUTURE: A NIGHTMARISH
WORLD INFECTED BY A VIRUS THAT TURNS MOST
OF THE POPULATION INTO ZOMBIE-LIKE DRONES.
WILL THE SYNTHETIC HUMAN ZOICHI KANOE BE
MANKIND'S SALVATION?

MANGA ON SALE AT
WWW.VIZSIGNATURE.COM
ALSO AVAILABLE AT YOUR
LOCAL BOOKSTORE OR
COMIC STORE.

ISBN 978-1-4215-3184-7
$12.99 US $16.99 CAN £8.99 UK

VIZ SIGNATURE

BIOMEGA © 2004 by Tsutomu Nihei/SHUEISHA Inc.

Hey! You're Reading in the Wrong Direction!

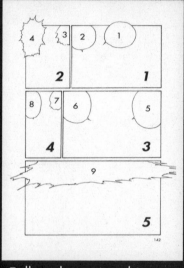

This is the _end_ of this graphic novel!

To properly enjoy this VIZ graphic novel, please turn it around and begin reading from **right to left.** Unlike English, Japanese is read right to left, so Japanese comics are read in reverse order from the way English comics are typically read.

Follow the action this way

This book has been printed in the original Japanese format in order to preserve the orientation of the